Evening Standard

The London Pub & Bar Guide 1999

EDWARD SULLIVAN

SIMON & SCHUSTER

A VIACOM COMPANY

First published in Great Britain by Simon & Schuster, 1998
A Viacom Company

Simon & Schuster Ltd
Africa House
64-78 Kingsway
London WC2B 6SX

Design: Neal Cobourne and Moore Lowenhoff
Typesetting: Stylize Digital Artwork
Cover photograph: Dillon Bryden. Photographed at the Elephant & Castle,
Holland Street, Kensington

A CIP catalogue record is available from the British Library

ISBN 0-671-02204-0

Printed and bound in Italy

Also published in this series:
Children's London

HOW TO USE THIS GUIDE
Pubs and bars are listed alphabetically. Every effort has been made to
obtain and ensure accurate information. Details can vary so please check
before a visit.

OPENING HOURS
Licensing hours may change during the course of this Guide but are deemed
accurate at the time of press.

BANK HOLIDAYS
Our research tells us that Bank Holiday food and service hours can alter
dramatically. We recommend that you check details in advance.

CONTENTS

190

190 Queensgate, SW7; 0171 581 5666

The bar of the restaurant opens late for members but is also accessible to those who have been dining here. It has been described to me as one of the easiest places to pull in London, and judging by the number of singles and same-sex groups who frequent it, I can see why.

OPEN bar: 11.00-01.00 (Mon-Sat), 11.00-midnight (Sun)

FOOD bistro: 07.00 (breakfast) -23.00 (Mon-Sun)

CREDIT CARDS all major cards

NEAREST TUBE STATIONS Gloucester Road, South Kensington

ABBAYE

55 Charterhouse, EC1; 0171 253 1612

The former Hubble & Co. seems to have emigrated. In its place comes this Belgian-style bar with a quality food-focus. Good place to take a date, useful for after-work drinks and a truly excellent place to eat.

OPEN 11.30-22.30 (Mon-Fri), Saturdays and Sundays private parties only (have late license until 3am Sun-Thurs, until 6am Fri-Sat)

FOOD as opening times

CREDIT CARDS all major cards, not Diners

DRAUGHT BEERS Stella Artois, Leffe Blonde, Leffe Brune, Hoegaarden, Belle-Vue Kreik

Private room seats 90 or 120 standing, Sat/Sun private bookings for up to 200 people

NEAREST TUBE STATION Farringdon

ADAM AND EVE

81 Petty France, SW1; 0171 222 4575

Petty France is where you go to get a new passport. It can be a slow process, so my advice is to collect your number announcing how long the wait is likely to be and pop down the road to the Adam and Eve where they're used to all that form filling. This used to be a fair to middling lager house until Scottish and Newcastle gave it a personality transplant. It has been one of their real ale houses for a couple of years now, bare boards, quick pies with flaky pastry lids and all. The ales are Scottish & Newcastle regulation issue but, happily, they serve three different guest ales every week.

OPEN 11.00-23.00 (Mon-Sat), 12.00-15.00 (Sun)

FOOD 11.00-23.00 (Mon-Fri), 12.00-15.00 (Sat & Sun)

CREDIT CARDS all major cards

DRAUGHT BEERS Courage Best, Courage Directors, John Smith's Extra Smooth, Theakston Best, Theakston Old Peculier, Theakston XB, three guest ales, Beck's, Foster's, Guinness, Scrumpy Jack

Wheelchair access to venue

NEAREST TUBE STATION St James's Park

ADELAIDE

143 Adelaide Road, NW3; 0171 722 3777

Anyone familiar with what's been going on in Clapham in recent years will know the works of Anne and Tom Halpin, creators of The Sun, The Falcon and The Railway. I suspect the Halpins have a job lot of yellow paint for their venues but so much has been used at the Adelaide that we might now start to see the beginning of the end of it. It's a beautiful conversion though, their best to date. Lots of tender loving care and money seem to have been spent on transforming what was The Viceroy into this huge modern foody pub which Chalk Farm must be quite pleased to have on its doorstep. I've been a couple of times since the opening (champagne-induced, memory-losing) bash and each occasion has been quite different. Weekends can be quite sexy affairs with a good following of pre-clubbers and older people like me who just want a few jars of anything to forget their woes. I popped back again one lunchtime to sample the food, only to be foiled as it was the chef's day off. I didn't understand that and am not particularly interested in a chef's social habits, especially when I'm hungry. However, they do rustle up bowls of soup and panini toasted sandwiches (available every day for a fiver with a drink included) which were actually just the ticket, but I do mean to go again and sample some of the dishes from the much more interesting every-day-apart-from-Monday menu. It's a real shame there are no cask ales, but it has a good atmosphere, decent décor and furnishings, and good luck to it!

OPEN *11.00-23.00 (Mon-Sat), 12.00-22.30 (Sun)*
FOOD *12.30-14.30 (Mon-Fri) 12.30-22.00 (Sat-Sun)*
CREDIT CARDS *all major cards, except AmEx and Diners*
DRAUGHT BEERS *Staropramen, Grolsch, Tennent's Pils, Tennent's Extra, Guinness, Caffrey's, Dry Blackthorn*
Wheelchair access. Private room seats 250
NEAREST TUBE STATIONS *Chalk Farm, Swiss Cottage*

ADMIRAL CODRINGTON
17 Mossop Street, SW3; 0171 581 0005

This famous old Chelsea pub will get a paragraph or two in the history of our times. The 70s and 80s were its heydays when it was, quite simply, *the* place to be. It became the unofficial headquarters of the Sloane Rangers who referred to it by its nickname. During Thatcher's reign (and almost exactly to those dates) The Cod was in the safe hands of Mel Barnett and his wife, model Irene Dunford. For many a social season they encouraged the young, the beautiful and the rich to whoop it up, and whoop it up they did. Its famous clientele included the then Lady Diana Spencer, and I hear that both her ladies-in-waiting met their future spouses there, and Fergie and Prince Andrew apparently used the pub to meet in secret to discuss their wedding arrangements.

Such was the success that when the lease came up for renewal in 1990, jealous Bass wanted it back. The Marquess of Bath – Viscount Weymouth as he was then – led a long campaign, gathered 3,000 or so names and pleaded with the brewers to leave it alone. The campaign failed. Mel stormed out of the pub declaring, 'I will never set foot in that pub again – unless I own it.' The customers left along with the Barnetts, and Bass struggled with the place for years, so much so that at the end of 1996 they decided to sell the lease. Enter Mel and Irene once again. They had come home. It took some time for The Cod to find its feet again and it may never quite recreate those glory days of yesteryear, but it is markedly improved. It has become a destination once again, and long may it remain so.

OPEN *11.00-23.00 (Mon-Sat), 12.00-22.30 (Sun)*
FOOD *12.00-15.00 (Mon-Fri), 18.30-21.00 (Mon-Thurs), 13.00-16.00 (Sun)*
CREDIT CARDS *all major cards*
DRAUGHT BEERS *Bass, Fuller's London Pride, Greenall's IPA, Carling Black Label, Grolsch, Guinness, Dry Blackthorn, Caffrey's, Staropramen*
Wheelchair access to venue. Private room: conservatory with cocktail bar, seats 30
NEAREST TUBE STATION *South Kensington and Sloane Square*

ALBERO & GRANA
Chelsea Cloisters, Sloane Avenue, SW3; 0171 225 1048

My approach to this wine and cocktail bar was blocked by the doorman who asked 'Can I help you?' I resisted the temptation to say that I had come to pay my mortgage or to buy a tin of beans and some frozen chips for my supper. Of course what he really meant was 'What on earth does a person like you think you're doing coming into a place like this.' I stated the bleedin' obvious and said I had come for drinks, which foxed him sufficiently to allow me in. Subsequent investigations revealed they don't like large numbers of 'single-sex' groups turning up, presumably for fear of people enjoying themselves. The smoky, chrome-modern interior would have been spacious were it not for the proliferation of pillars and the clientele comprises the It boys and girls of Chelsea who have nothing better to do than fritter away their trust funds. Such is my presumed status, I was immediately offered the lesser 'bin end' wine list and, not one to be down-trodden, I demanded the same drinks list as the Its. It was worth it. The wines are world varied and cleverly collected but it was the cocktails which impressed me most, and the knowledgeable bar staff produce them with enough theatre and élan to make them an essential sample. I'm only reluctant to give it a positive vote on the basis that the doorman might well climb inside the bar himself and not allow any more of us is in, but I do rate it, despite the cold feeling of the place and the fact that I spent my last mortgage payment on a night out with my mates.

OPEN 12.00-23.00 (Mon-Sat), 12.00-22.30 (Sun)
FOOD opening hours
CREDIT CARDS all major cards
NEAREST TUBE STATION South Kensington

THE ALBERT

52 Victoria Street, SW1; 0171 222 5577

When it comes to Victorian values you can't beat The Albert. Richly accoutred, nobly disposed, it is the very model of a high Victorian public house. Today, gleaming new towers attempt to dwarf The Albert. It remains steadfastly undwarfed. With its fine engraved windows, removed and stored during the war, its rich decorations, its gleaming bar and noble staircase, it is in splendid form. It needs a staff of 28 to keep it running smoothly, more in the summer. There is quick food in the bar and a busy carvery on the first floor, and tourists with much to see in the neighbourhood find here a welcome respite from sore feet and history. The three-course meal runs in at £14.95 including service and the wine list boasts a gentle, reasonably priced selection of bottles.

This is New Scotland Yard's local and MPs use it a lot. With the Houses of Parliament just up the street they appreciate the division bell in the restaurant and, after a drink or two, may well start to think that one day their picture may join the portraits of Prime Ministers, from the Marquis of Salisbury to John Major, lining the broad staircase. Mrs Thatcher unveiled her portrait herself. The Queen used to meet foreign heads of state at Victoria Station. As she bowled along Victoria Street with her guest in the state landau she would point out the pensive young man holding a rose on the pub sign – Albert, her great-great-grandfather.

OPEN 11.00-23.00 (Mon-Sat), 12.00-22.30 (Sun)
FOOD bar 11.00-22.30 (Mon-Sat), 12.00-22.00 (Sun); carvery 12.00-21.30 (Mon-Sun)
CREDIT CARDS all major cards
DRAUGHT BEERS Courage Best, Courage Directors, Theakston, Foster's, Holsten, Kronenbourg, Miller, Guinness, Strongbow, John Smith's Extra Smooth, two guest ales
Wheelchair access to venue. Private room seats 26
NEAREST TUBE STATION St James's Park

ALBERTINE

1 Wood Lane, W12; 0181 743 9593

This is a bar for the connoisseur of wines rather than the session drinker, with a wide-ranging list that has some good value, quality offerings. The success of Albertine is down to its having resisted the temptation to become a restaurant. You can eat, of course – the menu includes Greek salad (£4.60) and leek and mushroom quiche (£4.30) – but food isn't the prime motive of this bar. It has the appearance of a musty 80s wine bar, with

dark wooden tables and candle-wax-coated bottles. Table service is all that's lacking to make this an almost perfect place for the wine lover.
OPEN *11.00-23.00 (Mon-Fri), 18.30-23.00 (Sat)*
FOOD *12.00-22.45 (Mon-Fri), 18.30-22.30 (Sat)*
CREDIT CARDS *all major cards, not AmEx*
Wheelchair access to venue. Private room: 30 seated, 40-50 standing
NEAREST TUBE STATION *Shepherd's Bush*

THE ALBION
10 Thornhill Road, N1; 0171 607 7450
This dear old ivy-covered, graceful coaching inn belongs to a quieter, more rural time. The delightful Thornhill Road is lined with Georgian houses, and if going to The Albion means making a detour, then make it. It is an elegant, prosperous pub. The roomy bar used to have a restaurant area, but the demand for the hearty cooked lunches and suppers had grown to such an extent that they now serve them throughout the pub. The star turn at The Albion, though, is the beer garden at the back – big, quiet and extraordinarily pleasant in the summer with its trellis and roses and picnic tables. A new menu hasn't proved enormously popular, but it remains a popular pub.
OPEN *11.00-23.00 (Mon-Sat), 12.00-22.30 (Sun)*
FOOD *bar 12.00-15.00 and 18.00-21.30 (Mon-Fri), 12.00-22.30 (Sun)*
CREDIT CARDS *all major cards*
DRAUGHT BEERS *John Smith's Extra Smooth, Theakston Best, Theakston XB, Foster's, Löwenbräu, Guinness, Strongbow, Beck's*
Wheelchair access to venue
NEAREST TUBE STATION *Highbury & Islington, Angel*

G. E. ALDWINKLES
154 Fleet Road, NW3; 0171 485 2112
G. E. Aldwinkles? Who he? The truth must out. He was made up. Still, so was Mr Pickwick, whom he much resembles, and new owners thought a change might perk this old Hampstead pub up a bit. It had been the White Horse for its first 100 years or so and it certainly needed something. Let's see what old G. E. Aldwinkles can do, thought Regent Inns.
   Regent Inns is emerging as an interesting contender in the highly competitive pub business. The driving force is David Franks who bought his first pub in 1977, soon had a couple of dozen, went public in 1993 and expects a turn-over of well over £31 million this year. The company has 60 pubs in London as I write and ambitious plans for a great many more. G. E. Aldwinkles has certainly smartened up the old White Horse, uncovering its original floor tiles, restoring its enamel plate ceiling and its nice horseshoe bar, replacing gloomy windows with clear glass, improving the food. The cellar bar had become a tremendous dump. Now people book it for parties and it is becoming known as a Saturday night comedy venue called The Hampstead Clinic. In the old days the White Horse did bed and breakfast in its upstairs rooms. The staffs of several company pubs lodge in them now.
OPEN *11.00-23.00 (Mon-Sat), midday-22.30 (Sun)*
FOOD *10.00-15.00 and 18.00-19.30 (Mon-Sat), midday-17.00 (Sun)*
CREDIT CARDS *all major cards*
DRAUGHT BEERS *Kronenbourg, Foster's, Holsten, Stella, Heineken, Guinness, Beamish Black*
Wheelchair access to venue, not to loos
NEAREST TUBE STATION *Belfont Park*

ALEXANDRA
14 Clapham Common Southside, SW4; 0171 627 5102
This tall, impressive, tile-fronted building is handy as the first port of call when leaving the tube at the south side of Clapham Common. The exterior disguises a vast barn-like interior, with a combination of low and high-

beamed ceilings, wooden floors, tables, chairs and walls, and the occasional step in the floor where you least expect it. The crowd is mostly young. Although it's a large bar, it fills up quickly at weekends.

OPEN *11.00-23.00 (Mon-Sat), 12.00-22.30 (Sun)*

FOOD *12.00-15.00 and 18.30-22.30 (Tues-Fri), 12.00-16.00 and 18.30-22.30 (Sat-Sun)*

CREDIT CARDS *all major cards*

DRAUGHT BEERS *Courage Best, Courage Directors, John Smith's Extra Smooth, Foster's, Kronenbourg, Miller, Guinness, Scrumpy Jack, Irish Red Ale, Independent Lager, Guinness Cold Flow*

Private room: 150 seated, 250 standing

NEAREST TUBE STATION *Clapham Common*

THE ALEXANDRA

33 Wimbledon Hill Road, SW19; 0181 947 7691

The Alex is one of Young's flagships, number one for liquor sales, they say in ringing tones. My man in Wimbledon is not surprised. He writes: 'The Alex is an institution in Wimbledon, a busy town centre pub, classically Victorian and over recent years it has been very carefully refurbished. The old public bar, for instance, is the Wine and Ale Bar now, all beams and brickwork and huge barrels to put plates and glasses on, an open log fire spit-roasting beef and turkey on cold winter days and a staircase leading to the new roof garden where, again in the winter, you will encounter Wimbledon's first rooftop marquee. In the summer you will meet a barbecue. A no-smoking bar leads to the Green Bar, now predominantly red actually, and go past the counter where pub meals are served and you are in the wine bar, Young's first, where you can eat and drink till 1 am on Friday and Saturday nights. It is, as it always was, a place where people do business, do lunch, recover from shopping. The station is only a few minutes' walk away and some regularly break their journeys to the further-flung outposts of network Southeast for a little something at The Alex. They can always catch the next train. Or the one after that...'

OPEN *11.00-23.00 (Mon-Sat), midday-22.30 (Sun), Wine bar to 1.00 (Fri-Sat)*

FOOD *midday-22.00 (Mon-Thurs), midday-21.00 (Fri-Sat)*

CREDIT CARDS *all major cards*

DRAUGHT BEERS *Ramrod Smooth, Young's Bitter, Young's Special, Young's Wheatbeer, Carling, Stella Artois, Young's Export*

Wheelchair access to venue

NEAREST TUBE STATION *Wimbledon*

ALL BAR ONE

The phonomenon that is All Bar One has been the success story of the decade and London seems to be the place where they succeed best. Some people criticise and say they are all the same wherever you go. Others praise and say they are all the same wherever you go. What you do get is consistency – wherever you find an All Bar One you know that it will be a spacious bar with library-style wine racks, a high standard of catering, a good range of beers and wines, and friendly, efficient staff. This is the All Bar One standard offer. It is what they call a retail brand in the Bass portfolio of eating and drinking venues, and it has proved so successful that Bass are going to expand it throughout the country as well as increasing its London presence. This is not to be sighed at. All Bar Ones are a very welcome addition to any high street, and the crowds who pile into them bear testament to this.

Branches at:

CANARY WHARF 42 Mackenzie Walk, South Colonnade, E14; 0171 513 0911

   NEAREST RAILWAY STATION *Canary Wharf (DLR)*

CHISWICK 197-199 Chiswick High Road, W4; 0181 987 8211

   NEAREST TUBE STATION *Turnham Green*

CITY (EC2) 34 Threadneedle Street, EC2; 0171 614 9931
　　NEAREST TUBE STATION *Bank*
CITY (EC4) 103 Cannon Street, EC4; 0171 220 9013
　　NEAREST TUBE STATION *Cannon Street*
CITY (EC4) 44-46 Ludgate Hill, EC4; 0171 653 9901
　　NEAREST TUBE STATIONS *Blackfriars, St Paul's*
CITY (SE1) 28-30 London Bridge, SE1; 0171 940 9981
　　NEAREST TUBE STATION *London Bridge*
CLAPHAM 32-38 Northcote Road, SW11; 0171 801 9951
　　NEAREST RAILWAY STATION *Clapham Junction*
FULHAM 587-591 Fulham Road, SW6; 0171 471 0611
　　NEAREST TUBE STATION *Fulham Broadway*
FULHAM 311-313 Fulham Road, SW10; 0171 349 1751
　　NEAREST TUBE STATIONS *Fulham Broadway, South Kensington*
HIGHGATE 1-3 Hampstead Lane, Highgate, N6; 0181 342 7861
　　NEAREST TUBE STATION *Highgate*
W1 289-293 Regent street, W1; 0171 467 9901
　　NEAREST TUBE STATION *Oxford Circus*
W1 3-4 Hanover Street, W1; 0171 518 9931
　　NEAREST TUBE STATION *Oxford Circus*
RICHMOND 11 Hill Street, Richmond; 0181 332 7141
　　NEAREST TUBE STATION *Richmond*
ST JOHN'S WOOD 60 St John's Wood High Street, NW8; 0171 483 9931
　　NEAREST TUBE STATION *St John's Wood*
SUTTON 2 Hill Road, Sutton; 0181 652 3521
　　NEAREST RAILWAY STATION *Sutton*
WANDSWORTH 527-529 Old York Road, SW18; 0181 875 0111
　　NEAREST RAILWAY STATION *Wandsworth Town*
WIMBLEDON 37-39 Wimbledon Hill Road, SW19; 0181 971 9871
　　NEAREST TUBE STATION *Wimbledon*
EC1 91-93 Charterhouse Street, EC1; 0171 553 9391
　　NEAREST TUBE STATION *Farringdon*
CROUCH END 2-4 The Broadway, Crouch End, N8; 0181 342 7871
　　NEAREST RAILWAY STATION *Crouch Hill*
SOHO 36-38 Dean Street, W1; 0171 479 7921
　　NEAREST TUBE STATION *Tottenham Court Road*
WC2 19 Henrietta Street, WC2; 0171 557 7941
　　NEAREST TUBE STATION *Covent Garden*
ISLINGTON 1 Liverpool Road, Islington, N1; 0171 843 0021
　　NEAREST TUBE STATION *Highbury & Islington*
HOLBORN 58 Kingsway, Holborn, WC2; 0171 269 5171
　　NEAREST TUBE STATION *Holborn*
LEICESTER SQUARE 48 Leicester Square, WC2; 0171 747 9921
　　NEAREST TUBE STATION *Leicester Square*
NOTTING HILL 126-128 Notting Hill Gate, W11; 0171 313 9362
　　NEAREST TUBE STATION *Notting Hill Gate*
W1 7-9 Paddington Street, W1; 0171 497 0071
　　NEAREST TUBE STATION *Baker Street*

THE ALMA TAVERN
499 Old York Road, SW18; 0181 870 2537
Every Victorian schoolboy knew what the Alma was. Alma, battle of;
famous victory; Crimean War, 1854. The Alma Tavern was built in Old
York Road 12 years later, a hotel at first but now a much admired
Victorian pub. It stands directly opposite Wandsworth Town station and
after victory or defeat at Twickers, rugger-buggers bound for Waterloo see
The Alma's elegant Frenchified dome and pour off the train and straight
into the bar. They tend to get home a little later than intended. The Alma is
a prosperous pub faced by shiny glazed tiles, bright green, and inside

there are lovely painted mirrors, gold mosaic medallions, a classical plaster frieze and a fine mahogany staircase leading out of the bar. They have all been scrupulously restored. In winter a fire blazes in the art deco fireplace and a handsome 1920s range heats the separate dining room. There are morning papers on the bar, a huge baker's dough table and a little French cash kiosk in the dining room. They cultivate Frenchness at The Alma, sell croques monsieur and croques madame, also a lot of wine. Indeed they have now taken to printing 'hôtel de la gare' on the menus. 'Tongue in cheek', says Charles Gotto, the licensee.

The Alma has become a big rugger pub and rugby nights are terrific occasions there. Doesn't the pub fear for the health of its painted mirrors? 'Why?' says rugger fan Gotto. 'They are as good as gold.'

OPEN *11.00-23.00 (Mon-Sat), midday-22.30 (Sun)*
FOOD *Bar: midday-22.30 (Mon-Sat), midday-16.00 (Sun), 10.00-13.00 (Sat-Sun) breakfast*
Restaurant: midday-15.00 (Mon-Sat), 19.00-22.30 (Mon-Sat), midday-16.00 (Sun) Lunch
CREDIT CARDS *all major cards*
DRAUGHT BEERS *Ramrod Smooth, Young's Bitter, Young's Special, Young's First Gold, Stella Artois, Young's Pilsner, Young's Export, Scrumpy Jack*
Wheelchair access to venue. Private room seats 70
NEAREST RAILWAY STATION *Wandsworth Town*

ALPHABET
61-63 Beak Street, W1; 0171 439 2190
The *Evening Standard* Bar of the Year in 1998. Rightly so too. It is attracting a large eclectic following of street-fashionable twentysomethings along with the usual, earthy Soho set. There's no draught beer so it's a bottle-sucking joint, and it also has a decent range of 20 New World wines, all under £20 a bottle, with champagne at £21. There's a downstairs bar with adjustable car seats and a street map of Soho on the floor. The food is excellent, and the menu changes regularly. Last year I predicted that it would become one of the hippest places in town. It has achieved that status, which means that getting in can be quite tricky on busy nights.

OPEN *11.00-23.00 (Mon-Sat)*
FOOD *11.00-22.00 (Mon-Sat), Bar Menu: 16.00-23.00*
CREDIT CARDS *all major cards, not Diners or AmEx*
Wheelchair access to venue
NEAREST TUBE STATION *Piccadilly Circus and Oxford Circus*

THE AMERICAN BAR
Savoy Hotel, Strand, WC2; 0171 836 4343
This bar is much more relaxed of late, but the dress code of jacket and tie should be observed – certainly no denims. Spirits are served as doubles for around £5 and bottled beers start at £4. Stylish, sophisticated surroundings make this a place where business people can happily punish their expense accounts. Service is somewhat stilted but friendly and efficient, and the kettle chips, almonds and olives are constantly replenished. All in all, it is rather a good deal.

OPEN *11.00-23.00 (Mon-Sat), 12.00-15.00 and 19.00-22.30 (Sun)*
CREDIT CARDS *all major cards*
NEAREST TUBE STATION *Temple and Embankment*

THE ANCHOR, BANKSIDE
34 Park Street, SE1; 0171 407 1577
Bankside has certainly gone up in the world. In Shakespeare's day it was all slums and stews but look at it now, a riverside walk, the new Globe Theatre opening at last and a famous old inn, immaculate in every particular. Dr Johnson often supped here with his good friend Mrs Thrale

whose husband owned it and the brewery next door. It became a sort of Groucho Club with Oliver Goldsmith, David Garrick and Edmund Burke holding court. Today's Groucho cannot always offer conversation on quite such a level, but it is a fine old pub with five bars, a minstrels' gallery, a private 18th-century dining room, a new riverside terrace with serried ranks of picnic tables, a garden terrace, a barbecue and a most superior restaurant. Sam Wanamaker often ate here when his wonderful Globe was taking shape nearby. He always had table 7, the one in the window. It is not a pub you can leave quietly. In the creaking Olympics The Anchor's floorboards would take gold.

OPEN *11.00-23.00 (Mon-Sat), midday-22.30 (Sun)*

FOOD *Bar: midday-21.00 (Mon-Sun); Restaurant midday-14.30 and 18.00-21.30 (Mon-Sun)*

CREDIT CARDS *all major cards*

DRAUGHT BEERS *Bass, Flowers, Thomas Greenall's Original, Foster's, Kronenbourg, Stella Artois, Murphy's, Dry Blackthorn, Strongbow, Caffrey's, plus nine cask-conditioned bitters changed on a weekly basis*
Private room seats 50

NEAREST TUBE STATION *London Bridge*

THE ANGEL

101 Bermondsey Wall East, SE16; 0171 237 3608

There has been an inn here in Rotherhithe since the 17th century, built on piles at the water's edge and always in the thick of things, around it a warren of tenements, boatyards and general riverside carrying-on. There were at least four little bars on the ground floor, the haunt of sailors, pirates, smugglers, press gangs, bawds, I suppose. Pepys knew it well and Judge Jefferies watched the hangings on Execution Dock from the balcony. Sometimes he watched the hangings in one pub, sometimes in another but, disagreeable to the last, he appears to have chosen The Angel to haunt. There is still a balcony, narrow but with a bench to sit on, and a new flagged terrace with tables and chairs and the river passing by. The Angel has been rebuilt a few times in its day but it has done well to survive at all, what with hard times and the blitz. Even the dockers have gone now but old Rotherhithe meets new Rotherhithe in the bar and business lunchers from the City use the restaurant upstairs, a serious eatery with formally dressed waiters and a fine view of Tower Bridge and the City. It is open in the evenings too. Almost at the front door is an outcropping of ruin in the centre of a field and a notice telling us that this is the remains of Edward III's moated manor house, begun in 1353. Edward III was A Good Thing, 'the greatest warrior king in Christendom' in Antonia Fraser's view. He had nothing at all to do with The Angel Tavern.

OPEN *11.30-23.00 (Mon-Sat); midday-22.30 (Sun)*

FOOD *bar midday-14.30 and 18.30-21.30 (Mon-Sun); restaurant: midday-14.00 and 19.00-21.30 (Mon-Fri), 19.00-21.30 (Sat), midday-14.30 (Sun)*

CREDIT CARDS *all major cards*

DRAUGHT BEERS *Caffrey's, Thomas Greenall's Original, Worthington's Best, Foster's, Stella Artois, Murphy's, Strongbow*
Private room seats 50

NEAREST TUBE STATION *Rotherhithe*

ANGLESEA ARMS

15 Selwood Terrace, SW7; 0171 373 7960

The Anglesea Arms was Lady Joseph's pub. It had been a personal gift to her from her husband, Sir Maxwell Joseph, chairman of Grand Met. She loved it and would have no changes made. When she died it passed to her family which, happily, sees things as she did, so the Anglesea remains wonderfully reassuring, everything substantial, nothing too smart, on all sides evidence of tender loving care. There are no juke boxes, no fruit machines, no television. The hours are unchanged too, and time is called at 3pm so that the bar gets a clean and a rest in the afternoon. The Anglesea is an early Victorian Free House, an integral part of a prosperous South Kensington terrace. There is a large saloon bar and a smaller bar down some steps known as the cubby, very cosy with a fire in winter. Then there is a stretch of forecourt that some would say was the jewel in its crown. It is a hugely popular place to drink in the summer. The Anglesea was the Evening Standard's Pub of the Year in 1988.

OPEN 11.00-23.00 (Mon-Sat), midday-22.30 (Sun)

FOOD midday-15.00 (daily)

CREDIT CARDS all major cards, not AmEx

DRAUGHT BEERS Adnams, Broadside, Brakspear, Brakspear Original, London Pride, Carlsberg Export, Grolsch, Heineken, Stella Artois, Guinness, Dry Blackthorn, Wadworth 6X, Hoegaarden, Freedom, Czech Budweiser, one guest beer

NEAREST TUBE STATIONS South Kensington, Gloucester Road

THE ANTELOPE

22 Eaton Terrace, SW1; 0171 730 7781

This deeply traditional, low-ceilinged, snug little pub sits in the heart of Sloaneland and attracts the residents of the Eatons, who pop in for a power-drink, peruse the financial pages and ponder over the state of their portfolios. It is more than 200 years old, which means that much of Belgravia grew up around it. When the houses arrived the Antelope obligingly provided two front doors, one for the grander household staff led by the butler, the other for the lowlier persons. Once inside, partitions kept them decently apart. There are still the same number of front doors.

Lunch is a comfortable and sedate affair but in the evening the floppy-haired, pin-striped suits meet up with power-dressed women wearing Alice bands for beers, beers and more beers. If you're not one of the privileged few to get pride of place on the bar stools, you may struggle to be noticed. The scene can resemble that of a trading floor, with outstretched arms clutching handfuls of money trying to catch the eye of the bar person. They used to spill out on to the pavement in the summer, but that's all changed now – it apparently upsets those neighbours who don't use the pub. Fanny Craddock (remember her?) once said its little paneled restaurant recaptured the flavour of the old chop-house, and that is still the aim – good plain cooking.

OPEN 11.30-23.00 (Mon-Sat), 12.00-15.00 and 19.00-22.30 (Sun)

FOOD 12.00-15.00 and 18.00-22.00 (Mon-Sat)

CREDIT CARDS all major cards

DRAUGHT BEERS Adnams, Tetley's, Marston's Pedigree, Carlsberg, Castlemaine XXXX, Stella Artois, Guinness, Dry Blackthorn, three guest ales Wheelchair access to venue, not to loos. Private room seats 40

NEAREST TUBE STATION Sloane Square

THE ARCHERY TAVERN

4 Bathurst Street, W2; 0171 402 4916

The Archery Tavern is a pretty country pub tucked away behind Bayswater Road, the archer's pub, rooted in the great days. It was built in 1839 on what used to be Thomas Waring's archery range, and he is the fine chap drawing his bow on the inn sign. He was a famous archer in his day. Waring is still there but I'm sorry to say he is just about the only archer who is. It is not that there aren't any archers these days. There are archery clubs all around London – in fact the London Archers are just across the park. They shoot three or four times a week on a strip of land attached to Kensington Palace. But, let's face it, there are nearer pubs. So The Archery Tavern has to depend on drinkers with other interests, and it has no problem there. People love it. It is so genuinely old-fashioned and it has some excellent Badger ales. A popular quiz night is running on Sundays at the time of writing and, no arguing with the landlord, Tony O'Neill—he sets the questions. The food is prepared on the premises and its fairly extensive menu of light snacks and main meals includes the steak and ale pie (£5.95). The pinball and satellite TV seem slightly incongruous, but these appear to be the ubiquitous features of a Hall & Woodhouse pub.

OPEN *11.00-23.00 (Mon-Sat), 10.30-22.30 (Sun); early opening at the weekend for breakfast*
FOOD *12.00-22.00 (Mon-Fri), 10.30-22.00 (Sat-Sun)*
CREDIT CARDS *all major cards*
DRAUGHT BEERS *Badger's Best, Badger IPA, Black Adder, Tanglefoot, Hofbräu lagers, Guinness, Dry Blackthorn, Dempsy's, Archery Bitter*
Private room seats 40
NEAREST TUBE STATION *Lancaster Gate*

THE ARGYLL ARMS

18 Argyll Street, W1; 0171 734 6117
Round the corner from Oxford Circus, actually squashed up against the side of the Underground station, is this spectacular Victorian pub. It gets packed at lunchtime. It is busy in the afternoon. You can't move in the evening. The Victorians knew about pubs all right.

   This Argyll is the business. First of all it looks so great from the front – all that show – so of course you go in, and Victoria Regina! You are in a glittering mirrored corridor with etched glass partitions opening on small numbered bars. Straight ahead is the big saloon bar, bags of space, bags of swank and behind that is the dining room. Every bit is full of people talking. The small bars at the front are lovely. They give you your own bit of counter and some space of your own. People liked that in 1868 and they like it now, but all over London grand Victorian pubs like this one are losing the partitions they were born with. They haven't done it at The Argyll, so cheers for it and back to our tour. Up the massive mahogany staircase and you are in another big bar. Victorian pastiche up here but in the spirit of things and a fine view of the London Palladium across the road. That is where Argyll House stood, a great mansion that came down in the 1860s. The original Argyll Arms came down too and this one went up in its place. Nicholson's get high marks for keeping it in such sparkling nick. They always seem to be fitting new carpets, there is hidden air conditioning and they recently spent £50,000 on the loos. Gents using the gents now find themselves facing framed pages of that day's *Financial Times*, thus enabling them, as Kipling advised, to fill each unforgiving minute with sixty seconds worth of distance run. You might suppose a bar so near Oxford Circus to be on the front line, but there is very little trouble. An 'acceptable standard of dress' is required and the big man on the door on Saturday nights enforces this.

OPEN *11.00-23.00 (Mon-Sat), 12.00-21.00 (Sun)*
FOOD *11.00-19.00; hot salt-beef sandwiches up to 21.00 (Mon-Sun)*
CREDIT CARDS *all major cards*
DRAUGHT BEERS *Adnams, Calder's Cream Ale, Tetley's, Carlsberg, Castlemaine XXXX, Stella Artois, Guinness, Dry Blackthorn, guest ales which change on a regular basis*
Wheelchair access to venue, not to loos. Private room: 30 seated, 70 standing
NEAREST TUBE STATION *Oxford Circus*

ATLANTIC BAR AND GRILL

20 Glasshouse Street, W1; 0171 734 4888
The design is that of a 30s cruise liner gliding gently across the Atlantic in search of the rich spoils of the New World. Going down the wide sweeping staircase into the bar and restaurant area, you will encounter Harry's Bar (presumably the first-class lounge); the calm atmosphere here is mainly due to the man on the door controlling the numbers. The main bar is vast, with

high ceilings, a large island bar and plenty of deck space for drinking cocktails. The City boys on the pull and office party girlies who look like they might have a long train journey home in an easterly direction seem to enjoy the vibrant, chatty environment and opportunistic atmosphere.

Surprisingly, the Atlantic still manages to draw a big crowd in the evenings despite having the most tedious door policy in London: 'At the discretion of the door'. I take for this that if you're a mate of the clipboard girly on the door then you're OK; the rest of us have to suffer the humiliation of being held in line while others breeze on in. A tip is to book a table to eat and then do what you like once inside, but turning up with a large gang is not recommended. Afternoons are the easiest times to get in, when they'll probably welcome you with open arms. In theory, you can get in here, without paying, until 3am, but unfortunately, the bat on the door has the last word, so unless she's flown off to hang upside down somewhere you may have a bit of a time of it. The owner is Oliver Peyton; call him and tell him I said he was a spoil sport.

OPEN *12.00-03.00 (Mon-Sat), 18.00-22.30 (Sun)*
FOOD *bar 12.00-03.00 (Mon-Sat), 18.30-22.00 (Sun); restaurant 12.00-15.00 and 18.00-midnight (Mon-Fri), 18.00-midnight (Sat); 19.00-midnight (Sun)*
CREDIT CARDS *all major cards*
DRAUGHT BEERS *Mash, Hoegaarden, a guest ale*
Wheelchair access to venue. Private room seats 70
NEAREST TUBE STATION *Piccadilly Circus*

THE AUDLEY

41 Mount Street, W1; 0171 499 1843
Pubs do not come much grander than The Audley. Mount Street – the heart of Mayfair – Berkeley Square at one end, Park Lane at the other. We have the first Duke of Westminster to thank for it. In the early 1880s he was having Mount Street rebuilt and his architects included drawings for a large glitzy public house. He sent them right back, giving them clearly to understand that a gin palace was not what he had in mind. So The Audley was built in red brick and pink terracotta, neo-French Renaissance like the rest of the street, a style that would not offend the most fastidious gentleman's gentleman.

Like all pubs of its generation The Audley mirrored the class divisions of the world outside. It was cut up into a parish of separate bars, each with its own social nuances. Mahogany and glass partitions hid each group of customers from each other, while narrow hinged screens hid customers from staff. The screens and partitions have long gone, of course, and we can see, as the original customers could not, all the superb plaster ceiling and the whole of the splendid bar itself. The original chandeliers have survived – so have the clocks, so has its general air of being rather a cut above which, indeed, while in The Audley, we all are. Overseas visitors often very much take to the paneled dining room upstairs. You eat formally and substantially here in the well-known English manner – several courses, Stilton, port. Open all week.

OPEN *11.00-23.00 (Mon-Sat), 12.00-22.30 (Sun)*
FOOD *bar 11.00-21.15 (Mon-Sun); restaurant 12.00-15.00 and 17.30-21.30 (Mon-Sat), 12.00-15.00 (Sun)*
CREDIT CARDS *all major cards*
DRAUGHT BEERS *Courage Best, Courage Directors, John Smith's Extra Smooth, Theakston Best, Beck's, Foster's, Kronenbourg, Guinness, Strongbow*
Wheelchair access to venue. Private room: jazz-theme room seats 120
NEAREST TUBE STATIONS *Green Park, Marble Arch*

THE AUSTRALIAN

29 Milner Street, SW3; 0171 589 3114

Here's a sports report. In 1878, Australia, on its second tour, played two matches on the smart new cricket pitch on Prince's Green, now occupied by Lennox Gardens. The first was against the Gentlemen of England. All three Grace brothers turned out for the Gentlemen who won by an innings and one run. The Australians then played the Players of England. The match was unfinished. It was a golden age. Dr Grace was in his prime, everyone was playing for the fun of it, England nearly always won and Australian cricketers far from home found a refreshment stop much to their liking in this wide, leafy street that led directly to the cricket ground. The pub they adopted later renamed itself The Australian and there it still is in Milner Street, three handsome storeys covered in Virginia creeper, a very fine English pub. Over the years the collection of memorabilia has built up to the extent that this is now almost a perfect museum of cricket. The rickety interior is a comfortable place to sip on the Pimms and enjoy the fine real ales and good-quality English fare. You used to be able to eat outside but neighbours objected, sigh, so in came the tables. There are still benches outside. You can sit on them but only until 9pm. Touring sides have long since moved on to pastures new but you will find Australians in here. Behind the bar.

OPEN *11.00-23.00 (Mon-Sat), 12.00-22.30 (Sun)*

FOOD *bar 11.00-21.15 (Mon-Sun); restaurant 12.00-15.00 (Mon-Sat) and 18.00-21.00 (Mon-Thurs), 12.00-14.30 (Sun)*

CREDIT CARDS *all major cards, not AmEx*

DRAUGHT BEERS *Adnams, Marston's Pedigree, Tetley's, Carlsberg, Carlsberg Export, Castlemaine XXXX, Guinness, Dry Blackthorn, guest ales*

NEAREST TUBE STATIONS *Knightsbridge, Sloane Square*

BABUSHKA

173 Blackfriars Road, SE1; 0171 928 3693

Gary Hibberd and John O'Donnell, a couple of guys from the rag trade, spotted a gap in the market for providing decent quality bars and eateries in previously unpopular areas. This bar – the old King's Head – was their first venture. They gutted it, reopened it, and in a matter of weeks it was necessary to make bookings for lunch – the Modern British cuisine was clearly an instant hit. The assembly of small rooms was knocked through to create one large bar stripped down to its bare brick and girders with a Dali-esque mural along one wall. There's a lounge area at the back with a grand piano, and an enormous beer garden for barbecues. In the evenings they whip off the napery and play host to a throng of after-work drinkers. At weekends the volume rises even more as pre-clubbers prepare for a long night at the nearby Ministry of Sound. Sundays have become a bit of an event, featuring Enigma, a daytime club scenario organised with the Ministry, who bring in five DJs for a glam, mostly gay event. They have a picker on the door (a new name for bouncer) and the more glam you are, the more likely you are to be picked.

OPEN *12.00-23.00 (Mon-Wed), 12.00-midnight (Thurs-Fri), 20.00-midnight (Sat)*

FOOD *12.00-16.00 (Mon-Fri)*

CREDIT CARDS *all major cards*

DRAUGHT BEERS *Caffrey's, London Pride, Carling Black Label, Carling Premier, Grolsch, Guinness, Dry Blackthorn, Staropramen*

Private room: 200 seated, 350 standing

NEAREST TUBE STATIONS *Waterloo, Blackfriars*

BABUSHKA

125 Caledonian Road, N1; 0171 837 1924

An even better conversion style-wise than its sister in Blackfriars Road (qv), this branch is split on three levels with a long ground-floor bar, an upstairs lounge filled with chesterfields, and a restaurant on the next level with views over the Regent's Canal. The food is really of a very high standard: pan-fried tuna with sweet and sour tomatoes (£7.25) and ricotta and leek strudel with tomato jam (£5.75). Extras are extra. If you live near the Caledonian Road you're quite lucky; if you don't, it's worth a trip. Not many people seem to know about the restaurant and, as with many a quiet place, the service can be slow. Things really get going on Sunday nights with a glam club, Pushka, where you're likely to find trannies dancing on the bar.

OPEN *12.00-23.30 (Mon-Fri), 19.00-23.30 (Sat)*

FOOD *bar 12.00-16.00 (Mon-Fri), 18.00-22.00 (Sat); restaurant – bookings only*

CREDIT CARDS *all major cards*

Wheelchair access to venue, not to loos. Private room: dining room for hire overlooking river, 40 seated, and lounge bar 40 seated, 60 standing

NEAREST TUBE STATION *King's Cross*

BABUSHKA

41 Tavistock Crescent, W11; 0171 727 9250

The third and probably not final venue from the team of Hibberd and O'Donnell opened in January 1997 in the farther-flung fields of Notting Hill. It's similar in design to the other Babushkas but is essentially a night-time venue. DJs perform every night of the week – house, hip-hop, jazz, soul. They even do flamenco dancing on Saturday at lunchtimes. There's a wide range of bottled beers, and the fridges can sometimes struggle to keep them chilled. I have my very own bottle of Polish Pure Spirit (79.9%) which is kept behind the bar for any personal emergencies I might decide to have. It's the only place I know where it can be rocking on a Saturday afternoon.

OPEN *17.00-23.00 (Mon-Fri), 12.00-23.00 (Sat-Sun)*

FOOD *as opening hours – bar food only*

CREDIT CARDS *all major cards*

DRAUGHT BEERS *Adnams, Kilkenny, Old Speckled Hen, Carlsberg, Löwenbräu, Guinness, Strongbow*

Wheelchair access to venue. Private room seats 50, 100 standing

NEAREST TUBE STATION *Westbourne Park*

THE BACKPACKER

126 York Way, N1; 0171 278 8318

This is, quite possibly, the most famous Australasian hang-out in the world, known to every man, woman and beast with any Antipodean connection whatsoever. As soon as Aussies and Kiwis arrive in London, this is where they head to party. And what a party! The action starts on Friday night with cheap drinks to oil the wheels. The party goes on until the early hours and then they do it all over again on Saturday. Sunday is an even bigger day. This is when Aussies and Kiwis go to Church. The Church is the venue nearby which holds up to 1,000 people. Often, 1,000 people go there. If you have an English accent, keep it down a bit, as admission is to Aussies and Kiwis first, with the rest of the world some way down the list. From noon until 3.30pm on a Sunday you can down the tinnies or drink Squashed Frog and be entertained by comedians, singers, bands, male and female strippers, Australasian music and party games you wouldn't want your mother to know about. Then, if you can take the pace, it's back to The Backpacker, where the party goes on until midnight. Bonza!

OPEN *16.30-02.00 (Fri), 18.00-02.00 (Sat), 15.30-midnight (Sun)*

CREDIT CARDS *none taken*

DRAUGHT BEERS *John Smith's Extra Smooth, Foster's, Holsten Export, Guinness, Scrumpy Jack, Strongbow, Kronenbourg, Stella*
NEAREST TUBE STATIONS *King's Cross, Kentish Town*

BALLS BROTHERS

Balls Brothers haven't ventured very far outside the City, where they seem to have got the formula for food and wines just right. All their branches are of a high standard, clean, comfortable and often air-conditioned. They have established a traditional style, and City folk take to it very well. The staff are friendly and knowledgeable about the wines offered from the list and the selection of specials chalked up on the blackboard.

Balls Brothers restaurants with wine bars:
OPEN *11.00-21.00 (Mon-Fri)*
A la carte restaurant 12.00-15.00 (Mon-Fri)
Bar food – sandwiches 11.00-21.00 (Mon-Fri)
CREDIT CARDS *all major cards*

CITY (EC2) 5-6 Carey Lane (off Gutter Lane), EC2; 0171 600 2720
    NEAREST TUBE STATION *St Paul's*
CITY (EC2) Gows Restaurant, 81-82 Old Broad Street, EC2; 0171 920 9645
    NEAREST TUBE STATION *Liverpool Street*
CITY (EC2) Moor House, London Wall, EC2; 0171 628 3944
    NEAREST TUBE STATION *Moorgate*
CITY (EC3) 52 Lime Street, EC3; 0171 283 0841
    NEAREST TUBE STATION *Bank and Liverpool Street*
CITY (EC3) St Mary at Hill, EC3; 0171 626 0321
    NEAREST TUBE STATION *Monument*
CITY (EC4) Bucklersbury House, Cannon Street, EC4; 0171 248 7557
    NEAREST TUBE STATION *Cannon Street*
SOUTHWARK Hay's Galleria, Tooley Street, SE1; 0171 407 4301
    NEAREST TUBE STATION *London Bridge*
SOUTHWARK The Hop Cellars, 24 Southwark Street, SE1; 0171 403 6851
    NEAREST TUBE STATION *London Bridge*
WEST END 20 St James's Street (entrance Ryder Street), SW1; 0171 321 0882
    NEAREST TUBE STATION *Green Park*

Balls Brothers wine bars:
CITY (EC2) 11 Bloomfield Street, EC2; 0171 588 4643
    NEAREST TUBE STATION *Liverpool Street*
CITY (EC2) 6-8 Cheapside, EC2; 0171 248 2708
    NEAREST TUBE STATION *St Paul's*
CITY (EC2) Kings Arms Yard, EC2; 0171 796 3049
    NEAREST TUBE STATION *Bank*
CITY (EC2) 42 Threadneedle Street, EC2; 0171 628 3850
    NEAREST TUBE STATION *Bank*
CITY (EC3) Mark Lane, EC3; 0171 623 2923
    NEAREST TUBE STATION *Tower Hill*

BAR AQUDA

13-14 Maiden Lane, WC2; 0171 557 9891
My estate-agent friend, Tarquin, badgered me to go along with him to London's newest gay bar, pronounced like Barracuda. Not sure I liked the idea of watering holes with shark prices, but I went along anyway and ended up having a jolly snappy time. I knew this place from old. A few years ago it was a sleepy little pub called the Peacock and then the brewers, Bass, spent a small fortune converting it into one of the modern genre of theme bars, Bar Coast. It didn't work, so recognising the seemingly endless wealth of the pink economy, they handed it over to their ever-increasing and successful portfolio of gay bars.

Little has changed from the Bar Coast days: a modern minimalist interior housing a café-style operation with decent food during the day and an opportunistic environment in the evening. Tarquin clearly preferred the evenings. He seemed to know, or have known, half the clientele and was clearly intent on getting to know the rest. 'It's packed full with cuties,' he exclaimed as he went off to air-kiss an old acquaintance. Indeed it was, although most of the men looked like they went to the same hairdresser who only does a number-one cut with a bouffant fringe. There were plenty of women there too and I felt that the bar was decidedly hetero-friendly. I was a bit disappointed with the somewhat expensive drinks list. Surely gay people don't survive on a diet of alcopops, bottled beers and Grolsch? But then again, looking at the physiques of most of them, they may well have it sussed.

OPEN *midday-23.00 (Mon-Sat), midday-22.30 (Sun)*
FOOD *midday-19.30 every day*
CREDIT CARDS *all major cards, not AmEx*
Wheelchair access to venue and loos
NEAREST TUBE STATION *Covent Garden*

THE BARLEY MOW

Narrow Street, E14; 0171 265 8931
In the days when canals served most of the country, the lock at the entrance to the Limehouse Basin was the way in from the Thames to the whole system. The basin had ten acres of water, four acres of quays and wharfs, and the river lock and the dockmaster controlled it all from the big customs house on the river bank.

The Limehouse Basin is a marina now and dockmaster and customs house both have new names and new roles. The dockmaster has become the harbourmaster, with new offices in the dock. The customs house has become The Barley Mow. This is a dramatic turn of events for any building, particularly one with such an official, not to say bossy, past. It has to be said that the customs house makes a surprisingly good pub. It is a listed building – 'red brick, domestic, early 18th century style with rusticated stucco quoins' is how the list describes it – so when Taylor Walker took it over in the late 80s it couldn't be altered too much. Still it provides an extra large bar, a sizeable restaurant, a big function room upstairs and a huge canopied riverside terrace. There was also an historic name waiting for it – The Barley Mow, after Taylor Walker's famous old brewery, the Barley Mow.

OPEN *12.00-23.00 (Mon-Sat), 12.00-22.30 (Sun)*
FOOD *12.00-14.30 and 18.30-22.00 (Mon-Sat); 12.00-22.00 (Sun)*
CREDIT CARDS *all major cards*
DRAUGHT BEERS *Burton, Tetley's, Carlsberg, Guinness, Dry Blackthorn, Carlsberg Export, Stella*
Wheelchair access to venue
NEAREST RAILWAY STATION *Limehouse*

THE BARLEY MOW

8 Dorset Street, W1; 0171 935 7318
A traditional, real-ale drinkers' pub from the Nicholson stable that quietly serves the locals to Dorset Street and Gloucester Place. You wouldn't imagine this, but when there's a big game being played at Wembley, the place is overrun with supporters. Why so? Because it's just around the corner from Baker Street station and the traveling fans tend to use it as a resting place.

Martin McDonald, the manager of 12 years, tells me the Beatles played darts here in the early 60s and would order up sausage, beans and chips while they played. The dartboard has gone, alas, but they still serve up a mean plate of sausage, beans and chips. The Barley Mow is full of authentic reminders of days gone by. Brass price lists are countersunk in the bar but are almost illegible now which is just as well as the prices are more than a hundred years out of date. The pub still has an old brass tap labelled Old Tom, which used to dispense gin. You brought your own jug and they filled it up. The best seats in the house are the two pawnbroker booths. Each has a pair of facing benches, a door with a lock and its own stretch of counter. The deal was you slunk in with the family silver under your jacket, did the deal and slunk out again. These days, people lucky enough to find a free booth tend to stay there for the rest of the evening.

OPEN *11.00-23.00 (Mon-Fri); often closed on Sat for private parties*
FOOD *11.00-15.30 (Mon-Fri)*
CREDIT CARDS none taken
DRAUGHT BEERS *Adnams, Brakspear, Calder's Cream Ale, Marston's Pedigree, Tetley's, Carlsberg Export, Castlemaine XXXX, Guinness, Addlestones Cask, Stella*
NEAREST TUBE STATION *Baker Street*

BAR M AT THE STAR AND GARTER
4 Lower Richmond Road, SW15; 0181 788 0345
When Glendola Leisure transformed The Star & Garter two years ago they breathed a new lease of life into a crumbling riverside pub. Bar M has been thoroughly refurbished, offering something just a little different to the Putney toper. It has one very long room fronting on to the river, a bar on the opposite wall, a highly polished light oak floor and a carpeted raised level running underneath the windows. The beers aren't to write about, but it does have a decent enough food menu and a small, if expensive cocktail list. Its pride of course is the river view, but the design means that too few customers can enjoy it.

OPEN *11.00-23.00 (Mon-Sat), 12.00-22.30 (Sun)*
FOOD *12.00-22.00 (Mon-Sat), 12.00-21.00 (Sun)*
CREDIT CARDS all major cards
DRAUGHT BEERS *Kilkenny, Tetley's, Foster's, Kronenbourg, Guinness, Dry Blackthorn*
Private room: 120 seated for dinner; Cellar Room 120 standing
NEAREST TUBE STATION *Putney Bridge*

BAR OZ
51 Moscow Road, Bayswater, W2; 0171 229 0647
Another experiment at branding by S & N who apparently think we're all going to adopt Australian habits to celebrate the Sydney 2000 Olympic Games. I won't be, and neither will anybody else judging by the fact that no more Bar Oz's are planned for London. Terrible!

OPEN *11.00-23.00 (Mon-Sat), 12.00-22.30 (Sun)*
FOOD *11.00-22.00 (Mon-Sat), 12.00-22.00 (Sun)*
CREDIT CARDS none taken
DRAUGHT BEERS *Beamish Red, John Smith's Extra Smooth, Beck's, Foster's, Kronenbourg, Beamish, Strongbow*
Wheelchair access to venue
NEAREST TUBE STATIONS *Queensway, Bayswater*

THE BARROW BOY AND BANKER
6-8 Borough Street, SE1; 0171 403 5415
Another excellent bank conversion from the Fuller's portfolio on the south side of London Bridge, close enough for the bankers of the City and the barrow boys of Borough High Street. It has one large, almost circular room, spacious banquettes and plenty of tables to sit at. There can be a bit of a fight for a seat in the evenings and there's often a scrum at the bar. You can normally escape to an even bigger bar upstairs, although this is sometimes closed for private functions.

OPEN *11.00-23.00 (Mon-Fri)*

FOOD *12.00-20.00 (Mon-Fri)*
CREDIT CARDS *AmEx, Mastercard, Visa, Switch*
DRAUGHT BEERS *Chiswick Bitter, ESB, Fuller's seasonal ale, London Pride, Carling Black Label, Grolsch, Heineken, Stella Artois, Guinness, Scrumpy Jack, a guest ale*
NEAREST TUBE STATION *London Bridge*

BAR ZOLA
33 Wellington Street, WC2; 0171 836 0038
When you've had a long day at the office, want a bit of fun, a few drinks, fairly loud music in a post-modernist environment, and you might just be up for pulling someone, then this is a great place. It fills up quickly in the evenings with suited boys and skirted girls looking for a bit of action. They're not looking for ales you understand. This is a lager-swilling, cocktail-tippling and shooter-downing clientele.

The drinks list boasts Slippery Nipples, Blow Jobs, Orgasms and Brain Haemorrhages. There is still a market for this type of thing.
OPEN *11.00-23.00 (Mon-Sat), 12.00-22.30 (Sun), happy hour 16.00-19.00*
FOOD *12.00-17.00 (Mon-Sat)*
CREDIT CARDS *all major cards*
DRAUGHT BEERS *Staropramen, Kronenbourg, Foster's*
Wheelchair access to venue. Private room: 80-100 seated, 120 standing
NEAREST TUBE STATIONS *Covent Garden, Charing Cross*

BEACH BLANKET BABYLON
45 Ledbury Road, W11; 0171 229 2907
Striking, stylish, sexy and sophisticated, this bar quickly became a mecca for fashionable Notting Hill when it opened in 1991. It was then owned by Carmel Azzopardi (now of The Cross Keys in Chelsea, qv) and was designed by Tony Weller. It makes a decent job of the food it serves – you find the restaurant by winding your way behind the bar, along a gangplank and down the spiral stairway into the cosy cellar. The menu changes regularly but the evening dishes currently include wild mushroom and spinach fricassee (£11.25), rib-eye steak with fries (£12.75) and roast lamb with bashed mids and broccoli (£13.50). Side dishes are an extra £3, and with starters from £3.95 and desserts from £3.50, this can prove to be an expensive night out. The brunch menu is cheaper and includes Eggs Benedict on muffins (£3.95) and the Babylon Breakfast with lamb and mint sausages (£8.50). BBB has been much copied but remains the original New Age bar, and is a very useful port-of-call in the Notting Hill crawl.
OPEN *12.00-23.00 (Mon-Sat), 12.00-22.30 (Sun)*
FOOD *12.00-23.00 (Mon-Sun)*
CREDIT CARDS *all major cards*
Three private rooms: 40, 30 and 50 seated, 100 standing
NEAREST TUBE STATION *Notting Hill Gate*

THE BEAUFOY ARMS
18 Lavender Hill, SW11; 0171 228 9246
This is London's leading reggae pub and the sound is up to blast off, although there's no live music. Strictly for reggae lovers only, with elements of dancehall, ragga and the safe side of jungle. Every night is reggae night but Saturday is disco time. There is traditional West Indian food all day – jerk chicken and pork, dumplings, curried goat and rice, salt fish, patties, breadfruit, fritters – and the strategically placed mirrors tell you that there are exotic dancers about. Exotic, as I had to explain to a colleague last year, means they take their clothes off.
OPEN *11.00-midnight (Mon-Sat), 11.00-23.00 (Sun)*
FOOD *as opening hours*
CREDIT CARDS *all major cards*

DRAUGHT BEERS *Webster's, Budweiser, Carlsberg, Foster's, Holsten, Red Stripe, Guinness, Dry Blackthorn*
Wheelchair access to venue
NEAREST RAILWAY STATION *Clapham Junction*

THE BEEHIVE
407-409 Brixton Road, SW9; 0171 738 3643
The Beehive is a busy well-run pub in the busiest bit of Brixton, and it makes a bold claim. It is, it says, the only pub in Brixton with no music. No music of any kind. It even switches off the music in its games machines. Its customers seem to like this. They also seem to like the big non-smoking bit, something all J. J. Wetherspoon pubs have. At any rate the turnover goes up. There was a shoeshop there before. It had music.
OPEN *11.00-23.00 (Mon-Sat), 12.00-22.30 (Sun)*
FOOD *11.00-22.00 (Mon-Sat), 12.00-21.30 (Sun)*
DRAUGHT BEERS *Directors, Theakston Best, Summer Lightning, Spitfire, Scrumpy Jack, two guest ales*
Wheelchair access to venue, not to loos
NEAREST TUBE STATION *Brixton*

BELGO CENTRAAL
50 Earlham Street, WC2; 0171 813 2233
The bar of this excellent beer outlet is too small to be of any consequence, but its main attraction is you can get a healthy selection of take-away bottles to sample on the Tube journey home. The best way to appreciate Belgo's offerings is to book a table in the restaurant and slowly, slowly plough your way through the 101 different Belgian beers on offer. You could go to Belgium and travel the length and breadth of the country in search of the perfect beer, but why bother when the best of its beer industry is brought to us right here? If Belgo is a theme bar then let us have more of them. It takes a lot to impress me but I can't imagine spending a better night anywhere (without having sex). I used to be put off by its moules'n'frites theme but several recent, and obviously addictive, visits have shown me that Belgium should be as cherished for its food as it is for its beer. Who else would use some of the finest beer in the world to make a stew? and why didn't someone turn me on to the idea of Leffe Blonde ice-cream when I was seven years old? If you appreciate your beers and enjoy the art of good cooking, you could do little better than to spend several orgasmic nights at Belgo.
OPEN *midday-23.30 (Mon-Thurs), midday-midnight (Fri-Sat), midday-22.30 (Sun)*
FOOD *during opening times*
CREDIT CARDS *all major cards*
DRAUGHT BEERS *Hoegaarden, Jupiler, Leffe Blonde, De Koninck, Leffe Brune, Belle-Vue Kriek, Vestmalle Dubbel*
Wheelchair access to venue and loos. Private room seats 55
NEAREST TUBE STATION *Covent Garden*

Branch at:
BELGO NOORD 72 Chalk Farm Road, NW1; 0171 267 0718

BELL AND CROWN
72 Strand on the Green, W4; 0181 994 4164
Strand on the Green wanders for half a mile along the river bank at Chiswick with beech trees and weeping willows and lovely 18th-century houses. As if this wasn't enough, it has three of London's most attractive pubs. If you walk along this riverside path starting at Kew Bridge you come to The Bell and Crown first, then The City Barge, then The Bull's Head. Meanwhile you will have passed houses in which John Zoffany chose to live and later Hugh Cudlip, Nancy Mitford, Margaret Kennedy,

Goronwy Rees and Dylan Thomas. Most of them will have known at least one of these pubs. Dylan Thomas, of course, will have known them all.

The Bell and Crown is marginally the biggest and is a well appointed, comfortable old pub with an air of no expense spared. The polished central counter serves a number of separate drinking areas, one around a corner, one down a flight of stairs, one over there, and there is a spacious conservatory, now a non-smoking area. There's no music ever, no games of any sort. The conservatory, seems a bit cut off in winter but in the summer the whole pub seems to turn towards the river, the conservatory becomes part of the outdoors, a terrace under a green awning beneath it and beneath that a patio by the tow path filled with picnic tables under umbrellas. If you can't get a seat in any of these places you can sit on the river wall. People do in great numbers.

OPEN *11.00-23.00 (Mon-Sat), midday-22.30 (Sun)*
FOOD *11.00-22.00 (Mon-Sat), midday-17.00 (Sun)*
CREDIT CARDS *AmEx, Mastercard, Visa*
DRAUGHT BEERS *Chiswick, ESB, Fuller's IPA, Carling Black Label, Grolsch, Stella Artois, Guinness, Scrumpy Jack, Strongbow, London Pride*
Wheelchair access to venue. Private room seats 40
NEAREST RAILWAY STATION: *Kew Bridge*

BELLE VUE

1 Clapham Common Southside, SW4; 0171 498 9473
Three large pubs and a good many smaller ones ring Clapham Common underground. The biggest and glossiest is the huge mock-Tudor Goose and Granite, formerly The Plough, one of London's most lavishly refurbished pubs with every mod con – air-conditioning, a no-smoking area, disabled loos, a vast flagged beer garden. Opposite is the stately Alexandra with its splendid mid-Victorian façade with bands of coloured brickwork, cast iron window boxes and magnificent dome. Then, on the corner, there's The Belle Vue, smaller, much more modest but having a good go.

The Belle Vue opened in 1914, not very good timing you might think, and until recently it was suitably downcast, a gloomy old pub. When Yandi Savage and Paul Seymour took it over it began to cheer up. The old curtains went and the dim frosted windows, the walls were painted a dusty pink and the food improved but they had hardly been open ten minutes before a cigarette end in a waste basket set the place alight. The fire was serious enough to close the place down for months. Back to square one. It is open again now. The burned-out bar counter has been replaced, the walls are dusty pink again and once again modish modern cooking is bringing young customers in. This part of Clapham is increasingly lively with lots of new places to eat and drink. The Belle Vue, with its symbolic address, 1 Clapham Common, seems, for a change, to be in the heart of things.

OPEN *midday-23.00 (Mon-Sat), midday-22.30 (Sun)*
FOOD *midday-16.00 and 18.30-22.30 (Mon-Sun)*
CREDIT CARDS *none taken*
DRAUGHT BEERS *John Smith's Extra Smooth, Foster's, Kronenbourg, Beamish*
NEAREST TUBE STATION *Clapham Common*

BELUSHI'S

9 Russell Street, WC2; 0171 240 3411
This rather rakish Covent Garden venue has the feel of a student-union bar, with pictures plastered over the walls and limited Blues Brothers memorabilia.

OPEN *11.00-midnight (Mon-Sat), 12.00-22.30 (Sun)*
FOOD *as opening hours*
CREDIT CARDS *all major cards, not AmEx*
DRAUGHT BEERS *Beamish Red, John Smith's, Coors, Foster's, Kronenbourg, Guinness*
Private room: 30 seated, 40 standing
NEAREST TUBE STATION *Covent Garden*

BIERREX

22 Putney High Street, SW15; 0181 785 0266

Putney High Street is coming alive somewhat with yet another useful drinking venue opening near the river end of the street. BierRex has been operating for over a year now, offering a decent range of European bottled and draught quality beers and lagers. There is a short line of casual booths on the right as you enter. Pass the bar and you come to a larger room with sofas, armchairs, decent-sized dinner tables and a 40-foot-wide, glass-covered, rear-illuminated Chimay mural. French windows open up in the warm weather.

OPEN *11.00-23.00 (Mon-Sat), 11.00-22.30 (Sun)*
FOOD *12.00-21.00 (Mon-Fri), 11.00-22.00 (Sat), 11.00-15.00 for breakfast and 15.00-22.00 normal menu (Sun)*
CREDIT CARDS *all major cards, not AmEx*
DRAUGHT BEERS *De Koninck, Hoegaarden, Leffe Blonde, Stella Artois, Belle-vue Kriek, Caffrey's, Dab, Vokler Cider, Grolsch, Budvar Budweiser*
Wheelchair access to venue and loos
NEAREST TUBE STATION *Putney Bridge*
NEAREST RAILWAY STATION *Putney*

Also at:
2-3 Creed Lane, EC4; 0171 329 3118

BILL BENTLEY'S

18 Old Broad Street, EC2; 0171 588 2655

Bill Bentley set up Bill Bentley's some 27 years ago in the form of a wine bar in Beauchamp Place. Since then it has grown to a chain of six wine bars and restaurants, which was acquired by Finch's and subsequently by Young's. Bill Bentley has retired now and so has the bar in Beauchamp Place, but five bars still remain in the City, including this one. It is easy to stray past, and you'd be surprised to discover that it has an outside seating area beyond the modern, long and narrow bar. There's a short terrace overlooking a split-level patio – if you can manage the steps, you can sit and listen to the hum of the air-conditioning extractor fan. The walls surrounding the patio are so high that I doubt the sun ever peeps through. Food is served at lunchtimes – mostly fish and meat dishes – with main courses running in at £6.90 for fish cakes and £12.95 for a fresh crab salad. There are almost 70 wines on the list, starting at £8.80 for the house, with a decent selection in the £10-£20 range. It's very business-like during the day, and a decent place to hang out on a summer's eve.

OPEN *11.00-21.30 (Mon-Fri)*
FOOD *11.45-15.00 (Mon-Fri)*
CREDIT CARDS *all major cards*
NEAREST TUBE STATIONS *Bank, Liverpool Street*

Branches at:
CITY (EC2) 202 Bishopsgate, EC2; 0171 283 1763
   NEAREST TUBE STATION *Liverpool Street*
CITY (EC3) 5 The Minories, EC3; 0171 481 1779
   NEAREST TUBE STATION *Oldgate, Tower Hill*
CITY (EC3) 1 St George's Lane, off Botolph Lane, EC3; 0171 929 2244
   NEAREST TUBE STATION *Monument*
CITY (EC3) WILLY'S WINE BAR 107 Fenchurch Street, EC3; 0171 480 7289

THE BLACKBIRD

209 Earls Court Road, SW5; 0171 835 1855

A funny thing happened to the Earls Court Road branch of Barclay's Bank. One day it turned into a pub. Fuller, Smith and Turner, the Chiswick brewer, is doing this to banks. It has found they make excellent Ale and Pie houses so Nat Wests in Fulham Road and Surbiton have become the Stargazey and the Denby Dale, the Martins in Tottenham Court Road is now the Jack Horner and the old Bank of England in Fleet Street has become, you will never guess, the Old Bank of England. Your bank next.

To look at it now you would never guess that The Blackbird had ever been anything but a pub. The builders knew though. They had a terrible job converting it. The walls were feet thick and reinforced. It took one man eight days to cut a reasonable opening between two vaults to make one decent-sized beer cellar. The kitchens are down here too and they keep the manager in the old bank safe; it is his office now. Well, they don't want to lose him. Upstairs in the banking hall, I beg your pardon, the saloon bar, the pillars are original and so is the mahogany panelling but the rest is a 1990s version of the 1890s, the golden age of pub interiors. This, though, is the golden age of pub pies, says Fuller's – steak and ale, chicken and bacon. No blackbirds though!

OPEN *11.00-23.00 (Mon-Sat), midday-22.30 (Sun)*
FOOD *midday-21.00 (Mon-Sun)*
CREDIT CARDS *Visa, Mastercard*
DRAUGHT BEERS *Chiswick Bitter, ESB, Fuller's Cream Ale, London Pride, Carling Black Label, Grolsch, Stella Artois, Guinness, Scrumpy Jack*
NEAREST TUBE STATION *Earls Court*

THE BLACK CAP

171 Camden High Street, NW1; 0171 485 1742
Every day of the week stars of the gay pub circuit will be performing somewhere. Elaborately wigged, extravagantly gowned, tottering on the highest heels, these starry ladies are in great demand. Some sing, belting out standards like Ethel Merman but louder. Some mime to Shirley Bassey or kd lang but the top stars are the stand-up comics, formidable dames not to be crossed. They have strong personalities and a large following. Wherever they play – The White Swan in Commercial Road, The Two Brewers in Clapham High Street, The Royal Oak in Hammersmith, The Salmon and Compasses in Islington, The Gloucester in Greenwich, The Royal Vauxhall Tavern in Kennington Lane, The Queens Arms in Lewisham – they get a welcome that would not disappoint Miss Bassey herself.

The Black Cap in Camden Town is the London Palladium of late-night drag. It has one long cabaret bar that opens at 21.00 and closes at 2am the music turned up to the threshold of pain. It is dimly lit and crowded, with a bar counter running most of its length, stopping to make room for a wider open space and a stage at the far end. The audience – mostly gay men, some gay women – pack the space in front of the stage as midnight approaches. Upstairs there has been a sensational transformation. Half a million pounds has been spent on Shufflewick's Bar, which is now extremely smart and stretches the length of the building, opening on to Fong Terrace, a splendid new roof garden full of tables. It keeps its unpublike hours during the week – noon to 2am. The bar is named after Mrs Shufflewick, a great drag artist who often appeared downstairs. The terrace is named after HIH Regina Fong, a star of the moment who reigns in the cabaret bar every Tuesday night.

OPEN *midday-2.00 (Mon-Thurs), midday-3.00 (Fri-Sat), midday-22.30 (Sun)*
FOOD *midday-21.00 (Mon-Sun)*
CREDIT CARDS *all major cards, not AmEx*
DRAUGHT BEERS *Caffrey's, Worthington, Carling Black Label, Carling Premier, Grolsch, Guinness, Red Rock*
Wheelchair access to venue
NEAREST TUBE STATION *Camden Town*

THE BLACKFRIAR

174 Queen Victoria Street, EC4; 0171 236 5650
The Blackfriar is a famous, much photographed pub, an outstanding example of art nouveau and funny with it. It is the wedge-shaped building

opposite Blackfriars Station, built in 1875 on the site of the old Dominican monastery you hear about, and it is still a monastery of sorts. That must be the Abbot, hands folded over his tummy, beaming down over the front door while jolly junior monks exuberantly point the way in. Inside, in a treasurehouse of multi-coloured marble, you find their brother monks having the time of their lives, drinking, singing, fishing, sleeping it off. Theirs, clearly, are the mock-serious wise saws. 'Wisdom is Rare', 'Industry is All' and 'A Good Thing Is Soon Snatched Up'. It is a leisurely pub with comfortable hours – 11.30am to 11pm, bar snacks lunchtime only. Office workers pop in for a drink on their way home, so it has a busy time early in the evening, and on warm evenings a happy crowd in suits, collars and ties gathers on the pavement outside. The Blackfriar doesn't open at all at weekends. As the monks say, industry is all.

OPEN *11.30-23.00 (Mon-Fri)*
FOOD *midday-14.30 (Mon-Fri), 17.30-21.00 (Mon-Thurs)*
CREDIT CARDS *Mastercard, Visa*
DRAUGHT BEERS *Adnams, Brakspear, Calder's Cream Ale, Marston's Pedigree, Tetley's, Carlsberg Export, Guinness, Dry Blackthorn, Carlsberg Pilsner, Stella Artois*
Wheelchair access to venue, not to loos
NEAREST TUBE STATION *Blackfriars*

BLACK LION

2 South Black Lion Lane, W6; 0181 748 7056
Walk along the river from Hammersmith Bridge, first the Lower Mall and then the Upper, and you pass five very different and interesting pubs. This is the fifth you come to.

The Black Lion appears in A. P. Herbert's *The Water Gypsies* lightly disguised as the Black Swan and is, like the others, old. Like the others it has lovely views of the river and provides a pleasant place to eat and drink outside. In The Black Lion's case it is a garden shaded by a massive chestnut tree even older, they say, than the pub. But things can change even at the most historic old pub. For as long as anyone can remember The Black Lion had a skittle alley. This is where A. P. Herbert used to play. In his day there were still skittle alleys in at least 50 London pubs but slowly, remorselessly the number dwindled. The Black Lion's alley, a particularly good one, was one of the few survivors but it was well known and seemed safe enough. Alas for skittles! It too has now been scrapped, replaced, sadly, by a few extra tables. It wasn't making money says the new manager, not a chap to beat about the bush. What will the pub ghost make of this? There have been reports of a ghost at The Black Lion for a good 200 years, some quite recent. Down-to-earth Australian barmen heard it clumping round on the top floor and the manager of the day told me he had actually seen it. He did not mind ghosts, differing in this regard from Mr Francis Smith, an excise officer, who set out to investigate The Black Lion ghost in 1804. He laid in wait for it, his fusee primed and loaded. At midnight the phantom appeared and Mr Smith shot it. Beneath the apparition's shroud was found the dead body of Mr Thomas Milward, a bricklayer. The hauntings, for the moment, ceased.

OPEN *11.00-23.00 (Mon-Sat), midday-22.30 (Sun)*
CREDIT CARDS *Mastercard, Visa*
DRAUGHT BEERS *Theakston Best, Courage Best, Foster's, Holsten Export, Kronenbourg, Guinness, Beamish, Strongbow*
Wheelchair access to venue. Private room seats 44
NEAREST TUBE STATIONS *Ravenscourt Park, Stamford Brook*

THE BLENHEIM

27 Cale Street, SW3; 0171 349 0056

London seems to have been particularly taken with the Duke of Marlborough's distant exploits. So many Blenheim Closes, Crescents and Gardens. Eighteen Blenheim Roads, several pubs. Here is one built in 1824 and called The Blenheim 120 years after the famous victory. This Blenheim is a handsome four-storied Georgian pub tucked away in a quiet back street and life has not been easy. The first floor has been a bar, a pool room, a Thai restaurant. It is now used for private parties. The back bar was a mortuary at one time and the great gale of 1987 did its best to make it one again, sending the chimney crashing through the skylight. The Blenheim seemed to go into a serious decline after that and when its lease reverted to the Cadogan Estates in 1991 it closed down. Two years later a local entrepreneur bought the lease and spent a lot of money putting it to rights. He made a good job of it with lanterns from a church in Halifax, oak floorboards from old French railway carriages and radiators from County Hall, but it didn't work and The Blenheim closed again. Its latest chapter seems promising. Badger Inns have it now and Tony and Lynn O'Neill are running it. The place has a buoyant, cheerful air. Lynn was British Freestyle Ski Champion for two years in the 1980s. They were famous victories too.

OPEN 11.00-23.00 (Mon-Sat), midday-22.30 (Sun)
FOOD midday-14.30 and 18.00-22.00 (Mon-Sun)
CREDIT CARDS all major cards
DRAUGHT BEERS Badger, Dorset IPA, Tanglefoot, Dempsey's, Hofbräu, Pilsner, Premium Export, Guinness, Dry Blackthorn
Private room seats 35
NEAREST TUBE STATIONS Sloane Square, South Kensington

THE BLIND BEGGAR

337 Whitechapel Road, E1; 0171 247 6195

On 8 March 1966 George Cornell of the Richardson gang was drinking in The Blind Beggar in Whitechapel Road when Ronald Kray walked into the bar and shot him dead. It is a scene that has passed into legend: the crowded bar, the Walker Brothers hit on the juke box, the shots in the air from Kray's minder, customers diving for the floor, the two gangsters facing each other for a long moment. 'Well, look who's here,' Cornell said, whereupon Kray raised his Mauser 9mm and shot him through the forehead.

The Blind Beggar already had a place in the history of the East End. In 1865 the young evangelist William Booth had spoken at an open air meeting on the pavement outside. This was the genesis of the Salvation Army. Parties of Salvationists regularly arrive on William Booth tours, but alas it is the other event that holds centre stage. The Blind Beggar has been refurbished time and again. A big conservatory has been added and a beer garden tacked on at the side, and people drinking in the comfortable modern bar with its button-backed sofas and red-shaded wall lights talk of other things. All the same, almost 30 years later, The Blind Beggar is still the pub where Ronnie Kray, hearing that George Cornell had called him a fat poof, sought him out and shot him down. The Blind Beggar is up for sale as I write, has been for three years. The lease is ever shorter but the price remains the same: £150,000 for the 14 years remaining.

OPEN 11.00-23.00 (Mon-Fri)
FOOD 11.30-15.00 (Mon-Fri), midday-15.00 (Sat)
CREDIT CARDS none taken
DRAUGHT BEERS John Smith's Extra Smooth, Webster's Yorkshire Bitter, Carlsberg, Foster's, Holsten, Kronenbourg, Guinness, Strongbow, Directors, Courage Best
Wheelchair access to venue. Private room: conservatory stands 30
NEAREST TUBE STATION Whitechapel

THE BLUE ANCHOR

13 Lower Mall, W6; 0181 748 5774

The Blue Anchor is the first of the pubs on Hammersmith's riverside coming from Hammersmith Bridge, a handsome old place at least 300 years old. There have, of course, been changes along the way, not least to its name. It started out as the Blew Anchor and Washhouses but as time passed it gave up washing and its spelling improved. The Victorians installed a host of partitions, our generation took them down, and so it goes. The old panelling survives though, as does the beautiful pewter bar counter.

The Blue Anchor is popular with the rowing club next door and goes in for old rowing photographs. Someone seems to have left their oars behind. There is a rather sombre collection of World War I artefacts – helmets, gasmasks and so on – and banknotes of many lands are pasted up over the bar counter. This is a busy pub in the summer. Its customers fill the picnic tables lining the river wall and there are cool marble-topped tables for them inside. The Georgian bow window has a view of the bridge, the river and the riverside path which used to be much enjoyed by Gustav Holst who taught at the St Paul's Girls School in Hammersmith for 35 years. Indeed it is said that he was inspired to write his Hammersmith Prelude and Scherzo for military band sitting at this window.

OPEN *11.00-23.00 (Mon-Sat), midday-22.30 (Sun)*

FOOD *midday-14.30 and 18.00-21.00 (Mon-Sat); midday-14.30 (Sunday lunch)*

CREDIT CARDS *Eurocard, Delta, Mastercard, Visa*

DRAUGHT BEERS *Courage Best Bitter, Courage Directors, Young's Special, Foster's, Holsten Export, Kronenbourg, Guinness, Scrumpy Jack, Speckled Hen Wheelchair access to venue. Private room seats 38*

NEAREST TUBE STATION *Hammersmith*

BLUES BAR

20 Kingly Street, W1; 0171 287 0514

Ain't Nothin' But ... – the Blues Bar is its Sunday name – is a hang-out for students of all ages. For a major venue which is a legend in Kingly Street, it's surprisingly small and dark, with a handkerchief-sized stage, three rows of tiny tables squashed together and an assortment of stray guitars, album covers and photographs adorning the walls. This ain't gonna win any awards for style, decor or service, but it is a fun, intimate bar with live music every night of the week.

OPEN *17.30-01.00 (Mon-Thur), 17.30-03.00 (Fri), 18.30-03.00 (Sat), 20.00-midnight (Sun)*

CREDIT CARDS *none taken*

DRAUGHT BEERS *Foster's, Kronenbourg*

NEAREST TUBE STATION *Oxford Circus*

BOOTSY BROGAN'S

1 Fulham Broadway, SW6; 0171 385 2003

There's nothing much Irish about this bar, which opened in the early part of 1997, replacing the very naughty Swan, which previously occupied this spot. The interior, designed by the people who did its sister pub, Waxy O'Connor's (qv), is a massive wooden structure of steps and platforms circumnavigating the central island bar. Wander around, up and down, and perplexingly you'll end up where you started but on a higher level.

Bootsy Brogan's is extremely popular at weekends, so a couple of very polite doormen are employed to keep control of the numbers of young Fulham drinkers in what is a useful addition to an increasingly acceptable crawl of drinking venues around the Fulham Broadway.

OPEN *11.00-23.00 (Mon-Sat), 12.00-22.30 (Sun)*

FOOD *bar 11.00-22.00 (Sun & Wed), 11.00-20.00 (Thurs-Sat);*

CREDIT CARDS *all major cards, not AmEx*

DRAUGHT BEERS *Caffrey's, Kilkenny, Tetley's, Foster's, Holsten, Guinness, Dry Blackthorn*
Wheelchair access to venue
NEAREST TUBE STATION *Fulham Broadway*

LA BOUFFE

11-13 Battersea Rise, SW11; 0171 228 3384
In a row of up-graded shops and cafés on Battersea Rise, La Bouffe stands out as one of the most inviting. It has a small terrace by which you enter the bar, an enormous mural by the ex-manager Johnny Reid, and a soothing cream and green painted interior. It needs to be soothing as the atmosphere can get quite frenetic in the evenings. It's a friendly place, though, and the staff cope well with the seemingly insatiable palate of the Battersea toper. They have draught Hoegaarden and St Omer, and get through lashings of Calvados.
OPEN *11.00-23.00 (Mon-Sat), 11.00-22.30 (Sun)*
FOOD *bar 11.00-22.30 (Mon-Sat), 11.00-22.00 (Sun); restaurant 12.00-15.00 and 19.00-23.00 (Mon-Sat), 12.00-15.00 and 19.00-22.30 (Sun)*
CREDIT CARDS *all major cards*
DRAUGHT BEERS *Hoegaarden, St Omer, Murphy's*
Wheelchair access to venue and loos
NEAREST TUBE STATION *Clapham Common*
NEAREST RAILWAY STATION *Clapham Junction*

THE BOX

32-34 Monmouth Street, WC2; 0171 240 5828
This is an unobtrusive, mostly gay bar behind a fairly nondescript modern shop front close to Seven Dials. The ground floor is café-style during the day, but they whip off the menus in the evening and the place gets down to the more serious business of consuming alcohol. Frozen margaritas, jugs of beer, wines and cocktails oil the proceedings, and the downstairs lounge bar holds many charity and themed events. The last Friday of every month is Fab Friday – party, party, party! Sundays are Box Babes – ladies' night.
OPEN *11.00-23.00 (Mon-Sat), 12.00-22.30 (Sun)*
Last Friday of the month 11.00-01.00 (party night)
FOOD *bar 11.00-17.30 (Mon-Sat), 12.00-19.00 (Sun)*
CREDIT CARDS *all major cards*
DRAUGHT BEERS *Box Lager, Red Stripe, Nastro Azzurro*
Wheelchair access to venue and loos. Private room: 60-80 standing
NEAREST TUBE STATION *Leicester Square, Covent Garden*

BRASSERIE ROCQUE

Unit G, Broadgate Circle, EC2; 0171 638 7919
A bar brasserie with concertina doors opening on to the lower level of Broadgate Circle, where the crowds spill out in the fine weather. At lunch the place is split into a bookable restaurant and an unbookable brasserie. Three courses in the restaurant will set you back £27.50; the brasserie offers a marginally cheaper similar menu but you can, of course, have just one course. In the evening the place is turned over to a drinking venue. Brasserie Rocque, they say, is named after John Rocque, a Huguenot whose finely detailed maps of London brought him great acclaim.
OPEN *11.30-22.00 (Mon-Fri)*
FOOD *restaurant and brasserie 11.30-15.00 (Mon-Fri); snacks available after 15.00 (Mon-Fri)*
CREDIT CARDS *all major cards*
Wheelchair access to venue and loos
NEAREST TUBE STATION *Liverpool Street*

BREAD AND ROSES

68 Clapham Manor Street, SW4; 0171 498 1779

New Labour? New philosophy on fund-raising. The party formerly known as the Opposition is capitalising on our marginal propensity to consume and dispose of our income in pubs and bars. Bread & Roses – a Workers' Beer Company free house owned by the Battersea & Wandsworth Trades Union Council – is proving to be a useful fund-raising tool. The name apparently comes from a movement song written during a strike of women textile workers in the USA in 1912: 'Our lives shall not be sweated from birth until life closes/Hearts starve as well as bodies/Give us bread but give us roses!' The Bread & Roses publicity material goes on: 'They won the right to a 54-hour working week; their struggle was not just for money but for a better quality of life, and that struggle continues.'

The philosophy might be the same but the bar has been stylised and adapted for the modern campaigner: highly polished wooden floors, purple and green painted walls (colours of the Suffragettes) and a large conservatory at the back leading out to a small garden with barbecue facilities. The vittles include a variety of flavoured bangers supplied by Simply Sausages – simply delicious. Wine flows endlessly and the house beer (Worker Ale) has apparently been recently sampled by the Camra people – disguised as rotund pullover-wearers hiding behind bushy beards. We await their verdict. As you might expect, there are free coffee mornings on Tuesdays for mothers with toddlers and the same on Thursdays for pensioners. Whether or not this is to be a new range of theme bars with branches in Parliament Square and the head office in Downing Street remains to be seen. Meanwhile, the rest of us can eat with a conscience and drink to the cause. *Na zdorovye!* As they say in Clapham.

OPEN *11.00-23.00 (Mon-Sat), 12.00-22.30 (Sun)*

FOOD *12.00-15.00 and 18.30-22.00 (Mon-Thurs), 12.00-15.00 and 18.30-22.00 (Sat), 13.00-16.40 and 18.30-22.00 (Sun)*

CREDIT CARDS *all major cards*

DRAUGHT BEERS *Adnams, Calder's Cream Ale, Worker's Ale, Carlsberg, Löwenbräu, Guinness, Budvar, Burrow Hill, Cider*

Wheelchair access to venue and loos – ground floor only. One private room: 40 seated, 80 standing

NEAREST TUBE STATION *Clapham Common*

BRENDAN O'GRADY'S

67-69 Kennington Road, SE1; 0171 928 5974

You feel out of it if you don't have an Irish pub round the corner nowadays. Everyone else does. Kennington has got one now, this one, an old Victorian pub that used to be Charlie Chaplin's local. It was the last place he saw his father alive. He writes most touchingly of it in *My Early Life*. It was called The Three Stags in those days, indeed it was The Three Stags for about 100 years, but in June 1995 Greene King, whose pub it is, decided it should have a new lease of life and that, begorra, is what it got. Almost £200,000 was spent on it and when it reopened three months later it had become Brendan O'Grady's. It was bright green inside and fitted out with cosy Victorian snugs. There's Irish food now and Irish music and a sea of Irish stout and if you sit down a minute an Irish colleen from Kennington asks what you are wanting and brings it over. Bringing a drink to your table, that is the Irish way so it is. It is far, far removed from the English way. The English like it a lot. When it was The Three Stags charabancs would bring regular parties of American tourists who would be charmed by lovable cockneys engaged by the manager to do lovable cockney things. Everyone always ended up doing the Lambeth walk. Tourists still come. Well the pub is still opposite the Imperial War Museum and Captain Bligh's house is still two doors away and now there's the lovable Irish carry-on at the Brendan O'Grady and a wonderfully Irish landlord, Brendan

McCann by name, with a splendid voice and a great way with an Irish ballad. Was Greene King right to change this typical south London pub into a typical Dublin pub? 'The takings,' says Greene King 'have quadrupled.'

OPEN *midday-23.00 (Mon-Sat), midday-22.30 (Sun)*
FOOD *midday-18.00 (Mon-Sat), midday-15.00 (Sun)*
CREDIT CARDS *all major cards*
DRAUGHT BEERS *IPA, Abbot Ale, Guinness, Kilkenny, Harp, Kronenbourg, Carling Black Label, Wexford*
Wheelchair access to venue
NEAREST TUBE STATION *Lambeth North*

BRIEF ENCOUNTER

42 St Martin's Lane, WC2; 0171 240 2221

Brief encounters are what it's all about at Brief Encounter. This is a long-established gay venue which has just had £650,000 spent on it, making it ready for even more encounters. I'm not sure the people who frequent the bar are that bothered about the decor, but nevertheless it looks a whole sight prettier these days. The diminutive basement bar is where all the action is: loud music, DJs, close encounters of any particular kind. Upstairs, the unlit, even smaller bar is rather quieter, but packed with City-suited after-work drinkers and an eclectic mix of others looking to create a brief moment of time.

OPEN *11.00-23.00 (Mon-Sat), 12.00-22.30 (Sun)*
CREDIT CARDS *all major cards*
NEAREST TUBE STATIONS *Leicester Square, Charing Cross*

BROMPTON'S AND THE WARWICK BAR

294 Old Brompton Road, SW5; 0171 370 1344

Brompton's is a long-established, extremely busy, late-night gay venue in Earls Court. The newly refurbished upstairs bar, with its own separate entrance, is now called the Warwick Bar, and is open all day until 2am. It serves food (S & N's Sizzler menu) until 9pm, but then they get on with the business of social interaction. Men of all ages fill this place nightly.

OPEN *Brompton's 22.00-02.00 (Mon-Sat), 22.00-midnight (Sun)*
Warwick Bar 18.00-02.00 (Mon-Sat), 20.30-midnight (Sun)
FOOD *18.00-21.00 (Mon-Sat)*
CREDIT CARDS *none taken*
DRAUGHT BEERS *Directors, John Smith's, Budweiser, Foster's, Kronenbourg, Beamish, Strongbow*
Private room seats 25 seated, 50 standing
NEAREST TUBE STATION *Earls Court*

BROWNS

1 Hackney Road, E2; 0171 739 4653

Men in City suits line their briefcases up next to each other. They stand quietly and alone at the bar, holding their drinks close to their chests. On the other side of the room a group of young men from an office party are being loud and obnoxious, but the squat, thick-set bouncer (who appears to be missing his neck) is keeping a close eye on them. A bikini-clad girl in stilettos wanders towards me, thrusting a glass full of money in my face (mostly coins but it includes a few strategically placed fivers). 'I'm dancing next,' she declares, shaking the glass. I try all my excuses (no change, waiting for a friend ...) but she won't budge. I put in 50p – she still doesn't budge. A pound later and she moves along to another customer. You tip before you see here, and with the cast of dancers changing with each record it cost me a small fortune. On to the stage they go, discarding all their clothes and stretching parts of the body you wouldn't normally see stretched in public. The office party cheer them on. The men on their own by the bar pretend not to be looking. There are curtained-off rooms so that

you can watch a dancer in the privacy of your own cubicle. It's £10 to watch on your own, £15 to share with a friend or £20 for three in the audience. There are house rules to be followed. One, purchase your tokens at the bar. Two, inform the manager of your name, the number in your group and the name of the dancer of your choice. Three, you will be given a token and a number, and the DJ will call you when your dancer is ready. Go to the table area (in the cubicle) and give your token to the dancer. Four, any person who touches the dancer will be ejected from the premises.
OPEN *12.00-midnight (Mon-Sat), 12.00-19.00 (Sun)*
CREDIT CARDS *all major cards*
DRAUGHT BEERS *Guinness, Dry Blackthorn, Scrumpy Jack, Carlsberg, Castlemaine XXXX, Tetley's, John Bull, Löwenbräu, Carlsberg Export Wheelchair access to venue. Private rooms seat 1,2,3,4,5 or 6. Stripping and table top dancing*
NEAREST TUBE STATIONS *Old Street, Shoreditch, Liverpool Street*

BROWNS
82-84 St Martin's Lane, WC2; 0171 497 5050
The old Westminster County Court has undergone a spectacular conversion to create one massive room, beautifully furnished, simply decorated and as sumptuous as a Victorian parlour. The proliferation of palms, hanging baskets and greenery blends rather well with the cream-painted walls and highly polished woodwork. The high bar-back shows off an impressive display of spirits, cocktail ingredients, wines and bottled beers. There are plenty of staff, all smartly uniformed in white shirts with their ties tucked into them. On the visits I made, they were all remarkably efficient, expert cocktail-makers, very friendly and highly industrious. The bar appeals to an upmarket clientele, mostly in their twenties and thirties, but has resisted the temptation to rob us blind. Free-poured cocktails are £4.35-£4.55, the choice of more than 30 wines sit in the £9.95-£27.95 range, bottled beers are £2.65 and there is a small but quality choice of sparkling wines and champagnes (£18.50-£69.50 for a Perrier Jouet Belle Epoque). The food is firmly rooted in what is fast becoming the Modern British tradition, and is well presented and reasonably priced. There are deals to be had on the food at lunch (under £5), and a pre-theatre menu offers two courses for £9.95 (until 6.30pm). This is the third Browns in London and certainly the most spectacular. Browns was started in 1973 by Jeremy Mogford when he opened his first bar in Brighton. He followed the student trail for a while before pitching to a more up-market clientele in London. It seems to have worked.
OPEN *12.00-midnight (Mon-Thurs), 12.00-00.30 (Fri-Sat), 12.00-23.00 (Sun)*
FOOD *bar 12.00-midnight (Mon-Thurs), 12.00-00.30 (Fri-Sat), 12.00-23.00 (Sun); restaurant 12.00-midnight (Mon-Thurs), 12.00-midnight (Fri-Sat), 12.00-23.00 (Sun)*
CREDIT CARDS *all major cards*
Wheelchair access to venue and loos. Private room: 200 seated, 300 standing
NEAREST TUBE STATION *Leicester Square.*

Branches at:
SW3 114 Draycott Avenue, SW3; 0171 584 5359
　NEAREST TUBE STATION *South Kensington*
W1 47 Maddox Street, W1; 0171 491 4565
　NEAREST TUBE STATION *Oxford Circus, Bond Street*

BULL AND GATE
389 Kentish Town Road, NW5; 0171 485 5358
A series of murals in the main bar show The Bull and Gate standing proudly alone in an idyllic Kentish Town. Nowadays it is dwarfed by the Forum next door. Still, it has kept its cheerfully ornate exterior which is

echoed inside with two bars, one for customers who go for the beer, the other for the choosier ones who go for the music. It specialises in breaking new bands with at least three playing every night of the week in a music room beyond the little bar. The music room is basic but it does have tables and chairs along each side now. Most of the indie acts that play here are entirely unknown so you can usually find somewhere to sit. Nirvana, Carter and Suede all played here in their early days, so you never know. Today's band at The Bull and Gate could be playing next door at the Forum tomorrow.

OPEN *Bar: 11.00-23.00 (Mon-Sat), midday-22.30 (Sun); Music bar 11.00-midnight (Mon-Sun)*

CREDIT CARDS *none taken*

DRAUGHT BEERS *Bass, Hand Pump, Toby, Carling Black Label, Carling Premier, Foster's, Kronenbourg, Staropramen, Guinness, Scrumpy Jack, Strongbow, Holsten Export, Grolsch*

NEAREST TUBE STATION *Kentish Town*

BULL'S HEAD

15 Strand on the Green, W4; 0181 994 1204

The Bull's Head admires but does not altogether trust the river that runs beneath its windows at Strand on the Green. Every month it washes over the tow path. Four or five times a year it covers the benches against the pub walls. It has not got into the pub itself since New Year's Eve 1977, when it swamped the saloon bar and the authorities promise that this won't happen again. Still, you don't take the Thames for granted. High tide, low tide, this is a lovely site for a pub. District Line trains rattle across the railway bridge almost overhead but it is surprising how quickly you get used to that, and the swans on the foreshore take no notice, nor does the heron on the post in the river, the cormorants on Oliver's Island nor, indeed, the customers of The Bull's Head. It has been there for almost 400 years now and has been expanding lately. It took over two of the pretty cottages on its right for the staff and the one on its left for extra room but from the outside you could never tell. There's an old plan of the interior dated 1803 on the wall and the pub seems much the same. The main bar with its old beams and nicotined ceiling is much as it was, and so are the outhouses and the entrance hall they call the games room because that is where the darts board is. There is a big flagged room next to it, where people eat, and picnic tables just off the tow path for sunny days. There is meant to be a secret tunnel to Oliver Island which is said to have saved Oliver Cromwell's bacon during the Civil War. No one lives on the little island now.

OPEN *11.00-23.00 (Mon-Sat), midday-22.30 (Sun)*

FOOD *11.00-17.00 (Mon-Sun)*

CREDIT CARDS *all major cards*

DRAUGHT BEERS *Wadworth 6X, Theakston Old Peculier, Greene King IPA, Courage Directors, Holsten, Foster's, Kronenbourg, Guinness, Strongbow*

NEAREST RAILWAY STATION *Kew Bridge*

BUNCH OF GRAPES

207 Brompton Road, SW3; 0171 589 4944

Visitors from foreign parts have been known to fly into Heathrow at first light, check into their hotel and make straight for The Bunch of Grapes. It is one of the London pubs in every guidebook. Year after year it stays a very classy pub. It is a protected building of course and looks it – granite piers, painted stucco Corinthian columns, a cast iron balcony and what about the spectacular painted mirrors, the etched glass and the splendid mahogany set piece in the bar: a hand-carved vine: with the ripest grapes? In its high Victorian days The Bunch of Grapes had six bars with a separate entrance to each. It still has four bars and three entrances and has kept a lot of the old partitions and a set of snob screens in good working order.

A fifth bar is now planned for the first floor, currently part of the landlord's quarters. If the planners agree, it will get the no-smoking area that pubs of this quality need these days. The character of the pub will not be dented. The food will remain stalwartly English, cooked by the landlord's wife, and the firmly worded notice on the main street doors will stay: 'The management regrets that people in dirty clothing will not be served.'

OPEN 11.00-23.00 (Mon-Sat), midday-22.30 (Sun)
FOOD 11.00-17.00 (Mon-Sun) downstairs
Restaurant: 17.00-22.00 (Mon-Sun)
CREDIT CARDS all major cards
DRAUGHT BEERS Courage Best, Courage Directors, John Smith's Extra Smooth, Foster's, Guinness, Strongbow, Beck's, Kronenbourg, one guest beer
Wheelchair access to venue, not to restaurant
NEAREST TUBE STATIONS Knightsbridge, South Kensington

BURLINGTON BURTIE

39-45 Shaftesbury Avenue, W1; 0171 437 0847
When it comes to sites for pubs it must be hard to beat the stretch of Shaftsbury Avenue sandwiched between the Gielgud Theatre and the Queen's. It has always done well but this year it has really hit it. There should be enough room. There's a big ground floor bar and a Hello Dolly staircase which takes you to a broad gallery with an eye-level view of upper deck passengers in passing double-decker buses, but upstairs, downstairs, both get packed. There are comfortable armchairs and sofas in there somewhere but you can't see them for the people, and the place is even more heaving now that it has a late night music and dancing licence. This keeps it going full tilt until 1am with live bands nightly and a disco every Friday and Saturday. The bar in the basement has not been such a smash but it now has Sky TV for big sports occasions and you can rent it for parties or whatever. A sandwich board on the pavement recommends Bertie's traditional fish and chips. Do you remember Bertie? The one who rose at 10.30 am and sauntered along like a toff? Who walked down the Strand with his gloves in his hand and walked back again with them off? Before my time.

OPEN midday-1.00 (Mon-Sat), midday-22.30 (Sun)
FOOD midday-19.00 (Mon-Sat)
CREDIT CARDS all major cards
DRAUGHT BEERS Foster's, CBL, Stella, Kronenbourg, Carling Premier, Murphy's, Caffrey's, Dry Blackthorn, Greene King, Brakspear
Wheelchair access to venue
NEAREST TUBE STATION Piccadilly

CACTUS BLUE

86 Fulham Road, SW3; 0171 823 7858
An irresistible tequila bar on the Fulham Road created by restaurant proprietor, Brian Stein – owner of the Maxwell Restaurant group. At the back there's a conservatory restaurant serving light dishes from quesadillas and tamales to main courses of crawfish chalupas (£9.95), lobster succotash (£12.95) and fried chicken salad (£7.95). There are dozens of different tequilas from all over the world, no draught beers but plenty of bottled beers and cocktails. If you're sitting upstairs, a mechanical tray raises the drinks from the main bar. Those who sit at the bar bounce up and down on the spring-loaded bar stools – irritating to watch, impossible not to do.

OPEN 17.30-23.45 (Mon-Fri), 12.00-23.45 (Sat-Sun)
FOOD bar as opening times; restaurant 17.30-23.00 (Mon-Fri), 12.00-23.00 (Sat), 12.00-22.00 (Sun)
CREDIT CARDS all major cards
Wheelchair access to venue
NEAREST TUBE STATION South Kensington

CAFÉ BOHÈME

13 Old Compton Street, W1; 0171 734 0623

Extraordinarily popular venue which could be a hundred times its current bijou size and still be packed. People stand on the pavement so they can be a part of the bohemian experience. There's live jazz on Wednesday afternoons and acoustic funk on Sunday evenings. A great bar but just a tad too small for comfort, so you might want to consider booking a table in the restaurant.

OPEN *08.00-03.00 (Mon-Wed), 24 hours (Thurs-Sat)*
FOOD *as opening hours*
CREDIT CARDS *all major cards*
DRAUGHT BEERS *White Beer, Stella Artois*
Wheelchair access to venue
NEAREST TUBE STATION *Leicester Square, Piccadilly Circus*

CAFÉ LATINO

25 Frith Street, W1; 0171 287 5676

Do you remember Diva – the bar with transvestite waiting staff? Café Latino has taken its place. It is painted orange and blue – the only colours available to designers last year – so the Latin flavour is not strong, although it manages to capture a certain taste with its food and drinks. Tapas range between £2.50 and £3.95 and you can buy a platter of six different types for £9.50. There is a fuller menu of antojotos (starters, £3.25-£6.50), platillos fuertes (substantial dishes, £5.25-£7.95). Cocktails – Cuba libra and frozen margaritas – are £4.95. A large spiral staircase occupies much of the ground floor and takes you up to the larger, brighter room with glitter sprinkled over the seats and floor. The basement bar is the best: cosy, intimate and perfect for a drinks party of 15-20 people. It attracts a very mixed clientele – the management have clearly decided not to jump, overtly, on any particular bandwagon.

OPEN *12.00-midnight (Mon-Wed), 12.00-01.00 (Thurs-Sat), 15.00-22.30 (Sun)*
FOOD *as opening hours*
CREDIT CARDS *all major cards*
Two private rooms seat 25 and 35
NEAREST TUBE STATIONS *Leicester Square, Tottenham Court Road*

CAHOOTS

2 Elystan Street, SW3; 0171 584 0140

I've been in cahoots with Cahoots to keep quiet about the place, as to chance across this bar is a pleasure indeed. Scottish & Newcastle established Cahoots to try out a new theme for some of its bars but sadly didn't follow this up. It has a prime location overlooking the small area of land known locally as Chelsea Green and has a rather smart interior of exposed walls with green foliage. On a summer's day, the windows fold back to allow a gentle breeze to cool the bar and there are few better venues for a relaxing drink. The interesting menu of burgers, sandwiches, chilli and pasta dishes lets itself down a little in the presentation – they might try disguising the fact that they use a microwave to heat the food.

OPEN *11.00-23.00 (Mon-Sat), 12.00-22.30 (Sun)*
FOOD *11.00-22.00 (Mon-Sat), 12.00-21.00 (Sun)*
CREDIT CARDS *all major cards*
DRAUGHT BEERS *John Smith's Extra Smooth, Coors, Beck's, Beamish*
Wheelchair access to venue and loos
NEAREST TUBE STATION *Sloane Square*

THE CAMDEN HEAD

Camden Walk, N2; 0171 359 0851

The dealers of Camden Passage, one of London's nicest antique markets, have a great prize in The Camden Head. If an antique has to be 100 years old, well, The Camden Head is nearly there. It was built in 1899 with Queen Victoria nearing the end of her long reign, and it is a beautiful public house, perfectly proportioned, richly appointed with lovely engraved glass and brilliant-cut mirrors. It stands, a choice example of the high-Victorian golden age of pub design with exuberant hanging baskets and its terrace spread before it at a commanding point in the market, and if whatever you search for still eludes you, there at the critical moment is The Camden Head. You can choose between a red plush banquette and one of the stools around the imposing island bar counter, or, on fine days, return with your glass to the large parasols on the terrace. It may be quite a while before you feel inclined to return to the fray.

OPEN *11.00-23.00 (Mon-Sat), midday-22.30 (Sun)*
FOOD *as opening hours*
CREDIT CARDS *all major cards*
DRAUGHT BEERS *Directors, John Smith's Extra Smooth, Theakston Best, Guinness, Beck's, Foster's, Kronenbourg, Beamish, Strongbow, plus a guest ale*
Wheelchair access to venue. Private room: 30 seated, 55 standing
NEAREST TUBE STATION *Angel*

THE CANNON
95 Cannon Street, EC4; 0171 626 8480

Look into this busy City pub at lunchtime. Who can these young men be, this flock of exotic birds in their brightly-coloured floppy cotton jackets – yellow, pale green, deck-chair striped – milling about and talking ten to the dozen? I will tell you. They are futures traders, formidable young men who spend their working day battling it out in the financial mêlée of London's Futures Exchange in Cannon Bridge, just round the corner. If they ply their alarming trade with sufficient brilliance they will become rich in a fortnight or so. If they are too brilliant their employers may lose every penny they have. Such a profession imposes its own strains, and you need a drink, and these particular futures traders feel at home in The Cannon. Its juke box is even louder than the trading pits. Furthermore it is mainly a lager house and they know that the cook does a daily joint for hot meat sandwiches. City men are keen carnivores.

Thus restored, it is back to the future in the afternoon for the bright jackets. Their wearers will be looking into The Cannon again, this time in civvies, on the way to their trains.

OPEN *11.00-23.00 (Mon-Fri)*
FOOD *as opening hours*
CREDIT CARDS *all major cards*
DRAUGHT BEERS *Bass, Caffrey's, Greene King IPA, London Pride, Carling Black Label, Carling Premium, Grolsch, Guinness, Dry Blackthorn*
Wheelchair access to venue
NEAREST TUBE STATION *Cannon Street*

CANTALOUPE BAR & GRILL
35 Charlotte Road, EC2; 0171 613 4411

Opening a decadent bar on the fringes of Shoreditch and the City proved to be a very good move indeed. It still attracts a mass following, but it's easy to feel out of place unless you sport a retro haircut, wear designer labels and enjoy lolling around and shooting the breeze to the beat of the interesting, if not dubious mix of musical mayhem. It has been expanded recently to allow for a new bar and a discreetly tucked-away restaurant area. Sadly, the loos are no closer, so you still need to plan your ablutions well in advance. Management complacency seems to be creeping in but nobody seemed to mind the sticky pools of beer on the tables, the over-flowing ash-trays and the curious refraction of light from the empty-glass mountain being erected. Half-way down my first bottle of wine, a ciggy panic (i.e. none) prompted a quick dash to the bar where, after a long wait, I was refused the necessary change unless I bought something else. Even pointing out that I was running what was going to be rather an expensive looking bill didn't wash, so I opted not to poke his lights out and struck a deal with a fellow punter instead.

Suitably replenished with ciggies, we decided to eat and were accidentally given two separate menus – for the bar, and for the restaurant. Typical of me to choose from the 'wrong' menu and be refused, but I find if you kick up enough fuss people generally come around to your way of thinking. I have to say that the food was really rather good. The restaurant menu changes regularly and can include grilled chilli and spinach polenta, steaks and a variety of fish dishes with an average price of £8-£9. Bar snacks can include garlic and herb pork suasages with roast onion mash and a red wine sauce, garlic and chilli chicken wings or a plate of olives or chips. If you want ketchup or mayo on your chips, you need to fork out an extra ten pence each. So irritating. I did wonder if I was the only person in Cantaloupe who had ever heard of customer service. Have bar owners really disappeared inside themselves? Maybe so. Still, if you name a bar after a melon, what can you expect?

OPEN *11.00-midnight (Mon-Fri), 18.00-midnight (Sat), 12.00-22.30 (Sun)*
FOOD *as opening hours*
Restaurant: 12.00-15.00 and 18.00-23.30 (Mon-Fri), 19.00-23.30 (Sat), 12.00-16.00 (Sun)
CREDIT CARDS all major cards
DRAUGHT BEERS Budweiser, Heineken, Stella Artois, Boddingtons, Murphy's, Wadworth 6X
Wheelchair access to venue
NEAREST TUBE STATIONS Old Street, Liverpool Street

CAPTAIN KIDD

108 Wapping High Street, E1; 0171 480 5759
Captain Kidd is a large and exuberant theme pub built on a magnificent site on the river at Wapping. The theme is, of course, Captain Kidd, the 17th-century privateer. His story is graphically told on the walls of the bar. He was cruelly and, many now think, unjustly done to death on nearby execution dock yard by The Town of Ramsgate. The Town of Ramsgate, small and introvert, is the genuine article. This is an exuberant modern pastiche, and it is proving a great success.

A seemingly ancient archway takes you down a cobbled path to a big, cheerful ground-floor bar with a flagstone floor and genuinely brand-new 17th-century features. Above it is the Café Brasserie Bar where children can have drinks and play video games. Food is served all day here, and there is a more formal restaurant on the floor above that. Each floor has fine river views, though the big river terrace at the side has the best with Canary Wharf mistily downstream. Captain Kidd seems to have been here forever, massive timbers supporting the ancient structure, open tread wooden stairs leading uncreaking from floor to floor, all bleached and split, you might suppose, by centuries of spray and sun. You would suppose wrong. Captain Kidd is what you might call ship-shape and Sam Smith fashion and it is a fine addition to tourist London. It is sure to give the genuinely old pubs of Wapping a run for their money.

OPEN *11.00-23.00 (Mon-Sat), 12.00-22.30 (Sun)*
FOOD *restaurant 12.00-15.00 and 18.30-23.00 (Mon-Sat), 12.00-15.00 and 18.30-21.30 (Sun)*
CREDIT CARDS all major cards
DRAUGHT BEERS Old Brewery, Sovereign Best, Ayingerbräu, Ayingerbräu Pils, Ayingerbräu Prinz, Samuel Smith's Stout, Samuel Smith's Special Reserve
Private room seats 50
NEAREST TUBE STATION Wapping

CARAVAGGIO
107-112 Leadenhall Street, EC3; 0171 626 6206
A restaurant by day, a bar in the evening. The blue-lit exterior of this former banking hall draws you towards the place. The entrance hints quite strongly at a hotel foyer, with its display cabinets and very high-tech reception area. The conference-style seating area is on the ground floor with a gallery above. The only draught beer is Bitburger but they do a wide range of spirits and a massive wine list.
OPEN 11.30-23.00 (Mon-Fri)
FOOD 11.30-15.00 and 18.30-22.00 (Mon-Fri)
CREDIT CARDS all major cards
DRAUGHT BEERS Bitburger
NEAREST TUBE STATION Bank
NEAREST RAILWAY STATIONS Fenchurch Street, Liverpool Street

THE CARTOONIST
76 Shoe Lane, EC4; 0171 353 2828
When the newspapers left Fleet Street, taking their cartoonists with them, The Cartoonist, a bright modern pub in Shoe Lane took it hard. At a stroke it lost many of its most free-spending, which is to say booziest, customers. The pub struggled. Scottish & Newcastle called in Front Page Pubs, a small chain of quality pub operators, who spruced the place up and introduced their own range of meals and wines. They called it The Cartoon Page. A year later and Front Page Pubs were pulling out of the deal. They tell me that the big noises at S & N, who are hardly renowned for their food, insisted that they use their own official food suppliers. Front Page couldn't agree and withdrew, taking their name with them. It is The Cartoonist once again. Margaret Thatcher, Tony Benn, Ken Livingstone, Frank Bruno, Terry Venables and Terry Waite (twice, once before, once after) have all been here to receive the Cartoonist Club of Great Britain's annual award.
OPEN 11.00-23.00 (Mon-Fri)
FOOD 12.00-21.00 (Mon-Fri)
CREDIT CARDS all major cards
DRAUGHT BEERS Courage Best, Courage Directors, John Smith's, Theakston XB, Foster's, Kronenbourg, Guinness, Strongbow
Private room seats 40
NEAREST TUBE STATION Chancery Lane, Blackfriars

THE CAT AND THE CANARY
1-24 Fisherman's Walk, E14; 0171 512 9187
For those who have chosen or been forced to work in or around Canary Wharf, here is a refuge. You get off the Docklands Light Railway at the wharf, go down the escalator and through the North Colonnade door and there it is, a dark pubby pub that has been there for ever. Well, since June 1992. That is for ever on Canary Wharf. Most of the woodwork is pretty old, as it happens. It came from redundant Victorian churches and includes some impressive pews and a telephone kiosk that used to be a pulpit. Innocent visitors who board the Docklands Light Railway by mistake should not be misled by the ecclesiastic interior. Let them be warned that the *Daily Telegraph*, the *Daily Mirror* and *The Independent* are all nearby, not to mention financiers by the dozen. The Cat and Canary has a sunny patio, good cask ales, bar billiards and darts. The Oak Room is a secluded place to avoid the hoi polloi, and there's another cosy corner known as the cuddy, said to be reserved for the exchange of rumours by *Daily Telegraph* personnel.
OPEN 11.00-23.00 (Mon-Fri)
FOOD 12.00-15.00 (Mon-Fri)
CREDIT CARDS all major cards

DRAUGHT BEERS *Chiswick Bitter, ESB, London Cream Ale, London Pride, Carling Black Label, Tennent's Extra, Grolsch, Heineken, Guinness, Strongbow, Stella Artois, one guest ale*
Wheelchair access to venue and loos
NEAREST RAILWAY STATION *Canary Wharf (DLR)*

THE CATCHER IN THE RYE

317 Regents Park Road, N3; 0181 343 4369
The Catcher in the Rye looks rather as if three small buildings have been knocked together. This is what happened, actually. A shop, a solicitor's office and another shop each gave its all to this nice modern pub with several little bars. People play chess and backgammon here, and they have recently installed air conditioning. The Catcher's best seller is a low-gravity bitter which it has specially brewed for it in Suffolk. *The Catcher in the Rye* is a novel by J.D. Salinger.
OPEN *11.00-23.00 (Mon-Sat), 12.00-22.30 (Sun)*
FOOD *12.00-14.30 and 19.00-22.30 (Mon-Sun)*
CREDIT CARDS *Visa, Mastercard*
DRAUGHT BEERS *Bass, Caffrey's, Catchers, Theakston XB, Foster's, Heineken, Dry Blackthorn, Murphy's, Carling Premier*
NEAREST TUBE STATION *Finchley Central*

CENTRAL STATION

37 Wharfdale Road, N1; 0171 278 3294
The owners of Central Station, Duncan Irvine and Martin Mason, won the licensed industry's UK Entrepreneur of the Year award in 1997. Pink Paper gave it the UK Pub of the Year award, and readers of *Scene Update* voted it their 'favourite pub'. Duncan and Martin bought the place in 1991, and it seems to get a bigger following as each year passes. There's nightly entertainment on the ground floor, live music, drag cabaret, strippers, quiz nights. Upstairs is the café bar and two function rooms where any non-profit-making gay group can meet without charge. About 50 such groups regularly meet here. There's a new roof garden, facing west, as roof gardens should, and a nightclub in the basement, dark and loud and late to bed. Famous punters are drawn to the happy-go-lucky nightlife, and I hear tell that they regularly include Jean-Paul Gaultier, Jimmy Somerville and Julian Clary. They must all be insomniacs – just look below for the hours that Central Station keeps.
OPEN *17.00-02.00 (Mon-Wed), 17.00-03.00 (Thurs), 17.00-04.00 (Fri), 12.00-04.00 (Sat), 12.00-midnight (Sun)*
FOOD *as opening hours*
CREDIT CARDS *all major cards*
DRAUGHT BEERS *Courage Directors, Courage Best, Foster's, Holsten, Kronenbourg, Guinness, Beamish, Scrumpy Jack*
Meeting room for gay groups. Four rooms for hire: 12-60 seated, 20-140 standing
NEAREST TUBE STATION *King's Cross*

Also at:
80 Brunner Road, Walthamstow E17,
NEAREST TUBE STATION *Walthamstow Central*

THE CHAMPION

1 Wellington Terrace, Bayswater Road, W2; 0171 229 5056
As I write, big changes are in the offing for this long-established, uncamp, uncomplicated gay local. This will include removing the massive heptagonal bar and replacing it with a linear bar against one wall that will undoubtedly allow more room for manoeuvre. There will be a new light and sound system that will create a party atmosphere. Karaoke comes and karaoke goes. At the moment it's in, but budding Shirley Basseys should check first.

OPEN *12.00-23.00 (Mon-Sat), 12.00-22.30 (Sun)*
CREDIT CARDS *all major cards*
DRAUGHT BEERS *Caffrey's, Worthington, Carling Black Label, Carling Premier, Grolsch, Red Rock*
NEAREST TUBE STATION *Notting Hill Gate*

THE CHAMPION
12-13 Wells Street, W1; 0171 323 1228
The most notable thing about The Champion is its quite remarkable windows. When Samuel Smith bought the pub in the 80s the company commissioned a series of big stained-glass windows from Anne Sotheran of York. They are now splendidly in situ, filling two whole walls. Each celebrates a different champion – Fred Archer, Captain Webb, W. G. Grace – and they fill the bar with an extraordinary light.
OPEN *11.30-23.00 (Mon-Fri), 11.30-23.00 (Sat), 12.00-22.30 (Sun)*
FOOD *as opening hours (not Sun)*
CREDIT CARDS *all major cards, except AmEx*
DRAUGHT BEERS *Samuel Smith's Mild, Ayingerbräu, Samuel Smith's Extra Stout, Sovereign Best, Old Brewery, Cider Reserve*
Wheelchair access to venue, not to loos. Private room: 110 standing
NEAREST TUBE STATION *Oxford Circus*

THE CHANDOS
29 St Martin's Lane, WC2; 0171 836 1401
Samuel Smith, the Yorkshire brewer, took no chances on unknown, untried southern builders when they bought this busy London pub. There was a lot to be done so they brought men down from Yorkshire to do it.

People hardly recognised the old Chandos when it reopened. The building seemed to have been totally refaced. It had a gleaming black and gold fascia and immaculate new stucco, and it was quite different inside – new fittings, new paneling, new just about everything. Victorian mahogany drinking booths, hand-made by the joiners from Tadcaster, lined the walls of the big downstairs bar. Pairs of button-back leather sofas faced each other across coffee tables in the grandly named Opera Room upstairs. The Yorkshiremen, well pleased, went home again. The Opera Room has its own staircase to the street, opens for breakfast at 9am, and subsequently offers coffee, lunch, tea and supper. It is a useful, well-turned-out pub in a great position. If you are passing, wave to the burly cooper working on the ledge three floors up. He has been doing something to a barrel up there all day and all night for years now.
OPEN *11.00-23.00 (Mon-Sat), 12.00-22.30 (Sun)*
FOOD *09.00-21.00 (Mon-Sun)*
CREDIT CARDS *all major cards*
DRAUGHT BEERS *Samuel Smith's Old Brewery Bitter, Ayingerbräu, Samuel Smith's Extra Stout, Samuel Smith's Cider Reserve, Dark Mild*
NEAREST TUBE STATIONS *Charing Cross, Leicester Square*

THE CHELSEA POTTER
119 King's Road, SW3; 0171 352 9479
This Potter holds prime position on the King's Road for people-watching and sitting and watching the world go by. In the summer, the windows open up and the outside seating is always full to capacity. Shoppers and tourists keep it busy by day, when you can also enjoy some traditional pub fare. In the evenings, there isn't really room for food. The place fills up, the music pipes up, the lights go down and the performance of young people enjoying themselves begins. Vanda Stiglic runs the place. Old hands may remember her from The Shuckburgh (qv) in the 80s. She loves Chelsea pubs, so much so that she now has another one, The Resident (formerly The Phoenix), down the road in Smith Street.

OPEN *11.00-23.00 (Mon-Sat), 12.00-22.30 (Sun)*
FOOD *all day (Mon-Sun)*
CREDIT CARDS *all major cards, not AmEx, Visa, Mastercard*
DRAUGHT BEERS *Courage Best, John Smith's Extra Smooth, Beck's, Foster's, Kronenbourg, Strongbow, Directors, Beamish*
Wheelchair access to venue
NEAREST TUBE STATION *Sloane Square*

THE CHELSEA RAM

32 Burnaby Street, SW10; 0171 351 4008

This is a fine, handsome, bright and cheerful pub with big arched windows and a reputation for above-average quality food of a Modern British design (chicken breast marinated in honey and thyme; seared salmon with a salad of plum tomatoes, rocket, pumpkin seeds and Italian sauce; prices from £7.95). The decor, simple and understated with large tables and creaky wooden chairs, is fast becoming the rage of modern pub restaurants. It works well here, and the antique dealers, artisans and wealthy City types who frequent the place obviously delight in it. The Chelsea Ram serves Young's beers, 20 or so wines from the list (from £8.95) and a few champagnes (house £23.45). The pub was recently extended at the back, and a new skylight covers a very pleasant corner where the best seats are. You can't book tables but it's worth taking your chances for the excellent food.

OPEN *11.00-15.00 and 17.30-23.00 (Mon-Sat), 12.00-22.30 (Sun), 11.00-23.00 (Fri)*
FOOD *12.00-14.30 and 19.00-21.45 (Mon-Sat)*
CREDIT CARDS *Mastercard, Visa, Switch*
DRAUGHT BEERS *Ramrod Smooth, Young's Bitter, Young's Pilsner, Young's Export, Young's Special, Guinness, Strongbow, Stella Artois, Castlemaine XXXX*
Wheelchair access to venue. Private room seats 12
NEAREST TUBE STATION *Fulham Broadway*

CHESHIRE CHEESE

5 Little Essex Street, WC2; 0171 836 2347

This is not to be confused with Ye Olde Cheshire Cheese, though it often is. American visitors sometimes photograph it inside and out before discovering that there is a rather better-known Cheshire Cheese ten minutes' walk away. This, though, is quite an old pub, too, and a certain amount of haunting goes on here. A ghost pushed the fruit machine around at night, and managers alone in the pub at weekends sometimes hear the dumb waiter inexplicably on its way up. Abraham Pera, the present manager, says that he has gone to the cellar on occasions to discover previously stacked beer barrels strewn across the floor. It doesn't seem to worry him, though – he has a customer who dresses up as a 17th-century ghost and takes his other customers on a ghost trail of the area. The pub closes at weekends but during the week the saloon bar stays open all day. The dive bar's customers are noticeably younger. This is where the pool table and the music are.

OPEN *11.00-23.00 (Mon-Fri)*
FOOD *as opening hours*
CREDIT CARDS *all major cards*
DRAUGHT BEERS *Courage Best, Courage Directors, Theakston Best, John Smith's Extra Smooth, Foster's, Holsten, Kronenbourg, Strongbow, Guinness*
Wheelchair access to venue and loos. Private room: 26 seated, 50 standing
NEAREST TUBE STATIONS *Temple, Charing Cross*

CHRISTOPHER'S SPEAKEASY

18 Wellington Street, WC2; 0171 240 4222

During Prohibition in the USA a speakeasy was a place where alcoholic drink was sold illicitly. There's nothing illegal about this place, although there should be, as those of us who remember the rather charming upstairs bar are disappointed to find it newly relegated to a converted cellar to make more room for the restaurant. It never seems to get too busy, which is great for those who like to have a nice quiet night in the middle of Covent Garden. I think it's wonderful, and I'm going to keep quiet about it, as it's handy to know there's such a haven of tranquillity in an otherwise riotous area. The famous illustrations have joined the bar in the cellar, and they cover just about every inch of wallspace. I was so pleased with my loneliness that I almost ordered a sandwich to celebrate, but at £5 for a BLT, I thought that might be pushing the boat out just a bit too far.

OPEN bar 11.00-23.00 (Mon-Sat), 12.00-16.00 (Sun); restaurant 12.00-15.30 and 18.00-23.45 (Mon-Sat), 12.00-15.30 (Sun)

CREDIT CARDS all major cards

Private room: 50 seated, 90 standing

NEAREST TUBE STATION Covent Garden

CICADA

132-136 St John Street, EC1; 0171 608 1550

I liked this place immediately. That is until the staff got shirty with me for asking to see the downstairs room (a beautiful Oriental-style bar), only open at weekends. The main bar is very Clerkenwell, very agreeable, and has decent food. If they fire all the staff I'll go back – they can't even make a decent Martini.

OPEN midday-midnight (Mon-Fri), 18.00-midnight (Sat)

FOOD as above, last food orders 23.00

CREDIT CARDS all major cards

DRAUGHT BEERS Kronenbourg, Guinness, Leffe

Wheelchair access to venue and loos. Private room, accomodates 70, standing (buffet type functions only)

NEAREST TUBE STATIONS Angel, Farringdon

THE CIRCLE

Queen Elizabeth Street, SE1; 0171 407 1122

Wandering around the beautiful but somewhat soulless part of London that encompasses several docklands redevelopment projects, one can only muse at how far out of central London one has to go to be able to afford such luxurious conversions. On the basis of my income, I calculate that I could possibly run to a shell on an industrial estate somewhere between Haverfordwest and Abergaveny. The infrastructure has started to arrive in the area around Butler's Wharf, and The Circle bar and restaurant occupies the lower floors of one such warehouse conversion. The modern interior is somewhat predicatable for the area: polished wooden floors, stark white walls and, for a change, comfortable well-spaced seating with a galleried upper level overlooking the street. It attracts a decent number of the afterwork crew for the rather extensive drinks list and really rather good-quality food. Cocktails (from £6), wines (from £9.50) and spirits (from £3.50) are the thing to go for with whisky lovers being enticed to an interesting range of malts. I wasn't asked how I'd like my Bloody Mary, so figuring that was enough rope for anyone to hang themselves with I let her get on with it. Although I've had better, this one was nicely spicey and did the trick. The beer I'm afraid is the downside. Keg lagers and a Tetley's bitter didn't attract me and neither would the happy hour (5-7pm) offer of three Miller Genuine Draft for the price of two. I'd be mad if I had one. Weekends are an altogether more sedate affair, when you can ease your way through the afternoon over a hot brunch including a full breakfast (£4.35), Club sandwich with fries (£4.35) or a toasted tuna melt (£2.50). Delicious!

OPEN 11.30-midnight or 23.00 for drinkers (Mon-Sat), 11.00-22.30 (Sun)

FOOD set menu 11.30-14.30, 18.00-22.30; sandwiches 11.30-18.30

CREDIT CARDS all major cards accepted

DRAUGHT BEERS *Stella Artois, Carlsberg, Guinness, Strongbow*
Wheelchair access to venue. Private rooms seats 70, 100 standing
NEAREST TUBE STATIONS *London Bridge, Tower Hill*

CIRCUS

1 Upper James Street, W1; 0171 534 4000
Clinically chic basement bar with good-looking bar staff and a relaxed
seating area. Popular with local hairdressers and off-duty bartenders. Worth
joining to ensure entry when the crowds descend later on. Membership is
free but most have been given to friends of the management. Girls always
seem to get in but if you go early enough you should be OK – if the bouncer
likes you. If you get in, ask the bartenders for an application form. If
you're not a member, try suggesting you work at the Met Bar – it worked
for me last time.
OPEN *midday-01.30 every day*
FOOD *12.30-15.00 then 17.45-midnight*
CREDIT CARDS *all major cards*
NEAREST TUBE STATION *Piccadilly Circus*

THE CITTIE OF YORKE

22 High Holborn, WC1; 0171 242 7670
When the Yorkshire Brewers Samuel Smith made their first sally into London
in 1979 they bought Hennekey's – well known, long established and much
respected. They thus acquired six fine London pubs. This one sold only
wine for more than 100 years. It was surely the greatest prize. It was the
original Hennekey's and it was famous. It had evolved from an ancient inn
built in 1430 and was largely rebuilt every 200 years or so. It emerged in
its present form in the 1890s, and such a form! There is no pub in London
quite like this one
    The main bar resembles the great hall of a medieval manor rising to
a soaring trussed root and high Gothic windows. Along one wall is the
famous bar, shorter than it used to be but still one of the longest in Britain.
Above it huge iron-hooped wine butts sit on a stout timber gallery supported
by fluted iron pillars. Each butt once held 1,000 gallons of wine. They
were in active use right up to the outbreak of the last war, when they were
carefully drained. A well-placed bomb might have carried off the customers
in a tidal wave of amontillado. Small cubicles line the facing wall, a table
and four chairs in each. They were originally kept for lawyers and their
clients but they now have to take their chances like everyone else. The
cubicles are very popular, as is the massive stove on cold days. It was
made in 1815 and still works perfectly. Each of its three sides has an open
grate and there is no sign of a chimney. That is under the floorboards.
    Samuel Smith's made some alterations. They made a second, smaller bar at
the Holborn end and a long cellar bar downstairs and, of course, they gave it
a quaint new name. Well, there is a lot of 'ye oldery' about and there was a
pub called the Cittie of Yorke in these parts in times gone by. Furthermore,
olde Sam Smith does come from Yorke or not far offe. He brews good beer at
Tadcaster and this and only this is now sold at all his London pubs. As for The
Cittie of Yorke, it is clearly in good heart. It remains a spectacular pub.
OPEN *11.30-23.00 (Mon-Sat)*
FOOD *12.00-22.00 (Mon-Fri)*
CREDIT CARDS *AmEx, Mastercard, Visa, Switch*
DRAUGHT BEERS *Ayingerbräu Wheat Beer, Old Brewery Bitter, Samuel
Smith's Dark Mild, Ayingerbräu Pils, Samuel Smith's Extra Stout, Special
Reserve, Ayingerbräu Prinz*
Wheelchair access to venue. Private room seats 260
NEAREST TUBE STATION *Holborn, Chancery Lane*

THE CITY BARGE

27 Strand on the Green, W4; 0181 994 2148

I don't suppose The City Barge was a prime target during the war.
Presumably the landmine that got it was meant for the railway bridge.
It missed though, and knocked down most of this nice old riverside pub
instead. An elderly regular remembers arriving at the pub and finding the
roof gone and rubble up to 'here'. He got his drink as usual but, incredibly,
someone pinched Queen Elizabeth I's charter. It had been on the wall
and it hasn't been seen since. The ancient fireplace with its grate raised to
stop floods putting the fire out survived, so did the bar counter and the
parliamentary clock made without glass to save tax.

So The City Barge was patched up and after the war it was rebuilt on
the original 1484 foundations. The pub was the Navigator's Arms in those
days and Richard III was in the winter of his discontent. It is slightly bigger
now with an old bar and a new bar. You go down a few steps to the old
bar, which is much as it was before the bombing, small, homely, old
fashioned. The new bar is up a few steps, substantially larger with a long
counter and drinking booths. They had live music up here every weekend
until the neighbours complained.

Like The Bull's Head, its near neighbour, The City Barge has Oliver
Cromwell stories. It has Beatles stories too. A sequence of Help was filmed
here and John, Paul, George and Ringo had a few days filming by the
river. The bit where Ringo falls into the cellar was shot in the studio. The
City Barge doesn't have a cellar. The river tries to get in from time to time
without much success. The old pub has a watertight ship's door on the tow
path now.

OPEN *11.00-23.00 (Mon-Sat), 12.00-22.30 (Sun)*
FOOD *as opening hours*
CREDIT CARDS *Mastercard, Visa, AmEx, Switch*
DRAUGHT BEERS *Courage Directors, Theakston Best, Theakston Old Peculier,
Theakston XB, Foster's, Kronenbourg, Guinness, Strongbow*
Wheelchair access to venue
NEAREST RAILWAY STATIONS *Kew Bridge, Gunnersbury*

CITY PAGE

2a Suffolk Lane, EC4; 0171 626 0996

Front Page Pubs are doing a marvelous job in lifting the standards of some
of London's pubs and bars, and the City Page is the fifth in their slowly
expanding yet highly efficient portfolio. Being underground, almost like a
series of tunnels knocked together, it reminds you of those wine cellars
popular in the early 80s, and they seem to have found a carpet from that
era to complement the decor. Bollinger's the drink here. A Front Page pub
wouldn't have it any other way, and at £35 a bottle it comes in at rather
good value. It doesn't have great kitchen facilities so the menu is restricted
to sandwiches and salads (from £3.50). It's too bad these wonderful
cellars can't be air-conditioned. You can't tell by looking that this is a part
of the Page family.

OPEN *11.00-23.00 (Mon-Fri)*
FOOD *11.00-23.00 (Mon-Fri)*
CREDIT CARDS *all major cards*
No private room but venue can be hired for up to 200 people
NEAREST TUBE STATIONS *Cannon Street*

THE CLACHAN

34 Kingly Street, W1; 0171 734 2659

Kingly Street must always have been a pain for Liberty's, nipping in as it
does and cutting the great department store in two. The three-storey bridge
that crosses Kingly Street is just Liberty's trying to get from one bit of the
store to the other. Go under the bridge and on the left is a small but perfectly

formed public house, rather romantic, faintly Scottish, a turret on the corner adding a green copper dome to the skyline. This, until quite recently, was The Bricklayers and Liberty's owned it. What, though, was Liberty's to do with it? It did not want a pub. It wanted more space for warehousing. Perhaps ... But no. The Bricklayers was a protected building, as Liberty's itself is. A pub it had to stay. So in 1983 Nicholson's bought it, smartened it up and changed its name. It is now The Clachan, the old Scots word for meeting place, and Scots do on occasion meet there. There is a large air-conditioned bar, at least six real ales on tap and a good-sized clachan upstairs called the Highland Bar. The haggis is piped in on Burn's Night and pictures of bearded highland worthies decorate the walls, but apart from this Nicholson's has resisted smothering The Clachan in tartan.

OPEN 11.00-23.00 (Mon-Sat)
FOOD bar 11.00-20.30 (Mon-Sat)
CREDIT CARDS all major cards
DRAUGHT BEERS Tetley's, IPA, Kilkenny, Carlsberg, Carlsberg Export, Guinness, Blackthorn Cider, three guest ales
Wheelchair access to venue, not to loos. Private room seats 36
NEAREST TUBE STATION Oxford Circus

THE CLARENCE

53 Whitehall, SW1; 0171 930 4808
Ancient overhead timbers from a Thames pier, wonderful cellars under Whitehall, leaded windows throwing delicate patterns on the pale wooden floor, this is a most romantic old pub. It has tremendous appeal for tourists. It used to provide a jester for them every summer but this seemed a bit over the top and anyway he retired. They are pleased to find the settles and benches still there and the wooden floors, though sadly the gas lights went in the recent redecoration.

Inigo Jones's famous banqueting hall is just two blocks away. It was from one of its windows that Charles I stepped on to the scaffold to face the executioner. Every year roundheads and cavaliers mark the anniversary of this grisly event with a toast in The Clarence. I suppose the Clarence who gave his name to The Clarence was good old William IV, the sailor king. He was Duke of Clarence at the time. But this was the king who gargled two gallons of water every morning. Is he a suitable role model for a pub? Richard III's brother, poor perjured Clarence, would be better, drowning, as he did, in a butt of malmsey. Not that you get malmsey at The Clarence. It is a real ale house.

OPEN 11.00-23.00 (Mon-Sat), 12.00-22.30 (Sun)
FOOD 11.00-23.00 (Mon-Sat), 12.00-22.30 (Sun)
CREDIT CARDS all major cards
DRAUGHT BEERS Abbot Ale, John Smith's Smooth Cask Ale, Theakston Best, Theakston Old Peculier, Beck's, Foster's, Kronenbourg, Strongbow
Wheelchair access to venue. Private room seats 52
NEAREST TUBE STATIONS Charing Cross, Embankment

THE CLIFTON

96 Clifton Hill, NW8; 0171 624 5233
Two stories are told about The Clifton. One is that it was the country retreat of a rich man who got fed up with his London friends galloping over to drink his drink so he got a license and made them pay. The other is that the Prince of Wales, the one who became Edward VII, used to meet Lily Langtry there in the private bar. Well, he might have done. It is the sort of thing he did.

The Clifton is a substantial Georgian villa in a particularly pleasant street in St John's Wood. It has been a pub since 1834, and in recent years it has been beautifully restored and refurbished. The style is Edwardian of course. It is all pine paneling, polished floors with Persian rugs and ornate, open fireplaces and it is full of quiet corners for well-upholstered lovers to hold hands. In 1985 it was the Evening Standard Pub of the Year, the unanimous choice of the judges, and that year too an extremely nice conservatory was added. This is the restaurant now. There is a sunny terrace at the back and tables in the garden flanking the street, and in the winter it is particularly inviting with fires in each of the main rooms. Edward VII would probably have liked it even more now. For one thing, there are pictures of him everywhere. There are even more of his shapely mistress. There is even one of his wife.

OPEN *11.00-23.00 (Mon-Sat), 12.00-22.30 (Sun)*

FOOD *12.00-14.45 and 19.00-21.30 (Mon-Sat), 12.00-17.00 (Sun), no food Sunday evenings*

CREDIT CARDS *all major cards*

DRAUGHT BEERS *Adnams, Calder's Cream Ale, Pedigree, Tetley's, Carlsberg, Castlemaine XXXX, Guinness, Dry Blackthorn, Greene King Abbott, Stella Artois, one guest ale*

NEAREST TUBE STATIONS *St John's Wood, Maida Vale*

THE COACH AND HORSES

29 Greek Street, W1; 0171 437 5920

One of Soho's most celebrated pubs, The Coach and Horses, stands proud on the corner of Romilly Street and Greek Street. Inside, its red plastic stool covers, black Formica table tops and Basic Food Hygiene Certificate announce that this is a pub for serious drinkers. For many years *Private Eye* had its offices opposite the pub, which became a haunt of Richard Ingrams, Peter Cook, William Rushton, Michael Heath and Jeffrey Bernard. *Private Eye* still has its fortnightly lunches in an upstairs room, although lunches in the pub itself have been stopped. A sandwich in the bar is quite enough. The landlord, Normal Balon, is known to many as London's rudest landlord, a reputation borne out of much self-perpetuation, I suspect.

OPEN *11.00-23.00 (Mon-Sat), 12.00-22.30 (Sun)*

FOOD *sandwiches at bar*

CREDIT CARDS *none taken*

DRAUGHT BEERS *Burton Ale, Calder's Cream Ale, Marston's Pedigree, Tetley's, Carlsberg, Carlsberg Export, Löwenbräu, Guinness, Dry Blackthorn Wheelchair access to venue, not to loos*

NEAREST TUBE STATION *Leicester Square, Tottenham Court Road*

THE COAL HOLE

91 The Strand, WC1; 0171 836 7503

In the distant days of The Coal Hole's notoriety, it was a coalheavers' hang-out in old converted cellars off the Strand. It was very rough. The coalheavers drank and carried on, word got round and others started going, actors and the like. The coalheavers moved on to the Ship and Shovel, also still going strong, and The Coal Hole moved further along the Strand to proper premises in the Savoy buildings, where it is today. The main bar on the Strand is high and handsome with large windows, hanging banners and marble reliefs of frisking maidens, muses perhaps, or seasons. The cellar bar has been much smartened up lately. It has its own entrance and its own lively following. It is an interesting bar, wandering off downhill a bit, and at its far reaches is a locked gate, beyond which some steps lead down to a little windowless snug. This, they will tell you, is the coal hole. It certainly could be one. People drink in it sometimes. It is not for claustrophobics.

OPEN *11.00-23.00 (Mon-Sat), 12.00-18.00 (Sun)*

FOOD *11.00-16.45 (Mon-Sat), Sandwich menu 12.00-15.00 (Sun)*

CREDIT CARDS *Mastercard, Visa*

DRAUGHT BEERS *Tetley's, Timothy Taylor Landlord, Carlsberg, Castlemaine XXXX, Guinness, Addlestones, Stella Artois, Marston's Pedigree, Old Speckled Hen, one guest ale*

NEAREST TUBE STATIONS *Charing Cross, Covent Garden*

COATES

45 London Wall, EC2; 0171 256 5148

Corney and Barrow (qv), the rather up-market chain of City bars, goes down-market a little with its two Coates outlets. This one opened in 1991 and provides good value food in an up-beat atmosphere. The food is pizza – not a bad idea in a bar for City workers. In the evenings the atmosphere gets quite lively; there's karaoke on Wednesday and Friday and a disco on Thursday. As one of the researchers of this *Guide* put it: 'Essex nymphos by night and an easy place to pull on Thursdays'.

OPEN *11.00-23.00 (Mon-Sat), 12.00-22.30 (Sun)*

FOOD *12.00-17.00 and 19.00-22.00 (Mon-Sat)*

CREDIT CARDS *Mastercard, Visa*

DRAUGHT BEERS *Young's Ordinary, Young's Special, London Lager, Premium Lager, Guinness, Young's Oatmeal, Scrumpy Jack*

NEAREST TUBE STATION *Farringdon*

Also at: City
46 Cowcross Street, EC1; 0171 251 3128

COCKTAIL BAR AT THE CONNAUGHT

Connaught Hotel, 16 Carlos Place, W1; 0171 499 7070

If the entire country gave up smoking, there would be one last remaining humidor circulating the Cocktail Bar at the Connaught Hotel. This is where you'll find gentlemen sitting in big leather chairs puffing away on large Havanas or the like, sipping brandies and probably speculating on government policy, economic trends and profit forecasts of the major internationals. The bar is extraordinarily handsome, elegant, exclusive and serene with service that is military prompt yet very discreet. When I went with my colleagues, Andrew Jefford and Angus McGill, they were quietly and politely asked if they'd care to repair to the cloakroom where they would be furnished with ties. They didn't mind in the slightest, and the cloakroom attendant told them they now looked like a million dollars. They gave him a pound. Back in the bar we tucked in to the wonderful free nibbles, and suggested that this would be a great place for a clandestine meeting.

OPEN *11.00-15.00 and 17.30-23.00 (Mon-Sat), 12.00-14.00 and 19.00-22.30 (Sun)*

CREDIT CARDS *all major cards*

Wheelchair access to venue

NEAREST TUBE STATION *Bond Street*

THE COLEHERNE

261 Old Brompton Road, SW5; 0171 373 9859

The Coleherne is a cavernous Victorian pub in Earl's Court and the most famous gay pub in the world. The atmosphere is macho and menacing, with little of the gaiety of the usual gay pub. The Coleherne has two sets of customers, the ones in leather and the rest. Some stand holding bottles and staring straight ahead. Less flamboyant customers gather in large numbers on the other side of the bar. There is not a lot of conversation even among this group. The Coleherne isn't strong on conversation. Serial killer Colin Ireland, now serving life, met his victims here. During his trial there were said to be more reporters in The Coleherne than regular customers. Armistead Maupin's character Mouse, from his *Tales of the City* books, came here when he first visited London. It has recently had a rather drastic shake-up on the decor front. But this is The Coleherne. The old rules still apply.

OPEN *12.00-23.00 (Mon-Sat), 12.00-22.30 (Sun)*

DRAUGHT BEERS *Worthington's Best, Caffrey's, Grolsch, Carling Premier, Guinness, Red Rock*

CREDIT CARDS *all major cards*

Wheelchair access to venue and loos

NEAREST TUBE STATION *Earls Court*

THE COLLECTION

264 Brompton Road, SW3; 0171 225 1212

A 100-foot-long portal with an illuminated glazed floor leads you into this vast former Katharine Hamnett warehouse conversion housing a mezzanine restaurant and a café and bar on the ground floor. The 60-foot bar sweeps high and wide into the distance, rising with the peculiar inclination of the floor, which allows those of us who are vertically challenged to survey the proceedings from a confident position. And survey we will. It attracts beautiful and well-heeled people who compose themselves by resting in the café area or milling around the large open floorspace tippling cocktails and foot-tapping to the beat of the acid jazz. The impressive display of drinks served up by the appropriately friendly, comely staff makes you feel like experimenting with something expensive, which is rather handy, because you very probably will. Cocktails are £6 each and there are 17 on the menu to work through, but I have been assured that it is still cool to stand sucking beer from the neck of a bottle.

This isn't really a daytime venue – the only company might be the District Line trains rattling by outside. That's why I like it for lunch. From the Thai noodle menu I usually opt for beef teriyaki with yaki soba noodles (£6.95), but that's only because I like to say yaki soba. Getting in can be quite tricky so it's best not to go in large numbers, and most punters seem to be either City-smart or PR-groomed. It was founded by Daphne's and Pasha proprietor, Mogens (pronounced mo-ans) Tholstrup. He's the man who sold his empire to Belgo for several million and got to keep his job. Smart move.

OPEN 12.00-23.00 (Mon-Sat)

FOOD bar and restaurant upstairs 12.00-15.00 (Wed-Sat) and 19.00-23.30 (Mon-Sat); restaurant downstairs 12.00-23.00 (Wed-Sat), no lunch served Mon and Tues

CREDIT CARDS all major cards

Wheelchair access to venue and loos, not upstairs

NEAREST TUBE STATION South Kensington

COME THE REVOLUTION

541 King's Road, SW6; 0171 610 9067

The title has nothing to do with any affiliation of a political kind, and the owners would be very happy if you'd stop asking that question. Come the Revolution opened up nearly five years ago and was an immediate hit with the younger element of Fulham, since it's very handy for a couple of neighbouring clubs, Crazy Larry's and Embargo. It's loud, sometimes impossibly fashionable and occasionally a little bit eccentric. Food and music being the love of Fulhamites, the Thai chef Toni serves some formidable Thai dishes at remarkably cheap prices (nothing over £5.50). There is no let-up to the music: R & B Mondays, Latin American acoustic guitars on Tuesdays, happy house Wednesdays, a very loud but fabulous Japanese funk band on Thursdays, DJs Fridays and Saturdays, jazz on Sunday at lunchtime with a traditional English roast lunch and Caribbean and Creole in the evening. There's a minor escape from all this in the form of a wonderful walled garden at the back to while away the summer evenings. You can even while away the winter evenings now – they've installed a covering canopy and garden heaters. Did I mention the crushed velvet and velour furnishings? I wonder if they'll survive the next revolution.

OPEN 11.00-23.00 (Mon-Sat), 12.00-22.30 (Sun)

FOOD bar 12.00-15.00 and 17.30-21.30 (Mon-Sun)

CREDIT CARDS all major cards

DRAUGHT BEERS Calder's Cream Ale, Kilkenny, Beck's, Kronenbourg, Warsteiner

Wheelchair access to venue

NEAREST TUBE STATION Fulham Broadway

COMPTON ARMS

4 Compton Avenue, N1; 0171 359 2645

A quiet little country pub hidden away off Canonbury Square. There's a small cosy low-ceilinged bar and benches round cask tables under a friendly sycamore tree at the back. The 20th century encroaches. Crib and dominoes wait behind the bar but no one ever asks for them. There is still neither juke box nor gaming machine but Sky TV has arrived. The little Compton is always busy when Arsenal is at home.

OPEN *11.00-23.00 (Mon-Sat), midday-22.30 (Sun)*

FOOD *bar midday-15.00 and 18.00-21.00 (Mon-Fri), midday-21.00 (Sat-Sun)*

CREDIT CARDS *all major cards*

DRAUGHT BEERS *Abbot Ale, Greene King, Rayments, Wexford Cream Ale, Harp, Kronenbourg, Stella Artois, Guinness, Bulmers*

Wheelchair access to venue

NEAREST TUBE STATION *Highbury & Islington*

THE COOPERS' ARMS

87 Flood Street, SW3; 0171 376 3120

Good mannered, good natured, we have here a thoroughly well-bred pub with staff and customers in complete accord. Parents may raise an eyebrow to find Justin or Julian serving behind the bar but it is usually an enjoyable interlude, to be dined out on later. For the moment the City can wait. A massive buffalo head, a gift from a customer, presides over the bar, a baker's dough table occupies an extravagant amount of floor space, a splendid LMS long case clock looks as though it had been made for the end wall and two massive air filters on the ceiling keep the air clear and smokers and non-smokers in harmony. The brasserie style food is a major attraction. Upstairs is a useful room for special occasions with a magnificent 17-foot table, originally a draughtsman's table from a Jarrow shipyard. On Saturdays it is laden with food and drink as wedding guests pour up the stairs and into yet another reception. Chelsea Register Office is round the corner.

OPEN *11.00-23.00 (Mon-Sat), midday-22.30 (Sun)*

FOOD *12.30-15.00 and 19.00-22.00 (Wed-Sat)*

CREDIT CARDS *all major cards*

DRAUGHT BEERS *all Young's varieties, Beck's, Budweiser, Holsten, Michelob, Red Stripe, Stella Artois, Scrumpy Jack, Staropramen*

Wheelchair access to venue. Private room: 30 seated, 70 standing

NEAREST TUBE STATION *Sloane Square*

CORK AND BOTTLE

44-46 Cranbourn Street, WC2; 0171 734 7807

I think that this was possibly the first wine bar I went to in London. It's almost impossible to find – entry is via a narrow doorway in bustling Cranbourn Street – and you descend a flight of steps into the basement, where a couple of air-conditioned bars extend warren-like underground. The place opened in August 1971 and was one of the first wine bars of its day. It was always packed, and offered a wide, mostly palatable range of wines. In 1984 it was voted the very first *Evening Standard* Wine Bar of the Year, and its success seemed to roll on even with the dawning of a new generation of wine bars. The Cork and Bottle is more than 28 years old now, and I have been back several times in the past year to check it out. It's wearing well, clearly dating from the 70s but still remarkably popular and unpretentious. Some of the customers look as though they have been frequenting the place since 1971, and many probably have. The bar staff I encountered were quite laid back in that Antipodean style which can appear off-hand, but were very knowledgeable about the wines and seemed willing to help when people were struggling with the extensive list.

OPEN *11.00-midnight (Mon-Sat), 12.00-22.30 (Sun)*

FOOD *11.00-23.30 (Mon-Sat), 12.00-22.00 (Sun)*

CREDIT CARDS *all major cards*
NEAREST TUBE STATION *Leicester Square*

CORNEY AND BARROW

Corney and Barrow have been established in the City since 1870, but their latest bars were introduced in 1988, with the opening of the branch at Broadgate. This is the glass structure in the gardens of Exchange Square, Broadgate, where they hold regular croquet tournaments during the summer. Exchange Square is the smallest Corney and Barrow in the entire world, although it benefits from an upstairs and a rather large expansion on to the pavement outside. The Cannon Street branch opens at 8am for breakfast. The Eastcheap Corney and Barrow is in a basement close to Monument tube station, and is well frequented by local workers.

The branch at Broadgate Circle is the most spectacular. On the first level of the Circle, a mostly glass structure houses the highly modern bar with TV monitors displaying financial data. Its outside terrace sweeps wide on both sides, all but encompassing the Circle, and has plenty of seating space and large parasols to shade customers from the midday heat. These tables are bookable, and when events are going on in the Circle, there is no better place from which to watch them. You might see dancing – even dancing horses – or ice skating in winter months. The food here is restricted to sandwiches and the like – they don't really have the facilities in such a confined space. The clientele is predominantly City males, but in the evenings the crowd becomes much more mixed, and groups gather on the terrace, sipping wines, champagnes and bottled beers. A perfect location.

OPEN *11.00-22.30 (Mon-Wed), 11.00-23.00 (Thurs-Fri); Cannon Street opens at 08.00, Leadenhall Place at 09.30, Exchange Square, Canary Wharf and Broadgate at 10.00.*
FOOD *11.00-22.30 (Mon-Fri); Cannon Street 08.00-22.30*
CREDIT CARDS *all major cards*

Branches at:
CANARY WHARF 9 Cabot Square, Canary Wharf, E14; 0171 512 0397
    NEAREST RAILWAY STATION *Canary Wharf (DLR)*
CITY (EC2) 19 Broadgate Circle, EC2; 0171 628 1251
    NEAREST TUBE STATION *Liverpool Street*
CITY (EC2) 2b Eastcheap, EC2; 0171 929 3220
    NEAREST TUBE STATION *Monument*
CITY (EC2) 5 Exchange Square, Broadgate, EC2; 0171 628 4367
    NEAREST TUBE STATION *Liverpool Street*
CITY (EC3) 1 Leadenhall Place, EC3; 0171 621 9201
    NEAREST TUBE STATION *Bank, Monument*
CITY (EC3) 16 Royal Exchange, EC3; 0171 929 3131
    NEAREST TUBE STATION *Bank*
CITY (EC4) 44 Cannon Street, EC4; 0171 248 1700
    NEAREST TUBE STATION *Mansion House*
CITY (EC4) 3 Fleet Place, EC4; 0171 329 3141
    NEAREST TUBE STATION *St Paul's*
CITY (EC2) 12 Mason's Avenue, Basinghall Street, EC2; 0171 726 6030
WEST END 116 St Martin's Lane, WC2; 0171 655 9800

THE CORONET

338-346 Holloway Road, N7; 0171 609 5014
There used to be a cinema in Holloway Road called the Savoy. It opened in 1940 in the middle of the blitz and there were queues every night in spite of the blackout and the constant air raids. After the war it became the ABC, then The Coronet and then, in June 1983, it closed, it seemed, for ever. Wait though, this story has a happy ending. Come 1996 and enter J. D. Wetherspoon spending £1.5 million on the old building, buying and refitting it. It is now a most remarkable pub, possibly London's

biggest. It can accommodate more than 1,000 customers at a time and night after night it does. Its show biz antecedants are plain for all to see. It is unmistakably a one-time cinema and its neon sign, CORONET, splashed across the cream tiled frontage can be seen at night all along Holloway Road from Islington to Archway.

So in you go through the glass doors, across the foyer and down the flight of steps almost the width of the building and there, instead of the stalls, is this vast bar. The circle, now full of air-conditioning gear and such, still covers half of it and then the ceiling soars over the front stalls as ceilings did when cinemas were cinemas, and on every side images of the gods and goddesses of the silver screen look down, langorous and glamorous as ever, Fred Astaire, Ginger Rogers, Humphrey Bogart, Ingrid Bergman... it was once their job to fill The Coronet. Now the attraction is the building itself and the beer it sells at such amazing prices. The Coronet shifts vast quantities of Guinness and at £1.29 a pint who could wonder? Wetherspoon's rules apply: a no-smoking area bigger than some pubs I know and no TV, pool, pinball or music of any sort. You couldn't hear it anyway when the crowds pour in.

OPEN 11.00-23.00 (Mon-Sat), midday-22.30 (Sun)
FOOD 11.00-22.00 (Mon-Sat), midday-21.30 (Sun)
CREDIT CARDS AmEx, Delta, Mastercard, Switch, Visa
DRAUGHT BEERS Caffrey's, Courage Directors, John Smith's Extra Smooth, Theakston Best, Kronenbourg, McEwan's, Guinness, Dry Blackthorn, Greene King, Abbot Ale, Budweiser
Wheelchair access to venue and loos
NEAREST TUBE STATION Holloway Road

CORTS HOLBORN

78 High Holborn, WC1; 0171 242 4292

I revisited a part of town I thought I knew well, only to find its fortunes changed much for the better by the welcome addition of this beautiful modern bar and restaurant. It's rare for me to enjoy a lunch so much that I'll dash back again the same day to sample the evening atmosphere, but I was so taken with its design, food, drink and super-efficient air-conditioning system. I went with an old crony, Derek, for lunch. I boringly chose the chicken breast (£9.50) but was pleasantly surprised with the chargrilled vegetable salad and the chef's resistance to piling up the plate with fields of unwanted grassy ingredients. Derek had the seared tuna, wok-fried vegetables and soy chilli dressing (£10.50). He wolfed down a delicious dessert of chocolate quenelles, demolished the remainder of the wine and dashed back to work leaving me to foot the bill. The restaurant doesn't open in the evenings and, should the bar fill to overflowing, they ease the crush by using the dining area. When I ordered a two-pint jug of Hoegaarden (£6.80), I was asked how many glasses I wanted. 'Just the one, thanks,' I replied. I wasn't about to be disadvantaged twice in one day, so I let my drinking partners buy their own. By the end of the evening we had put away far too many beers, several bottles of Stormy Cape Chenin Blanc (£12.50) and a decent hammering of cocktails (from £5). The arrival of Corts has brought Holborn stratospherically upmarket. We need more places like this in London, please.

OPEN 11.30-23.00 (Mon-Fri), Saturday private parties only
FOOD 11.30-19.30 (Mon-Fri)
CREDIT CARDS all major cards, not Diners
DRAUGHT BEERS Stella Artois, Hoegaarden
Wheelchair access to venue and loos. Available for private hire to accommodate 250 on ground floor. Also have basement area called Absolutions which is a function room for 40 seated, 80 standing
NEAREST TUBE STATION Holborn

THE COW

89 Westbourne Park Road, W2; 0171 221 0021

Tom Conran's Cow is an Irish-style bar but not quite in the vein of those being churned out by the big brewers with monotonous regularity. 'Guinness and Oysters' boasts one sign. That's what they do in Ireland. This is a small pub with one long, narrow room that specialises in seafood. The upstairs restaurant is receiving much acclaim. It is in the hands of Francesca Melman (she of River Café and Alastair Little fame). The staff here are very knowledgeable and helpful with the menu. Tom himself will often be found in the bar, as will a gathering of other local celebrities. The Cow is unobtrusive, gentle and a calm place to spend an evening in this developing part of Westbourne Park.

OPEN *12.00-23.00 (Mon-Sat), 12.00-22.30 (Sun)*

FOOD *bar 12.30-15.00 and 18.30-22.30 (Mon-Sat), 12.30-16.00 (Sun); restaurant 19.30-23.00 (Mon-Sun)*

CREDIT CARDS *Eurocard, Mastercard, Visa, not AmEx or Diners*

DRAUGHT BEERS *ESB, London Pride, Hoegaarden, Red Stripe, Guinness, Fuller's Seasonal Beers, Belgian and Euro beers*

NEAREST TUBE STATIONS *Royal Oak, Westbourne Park*

THE CRESCENT

99 Fulham Road, SW3; 0171 225 2244

The rather bijou ground-floor bar fills up quickly and hides a much bigger basement area. It's clinically clean, modern and nicely air-conditioned. The food seems to be improving with each visit and although not especially cheap, provides a good quality alternative to the other rather more expensive restaurants in Brompton Cross. With a wine list in excess of 200 wines and useful descriptions to help you choose, this is surely a wine lover's fantasy.

OPEN *11.00-midnight (Mon-Fri), 10.00-midnight (Sat), 11.00-22.30 (Sun)*

FOOD *as opening hours until 30 mins before closing*

CREDIT CARDS *all major cards*

NEAREST TUBE STATION *South Kensington*

THE CRICKETERS

Maids of Honour Row, The Green, Richmond, TW9; 0181 940 4372

Ronnie Wood, the Rolling Stone whose local this is, liked The Cricketers so much he tried to buy it. He and his drinking pal, snooker superstar Jimmy White, pooled their loose change, made an offer. The owners stuck to their asking price, £400,000, and Greene King snapped it up instead. This, you may well think, was not a lot for an 18th-century Grade I listed building on Richmond Green, a dream location, but then again you may not have been inside it before the sale. The Cricketers was not only down at heel but it was having unappealing problems with the local yobbery. This changed very quickly with the arrival of new Greene King managers. 'Our customers now tend to be more suited than booted' says the new licensee, Grant Adlam, with satisfaction. That was the essential Stage 1 in The Cricketers' revival. Stage 2 has been putting in a new kitchen and improving the food. Stage 3 was the complete refurb of the whole pub. It has been noticed that cricketers who play cricket on the green on summer evenings usually end up in The Cricketers.

OPEN *11.00-23.00 (Mon-Sat), midday-22.30 (Sun)*

FOOD *midday-15.30 and 17.30-20.30 (Mon-Sat)*

CREDIT CARDS *all major cards*

DRAUGHT BEERS *Abbot Ale, Greene King IPA, Wexford Irish Cream Ale, Harp, Kronenbourg, Stella Artois, Guinness, Strongbow*

NEAREST TUBE STATION *Richmond*

CROCKER'S FOLLY

24 Aberdeen Place, NW8; 0171 286 6608

Frank Crocker was the man who built this hotel at the height of the Victorian railway boom. He'd been given a tip that Marylebone Station was to be built across the road and, being an entrepreneurial spirit, decided to buy the adjacent land which he hoped would result in his fame and fortune. The tip was not worth listening to. Marylebone Station was built where it is, and the desperate Mr Crocker jumped from one of the upper windows. The Crown Hotel – as he called it – faced difficult times. Today it is owned by Regent Inns, who spent a lot of money on making it look as marvellous as it does. There are marble columns, marble walls, marble counters, massive baronial fireplaces, rich mahogany fittings, plus a magnificent saloon bar and a noble public bar with nine cask ales on the hand pumps – worth a trip just for that. The cellars are as roomy as everywhere else. There is also a pleasant restaurant room, which used to be the billiard room and has an enormous fireplace, a pike in a glass case and a bust of Emperor Caracalla. No bust yet of Mr Crocker, but they will surely put one there one day. His ambition was the death of him, but he has left one of London's most impressive public houses and they changed the name to commemorate the man. Fame at last!

OPEN *11.00-23.00 (Mon-Sat), 12.00-22.30 (Sun)*

FOOD *bar 12.00-14.30 and 18.00-21.30 (Mon-Sat), 12.00-20.00 (Sun); restaurant 12.00-14.30 and 18.00-21.30 (Mon-Sat), 12.00-20.00 (Sun)*

CREDIT CARDS *all major cards*

DRAUGHT BEERS *Adnams, Brakspear, Caffrey's, Crocker's, John Smith's Extra Smooth, Theakston XB, Foster's, Kronenbourg, Stella Artois, Guinness, Dry Blackthorn, Gale's HSB, Hancock's, guest ales*

Wheelchair access to venue. Private room: 15 seated, 25 standing

NEAREST TUBE STATION *Warwick Avenue*

THE CROOKED BILLET

14 Crooked Billet, SW19; 0181 946 4942

The Crooked Billet is in the tiny hamlet of that name hard by Wimbledon Common, and it has been slipping in and out of local records for nearly 500 years. It first appears in 1509: a brewery and inn. Then we hear of Walter Cromwell, the father of Henry VIII's Lord High Chamberlain, retiring to the inn in 1513 and dying there. His bit of land gets called Cromwell's Half-Acre. A few years pass and the old inn is being rebuilt a little way off, then rebuilt again. The builders seem hardly to have been out of the place. The latest lot emerged only on Good Friday 1994 having given the old pub a thorough going over. When they finished, the settles in the new no-smoking area were the only original fittings left and breath was held while the oldest regular inspected his new local. The best he'd seen it, he said. The refurbished bar has proved popular but in fine weather people do as they have done for centuries; they sit with their drinks on the green opposite the Crooked Billet, enjoying the sunshine at the heart of Cromwell's Half-Acre.

OPEN *11.00-23.00 (Mon-Sat), midday-22.30 (Sun)*

FOOD *midday-14.30 and 18.30-21.30 (Mon-Sat), midday-14.15 and 19.00-21.00 (Sun)*

CREDIT CARDS *Mastercard, Visa*

DRAUGHT BEERS *Young's Bitter, Young's Special, Young's Pilsner, Young's Export, Guinness, Scrumpy Jack, Ramrod Smooth, First Gold*

Wheelchair access to venue, not to loos

NEAREST TUBE STATION *Wimbledon*

CROSS KEYS

1 Lawrence Street, SW3; 0171 349 9111

Not many people would get away with transforming such a memorable old Victorian pub with its cluster of small rooms, all mahogany and worn plush, the big old bar with the elaborate back fitting and the little garden behind. But transform it they did. The new Cross Keys was designed by Tony and Rudy Weller (of Beach Blanket Babylon fame, qv). Anyone who knows Beach Blanket Babylon, still the hippest bar around, will recognise the unique style of designer Tony Weller and his brother, Rudy, the sculptor, whose heroic bronze horses rear and snort on the corner of the Haymarket and Piccadilly Circus. You won't recognise it from the old place but they are to be forgiven for meddling with the past by making such a good job of it: large tables, low chairs, comfortable seating around the fireplace, high stools at pedestal tables, York stone-paved floor, modern bar counter against the far wall and a stone-moulded Friar Tuck above the fireplace, warming the parts of himself that need warming. A good section of the ceiling has gone, making way for a high gallery with a massive wrought-iron chandelier. The galleried balcony is often used as a gallery, with art exhibitions and a variety of other events. At other times it is home to office parties and wedding receptions. They have expanded upwards in the past year and there is now the most delightful dining room which is bookable for private parties.

Downstairs a walk to the back of the bar brings you into a large glass conservatory which houses the always-busy restaurant, for which it is usually advisable to book. The menu is limited, usually including meat, pasta and fish dishes but recent experiences suggest that the previous high standards in cooking are beginning to go astray. Despite my report last year that I had received sufficient complaints about attitudinal bar staff and a seeming reluctance to pour full measures into a pint glass, little has changed and standards can relax into lethargy at weekends.

OPEN 12.00-23.00 (Mon-Sat), 12.00-22.30 (Sun)
FOOD bar 12.00-14.30 and 18.00-20.00 (Mon-Sun); restaurant 12.00-15.00 and 19.00-23.00 (Mon-Sat), 12.00-16.00 and 19.00-22.00 (Sun)
CREDIT CARDS all major cards, not Diners
DRAUGHT BEERS John Smith's Extra Smooth, Theakston Best, Foster's, Kronenbourg, Guinness, Dry Blackthorn, Caffrey's, Directors
Wheelchair access to venue
NEAREST TUBE STATION Sloane Square

THE CROWN

116 Cloudesley Road, N1; 0171 837 7107

The Crown had been sitting happily tucked away behind Liverpool Road for the past hundred years when Fuller's decided to revamp it as one of their Bohemia pubs (or bulimia, as I thought the PR girl said). These concentrate on food (which is why I thought I'd heard her correctly). The renovation did not destroy any of the original features of the pub; it has simply had a lick of paint, a good polish and a general sprucing up all round. The old kitchen was gutted to make way for the new dining room. With so many pubs offering decent food these days, The Crown is probably not going to be a destination, but I would be very happy to have it in my neighbourhood.

OPEN 12.00-23.00 (Mon-Sat), 12.00-22.30 (Sun)
FOOD 12.00-15.00 and 18.00-22.00 (Mon-Sat), 12.00-16.00 (Sun)
CREDIT CARDS all major cards
DRAUGHT BEERS London Pride, Stella Artois, Guinness, Scrumpy Jack, Extra Special XB, Carling, Staropramen, Hoegaarden, two real ales, one changed on a seasonal basis
Wheelchair access to venue
NEAREST TUBE STATION Angel

THE CROWN

49 Tranquil Vale, SE3; 0181 852 0326

What a peaceful name for a street, Tranquil Vale, though it's not as tranquil as all that with the traffic howling past the door. Happily though, you can escape all this by slipping into the rather more tranquil Crown pub. There are not many older buildings than this in Blackheath village. The Crown was built in 1740 and has been a village alehouse, a stout warehouse, a staging post for horse buses and a boozy local. Now it is a village alehouse again, doing its best to keep modern times at bay with old floorboards, stout wooden furniture, traditional English pies on the menu and plenty of English ale in the cellar. It is a handsome, old-fashioned pub.

OPEN 11.00-23.00 (Mon-Sat), 12.00-22.30 (Sun)

FOOD 11.00-21.00 (Mon-Sat), 12.00-21.00 (Sun)

CREDIT CARDS all major cards

DRAUGHT BEERS Courage Best, Theakston Best, Theakston XB, Beck's, Foster's, Guinness, John Smith's Extra Smooth, Strongbow, three guest ales

NEAREST RAILWAY STATION Blackheath

THE CROWN AND GREYHOUND

73 Dulwich Village, SE21; 0181 693 2466

This is a story of two pubs, The Crown and The Greyhound. The Greyhound was the grand one with the ballroom and the pleasure grounds. The London-Sevenoaks stage stopped there twice a day. Charles Dickens dined there with the Dulwich Club, so Dulwich was where Mr Pickwick retired. No one thought much of The Crown, the small pub on the other side of the road. In 1895 the manager of the humble Crown bought the fine Greyhound and pulled it down. Three years later The Crown was pulled down as well, and a splendid new pub built on the site, the imposing Crown and Greyhound, which has been a centre of village life ever since. It is one of the biggest and most successful pubs in south London, so busy you can hardly move in the evenings. It has four bars, one non-smoking, the others joined by the original mahogany counter, and a lot of the original furniture, including high-backed Victorian settees of unusual discomfort. There is a busy restaurant, and every Saturday a wedding reception in the suite of function rooms. Lunch specials can include penne pasta with mince and mushrooms, vegetable moussaka or steak and mushroom pie (£5.25), and there's a simpler menu of jacket potatoes, sandwiches, and gammon and chips. The evening menu covers rainbow trout, tarragon chicken and Dijon pork (from £6.75). The garden is huge and full of tables, with steps taking you up to the nicest, greenest bit, and yet more tables under a magnificent horse chestnut tree.

OPEN 11.00-23.00 (Mon-Sat), 12.00-22.30 (Sun)

FOOD 12.00-14.30 and 18.00-22.00 (Mon-Sat), 12.00-15.00 (Sun)

CREDIT CARDS all major cards

DRAUGHT BEERS Burton Ale, Calder's Cream Ale, Kilkenny, Tetley's, Young's, Carlsberg, Carlsberg Export, Castlemaine XXXX, Guinness, Dry Blackthorn, Sweet Blackthorn, Stella Artois

Wheelchair access to venue, not to loos. Two private rooms: 25-90 seated, 30-110 standing

NEAREST RAILWAY STATION North Dulwich

THE CROWN AND SHUTTLE

Shoreditch High Street, E1; 0171 247 7696

A respectable East End local noted for its entertainment. At lunchtime and in the early evening exotic dancers dance exotically round the pool table, taking off all their clothes except their shoes. City workers in suits watch without comment or expression, and applaud politely as the dance concludes. Pool players later resume their interrupted game.

OPEN 11.00-23.00 (Mon-Fri)

CREDIT CARDS *none taken*
DRAUGHT BEERS *Courage Best, Webster's, Beck's, Carlsberg, Foster's, Holsten Export, Kronenbourg, Beamish, Guinness, Strongbow*
NEAREST TUBE STATION *Liverpool Street*

THE CROWN AND TWO CHAIRMEN
31 Dean Street, W1; 0171 437 8192
This is the story. Queen Anne was having her portrait painted. The painter was James Thornhill and he had a studio opposite this pub. She arrived for sittings in a sedan chair. The chairmen would put her down in Dean Street and while she tripped into the studio they would stagger into the pub. The Queen Anne portrait in the House of Commons is by Thornhill. Perhaps that was the one. She seems to have been very stately. The chairmen would have needed a drink. Anyway the picturesque name brings in the passing trade and the pub flourishes. A few years back Allied Domecq spent a vast amount of money reorganising the interior of this pub, dramatically increasing the drinking space. They did a wise thing as it happens, as the space has quickly filled up with new customers, who come to eat and enjoy the real ales. The crowd spill out on to the pavement in the warm weather, and seem to spend most of the day there. Best buys include the wonderful doorstep sandwiches and real chips.
OPEN *11.00-23.00 (Mon-Sat), 12.00-22.30 (Sun)*
FOOD *12.00-17.00 and 18.00-22.30 (Mon-Sun)*
CREDIT CARDS *all major cards*
DRAUGHT BEERS *Calder's Cream Ale, Marston's Pedigree, Old Speckled Hen, Tetley's, Budvar, Carlsberg, Guinness, Dry Blackthorn, Carlsberg Export, Stella Artois*
Wheelchair access to venue, not to loos. Private room: 50 seated, 120 standing
NEAREST TUBE STATION *Piccadilly Circus*

CRUSTING PIPE
27 The Market, Covent Garden, WC2; 0171 836 1415
On the lower level of the covered market hall, the tables and chairs in the courtyard belong to this wine bar, part of the Davys (qv) portfolio. Inside, it is a warren of old wine vaults with stone-flagged floors covered in sawdust. You would imagine that it would be full of tourists, and it often is. The cacophony of sound made by the nearby musicians and the applauding audiences lends a festive air to this and its neighbouring bars. Londoners seem to take over on weekday evenings. The wine list is the attraction, with a decent-sized range of quality wines which are constantly changing.
OPEN *11.30-23.00 (Mon-Sat), 11.30-18.00 (Sun)*
FOOD *bar as opening hours; restaurant 12.00-15.00 and 17.30-22.00 (Mon-Sat), 12.00-16.00 (Sun)*
CREDIT CARDS *all major cards*
NEAREST TUBE STATION *Covent Garden*

CRUTCHED FRIAR
Crutched Friars, EC3; 0171 264 0041
A Crutched Friar was a member of the mendicant (a less common word for begging) order of monks, who were suppressed in 1656. If you wander along Crutched Friar Street today, you will notice that many of the buildings recognise this link, with friars of all shapes and sizes integral to the architecture. The Crutched Friar we want to talk about is the new pub close to Fenchurch Street Station, and what a popular place it is. I've been several times now and still haven't managed to see the walls for the sheer enormity of the City crowds who go there after work. There are three long linear rooms, two of them on either side of what is really only a wide corridor, and they all get packed very quickly. There is also the tiniest of

terraces – you probably have to arrive at opening time to have a chance there – and a very agreeable patio garden at the back, from where you could hear your train whistling its departure, if they still whistled, of course.

OPEN *11.00-23.00 (Mon-Fri)*

FOOD *as opening hours*

CREDIT CARDS *all major cards*

DRAUGHT BEERS *Bass, Caffrey's, London Pride, Carling Black Label, Grolsch, Staropramen, Guinness, Cidermaster*
Wheelchair access to venue and loos

NEAREST TUBE STATION *Tower Hill*

NEAREST RAILWAY STATION *Fenchurch Street*

THE CUTTY SARK TAVERN

Ballast Quay, SE10; 0181 858 3146

Walk far enough along the river bank at Greenwich and you will come across a charming quay, a row of picturesque old houses, an ancient cherry tree and The Cutty Sark Tavern. If it's fine people will be sitting on the river wall having a drink. If not they will be in the bar with its old beams and comfortable wooden furniture or in the old panelled room upstairs having red mullet perhaps or the traditional whitebait. People sometimes travel miles to be here. The Cutty Sark has a sort of fan club and you can see why. It is a true period piece. It was The Union Tavern, and was built in 1804 as a small working men's pub for seafarers and riverboat men. It is now a listed building in the hands of licensee Sydney Haines. He changed the name in 1954 to welcome the last of the great tea clippers to her new home in Greenwich.

OPEN *11.00-23.00 (Mon-Sat), 12.00-22.30 (Sun)*

FOOD *12.00-21.00 (Sun-Fri), 12.00-19.00 (Sat), 12.00-21.00 (Sun)*

CREDIT CARDS *all major cards, not AmEx*

DRAUGHT BEERS *Bass, Caffrey's, Carling Black Label, Carling Premier, Tennent's Extra, Staropramen, Guinness, Dry Blackthorn, five traditional cask ales changed on a regular basis*
Wheelchair access to ground floor only, not to loos

NEAREST RAILWAY STATION *Maze Hill*

DALY'S WINE BAR

210 Strand, WC2; 0171 583 4476

The Royal Courts of Justice, where those learned judges have to decide on the most important legal issues in the land, is an extraordinarily austere experience for anyone involved. Television pictures are broadcast from the steps of the Courts so that the nation can share in the jubilation and disappointment of both sides. We've witnessed some remarkable scenes on these steps, and no doubt, off-camera, they repair to Daly's Wine Bar across the road to open a bottle or two. We're not talking draught beer, you understand; the fridge is stocked with a variety of fine wines and champagnes – Laurent Perrier (£34.50), Perrier Jouet (£32.50), Bollinger (£39.50) and Krug Grande Cuvée (£85). In the evenings it's still a legal hang out, being so close to all the chambers. This is presumably when the briefs try to lose their briefs to another brief. Considering this is a lawyers' den, there's an alarming number of anti-crime posters scattered around the place (Watch Out There Are Thieves About). But then again, if you consider what they charge, it almost makes you wonder!

OPEN *10.00-23.00 (Mon-Fri)*

FOOD *coffee and Danish pastries 10.00-12.00 and 15.00-17.00; 12.00-14.30 (Mon-Fri), sandwiches and hot specials*

CREDIT CARDS *all major cards, not Diners*
Wheelchair access to venue, not to loos. Private room: 80 seated, 100-200 standing

NEAREST TUBE STATION *Temple*

DAVYS

Davys is a long-established shipper of wines but is probably better known today as a company operating a large chain of wine bars. The theme for the bars, if we have to specify one, is a modern version of medieval England, and they've done a cracking job recreating the feel of an Olde English inn. Many of these places look as if they're hundreds of years old. They're not, of course, but you'll often find stone-flagged floors, old wooden-panelled walls, partitions, private booths, and, nearly always, sawdust on the floor. They're not all fully licensed, but you can always get wines, and many serve bottled and draught lagers, and in some cases draught ales. (Beware the Old Wallop ale, it can hit quite hard!) The limited food includes curious plates of ham off the bone, half-chickens, fish and beef dishes. The hours vary slightly at each location, so it's worth checking before you go, but Davys in EC postcodes open Monday-Friday only and close at either 9pm or 10pm.

Branches at:

BARBICAN (EC1) 15-17 Long Lane, EC1; 0171 726 8858
    NEAREST TUBE STATION *Barbican*
BARKING SPOTTED DOG/COLONEL JASPERS 15 Longbridge Road, IG11; 0181 507 7155
    NEAREST TUBE STATION *Barking*
BAYSWATER GYNGLEBOY 27 Spring Street, W2; 0171 723 3351
    NEAREST TUBE STATION *Paddington*
CANARY WHARF 31-35 Fisherman's Wharf, E14; 0171 363 6633
    NEAREST RAILWAY STATION *Canary Wharf (DLR)*
CITY (E1) GRAPESHOTS 2-3 Artillery Passage, E1; 0171 247 8215
    NEAREST TUBE STATION *Liverpool Street*
CITY (E1) VINEYARD International House, 1 St Katharine's Way, E1; 0171 480 6680 and 0171 480 5088 (Coffee House)
    NEAREST TUBE STATION *Tower Hill*
CITY (EC1) BOTTLESCRUE Bath House, 53-60 Holborn Viaduct, EC1; 0171 248 2157
    NEAREST TUBE STATION *Chancery Lane*
CITY (EC1) CITY PIPE Foster Lane, off Cheapside, EC1; 0171 606 2110
    NEAREST TUBE STATION *St Paul's*
CITY (EC1) CITY VAULTS 2 St Martin's le Grand, EC1; 0171 606 8721
    NEAREST TUBE STATION *St Paul's*
CITY (EC1) COLONEL JASPERS 190 City Road, EC1; 0171 608 0925
    NEAREST TUBE STATION *Old Street*
CITY (EC2) BANGERS 12 Wilson Street, EC2; 0171 377 6326
    NEAREST TUBE STATION *Liverpool Street, Moorgate*
CITY (EC2) BISHOP OF NORWICH 91-93 Moorgate, EC2; 0171 920 0857 and 0171 588 2581 (Bishops Parlour)
    NEAREST TUBE STATION *Moorgate*
CITY (EC2) CITY BOOT 7 Moorfields High Walk, EC2; 0171 588 4766
    NEAREST TUBE STATION *Moorgate*
CITY (EC2) DAVYS AT RUSSIAN ROW Russia Court, Russia Row, EC2; 0171 600 2165 (Ale & Port House) and 0171 606 7252 (Wine Rooms)
    NEAREST TUBE STATION *St Paul's*
CITY (EC2) PULPIT 63 Worship Street, EC2; 0171 377 1574
    NEAREST TUBE STATION *Moorgate*
CITY (EC3) BANGERS TOO 1 St Mary at Hill, EC3; 0171 283 4443
    NEAREST TUBE STATION *Monument*
CITY (EC3) CITY FLOGGER Fenn Court, 120 Fenchurch Street, EC3; 0171 623 3251
    NEAREST TUBE STATION *Bank*
CITY (EC3) CITY FOB below London Bridge, Lower Thames Street, EC3; 0171 621 0619
    NEAREST TUBE STATION *Monument*

CITY (EC3) HABIT 65 Crutched Friars, Friary Court, EC3; 0171 481 1131
   NEAREST TUBE STATION *Tower Hill*
CITY (EC4) 10 Creed Lane, EC4; 0171 236 5317
   NEAREST TUBE STATION *St Paul's*
CITY (EC4) SHOTBERRIES 167 Queen Victoria Street, EC4; 0171 329 4759
   NEAREST TUBE STATION *Blackfriars*
CITY (SE1) COOPERAGE 48-50 Tooley Street, SE1; 0171 403 5775
   NEAREST TUBE STATION *London Bridge*
CITY (SE1) MUG HOUSE 1-3 Tooley Street, SE1; 0171 403 8343
   NEAREST TUBE STATION *London Bridge*
CITY (SE1) SKINKERS 42-46 Tooley Street, SE1; 0171 407 9189
   NEAREST TUBE STATION *London Bridge*
COVENT GARDEN CHAMPAGNE CHARLIES 17 The Arches, Villiers Street, WC2;
   0171 930 7737
   NEAREST TUBE STATION *Charing Cross*
COVENT GARDEN CRUSTING PIPE 27 The Market, Covent Garden, WC2;
   0171 836 1415
   NEAREST TUBE STATION *Covent Garden*
COVENT GARDEN TAPPIT HEN 5 William IV Street, WC2; 0171 836 9839
   NEAREST TUBE STATION *Charing Cross*
CROYDON WINE VAULTS 122 North End, Croydon; 0181 680 2419
   NEAREST RAILWAY STATION *West Croydon*
FARRINGDON BURGUNDY BEN'S 02-108 Clerkenwell Road, EC1;
   0171 251 3783
   NEAREST TUBE STATION *Farringdon*
GREENWICH DAVYS WINE VAULTS 61-65 Greenwich High Road, SE10;
   0181 858 7204
   NEAREST RAILWAY STATION *Greenwich*
GREENWICH DAVYS COLONEL JASPERS 61-65 Greenwich High Road, SE10
   0181 853 0585
   NEAREST RAILWAY STATION *Greenwich*
HOLBORN BUNG HOLE Hand Court, 57 High Holborn, WC1;
   0171 831 8365 and 0171 242 4318 (Bung Hole Cellars)
   NEAREST TUBE STATION *Holborn, Chancery Lane*
HOLBORN TRUCKLES OF PIED BULL YARD Off Bury Place, WC1;
   0171 404 5338
   NEAREST TUBE STATION *Holborn*
ST JAMES'S CROWN PASSAGE 20 King Street, St James, SW1;
   0171 839 8831
   NEAREST TUBE STATION *Green Park*
ST JAMES'S TAPSTER 3 Brewers Green, Buckingham Gate, SW1;
   0171 222 0561
   NEAREST TUBE STATION *St James's Park*
SOUTHWARK BOOT AND FLOGGER 10-20 Redcross Way, SE1;
   0171 407 1184
   NEAREST TUBE STATION *London Bridge*
WEST END CHIV 90-92 Wigmore Street, W1; 0171 224 0170
   NEAREST TUBE STATION *Bond Street*
WEST END CHOPPER LUMP 10c Hanover Square, W1; 0171 499 7569
   NEAREST TUBE STATION *Oxford Circus*
WEST END DOCK BLIDA 50-54 Blandford Street, W1; 0171 486 3590
   NEAREST TUBE STATION *Baker Street*
WEST END LEES BAG 4 Great Portland Street, W1; 0171 636 5287
   NEAREST TUBE STATION *Oxford Circus*

DEACONS

Walbrook, EC4; 0171 248 1070
Obliquely opposite St Stephen Walbrook church is this modern bar neatly
sandwiched between a car park and a Japanese restaurant. This is a good

example of how City pubs cater for the young and those crazy for bar games. Loud music, computer games, gambling machines, more loud music and five pool tables attract large crowds in the evenings. If you stand outside – and many do – you can watch the commuters galloping down Walbrook towards Cannon Street at the end of the day. Don't stray to the other side of the wall, though – they don't like it if you do that.

OPEN *upstairs 11.00-22.00 (Mon-Wed), 11.00-23.00 (Thurs-Fri); downstairs sports bar 11.00-22.00 (Mon-Wed), 11.00-23.00 (Thurs), 11.00-midnight (Fri)*

OPEN *upstairs 11.00-22.00 (Mon-Wed), 11.00-23.00 (Thurs-Fri); downstairs sports bar 11.00-22.00 (Mon-Wed), 11.00-23.00 (Thurs), 11.00-midnight (Fri)*

FOOD *11.00-21.00 (Mon-Fri)*

CREDIT CARDS *all major cards*

DRAUGHT BEERS *Caffrey's, London Ale, Carling Black Label, Grolsch, Staropramen, Guinness, Red Rock*

Wheelchair access to venue. Two private rooms: 20 seated, 200 standing; no seating, 150 standing

NEAREST TUBE STATIONS *Cannon Street, Bank*

DE HEMS

11 Macclesfield Street, W1; 0171 437 2494

De Hems claims to be London's only Dutch pub. Does anyone doubt it? It looks Dutch. See its gable. It behaves Dutch. Proost. It's Dutch all right. The De Hems used to be called The Macclesfield – you find it in Macclesfield Street on the very edge of Chinatown. A few more yards down the street and it could have been London's only Chinese pub, but a Dutch sailor called de Hems took it over in the 1920s so it's Dutch plates, Dutch photographs, Dutch old masters. 'Orangjeboom Gezondheid' declares the mirror behind the bar, a friendly greeting apparently. It is a very friendly pub this one. The noise level rises as the evening goes on and the evening goes on until midnight, courtesy of a music licence. The ceiling is a subtle shade of nicotine, though the ceiling fans do their best and in the summer the doors fold right back, opening the whole bar to the air and other delights of Macclesfield Street. They call the upstairs bar 't'Oude Trefpunt', the old meeting place, and on the first Thursday of every month many Dutchies living in London meet there. On Wednesdays it's the comedy club. Orangjeboom means orange tree, the symbol of the Orangjeboom Brewery in Breda, near Rotterdam. There's a huge Orangjeboom pump on the bar pouring out prime Dutch ale and they now do draught Witte Raaf, one of the wheat beers the Dutch and Belgians like so much. It has a high creamy head and is so cloudy you can't see the bottom of the glass.

OPEN *midday-midnight (Mon-Sat), midday-22.30 (Sun)*

FOOD *midday-23.30 (daily), Dutch and English menu*

Oranjeboom Boom Comedy Show Wed nights 20.00-closing

CREDIT CARDS *all major cards*

DRAUGHT BEERS *Calder's Cream Ale, Leffe, Pedigree, Tetley's, Dry Blackthorn, Guinness, Dutch beers, Oranjeboom, Leffe, Blonde & Bruin, Witte Raaf and Speciality Dutch Gin (Geneverf)*

Wheelchair access to venue. Private room: 100 standing

NEAREST TUBE STATIONS *Piccadilly Circus, Leicester Square*

DETROIT

35 Earlham Street, WC2; 0171 240 2662

Betty, my butcher's wife, is having her very own meat crisis. The woman who reckons she can spot a decent meaty bone at 50 paces is beside herself with worry so I took her out on the razzle to cheer her up. After a long, boozy night in Covent Garden, we ended up in this dark, low-ceilinged, cave-like, basement bar where the temperature was already starting to rise. We settled ourselves in a cosy corner with a bottle of Pinot Grigio (£12.95) and then Betty decided it was time to dance. There is no dance floor but that didn't stop her strutting and shimmying to the DJ's music with anyone who showed even a vague interest. I dragged her back to the corner as our main mission was to go through the cocktail list (£4-£6.50). I enjoyed my Bombay Sapphire Martini (crisp and dry) and Betty had several Carole Channings on the basis that they get her very pissed in a short space of time. With one eye on the menu and the other on some poor unsuspecting guy in the corner, she asked, 'Do you think if I asked that guy for an Orgasm (£4), he'd give me one?' I told her to try it. She did. His name was Lionel. He was a trainee accountant from Tufnell Park with long sideburns and an HGV licence. I was beginning to feel 103 years old so went for the last bus home. I hear the meat crisis is all but over.

OPEN 17.00-midnight (Mon-Sat), 17.00-23.00 (Sun)
FOOD 17.00-23.00 (Mon-Sat), 17.00-22.30 (Sun)
DRAUGHT BEERS Stella Artois (½ pints only)
CREDIT CARDS all major cards
Wheelchair access possible via adjoining entrance. 2 private rooms, one seats 40, 80 standing, the other seats 60, 100 standing
NEAREST TUBE STATION Covent Garden

THE DEVEREUX

Devereux Mews, 20 Devereux Court, WC2; 0171 583 4562
In between Strand and Middle Temple is this elegant public house where lawyers gather to tipple over their briefs. It has a very pleasant bar, a room with books and comfortable chairs and a rather smart restaurant upstairs serving fish and chips (£6.95), rump steak (£9.95) and a range of chicken, pasta and vegetarian dishes. The pub was built in 1844, a good year for building pubs, and is now looking smarter than ever.

OPEN 11.00-23.00 (Mon-Fri)
FOOD 11.00-23.00 (Mon-Fri)
CREDIT CARDS all major cards
DRAUGHT BEERS Courage Directors, John Smith's Extra Smooth, Theakston Best, Theakston XB, Foster's, Beck's, Kronenbourg, Guinness, Beamish, Strongbow, special ales
Wheelchair access to venue
NEAREST TUBE STATION Temple

THE DICKENS INN

St Katharine's Way, E1; 0171 488 2208
Charles Dickens loved his pubs; he wrote about them often enough. Alas, he knew nothing of this pub, The Dickens Inn. It was just a riverside warehouse in his day, but in our day it was heaved on to wheels and transported to its new home here on St Katharine's Dock, a bustling part of London which draws the tourists to its pleasant yacht-occupied waters, shopping areas and bars. The old warehouse that is now The Dickens Inn has five separate bars and restaurants and a great number of staff to keep its visitors served. Authorities all over London seem to be in permanent combat with bars to stop their customers drinking outside, but The Dickens recently won a major battle and now its customers sit happily in one of the two terrraces whenever the sun shines. Tourists love it.

OPEN pub 11.00-23.00 (Mon-Sat), 11.00-22.30 (Sun); snack bar 11.00-15.00 (Mon-Fri), 11.00-17.00 (Sat), 12.00-17.00 (Sun); pizza & pasta restaurant 12.00-22.00 (Mon-Sun); Wheelers Restaurant 12.00-15.00 & 18.30-22.00 (Mon-Sat), 12.00-15.00 & 19.00-22.00 (Sun)
FOOD as opening hours
CREDIT CARDS all major cards

DRAUGHT BEERS *Foster's, Kronenbourg, Carlsberg, Budweiser, Beck's, John Smith's Bitter, Courage Best, Courage Directors, Beamish Red, Old Speckled Hen, Theakston Old Peculier, Guinness, guest ales*
Wheelchair access. Private room seats up to 120, 150 standing
NEAREST TUBE STATION *Tower Hill*

T. E. DINGWALLS

11 Camden Lock Place, NW1; 0171 267 0545
Camden Lock has one of the biggest markets in Europe and is apparently London's fourth biggest tourist attraction. On a summer's day it can get a quarter of a million visitors, and it sometimes seems that they are all trying to get a drink in T. E. Dingwalls. Dingwalls has certainly changed. It used to be a venue, a night club, a disco, the inmost place for clubwise kids. It was famously dark and sweaty and for most of the 70s and 80s it got the best dancers in town. Rhythm and Booze they called it, and every up-and-coming band had to play there. With the end of the 80s a rolling programme of renewal began in Camden Lock and in 1991 it was Dingwalls' turn. The whole building was taken apart and put together again, and when it reopened in 1992 the old venue was three times the size and had a pub on top, T. E. Dingwalls. It is a light, high, roomy pub, with bare boards, bare brick, open rafters and stairs from the bar to a mezzanine. There are seven real ales on the hand pumps, plus Tex-Mex food and a sensational terrace with wooden decking and parades of tables and benches. It is noisy and boisterous at the best of times but when the sun comes out the new T. E. Dingwalls is a magnet, with customers packing the terrace, the bank of the canal and the pub itself. One day in May 1994, it made history. It became the first pub in Britain to get an all-day Sunday licence. It can hardly wait to get the extra hour on Fridays and Saturdays.
OPEN *11.00-23.00 (Mon-Sat), 12.00-22.30 (Sun)*
FOOD *12.00-15.00 (Mon-Fri), 12.00-16.00 (Sat-Sun)*
CREDIT CARDS *Mastercard, Visa*
DRAUGHT BEERS *Abbot Ale, Boddingtons, Brakspear, Caffrey's, Ted's Tipple, Carling Premier, Foster's, Kronenbourg, Stella Artois, Guinness, Dry Blackthorn*
Wheelchair access to venue. Private room seats 500
NEAREST TUBE STATION *Camden Town*

DIRTY DICK'S

202 Bishopsgate, EC2; 0171 283 5888
The story goes that the bride-to-be of an 18th-century merchant, Nathaniel Bentley, died on their wedding day and, rather put out, Bentley locked the room in which the wedding breakfast was set, swearing it would never be re-opened. After that he neither changed his clothes nor washed. 'If you wash today,' he would say reasonably, 'you just have to wash again tomorrow.' He became quite a celebrity. People flocked to his hardware shop in Leadenhall Street, which daily grew dirtier, and when his landlord eventually got him out, Ye Olde Port Wine House in Bishopsgate bought the entire contents, rotting wedding breakfast, dead cats and all, and displayed them in its cellar bar. Ye Olde Port Wine House became Dirty Dick's. The artefacts stayed until the mid-1980s when they simply had to get rid of them. Dirty Dick's is owned by Young's now but it remains a very successful pub. The main bar with its wooden floor, old beams and copper counter is crowded and notably cheerful; the first floor restaurant, now called Hobson's, has been enlarged and done over, and the candle-lit Dive bar seems roomier since the clean-up and frankly a great deal more congenial. There's a photograph of it as it was. You will recognise the beams, the settles and the old wooden benches. If you miss the dead cats, look in the glass case at the bottom of the stairs.
OPEN *main bar: 11.00-23.00 (Mon-Fri), 12.00-15.00 (Sun), not open Saturdays*

Hobsons Bar/Dive Bar 12.00-21.00 (Mon-Fri)
FOOD *12.00-14.30 (Mon-Fri)*
CREDIT CARDS *all major cards*
DRAUGHT BEERS *Young's Bitter, Young's Special, Guinness, Scrumpy Jack, Carling, Stella Artois*
Wheelchair access on ground floor only, not to loos. Private rooms: 90-150 seated, 40-100 standing
NEAREST TUBE STATION *Liverpool Street*

DOG AND DUCK

18 Bateman Street, W1; 0171 437 4447
Tiny bar on the corner of Bateman Street and Frith Street that was Soho's Pub of the Year in 1991 and 1992. The Dog & Duck is still going strong, and has a fine reputation for real ales. It is very friendly, principally because, as it's so small, you get to know people intimately just by squeezing past.
OPEN *11.00-23.00 (Mon-Fri), 18.00-23.00 (Sat), 19.00-22.30 (Sun)*
CREDIT CARDS *none taken*
DRAUGHT BEERS *Landlord, Tetley's, Carlsberg Export, Castlemaine XXXX, Stella Artois, two guest ales*
Deaf club Sun evenings 19.00-22.30 upstairs bar
Wheelchair access to venue, not to loos. Private room holds 35
NEAREST TUBE STATIONS *Piccadilly Circus, Tottenham Court Road*

THE DOG AND FOX

24 Wimbledon High Street, SW19; 0181 946 6565
The Dog and Fox occupies an enormous site, dominating its bit of the High Street with an impressive display of turrets, decorated gables and pillared porticoes. Young's, whose pub it is, point out that the actual pub bit isn't all that big considering. It is just that it is backed up by what seems an acre or two of terrace between pub and High Street, and also by a whole Chinese restaurant and a ballroom, not used for balls much these days but essential for conferences, weddings, annual dinner dances and the like. It comes as a shock to hear that it used to be even bigger, that it once had eight public rooms and several hundred acres of land, but you can be too big, that seems clear, and Young's must be relieved that the late Victorians rebuilt it in its present modest proportions and set it back a bit so that the High Street could be widened. It is a very youthful pub these days, totally refurbished in the modern Victorian style that Young's and its customers like so much.
OPEN *11.00-23.00 (Mon-Sat), 12.00-22.30 (Sun)*
FOOD *12.00-14.30 (all week) and 18.00-21.00 (Sun-Thurs)*
CREDIT CARDS *all major cards, not AmEx*
DRAUGHT BEERS *Young's Bitter, Young's Export, Young's Premium Lager, Young's Ramrod Smooth, Young's Special, Guinness, Scrumpy Jack, Stella Artois, Carling Black Label*
Wheelchair access to venue, not to loos. Private room seats 120
NEAREST TUBE STATION *Wimbledon*

DOG HOUSE

187 Wardour Street, W1; 0171 434 2116
The tendency to party is somewhat at odds with the atmosphere of this cramped, air-conditioned, exuberantly colourful basement bar on the upper reaches of Wardour Street. The service is rugby-club style, so don't expect a lot. The staff profess to make decent cocktails while serving up an average range of bottled beers – no draught; you're already in the basement. The Dog House is independently owned and operated by Noel Cardew, who enforces a strict policy requiring men to remove their ties. I am told that ties intimidate the regular clientele, which might include people wearing skateboarding gear and the like. I must remember my tie the next time I'm wandering through Kensington Gardens; it'll keep the skateboarders away from me.

OPEN *17.00-23.00 (Mon-Fri), 18.00-23.00 (Sat)*
CREDIT CARDS *all major cards*
NEAREST TUBE STATION *Tottenham Court Road*

THE DOG STAR
389 Coldharbour Lane, SW9; 0171 733 7515
Coldharbour Lane is recognised by friend and foe alike as the frontline in
the battleground that Brixton once was. It is a workaday terrace, mostly
small shops with flats above. It begins with the famous Ritzy cinema, and
on the first corner along is the pub formerly known as The Atlantic. It has
a much-reported history under its former name when it was the scene of
riots and known as a drug venue. Once upon a time it was notorious for
refusing to serve West Indian customers. It became one of the first London
pubs with a black manager and the Evening Standard was soon reporting
that it was the nearest thing in London to a New Orleans bar. After a little
bit more bother it closed in 1995 and it remained closed for a short time.
Then, helped by Brixton Challenge, new owners spent £250,000 on putting
it to rights. It re-opened with a big party and lots of publicity as The Dog
Star. Twelve days later Brixton rioted again, looters robbed it of all its
stock, stole the brilliant new sound system, emptied the gaming machines
and set it alight. Undeterred, The Dog Star battled on. It is now packed
with musically hip youngsters, who adore the scrum of the crowds, the loud
music from the serious sound system and the pre-clubbing atmosphere.
There are also plans for a conservatory, a covered beer garden and a
gallery and new bar in the upper levels of the pub. Some say The Dog
Star is still a bit rough, but it manages to attract a mean following. There
are some large chaps on the door and when it's full you don't get in.
OPEN *12.00-01.00 (Mon-Thurs), 12.00-03.00 (Fri-Sat), 12.00-midnight (Sun)*
FOOD *12.00-15.00 and 19.00-22.00 (Mon-Thurs), 12.00-15.00 and
18.00-22.00 (Fri-Sat), 12.00-18.00 (Sun)*
CREDIT CARDS *all major cards*
DRAUGHT BEERS *Kilkenny, Tetley's, Carlsberg Export, Carlsberg Pilsner,
Löwenbräu, Guinness, Scrumpy Jack*
Wheelchair access to venue and loos. Private room seats 200
NEAREST TUBE STATION *Brixton*

DOME
354 King's Road, SW3; 0171 352 2828
Domes first appeared on our streets in 1983 when the theme team of Roger
Myers and Karen Jones formed a joint venture with brewers Courage to
transform old pub sites into something a little more innovative, mimicking
the traditional Paris café society. So the Bird in Hand in Hampstead became
the very first Dome, to be followed by this branch in Chelsea at the junction
of the King's Road and Beaufort Street. Domes make up a part of the
Pelican Group (with Café Rouge and Oriel), which was sold to Whitbread
in 1996, but is still run autonomously with Ms Jones at the helm. They've
tinkered with the brand over the years, improving the style, image, decor,
food and drink. The Chelsea Dome is as popular as ever, and I've made
many visits in the course of the past year. The important thing is you can
just go for drinks, and in Chelsea many people do. The atmosphere is quite
relaxed during the day (this is a good place for celebrity spotting); in the
evenings the Dome goes into overdrive as the crowds pack in, filling the
tables and the small conservatory at the back. During the summer months
the wood and glass walls fold away in traditional Paris fashion, so the buzz
from inside makes it quite difficult to walk past. The prix fixe three-course
menu of £4.99 is extraordinarily good value, and the salads, snacks and
sandwiches from the main menu are also reasonably priced. The relaxed
atmosphere tends to be taken a bit too seriously by the waiting staff, who
are excruciatingly slow, so it's probably not a place to visit for a quick fix.

Branches at:
CAMDEN 18 Chalk Farm Road, NW1; 0171 428 0998
    NEAREST TUBE STATION *Camden Town*
CITY 57-59 Charterhouse Street, EC1; 0171 336 6484
    NEAREST TUBE STATION *Farringdon*
COVENT GARDEN 32 Long Acre, WC2; 0171 379 8650
    NEAREST TUBE STATION *Covent Garden*
EARLS COURT 194-196 Earls Court Road, SW5; 0171 835 2200
    NEAREST TUBE STATION Earls Court
HAMPSTEAD 58-62 Heath Street, NW3; 0171 431 0399
    NEAREST TUBE STATION *Hampstead*
ISLINGTON 341 Upper Street, N1; 0171 226 3414
    NEAREST TUBE STATION *Angel*
KENSINGTON 35a-35b Kensington Court, off Kensington High Street, W8;
0171 937 6655
    NEAREST TUBE STATION *High Street Kensington*
OXFORD STREET Selfridges, 400 Oxford Street, W1; 0171 318 3937
    NEAREST TUBE STATION *Bond Street*
RICHMOND 26 Hill Street, Richmond, TW9; 0181 332 2525
    NEAREST TUBE STATION *Richmond*
SOHO 57-59 Old Compton Street, W1; 0171 287 0770
    NEAREST TUBE STATIONS *Tottenham Court Road, Piccadilly Circus*
WEST END 8-10 Charing Cross Road, WC2; 0171 240 5556
    NEAREST TUBE STATION *Leicester Square*
WIMBLEDON 91 High Street, Wimbledon Village, SW19; 0181 947 9559
    NEAREST TUBE STATION *Wimbledon*

THE DOVE

19 Upper Mall, W6; 0181 748 5405
A roll-call of just some of the people who have visited The Dove hangs over the fireplace in the bar. It is a remarkable list, a who's who of the theatre and cinema, life and letters and I bet they all loved it, these famous faces. This is, after all, the Pigeons of *The Water Gypsies*, the perfect riverside pub. It has always attracted artists and writers. William Morris lived next door, James Thomson, in an on-rush of patriotism, wrote 'Rule Britannia' upstairs, Ernest Hemingway drank here and so did Graham Greene. This, then, is the calibre of person you must expect to find as you step inside from the narrow alleyway, but first look in the room immediately on your right. If you can squeeze in you will be in what the *Guinness Book of Records* says is the smallest bar in the UK, big enough for four medium-sized drinkers, two of them sitting on stools at the bar. The four medium-sized drinkers are there most of the time. You will have to back out again into the dark, low-ceilinged, oak-beamed saloon bar, all black panelling, cushioned wall settles and copper-topped tables and you may decide to stay there, particularly in winter when the fire is on. Up those steps, though, are rooms serving food and rooms for eating in, and past them is the Dove of summertime, a verandah shaded by an old vine, a terrace overlooking the river, another terrace reached by a spiral staircase, sunny places, shady places and families of wild geese sailing by. Brian Lovrey has the tenancy, his son Gary is the new manager and both guard the old pub's character. No music. No gaming machines. The Dove has been a Fuller's house since 1796.
OPEN *11.00-23.00 (Mon-Sat), midday-22.30 (Sun)*
FOOD *midday-14.30 and 18.30-21.45 (Mon-Sat)*
CREDIT CARDS *Visa, Mastercard, Switch*
DRAUGHT BEERS *ESB, London Pride, Grolsch, Heineken, Guinness, Murphy's, Strongbow*
NEAREST TUBE STATION *Hammersmith*

DRAYTON ARMS

153 Old Brompton Road, SW5; 0171 373 0385

For grandeur and self confidence it is hard to beat the Drayton Arms. It is high Victoriana, all buff terracotta and purple brick. The interior is almost as grand as the exterior with beautiful art nouveau lanterns and a wonderful mahogany bar with wrought iron flourishes and marble columns. There is a much less attractive back room, but you can't have everything. The first pub on the site went up in 1847 and contained the largest single household in the area, the publican, his wife, their seven children and five servants. It was demolished in 1891 and up went this one, far bigger, infinitely grander and thankfully it has survived the thousand natural shocks that pubs are heir to. It is a listed building now but it still likes to let its hair down sometimes, and at 9pm every Friday and Saturday it becomes a lively venue for folk, jazz and assorted entertainers. The Webber-Douglas Academy has a small theatre for its student productions on the first floor – capacity houses every time I'm told. It seats 33.

OPEN *11.00-23.00 (Mon-Sat), 12.00-22.30 (Sun)*

FOOD *bar 11.00-15.00 and 18.00-20.30 (Mon-Sat), 12.00-17.00 (Sun)*

CREDIT CARDS *all major cards, not AmEx*

DRAUGHT BEERS *Bass, Hancock's Welsh Bitter, Carling Black Label, Staropramen, Guinness, Dry Blackthorn*

Wheelchair access to venue

NEAREST TUBE STATIONS *Gloucester Road, South Kensington*

THE DUBLIN CASTLE

94 Parkway, NW1; 0171 485 1773

This Victorian local in Camden Town won't win many design awards but that's not what it is all about. It has long been established as an influential music venue on the pub circuit. The front bar is invariably packed, though when you reach the small music room at the back you may well find a young band playing to just a handful of friends. It is not always the case, however. This was, after all, where Madness got their first break, and there have been some very special times recently. The night Blur played here is fully documented in a framed tabloid story behind the bar. It is rap, ska, R & B and every customer a critic at The Dublin Castle nowadays.

OPEN *11.30-midnight (Mon-Sun)*

CREDIT CARDS *none taken*

DRAUGHT BEERS *John Smith's Extra Smooth, Beamish Red, Kronenbourg, Carlsberg, Foster's, Holsten, Guinness, Strongbow*

Wheelchair access to venue, not to loos

NEAREST TUBE STATION *Camden Town*

DUKE OF CAMBRIDGE

228 Battersea Bridge Road, SW11; 0171 223 5662

1997 was a rather special year for the Duke of Cambridge. It was taken over by those quality pub operators Nick Elliot and Joanna Celvely whose successes are legendary at The Chelsea Ram and The Queens on Regent's Park Road (qqv). It received a dramatic facelift. The carpet went, the bare boards were stripped and polished, the curtains were replaced by louvres, the loos moved from one side of the pub to the other and a new kitchen was installed. Then the whole place was redecorated and refurnished. Finally, Dan Brinklow, the gifted chef from The Chelsea Ram, moved into his new kitchen and started cooking some of the best food you'll find in London's pubs. The new Duke of Cambridge opened in August to the delight of the locals. Two giant parasols cover the terrace at the front, from where you walk into a splendid room with plenty of space, newly varnished woodwork, large old tables, antique mirrors and cream painted walls. It's Young's beers, of course, which is no bad thing, and they've put together a carefully selected range of 26 bottled wines with four reds and

whites by the glass. By Christmas it was named the Evening Standard Pub
of the Year for 1998. Worth any number of visits.

OPEN *11.00-23.00 (Mon-Sat), 12.00-22.30 (Sun)*
FOOD *12.00-14.30 and 19.00-21.45 (Mon-Sat), 12.00-14.45 and 19.00-
21.30 (Sun)*
CREDIT CARDS *all major cards, not AmEx*
DRAUGHT BEERS *Young's, Stella Artois, Castlemaine XXXX, Guinness,
Strongbow*
*Wheelchair access to venue. Private room: 40 seated, 60 standing (from
August 1998)*
NEAREST RAILWAY STATION *Clapham Junction*

DUKE OF CUMBERLAND
235 New King's Road, SW6; 0171 736 2777

This is a big, swanky, four-storey pub looking across New King's Road to
Parsons Green. It has balusters, arched windows and soaring chimneys,
and is superbly fitted inside. The cost of such a display of mahogany,
engraved glass and so on was well spent. The pub was The Duke's
Head until a thorough renovation in 1971 when it became The Duke of
Cumberland and won the *Evening Standard* Pub of the Year competition.
The public bar at the back has now been merged with the great saloon
bar at the front, leaving the entire interior as one huge open-plan room.
There is a substantial television in a cupboard over the front entrance, but
a sporting event has to be very important for the cupboard doors to open.
The Duke of Cumberland is a fine upstanding public house, proud of the
character and achievements of the man whose name it now bears. A large
board, prominently displayed in the saloon bar, recalls that he murdered
his valet, committed adultery, sodomy and incest, blackmailed his brother,
indecently assaulted the wife of the Lord Chamberlain and plotted the
assassination of his niece, the future Queen Victoria. A man, in short, of
broad and varied interests, most suited to the role of King of Hanover,
which is what he became.

OPEN *11.00-23.00 (Mon-Sat), 12.00-22.30 (Sun)*
FOOD *12.00-15.00 and 19.00-22.30 (Mon-Sun)*
CREDIT CARDS *all major cards not Diners, AmEx*
DRAUGHT BEERS *All Young's bitters, Guinness, Carling, Stella Artois*
Wheelchair access to venue, not to loos
NEAREST TUBE STATION *Parsons Green*

THE DUKE OF EDINBURGH
299 Green Street, E13; 0181 472 2546

When West Ham are playing at home, this is where the action is. The
Hammers Bar with its football memorabilia and pool tables pulls them in.
They fill the main bar, too, and the yard at the back. Then they all go off
to the match and come back again afterwards. They have a big screen for
the away games. The fans like that.

OPEN *11.00-23.00 (Mon-Sat), 12.00-22.30 (Sun)*
FOOD *12.00-15.00 and 18.00-20.00 (Mon-Sun)*
CREDIT CARDS *none taken*
DRAUGHT BEERS *Caffrey's, Toby, Worthington's Best, Carling Black Label, Carling
Premier, Tennent's Pilsner, Guinness, Dry Blackthorn*
Wheelchair access to venue and loos
NEAREST TUBE STATION *Upton Park*

THE DUKE'S HEAD
8 Lower Richmond Road, SW15; 0181 788 2552

If you stand on Putney Bridge and look up river the first pub on the left is
the massive Star and Garter, a landmark, five storeys high with a tower
making six. As I write, it is facing a major refurbishment. No one, not even

the owners, knows what it will be like this time next year. The Duke's Head is the next pub along and I can confidently tell you what it will be like. It will be the elegant Georgian building it has always been, scrupulously preserved, rich in carved mahogany and fine etched glass. Some of this was lost in the war. A bomb in Fulham put a lot of windows out but they all have been carefully and expensively replaced.

Up-river rowing club boat houses line the bank shoulder to shoulder and The Duke's Head has always been deeply involved in rowing. At one time a boat builder built boats on the top floor, lowering the finished ones down on the hoist which is still there. For years Putney Town Boat Club used the front part of the pub's cellars as its boat house and rowing men and women still drink there as a matter of course. It is a peaceable place but it has one spectacularly busy day. That day, of course, is the day of the Boat Race and barmen are assembled to cope as best they may with the tremendous crowd. In 1995 the pub broke all its records for beer consumption – 16,000 pints.

OPEN *11.00-23.00 (Mon-Sat), midday-22.30 (Sun)*

FOOD *midday-14.30 (Mon-Sat), midday-15.00 (Sun)*

CREDIT CARDS *all major cards*

DRAUGHT BEERS *Young's Bitter, Special, Pilsner, Export, Stella, Scrumpy, Guinness*

Wheelchair access to venue

NEAREST TUBE STATION *Putney Bridge*

DUST

27 Clerkenwell Road, EC1; 0171 490 5120

The owners took over what was an empty space to create a new drinking venue, and if they're not careful this space will remain empty. Trying to be too many things to too many people usually doesn't work. It serves Abbot Ale and the excellent range of St Peter's ales by the bottle. Has the somewhat dubious air of a student bar without the students.

OPEN *11.30-23.00 (Mon-Wed), 11.30-midnight (Thur-Sat)*

FOOD *11.30-21.30 (Mon-Sat)*

CREDIT CARDS *all major cards, not AmEx*

DRAUGHT BEERS *Stella Artois, Hoegaarden, Guinness, Strongbow, De Koninck, Abbot's, IPA*

Wheelchair access to venue and loos

NEAREST TUBE STATION *Farringdon*

THE EAGLE

159 Farringdon Road, EC1; 0171 837 1353

The Eagle is basically a robust local boozer. When Michael Belben and David Eyre took it over, they made half the bar counter an open kitchen and started cooking the kind of things people have on their hols. Fay Maschler put it in her *Evening Standard London Restaurant Guide*, Egon Ronay gave it a star and Carlton Television voted it the Best Pub Restaurant of 1997. They must be doing something right. You see and smell what is being cooked, order your food from the bar and have a drink at your table. There's no booking at The Eagle, no quiet little table anywhere. People in the know get in either early or late. There are Italian sausages sizzling on the grill, crostini, fresh tuna, grilled squid and delicious pasta dishes. Nothing takes more than ten minutes. They also do good cask beers and get through a lot of wine. In the afternoon, when The Eagle empties, you can see what a nice old pub it is.

OPEN *12.00-23.00 (Mon-Sat), 12.00-17.00 (Sun)*

FOOD *12.30-14.30 and 18.30-22.30 (Mon-Fri), 12.30-15.30 and 18.30-22.30 (Sat), 12.30-16.00 (Sun)*

CREDIT CARDS *none taken*

DRAUGHT BEERS *Boddingtons Bitter, Marston's Pedigree, Wadworth 6X, Heineken, Hoegaarden, Stella Artois, Gambrinus, Guinness*
Wheelchair access to venue, not to loos
NEAREST TUBE STATION *Farringdon*

THE EAGLE

2 Shepherdess Walk, City Road, N1; 0171 553 7681
The words of the song that still makes this pub a household name are high on the side wall, so that all who turn into Shepherdess Walk from the City Road can read them:

Up and down the City Road
In and out the Eagle
That's the way the money goes
Pop goes the weasel!

The Eagle of the song was actually the Royal Eagle Music Hall, which stood on this site. It had pleasure grounds with fountains, gas devices, illuminations, cosmoramas, magic mirrors and the famous Grecian Saloon, and became so notorious that General Booth of the Salvation Army took it over to close it down. The whole lot was demolished in 1901, and this pub went up instead. It is looking very well just now, with its confident Edwardian frontage all spruced up and the handsome eagle on the cupola brightly gilded. There is also a big saloon bar with a new horseshoe-shaped bar and pictures of music-hall stars, plus a public bar with bar billiards and TV sport, and a big beer garden at the back. You have to get there early at lunchtimes in the summer or you don't get a table. The Eagle is part of local life, of course, but there is always the Pop Goes the Weasel bonus. It brings in the most unexpected people. The Brits know all the words. We learnt this song about pawning our tailor's iron or whatever at our mother's knee. Weird, really. It doesn't even rhyme.

Half a pound of twopenny rice
Half a pound of treacle
That's the way the money goes
Pop goes the weasel!

OPEN *11.30-23.00 (Mon-Sat), 12.00-22.30 (Sun)*
FOOD *11.30-22.00*
CREDIT CARDS *all major cards, except AmEx, Diners*
DRAUGHT BEERS *Bass, Worthington Cream Flow, Carling Black Label, London Pride, Staropramen, Grolsch, Guinness, Strongbow, two regular guest ales, occasional beer festivals*
NEAREST TUBE STATION *Old Street*

EAST ONE

175-179 St John Street, EC1; 0171 566 0088
I'm going back to this place in a hurry. Not only did I get well-made cocktails by Taro, who entertained me with his conjuring abilities, it also has some brilliant deals on its Oriental food. Could do with a better vodka selection.
OPEN *midday-15.30 then 17.00-midnight (Mon-Fri), 17.00-midnight (Sat)*
FOOD *as opening times*
CREDIT CARDS *all major cards*
Wheelchair access to venue and loos
NEAREST TUBE STATION *Farringdon*

ECLIPSE

157 Balham High Road, SW17; 0181 772 0082
Eclipse is a large venue split on three levels, each with its own bar and atmosphere. For an artistic ambience, head straight for the pink-upholstered upstairs bar, where the music is also louder but not to the point where miming is necessary in order to communicate. The venue is clean and comfortable throughout, with room for around 300 people. The clientele is mostly young locals.

OPEN *11.00-23.00 (Mon-Sat), 12.00-22.30 (Sun)*
FOOD *11.00-21.00 (Mon-Fri), 11.00-18.00 (Sat-Sun)*
CREDIT CARDS *all major cards*
DRAUGHT BEERS *Bass, IPA, Foster's, Stella Artois, Guinness, Blackthorn, Kronenbourg, Caffrey's, one guest ale, five traditional ales*
Wheelchair access to venue and loos. Private room: 100 standing
NEAREST TUBE STATION *Balham*

THE EDGAR WALLACE

40 Essex Street, WC2; 0171 353 3120
In 1975 The Essex Arms, a small pub in a little street off Fleet Street, was renovated and given a new name. Whitbread decreed that to mark the 100th anniversary of the birth of the writer Edgar Wallace it would henceforth be called The Edgar Wallace. The great man's daughter, Penny Wallace, loaned the pub a collection of photographs, letters, newspaper cuttings, playbills and other memorabilia. The Edgar Wallace Society, whose members include Miss Wallace, met in the first-floor restaurant. This pleasing custom has continued every year since, and the pub has had another going over. It is now one of Whitbread's real ale pubs, a Hogshead, with home-made food and ten real ales on the handpumps. Edgar Wallace was a great journalist. He wrote more than 170 novels and plays and films, including *The Four Just Men, Sanders of the River, The Ringer*, and when he died in Hollywood in 1932 they brought his body home on the Berengaria. He was a household name. Now he's on an inn-sign, smoking a cigarette.
OPEN *11.00-23.00 (Mon-Fri)*
FOOD *12.00-15.00 (Mon-Fri)*
CREDIT CARDS *all major cards*
DRAUGHT BEERS *Boddingtons, Flowers, Heineken, Hoegaarden, Stella Artois, Murphy's, Strongbow, up to 7 cask ales which change on a regular basis*
Wheelchair access to venue. Private room: 28 seated, 50 standing
NEAREST TUBE STATION *Temple*

THE EDGE

11 Soho Square, W1; 0171 439 1313
On the north side of Soho Square you will find this four-storey former office building, three of the floors now used as one of Soho's many gay bars. Every floor has its own bar – the ground floor is geared towards coffees and the like during the day, the first floor has a bigger seating area, and the top floor has its own dance floor. The prices aren't cheap, and bottled beers were warm when I was last there.
OPEN *12.00-01.00 (Mon-Sat), 12.00-22.30 (Sun)*
CREDIT CARDS *all major cards, not AmEx*
Private room: 50 standing
NEAREST TUBE STATION *Tottenham Court Road*

EDWARD'S

40 Hammersmith Broadway, W6; 0181 748 1043
Arriving by public transport at Hammersmith these days will bring you into the all-new, 700-years-in-the-construction Broadway Centre. If you take the King Street exit, the first sight to greet you is Edward's, one of Bass's latest generation of quality bars with something going on all day. Edward's opens for breakfast at 8am, moves into morning coffees at 10am and on to a rather good-quality pub lunch at 12pm. Then there's afternoon tea and a loud bang in the evening when the disco gets going. The beautiful function room upstairs with its cream walls and lovely windows has a new role, too, and its own name. It is now Upstairs at Edward's, hosting themed evenings with jazz, comedy and blues. Edward's occupies a splendid Victorian building, and Bass have taken good care of it in the

£500,000 restoration. It used to be called The Swan, and the swan still sways gently in the breeze on the inn-sign outside.
OPEN *08.00-23.00 (Mon-Fri), 10.00-23.00 (Sat), 10.00-22.30 (Sun)*
FOOD *08.00-20.00 (Mon-Fri), 10.00-20.00 (Sat), 11.00-20.00 (Sun)*
CREDIT CARDS *all major cards*
DRAUGHT BEERS *Bass, Caffrey's, London Pride, Carling Black Label, Carling Premier, Grolsch, Staropramen, Guinness, Cidermaster*
Wheelchair access to venue. Private room 60 seated, 120 standing
NEAREST TUBE STATION *Hammersmith*

Branches at:
1 Camden High Street, NW1; 0171 387 2749
    NEAREST TUBE STATION *Camden Town*
28-30 New Broadway, W5; 0181 567 9438
    NEAREST TUBE STATION *Ealing Broadway*
170 Uxbridge Road, W12; 0181 743 3010
    NEAREST TUBE STATION *Shepherd's Bush*

ELBOW ROOM
103 Westbourne Grove, W2; 0171 221 5211
Fancy a game of pool? There's plenty of elbow room in here, with seven pool tables to play on. It's well designed, decently laid out and serves brilliant burgers from an open kitchen. You hire the pool table by the hour. It's £6 before 7pm on weekdays, then £9 per hour later on. At weekends it's £6 before 5pm, then £9. You turn up, they write your name on a board and call you when it's your turn. Waiting around is a pleasurable experience – there's a restaurant/bar area at the front and away from the tables. Draught beers are £2.30 a pint and bottles are £2.30. There's no better way to while away an afternoon or evening. Perfect!
OPEN *12.00-23.00 (Mon-Sat) 12.00-22.30 (Sun)*
FOOD *12.00-22.30 (Mon-Sat), 12.00-22.00 (Sun)*
CREDIT CARDS *all major cards, not AmEx*
DRAUGHT BEERS *Boddingtons, Heineken, Hoegaarden, Stella Artois, Guinness*
Wheelchair access to venue
NEAREST TUBE STATIONS *Bayswater, Notting Hill Gate, Royal Oak, Queensway*

ELEPHANT & CASTLE
40 Holland Street, W8; 0171 937 0316
Quiz masters like to ask where this name came from, and the common answer is that it had something to do with the Infanta of Castile, but the Brits of the day got it wrong. There is another theory that it comes from the sign of the Cutlers' Company, and this is probably the true origin. But who cares? This is a perfectly agreeable pub, which has been run by Greg and Yvonne Porter for the past six years. Since their arrival the pub has won a clutch of awards for its floral displays, including the London in Bloom award for the best public house in 1994. It will doubtless win again, as Greg continues to apply the daily TLC to his pride and joy. While he's pottering away outside, Yvonne takes control of the kitchen and serves above-average pub grub most of the day. The Elephant & Castle is usually a quiet little pub, with conversation being the music to listen to, but be warned – it is regularly used by *Evening Standard* journalists, and they can be a rather boisterous bunch of customers.
OPEN *11.00-23.00 (Mon-Sat), 12.00-22.30 (Sun)*
FOOD *11.00-21.00 (Mon-Fri), 12.00-19.30 (Sat), 12.00-18.00 (Sun)*
CREDIT CARDS *all major cards, except AmEx*
DRAUGHT BEERS *Bass, Caffrey's, London Pride, Carling Black Label, Grolsch, Staropramen, Guinness, Dry Blackthorn*
NEAREST TUBE STATION *High Street Kensington*

THE ELEPHANT AND CASTLE

Newington Causeway, SE1; 0171 357 9134

There are five Elephant & Castles in London, and this one is actually in Elephant & Castle. The original pub was an 18th-century tavern which had the sense to pick a site where five major roads met. Then it became a stop on the Northern Line and the south London terminus of the Bakerloo, and got a place on the Monopoly board – and you can't get more famous than that. The planners promised to replace the old pub when they redeveloped the area after the war, and in the early 60s the work began – a vast new traffic system, a gargantuan shopping centre and Alexander Fleming House, a huge office complex designed by the internationally famous architect, Erno Goldfinger. The new pub had not been forgotten. When the redevelopment was completed, Alexander Fleming House appeared to have pupped. A smaller version stood in the lee of the big one, and a peculiarly uninteresting public house occupied the ground floor. It was called, of course, The Elephant & Castle.

These days, Goldfinger's building stands empty, its unhappy occupant, the Department of the Environment, having fled. Is this, then, the end for Erno Goldfinger's only pub? Well, no. The Goldfinger camp seems to have carried the day. The building has been sold to developers, who are about to turn it into 420 flats. This means that the pub will survive, and more than survive. It will surely get a thorough facelift. It may even find some admirers. Meanwhile it soldiers on. The pool table is in daily use, and so too is the juke box. Something very unexpected has happened to the view from The Elephant & Castle. The children's television programme Blue Peter invited its viewers to suggest improvements to their local environment. As a result the nearby electricity substation is now floodlit, the colours changing as they wash over it. You can see it all from the pub.

OPEN *11.00-23.00 (Mon-Sat), 12.00-22.30 (Sun)*

FOOD *12.00-15.00 (Mon-Sun)*

CREDIT CARDS *none taken*

DRAUGHT BEERS *John Smith's Extra Smooth, Ruddles Best, Ruddles County, Heineken, Stella Artois, Carling, Guinness, Scrumpy Jack, Strongbow Wheelchair access to venue*

NEAREST TUBE STATION *Elephant and Castle*

THE ENGINEER

65 Gloucester Avenue, NW1; 0171 722 0950

An unexpected chapter in the life of actress, Tamsin Olivier, started in the summer of 1994. Tamsin – daughter of Lord Olivier and Joan Plowright – and the artist, Abigail Osborne, were thinking of opening a restaurant. They looked at Primrose Hill and came across the rather run-down Engineer. Tamsin and Abigail loved the building, bought the lease and set about doing it up. They didn't hang about, and in five and a half weeks it was looking splendid. The saloon bar gleamed, restaurant tables lined the old public bar and filled the one-time snug, and there was an entirely new kitchen. Tamsin postponed her wedding, and people were beating a popular path to the door. The food, distinctly classy and not cheap, is a big draw at The Engineer. If you want a table in the restaurant, it is best to book, particularly in the evening. You can eat in the bar if you like, though it does get very crowded, and in the summer there's a big garden. Tamsin and Abigail are both in the thick of it, taking orders, serving, doing their stuff. The locals love it, and hope that the only boards Miss Olivier will tread in future are those of the floor of The Engineer.

OPEN *11.00-23.00 (Mon-Sat), 12.00-22.30 (Sun)*

FOOD *bar 12.00-15.00 and 19.00-22.30 (Mon-Sat), 12.30-15.30 (Sun); restaurant 12.00-15.00 and 18.30-22.30 (Mon-Sat), 12.30-15.30 and 19.00-22.00 (Sun)*

CREDIT CARDS *Mastercard, Switch, Visa*

DRAUGHT BEERS *Caffrey's, London Pride, Grolsch, Carling, Guinness, one guest ale*
Wheelchair access to venue and loos. Two private rooms: 16 and 32 seated, and garden
NEAREST TUBE STATIONS *Chalk Farm, Camden Town*

ENNISMORE ARMS

2 Ennismore Mews, SW7; 0171 584 0440

Charles Gray, narrator of the *Rocky Horror Picture Show* and a many times upper-crust villain in films, once said 'I prefer a pint at the local to drinking champagne in a dress suit'. True to his word, he has been a regular at the Ennismore Arms for many a year, and with such a handsome local, why wouldn't he? The Ennismore is what they call a decent pub in SW7 and it's so hidden away you're unlikely to stray past. The locals seem to like it that way.

OPEN *11.00-23.00 (Mon-Sat), 12.00-22.30 (Sun)*
FOOD *12.00-22.30 (Daily)*
CREDIT CARDS *all major cards*
DRAUGHT BEERS *Courage Best, Directors, Theakston Best, Foster's, Kronenbourg, Guinness, Strongbow, John Smith's Extra Smooth*
Wheelchair access to venue
NEAREST TUBE STATION *Knightsbridge, South Kensington*

ENTERPRISE

2 Haverstock Hill, NW3; 0171 485 2659

Directly opposite Chalk Farm tube is this three-storey, multi-coloured building, home to a very individual interpretation of an Irish-influenced bar. I say Irish-influenced rather than thematic, as in the case of the poorer examples seen at Scruffy Murphy's (qv) and Finnegan's Wakes (qv). The Enterprise is really rather a pleasant place to walk into, decorated with prints of the great literati, Behan, Wilde and the like. The big, almost square bar extends into the well-furnished room, with tables big enough to seat a large crowd. One wall is completely filled with books, adding to the scholarly feel. The erudite, unpretentious clientele can get quite lively in the evenings, but this is also a good daytime pub, and there are too few of them around these parts.

OPEN *11.00-23.00 (Mon-Sat), 12.00-22.30 (Sun)*
FOOD *sandwiches available as opening hours*
CREDIT CARDS *none taken*
DRAUGHT BEERS *Caffrey's, Budweiser, Foster's, Holsten Pils, Kronenbourg, Strongbow, Young's Bitter, Hoegaarden, Guinness*
Wheelchair access to venue and loos. Private room: 60 standing
NEAREST TUBE STATION *Chalk Farm*

THE ENTERPRISE

35 Walton Street, SW3; 0171 584 3148

Once a gloomy little local, The Enterprise is a celebration of upward mobility. For many years it has been one of London's most unpublike pubs, as the people of Knightsbridge choose to use it as a restaurant. It is a pub, it has a pub licence, but with Stella Artois being the only beer – and only available in half-pints – and the seats allocated to those who are eating, it feels and behaves like a restaurant. Ever since Diana, Princess of Wales, was seen having lunch here with her chums, it has been hard to get a table. You can't book – you turn up and take your chances. The Enterprise is handsome, stylish and reasonably expensive. Half a roast duck with prunes and pears, Dover sole, and artichoke heart with a spinach gratin and warm vinaigrette are just a few of the things which you may find on the menu. The tables are a little too close together for a private conversation, and the management has a rather irritating habit of levying a £1 cover charge. 'For napery,' they tell me. I was tempted to say I would do without. If you are invited to dinner at The Enterprise you know you can leave your cheque book at home – credit cards only, please.

OPEN *12.00-15.30 and 17.30-23.00 (Mon-Sat), 12.00-22.30 (Sun)*
FOOD *12.30-14.30 (Mon-Fri), 11.30-15.00 (Sat) 12.30-15.00 (Sun) and 19.00-23.00 (Mon-Sat) 19.00-22.30 (Sun)*
CREDIT CARDS *all major cards, not AmEx or cheques*
DRAUGHT BEERS *Stella Artois (half-pints only)*
Wheelchair access to venue
NEAREST TUBE STATIONS *South Kensington, Knightsbridge*

THE FALCON

33 Bedford Road, SW4; 0171 274 2428

The Falcon is the sister of the altogether successful Halpin chain of pubs in London. The Halpins are of course Anne and Tom Halpin who also own The Sun and The Railway in Clapham and The Adelaide in Chalk Farm (qqv). They've painted this pub a very bright and cheery egg-yolk yellow, which actually looks much better than it sounds. There's a terrace of picnic tables at the front before you go into the big single-roomed bar with its rickety old furniture, pool table and student atmosphere. At the back of the building there is an enormous beer garden with its own bar, which can seat upwards of 100 people, and very often does.

OPEN *12.00-23.00 (Mon-Sat), 12.00-22.30 (Sun)*
FOOD *12.00-20.30 (Mon-Thurs), 12.00-21.00 (Fri-Sun), closes later on summer barbecue nights*
CREDIT CARDS *all major cards*
DRAUGHT BEERS *Bass, Caffrey's, London Pride, Tennent's, Grolsch, Staropramen, Tennent's Extra, Guinness, Blackthorn*
NEAREST TUBE STATION *Clapham North*

THE FALCON

2 St John's Hill, SW11; 0171 924 8041

This is a handsome Victorian pub with large windows, flower baskets and copper lanterns. 'The longest bar in the UK' boasts their poster. It is in fact the longest continuous bar in the UK – there's a subtle difference. The Falcon's bar is circular, and at 125 feet it takes up to 12 bartenders to man it effectively. If you put a pint glass next to another one and so on all the way around the bar, you would need to drink 428 pints before you got back to where you started from. How's that for a challenge?

OPEN *11.00-23.00 (Mon-Sat), 12.00-22.30 (Sun)*
FOOD *12.00-19.00 (Mon-Sat)*
CREDIT CARDS *none taken*
DRAUGHT BEERS *Bass, Caffrey's, London Pride, Sadlers, Carling Premier, Grolsch, Guinness, Cidermaster, beer festivals*
Wheelchair access to venue and loos
NEAREST TUBE STATION *Clapham South*

THE FALCON

234 Royal College Street, NW1; 0171 485 3834

The Falcon, once a local boozer, then a Bohemian joint with a fringe theatre at the back, has become the place to catch the newest, hottest and brightest of the young rock bands.

Bands being bands, the newest and hottest are certain to be the loudest, and loud means trouble from the neighbours. Never mind, soft words and sound proofing, that is the answer, and all is well again in Royal College Street. Good guitar-led indie-rock bands play six nights a week under different banners at The Falcon. In the front bar, agreeably spartan with wooden floorboards, tables and chairs, the music is turned up to deafening. Move into the back room and it gets even louder, thanks to the new sound system, recently fitted as part of a major refurb. The walls, once nihilistically

black are now orangey-red, complemented by a new lighting rig. Along with the new air conditioning this makes The Falcon a remarkably smart venue and has boosted its popularity with bands and punters. It has shot up the leaguetable of North London pub venues, putting it firmly near the top.
OPEN *14.00-23.00 (Mon-Sat), 15.00-22.30 (Sun)*
FOOD *not serving yet but due to serve food shortly*
CREDIT CARDS *none taken*
DRAUGHT BEERS *Foster's, Kronenbourg, Beck's, John Smith's, Guinness*
Wheelchair access
NEAREST TUBE STATION *Camden Town*

FAT SAM'S

498-504 Fulham Road, SW6; 0171 386 7577
This is TGI Friday's without the style, and that is making the dangerous assumption that TGI's has any style at all. Drinks are fairly cheap but you'd have to be very hungry indeed to eat here.
OPEN *midday-23.30 (Mon-Wed), midday-01.30 (Thur-Sat), midday-22.30 (Sun)*
FOOD *midday-23.30 (Mon-Wed), midday-01.00 (Thurs-Sun)*
CREDIT CARDS *all major cards, not AmEx*
DRAUGHT BEERS *bottles at present, draught due to be offered soon*
Wheelchair access to venue, not to loos
NEAREST TUBE STATION *Fulham Broadway*

THE FENCE

67-69 Cowcross Street, EC1; 0171 250 3414
Happy-go-lucky wine bar close to Farringdon Station. Outside is particularly useful in the summer. Usually full of naughty City people out to play.
OPEN *11.00-23.00 (Mon-Fri)*
FOOD *midday-15.00 then 18.00-22.00 (Mon-Fri)*
CREDIT CARDS *all major cards*
Wheelchair access to venue and loos
NEAREST TUBE STATION *Farringdon*

FERRET AND FIRKIN

114 Lots Road, SW10; 0171 352 6645
This semi-circular old pub is the semi-circular corner where Lots Road heading for the river turns left and heads for Cheyne Walk. It now has the towers of the new Chelsea Harbour against the skyline. The Ferret and FIRKIN in the Balloon up the Creek is actually its full title, making it the longest pub name in London. The ferret and the balloon appear on the pub-sign, a rather cliquey set of regulars call themselves the Balloonatics and the brewhouse in the cellar produces copious quantities of a bitter called Balloon-astic. The best bitter is Ferret Ale (3.5%), and they make Dogbolter (5.6%) and Full Mash Mild (3.4%) too. The Ferret shows how well the classic FIRKIN style wears. The brass chandeliers, the ceiling fans, the wooden floor, the church pews – they will all last, you feel, for ever. The pews are unexpectedly roomy and comfortable. They come from a firm in the Midlands called Pew Corner. The Ferret serves food, substantial portions of an average quality (which actually is a compliment), which does the job for healthy appetites (those who want to put a lining on their stomachs before hammering back the beer). There is live music, too, usually fun rather than talented, but the sporty clientele may well be amused when the Chelsea Operatic Society do their jamming sessions.
OPEN *12.00-23.00 (Mon-Sat), 12.00-22.30 (Sun)*
FOOD *hot food 12.00-19.00 (Mon-Sun); sandwiches available up to closing time*
CREDIT CARDS *all major cards, not AmEx*
DRAUGHT BEERS *Balloonastic, Dogbolter, Ferret Ale, Full Mash Mild, Carlsberg, Guinness, Western Scrumpy, Stella Artois, Murphy's, one guest ale*

Wheelchair access to venue
NEAREST TUBE STATION *Fulham Broadway*

FILTHY MCNASTY AND THE WHISKEY CAFÉ

68 Amwell Street, EC1; 0171 837 6067

Coming up with creative names for Irish theme pubs is clearly a tricky business. Filthy McNasty and the Whiskey Café is clearly poking fun at itself, and why not? This two-roomed pub is rather fun and has resisted temptations to go overboard on the Irish memorabilia front. It's a decent local and I'd be rather pleased to have one near me.

OPEN *12.00-23.00 (Mon-Sat), 12.00-22.30 (Sun)*
FOOD *12.00-15.00 (Mon-Sat) and 18.00-21.00 (Mon-Sun), 12.00-16.00 (Sun)*
CREDIT CARDS *none taken*
DRAUGHT BEERS *Tetley's, Kilkenny, Stella Artois, Löwenbräu, Carlsberg, Carlsberg Export, Guinness, Dry Blackthorn*
Wheelchair access to venue and loos
NEAREST TUBE STATION *Angel*

FINCH'S

190 Fulham Road, SW10; 0171 351 5043

The public houses of Mr Henry Hobson Finch all had proper names of their own but almost all of them were known as Finch's. This one, the Finch's in Chelsea, was really called The King's Arms. The name appears, rather small but very permanently in wrought iron, above the entrance, but it has been Finch's to anyone who ever drank there since, oh, probably 1897, which is when Mr Finch bought it.

Young's bought all the Finches in 1991 and in this case at least it has accepted the reality of the situation. This Finch's really is Finch's now. 'FINCH'S' declares the fascia and a new pub-sign has gone up. On it is a large feisty-looking finch. Old Mr Finch would surely be pleased. He would be pleased, too, to see that his handsome Victorian pub, once considered so Bohemian, has kept so much of its splendid mahogany and brass, so many of its decorated mirrors and etched glass screens. Finch's tell me proudly that this is the last traditional public house in Chelsea. It isn't, of course, but in this particular stretch of the Fulham Road, with its lively bars, nightclubs and restaurants, Finch's does provide something a little less frenetic. That's not to say that this is a haven of tranquillity far from the madding crowd. On the contrary, it has quite a bit of life of its own, and is clearly not geared to attracting just one specific age group.

OPEN *11.00-23.00 (Mon-Sat), 12.00-22.30 (Sun)*
FOOD *12.00-14.30 (Mon-Fri)*
CREDIT CARDS *all major cards, not AmEx*
DRAUGHT BEERS *Young's Bitter, Young's Premium, Young's Special, Guinness, Scrumpy Jack, Stella Artois, Carling*
Wheelchair access to venue
NEAREST TUBE STATION *South Kensington*

THE FINE LINE

236 Fulham Road, SW10; 0171 376 5827

When my mate Will had yet another birthday, we did the traditional thing and allocated the entire day for eating and drinking. In the course of our journey, we came across this Fuller's conversion from its Ale & Pie house, The Stargazey. Fuller's have been branding pubs for sometime now, but it seems someone has finally woken up to the smell, the hops burning and decided that the modern genre of bars is attracting significant earnings. This is the Fuller's version of All Bar One, and it doesn't look half bad. The furniture has obviously been arranged by someone who never sits down, providing us with evidence that Fuller's have mastered the art of minimising the number of seating places from the maximum items of furniture it is possible to cram in. I pushed an elderly lady aside and staked my claim on one of the few spaces available. I ordered champagne (£32). It came with an ice bucket and was dumped in front of me. I asked for a towel. 'If you tell me what you want it for I'll decide if you can have one'. Now I didn't expect charm or wit from this staggeringly challenged moron from the London School of Mental Abeyance and I explained, very slowly, that water drips. I was given a bright blue J cloth. It reminded me my loo needs cleaning.

OPEN *midday-23.00 (Mon-Fri), 11.00-23.00 (Sat), 11.00-22.30 (Sun)*
FOOD *midday-22.30 (Mon-Thur), midday-21.00 (Fri), 11.00-21.00 (Sat), 11.00-22.00 (Sun)*
CREDIT CARDS *Visa and Mastercard*
DRAUGHT BEERS *London Pride, Caffrey's, Stella Artois, Carling, Freedom, Guinness*
Wheelchair access to venue
NEAREST TUBE STATIONS *Earls Court, Fulham Broadway, South Kensington*

Branch at:
Northcote Road, SW11; 0171 924 7387

FINNEGAN'S WAKE
This is Scottish & Newcastle's vision of the Irish theme pub, and the poor relation of the genre. S & N seem to have stopped rolling them out now, and in fact have one less than they had last year (see Shuckburgh Arms). The style of these pubs is rather basic, the Irishness coming from old posters from the Irish Tourist Board plastered over the walls and ceilings. They have Irish music, all right, and Irish-ish food, which is served almost all day. The Finnegan in question is apparently borrowed from the James Joyce novel *Finnegans Wake*, except that James Joyce didn't bother with an apostrophe.

Branches at:
EALING The Green, W5; 0181 567 2439
  NEAREST TUBE STATION *Ealing Broadway, South Ealing*
FULHAM 48 Fulham Palace Road, W6; 0181 748 3948
  NEAREST TUBE STATION *Hammersmith*
HOLBORN 63 Lamb's Conduit Street, WC1; 0171 405 8278
  NEAREST TUBE STATION *Russell Square*
ISLINGTON 2 Essex Road, N1; 0171 226 1483
  NEAREST TUBE STATION *Angel*
KENSINGTON 34 Gloucester Road, SW7; 0171 584 0020
  NEAREST TUBE STATION *Gloucester Road*
WEST HAMPSTEAD 37 Fortune Green Road, NW6; 0171 435 0653
  NEAREST TUBE STATION *West Hampstead*
WESTMINSTER 2 Strutton Ground, SW1; 0171 222 7310
  NEAREST TUBE STATION *St James's Park*

FINO'S WINE CELLAR
123 Mount Street, W1; 0171 491 1640
We spend a large amount of our social life underground, hiding away from predators, the elements and our bosses. In this underground wine bar you can hide away from the entire world, and it wouldn't surprise me if people were mistakenly locked in and left to contend with themselves for days on end. Can you imagine that? This is an old bar dating back some 25 years or so, and owned and operated by the Fiori family, who are still highly visible in the running of the place. It has one long bar with a function room, The Boardroom, at the back. Then it has some of the cosiest caves to be found in a London bar. Wandering around one evening I lost count of the number of little hideaways. I kept disturbing young, and some not so young, couples who were trying to be hidden away before they went home, separately, to their loved ones. What are they all doing so

deep underground – potholing? But back to the bar. It's efficiently run by a team of men, some wearing jackets and dickie bows, some wearing cellar aprons. They make fresh crisps on the premises which are given away free, as well as wonderful juicy beefburgers.

OPEN *11.00-23.00 (Mon-Fri), 17.30-23.00 (Sat)*
FOOD *12.00-15.00 and 18.00-23.00 (Mon-Sat)*
CREDIT CARDS *all major cards*
Private room seats 30
NEAREST TUBE STATION *Green Park*

Branch also at:
W1 North Row; 0171 491 7261

FIRKIN PUBS

David Bruce and his wife started the FIRKIN chain with an old Southwark pub, the one-time Duke of York, in 1979. Bruce opened the renamed Goose & FIRKIN after raising a loan against his home, and what he did here set the pattern for all the FIRKINs to come – plain wooden furniture, bare floorboards, one bar, a little stage with a piano, home-made food and, above all, a brewhouse in the cellar. This bold revival of an ancient tradition is still the heart of the FIRKIN philosophy, although it is not always economical or practical for all the pubs to have their own brewhouses. In the early Eighties FIRKINs were a novel addition to the London drinking circuit, combining facilities for young drinkers with a decent range of real ales and modern lagers. The people at Camra were quite pleased, as were the millions of customers who used them. By 1988 there were 187 pubs nationwide in the FIRKIN portfolio, which David Bruce then sold for £6.6 million, intending to retire on his £2 million profit. He later tried to get them back again, but failed, and in 1991 the FIRKINs arrived in the hands of Allied Domecq, who now operate this idiosyncratic chain. New ones – being added all the time – are staying true to the old philosophy, while the older ones are demonstrating how well they stand the test of time.

To date there are 46 FIRKINs in and around London. They all love their pub games – some have so many they wouldn't be out of place on a pleasure beach. I'm told FIRKINs attract all ages, but generally you'll find a relatively young clientele. They can get quite loud at times with their bands, discos and school common-room mentality. While the pubs clearly stand the test of time, the FIRKIN joke wears a little thin after a while – the FIRKIN food, the FIRKIN loos and the FIRKIN beers. As the beers are brewed in house, FIRKINs are always ready to rename a beer to recognise an event or occasion. In the summer of 1997 they introduced an Ice Cream Beer, flavoured with vanilla pods, to recognise National Ice Cream Week. Food is served all day, with a selection of burgers, pizzas, sandwiches and main meals of beef and Dogbolter Ale pie (£4.50), chilli (£3.95) and lasagne (£3.95). A FIRKIN, by the way, is a small wooden barrel with a capacity of nine gallons.

Branches at:
BATTERSEA FARADAY & FIRKIN 66a Battersea Rise, SW11; 0171 801 9473
     NEAREST TUBE STATION *Clapham South*
BAYSWATER FETTLER & FIRKIN 15 Chilworth Street, W2; 0171 723 5918
     NEAREST TUBE STATION *Paddington*
BLACKHEATH FAIRWAY & FIRKIN 16 Blackheath Village, SE3; 0181 318 6637
     NEAREST RAILWAY STATION *Blackheath*
BOW FLAUTIST & FIRKIN 588 Mile End Road, E3; 0181 981 0620
     NEAREST TUBE STATION *Mile End*
BROMLEY PHILATELIST & FIRKIN 27-28 East Street, BR1; 0181 464 2361
     NEAREST RAILWAY STATION *Bromley*
CAMDEN FUSILIER & FIRKIN 7-8 Chalk Farm Road, NW1; 0171 485 7858
     NEAREST TUBE STATION *Camden Town*

CHELSEA FERRET & FIRKIN 114 Lots Road, SW10; 0171 352 6645
NEAREST TUBE STATION *Fulham Broadway*

CITY PHEASANT & FIRKIN 166 Goswell Road, EC1; 0171 253 7429
NEAREST TUBE STATIONS *Barbican, Angel*

CLAPHAM FRIESIAN & FIRKIN 87 Rectory Grove, SW4; 0171 622 4666
NEAREST TUBE STATION *Clapham Common*

CLAPHAM FRINGELLA & FIRKIN 762-764 High Road, SW4; 0181 289 6473
NEAREST TUBE STATION *Clapham Common*

COVENT GARDEN FAUN & FIRKIN 18 Bear Street, WC2; 0171 839 3252
NEAREST TUBE STATION *Leicester Square*

COVENT GARDEN FLYMAN & FIRKIN 166-170 Shaftesbury Avenue, WC2;
0171 240 7109
NEAREST TUBE STATION *Leicester Square*

COVENT GARDEN FULMAR & FIRKIN 51 Parker Street, WC2; 0171 405 0590
NEAREST TUBE STATION *Holborn*

CROYDON FIDDLER & FIRKIN 14 South End, CR0; 0181 680 9728
NEAREST TUBE STATION *East Croydon*

EALING PHOTOGRAPHER & FIRKIN 23-25 High Street, W5; 0181 567 1140
NEAREST TUBE STATION *Ealing Broadway*

EPPING FOREST & FIRKIN High Street, CM16; 0181 680 9728
NEAREST TUBE STATION *Epping*

EUSTON FRIAR & FIRKIN 120 Euston Road, NW1; 0171 387 2419
NEAREST TUBE STATIONS *Euston, King's Cross*

EWELL FRIEND & FIRKIN High Street, KT17; 0181 393 1294
NEAREST RAILWAY STATIONS *Ewell East, Ewell West*

FULHAM PHARAOH & FIRKIN 90 Fulham High Street, SW6; 0171 731 0732
NEAREST TUBE STATION *Putney Bridge*

GREAT PORTLAND STREET FITZ & FIRKIN 240 Great Portland Street, W1;
0171 388 0588
NEAREST TUBE STATION *Great Portland Street*

GREENWICH FUNNEL & FIRKIN Greenwich High Road, SE10;
0181 305 2088
NEAREST RAILWAY STATION *Greenwich*

HARROW FORNAX & FIRKIN Northolt Road, HA2; 0181 422 0505
NEAREST TUBE STATION *South Harrow*

HOLLOWAY FLOUNDER & FIRKIN 54 Holloway Road, N7; 0171 609 9574
NEAREST TUBE STATION *Highbury & Islington*

HOMERTON FALCON & FIRKIN 360 Victoria Park Road, E9; 0181 985 0693
NEAREST RAILWAY STATION *Homerton*

ISLINGTON FINNOCK & FIRKIN 100 Upper Street, N1; 0171 226 3467
NEAREST TUBE STATION *Angel*

KEW FLOWER & FIRKIN Kew Gardens Station, TW9; 0181 332 1162
NEAREST TUBE STATION *Kew Gardens*

KINGSTON-UPON-THAMES FINANCIER & FIRKIN 43 Market Place, KT1;
0181 974 8223
NEAREST RAILWAY STATION *Kingston-upon-Thames*

LEWISHAM FOX & FIRKIN 316 Lewisham High Street, SE13; 0181 690 8925
NEAREST RAILWAY STATION *Ladywell*

MARYLEBONE FARRIER & FIRKIN 74-76 York Street, W1; 0171 262 1513
NEAREST TUBE STATION *Marylebone*

NOTTING HILL FROG & FIRKIN 96 Ladbroke Grove, W11; 0171 229 5663
NEAREST TUBE STATION *Ladbroke Grove*

PECKHAM PHOENIX & FIRKIN Windsor Walk, SE15; 0171 701 8282
NEAREST RAILWAY STATION *Denmark Hill*

PINNER FROTHFINDERS & FIRKIN Marsh Road, HA5; 0181 866 0766
NEAREST RAILWAY STATION *Pinner*

RICHMOND FLICKER & FIRKIN Duke's Yard, 1 Duke's Street, TW9;
0181 332 7807
NEAREST TUBE STATION *Richmond*

SHEPHERD'S BUSH FRINGE & FIRKIN 2 Goldhawk Road, W12;
0181 749 9861
NEAREST TUBE STATION *Goldhawk Road*
SOUTHWARK GOOSE & FIRKIN 47-48 Borough Road, SE1; 0171 403 3590
NEAREST TUBE STATIONS *Elephant & Castle, Borough*
SYDENHAM FEWTERER & FIRKIN 313 Kirkdale, SE26; 0181 778 8521
NEAREST RAILWAY STATION *Sydenham*
TOOTING FAITH & FIRKIN 1 Bellevue Road, SW17; 0181 672 8717
NEAREST TUBE STATION *Tooting Bec*
TOOTING FREEDOM & FIRKIN 96 Tooting High Street, SW17;
0181 672 5794
NEAREST TUBE STATION *Tooting Broadway*
WEST END FLINTLOCK & FIRKIN 108a Tottenham Court Road, W1;
0171 387 6199
NEAREST TUBE STATION *Warren Street*
WEST KENSINGTON FRIGATE & FIRKIN Blythe Road, W14; 0171 602 1412
NEAREST TUBE STATION *Olympia*
WEST SOHO FANFARE & FIRKIN 38 Great Marlborough Street, W1;
0171 437 5559
NEAREST TUBE STATION *Oxford Circus*

THE FITZROY TAVERN
16 Charlotte Street, W1; 0171 580 3714
This famous bohemian pub seems to have settled down to a respectable middle age now, looking nostalgically back at scandalous days gone by. Those were the days – the 1930s when free spirits gathered round Augustus John and Nina Hamnet in the boozy, high-spirited saloon bar; the war years when the Fitzroy Tavern adopted *HMS Fitzroy* and wore a banner saying 'We're Here for the Duration We Hope'; the 50s with an all-star cast, as the photographs on every wall show: George Orwell, Dylan and Caitlan Thomas, Tommy Cooper, Michael Bentine, a very pretty Barbara Castle, a very young Richard Attenborough ...

The regulars today are every bit as sparky of course – who can doubt it? Their time will come to be photographed, glass in hand and hung on the wall. Meanwhile the Fitzroy has been greatly spruced up by the new owner, Sam Smith, with a smart new carpet and modern wallpaper, swagged curtains, new comfortably upholstered seats. What would Augustus John have made of the piped music and the gaming machines? Well, he could always have gone downstairs to the panelled Writers and Artists Bar. No music or machines in there. This is where writers' groups and historical societies meet. I think he would have been back in the saloon bar quite soon though. It is still where the action is.
OPEN *11.00-23.00 (Mon-Sat), 12.00-22.30 (Sun)*
FOOD *12.00-14.00 & 18.00-22.00 (Mon-Thur), 12.00-14.00 (Fri); bar snacks 12.00-14.00 & 18.00-22.00 (Sat); roast 12.00-15.00 then bar snacks 18.00-22.00 (Sun)*
CREDIT CARDS *all major cards, not AmEx and Diner*
DRAUGHT BEERS *Samuel Smith's*
Wheelchair access. Private room seats 20, 40 standing
NEAREST TUBE STATION *Goodge Street*

THE FLASK
77 Highgate West Hill, N6; 0181 340 7260
The Flask in Highgate is one of London's best-loved pubs. People like it for its age, for its character, for where it is. This is a lovely bit of London, with an old church, trees and comely houses. The Flask was built in 1663, rebuilt in 1767, done over in 1910 and again six years ago in a thorough renovation that closed the old pub for three months. People who had feared the worst were relieved by what they found when it reopened. It

wandered along as always, up steps here, down steps there, ceilings still low, oak panelling and floorboards as they were. There are several rather quaint customs maintained by The Flask, for instance, the annual Swearing on the Horns. This is one of those Merrie Olde England things and involves a set of antlers and strange oaths. You then get the freedom of Highgate and a chance to kiss the prettiest girl in the room.

There is food all day at The Flask. They serve up to 1,500 meals a week, and in high summer half of Highgate seems to want to eat there. The forecourt has beautiful white wisteria and lots of picnic tables, which fill with people at the first glimpse of the sun. These tables are still occupied in the depths of winter, actually. The British, a hardy island race, sit snugly in their overcoats, warmed by ingenious outdoor heaters.

OPEN *11.00-23.00 (Mon-Sat), 12.00-22.30 (Sun)*
FOOD *12.00-14.30 (Mon-Sun), 18.00-21.15 (Mon-Sat), 16.00-21.15 (Sun)*
CREDIT CARDS *all major cards*
DRAUGHT BEERS *Adnams, Burton, Calder's Cream Ale, Murphy's, Tetley's, Young's Special, Carlsberg, Castlemaine XXXX, Stella Artois, Guinness, Dry Blackthorn, plus guest ale*
Private room: 16 seated, 25 standing
NEAREST TUBE STATIONS *Archway, Highgate*

THE FLASK

14 Flask Walk, NW3; 0171 435 4580

The current passion for bottled water is not new. It was a hot item in the 18th century too, much to the advantage of Hampstead, where medicinal springs were found that cured idleness, dissipation and frivolity. These rather glum waters were bottled in The Thatched House and sold to the public for 3d a flask. The Thatched House became the Lower Flask to distinguish itself from the Upper Flask, which was much grander, and both got a place in Eng. Lit. In his novel *Clarissa* Samuel Richardson let his heroine take tea in the Upper Flask. He described the Lower Flask, though, as a place where second-rate characters were to be found in swinish conditions. Never mind, the Lower Flask did well with its flasks of water, delivered by cart to pubs and coffee houses all over London, and in 1874 the old thatched building was replaced by the tiled and distinctly unswinish one we see today. It has been The Flask ever since. Nothing is now heard of Hampstead's spring, and idleness, dissipation and frivolity flourish. The Flask, made of Hampstead's nice yellow brick with big gas lanterns to guide you to the door, has always been a popular local. It has kept its separate public and saloon bars, and they are divided by a fine listed Victorian screen. A big conservatory was recently added at the back and is used for food, music hall nights, live jazz and whatever else comes to mind.

OPEN *11.00-23.00 (Mon-Sat), 12.00-22.30 (Sun)*
FOOD *12.00-15.00 (Mon), 12.00-15.00 and 18.00-21.00 (Tues-Fri), 12.00-16.00 and 18.00-21.00 (Sat), 12.00-16.00 (Sun)*
CREDIT CARDS *Mastercard, Visa, Switch*
DRAUGHT BEERS *Young's Bitter, Young's Special, Oatmeal Stout, Scrumpy Jack, Young's Pilsner, Young's Export, Carling Black Label, Stella Artois*
Wheelchair access to venue and loo. Private room: 25 seated, 50 standing
NEAREST TUBE STATION *Hampstead*

THE FOUNDERS ARMS

52 Hopton Street, Bankside (off Southwark Street), SE1; 0171 928 1899

This fine modern pub stands boldly on the riverbank on the south side of Blackfriars Bridge. It is hard to find the first time but is worth the effort. The Dean of St Paul's managed all right. He formally opened it in 1979. When you get there you have Young's beer, a glass-walled bar, a pleasant restaurant and a big riverside terrace, wonderful on a sunny day. Both bar and terrace give you a fine view of the river and one of the great views of St Paul's.

OPEN *11.00-23.00 (Mon-Sat), 12.00-22.30 (Sun)*

FOOD *12.00-21.00 (Mon-Sun);*
CREDIT CARDS *AmEx, Mastercard, Visa, Switch*
DRAUGHT BEERS *All Young's, Stella Artois, Carling Black Label, Guinness, Strongbow*
Wheelchair access to venue
NEAREST TUBE STATION *Blackfriars*

THE FOX AND ANCHOR

115 Charterhouse Street, EC1; 0171 253 4838
The days of the bummarees are long gone. Bummarees? Who they? They were the blood-spattered merchants of Smithfield Market who would often pop in for a pint at the end of their night shift. Things are a lot cleaner now. Don't tell Tony Blair but they've managed to retain their special license which means they open at 7am for breakfast. And what a breakfast! I reckon it's among the best I have had anywhere in the world.
OPEN *07.00-23.00 (Mon-Fri)*
FOOD *07.00-15.00 (breakfast/lunch menu) 17.00-23.0 evening menu) (Mon-Fri)*
CREDIT CARDS *all major cards*
DRAUGHT BEERS *Calder's Cream Ale, Tetley's, Carlsberg Export, Castlemaine XXXX, Guinness, Dry Blackthorn, Adnams, Pedigree, Stella Artois, two guest ales*
Private room seats 25
NEAREST TUBE STATIONS *Farringdon, Barbican*

THE FOX AND GRAPES

Camp Road, SW19; 0181 946 5599
Camp Road potters along on the west side of Wimbledon Common, where the golf courses are, and an attractive low black and white pub overflows on to the narrow pavement. This is The Fox and Grapes, which has been there, part of it anyway, since 1787. It has a cosy, comfortable bar with a low wooden ceiling supported by huge oak pillars. They call it Caesar's Bar after a certain J. Caesar who built the Roman fort up the road. The stables now form the lounge bar, a large, high room with a gas log fire, wood panelling and a beamed and raftered roof. The Fox and Grapes serves home-cooked food all day. Special occasions like Burns Night and St Patrick's Day are huge thrashes, when all the tables and chairs are cleared out of the lounge. The Fox and Grapes is popular with most ages, shapes and sizes. Plastic glasses are provided for younger drinkers heading for the Common; golfers stock up here after their morning rounds; and dog-walkers particularly like to pop in. Dogs, unusually, are welcome. Children too.
OPEN *11.00-23.00 (Mon-Sat), 12.00-22.30 (Sun)*
FOOD *12.00-21.300 (Mon-Sun)*
CREDIT CARDS *AmEx, Mastercard, Visa*
DRAUGHT BEERS *Courage Best, Courage Directors, John Smith's Extra Smooth, Foster's, Holsten Export, Kronenbourg, Guinness, Scrumpy Jack, Strongbow, Old Speckled Hen, one guest ale*
Wheelchair access to venue, not to loos. Private room: 30 seated, 50 standing
NEAREST TUBE STATION *Wimbledon*

FOX AND HOUNDS

29 Passmore Street, SW1; 0171 730 6367
When the Hound stops chasing the Fox in a hunting pack, as may well happen, this pub's name will become all the more important a piece of social history. We will be able to take our grandchildren in and show them the prints on the wall, depicting country life until circa 1998. The Fox and Hounds is only licensed to sell beer or wine, so it's a no-go for gin or any other spirits, come to that. There used to be lots of pubs like this – known

as beer houses, a Victorian notion. Beer, thought the licensing authorities of the time, was safer than gin for the working man. The Fox and Hounds may be the only such establishment left, and Diane Harvey, the licensee, doesn't mind at all.

The Fox and Hounds started out in the 1860s. The street door opened on to a small room with a wooden floor, settles round the walls and a couple of tables. The landlady would hand you your beer through a flap in her living-room door. Things hardly changed for a hundred years. One room for the pub, three for the licensees and their children. Family and customers shared one outside loo. The outside lav stayed, right up to 1980, by which time the whole character of the district had changed. What had been terraces of working men's cottages had become fashionable and expensive. In Passmore Street today the modish new shop on the corner is Lord Linley's, and if one of the small houses comes up for sale nowadays, the asking price is around £500,000. The pub has changed too, of course, but thankfully it has not been spoiled. It is actually quite nice to have inside loos, a bar counter and more room. The Fox and Hounds remains a period piece, with Mrs Harvey still running the show in the old way. She has been at the pub for 29 years, has survived successive attempts to pull it down, and endured building work that closed the pub altogether for five months. People love this very agreeable old pub, and long may it stay that way.

OPEN *11.00-23.00 (Mon-Sat), 12.00-22.30 (Sun)*
FOOD *all day*
CREDIT CARDS *none taken*
DRAUGHT BEERS *All Young's, Carling Export, Dry Blackthorn, Carling Black Label, Guinness*
Wheelchair access to venue
NEAREST TUBE STATION *Sloane Square*

THE FOX AND HOUNDS
41 High Street, Carshalton, SM5; 0181 715 1612
The Fox and Hounds has had a somewhat troubled past, but let's not dwell on that. Plans were made to relaunch the pub as a music venue, and relaunch it they did. It opened to a chorus of trumpets and trombones, with live jazz playing most nights of the week, attracting a different clientele and ridding the pub of its image as a rough old pool emporium. It was by this time a better-than-average local pub. There's not so much music now, but you'll still find jazz on Wednesdays and pop, rock or blues on Sundays. They have pop quizzes every other Thursday, and do a roaring trade when these are on. They're ale drinkers rather than lager swillers down here in Carshalton, and at under £2 a pint, who wouldn't be?

OPEN *12.00-23.00 (Mon-Sat), 12.00-16.00 and 19.00-22.30 (Sun)*
FOOD *12.00-14.30 and 18.00-20.30 (Mon-Fri), 12.00-14.30 (Sat-Sun)*
CREDIT CARDS *all major cards, not AmEx*
DRAUGHT BEERS *Benskins, Tetley's, Carlsberg, Carlsberg Export, Castlemaine XXXX, Guinness, Calder's, Dry Blackthorn, Stella Artois, six guest ales*
Wheelchair access to venue, not to loos. Private room seats 30
NEAREST RAILWAY STATION *Carshalton*

THE FOX AND PHEASANT
1 Billing Road, SW10; 0171 352 2943
Situated in a smart enclave off the Fulham Road known to estate agents as The Billings, this pub is worth seeking out. It is a little country pub created 200 years ago by knocking two small houses into one, and it cheers you up just to look at it. It is extraordinarily pretty now, with its hanging baskets and antique lanterns. Inside it is quite unmodernised and has exposed beams, leaded windows, basic hardwood tables and chairs, and a big log fireplace. The two rooms are separated by a central bar, and both have lots of sporting prints. There is an excellent walled beer garden at the

back, very popular in the summer. They have taken to doing basket meals at lunch and in the evenings for £2-£3.

A minor drawback, you may think, is the nearness of the Fox and Pheasant to Chelsea football ground. You can hear them score. Opening hours go a little peculiar when Chelsea play at home, as they try not to be the first port of call for the departing fans.

OPEN *12.00-22.30 (Mon-Sun)*

FOOD *12.00-15.00 and 19.00-21.30 (Mon-Sat), 12.00-15.00 and 19.00-22.30 (Sun)*

CREDIT CARDS all major cards

DRAUGHT BEERS *Abbot Ale, Greene King IPA, Budweiser, Carling Black Label, Harp, Kronenbourg, Stella Artois, Guinness, Strongbow, Greene King seasonal ales, one guest ale, one guest bitter*

NEAREST TUBE STATION *Fulham Broadway*

FREEDOM

60-66 Wardour Street, W1; 0171 734 0071

Although this bar is mostly gay, you really don't need to be to drink here. In fact, on my first trip, if it hadn't been for the fact that I saw a couple of men necking and a couple of women looking longingly into each other's eyes, I would hardly have known. Freedom has a plain glass frontage and minimalist decor with a few patches of colour in the banquettes, tables and chairs. Lots of people come to eat the pasta dishes, sandwiches and salads (main courses around £5, two courses £8.50), and there is an extensive cocktail list starting at £5. Bottled lagers are too expensive at £2.80 and £2.90, and the house wine is £12. The place has changed its image over the years, and may well be changing again in the near future.

OPEN *11.00-03.00 (Mon-Sat), 12.00-midnight (Sun)*

FOOD *as opening hours*

CREDIT CARDS all major cards, not AmEx and Diners

Private room seats 120

NEAREST TUBE STATION *Piccadilly Circus*

THE FREEMASONS ARMS

32 Downshire Hill, NW3; 0171 435 4498

What's with these Freemasons Arms? Do Freemasons meet in them, exchanging coded handshakes and doing good works? Some do, I dare say, but the lodges have other meeting places now, leaving London's four surviving Freemasons Arms to their own devices. This is a big, modern pub near Hampstead Heath, built in 1932 to replace an earlier Freemasons Arms that was having trouble standing up. It has a splendidly prosperous and expansive air, with ample bars and spacious sitting and dining rooms. There can be few bigger pubs in north London. The Freemasons has just undergone a bit of a refurbishment and is now becoming more food focused. The garden is vast, full of roses and picnic tables. It also has a sunken courtyard with a fountain and more tables, and a flagged terrace overlooking the fountain. Downstairs in the basement is a true rarity – a skittle alley in fine fettle with a 21-foot pitch and big hornbeam skittles set in a diamond formation. Every Tuesday and Saturday skittlers try to knock them over with massive *lignum vitae* cheeses. This game, London skittles, was once played in pubs all over the south of England. It is an endangered species now. How nice to find it alive and well in the Freemasons Arms.

OPEN *11.00-23.00 (Mon-Sat), 12.00-22.30 (Sun)*

FOOD *bar 12.00-22.00 (Mon-Sun); restaurant 12.00-22.00 (Mon-Sun)*

CREDIT CARDS Mastercard, Switch, Visa

DRAUGHT BEERS *Bass, Caffrey's Cream Ale, London Pride, Carling Black Label, Staropramen, Guinness, Cidermaster*

Wheelchair access to venue and loo

NEAREST TUBE STATION *Hampstead*

THE FRENCH HOUSE

49 Dean Street, W1; 0171 437 2799

Still a favourite watering hole of the chattering classes. It is officially the French House now. It used to be officially The York Minister but no one ever called it that. The French pub is what it is. Its Frenchness began with the splendidly moustachioed Victor Berlemont who bought the pub just before the First World War and through the 20s and 30s filled it with singers and actors and boxers. Maurice Chevalier came. So did Georges Carpentier. Then the war and the Free French took it over and General de Gaulle was writing his historic declaration of defiance to the Nazis in the room above the bar. The war over, Victor's son, Gaston, took charge. He had the stylish moustaches and strong personality of his father, and life at the French pub got more bohemian than ever. Brendan Behan sang and danced in the bar, Francis Bacon, Lucien Freud, Dan Farson et al got agreeably tanked up and Gaston opened yet another crate of champagne. The walls are filled with pictures of famous people who have frequented The French over the years, including Dylan Thomas, who once left the only manuscript of *Under Milk Wood* there. Gaston retired on Bastille Day, 1989, and happily new owners were at hand who had been drinking in the French pub for years, Noel Botham and Lesley Lewis.

There's some serious drinking goes on in The French. This small, single-roomed pub is enduringly popular, and people still spill out into the streets to escape the smoke-filled room, the actress who never quite made it, or the television stars of yesteryear proffering their autographs to anyone who will have them. It is, perhaps, one of the friendliest pubs in London, and going alone is recommended: it'll take seconds before someone draws you into a conversation. The French is quite good for celebrity spotting, but booze is a great leveller of egos, and most of the names here will have left their star status behind them at the Groucho Club – the natural pre-French House drinking venue. It sells Gauloise, Gitanes and an awful lot of Ricard. Its restaurant is much acclaimed and has a rather adventurous menu. After The French? You'll probably go off with your new-found friends to Blacks, further up the street, or to Jerry's, which is almost next door. Vive la French pub!

OPEN *12.00-23.00 (Mon-Sat), 12.00-22.30 (Sun)*
FOOD *bar 12.30-15.00 and 18.30-22.00 (Mon-Sat); restaurant 12.30-15.00 and 18.30-23.00 (Mon-Sat)*
CREDIT CARDS *all major cards*
DRAUGHT BEERS *John Smith's Extra Smooth, Kronenbourg, Guinness (half pints only)*
Private room seats 30
NEAREST TUBE STATION *Leicester Square, Piccadilly Circus*

FREUD

198 Shaftesbury Avenue, WC2; 0171 240 9933

This small, somewhat sinister basement bar tries to be relaxed but the jazz music dictates the pace. It's the sort of place where Brylcreemed girls and boys stop by for coffee and cake and spend hours reading newspapers.

OPEN *11.00-23.00 (Mon-Sat), 12.00-22.30 (Sun)*
FOOD *11.00-16.30 (Mon-Sat), 12.00-16.30 (Sun)*
CREDIT CARDS *none taken*
NEAREST TUBE STATIONS *Tottenham Court Road, Covent Garden*

THE FRIDGE BAR

1 Town Hall Parade, Brixton Hill, SW2; 0171 326 5100

Next door to the world-famous nightclub of the same name (to which you can gain entry for a small charge), this small, mostly gay bar has free admission – but get there early.

OPEN *10.00-02.00 (Mon-Thurs), 10.00-04.00 (Fri-Sat), 13.00-12.30 (Sun)*
FOOD *12.00-18.00 (Mon-Sun)*
various music shows each night

CREDIT CARDS *none taken*
DRAUGHT BEERS *Red Stripe, Kronenbourg, Guinness*
NEAREST TUBE STATION *Brixton*

THE FRONT PAGE
35 Old Church Street, SW3; 0171 352 2908
There was a moment of unease when the present owners took it over in
1986 and promptly changed the name. It had been The Black Lion until
then, indeed there had been a Black Lion on the site for at least 300
years, so not everyone was pleased to find that it had become The Front
Page. But the new régime has been popular. All sorts of people like this
pleasant, comfortable, easy-going Chelsea pub, with its well-stocked
cellars and good food. There is no music, and no fruit machines or fitted
carpets. The big windows fill it with light, and the social mix is Chelsea as
it used to be and still, sometimes, is. The locals go for lunch, actors
rehearsing at the parish hall down the street look in for a drink, audiences
from the Cannon cinema up the street go for pre-movie supper, and after
9pm crowds of young Chelsea denizens arrive. There is a private dining
room upstairs, the staff are young and cheerful, the regulars are all ages
and cheerful, and everyone gets on well.
OPEN *11.00-23.00 (Mon-Sat), 12.00-22.30 (Sun)*
FOOD *12.00-14.30 and 19.00-22.00 (Mon-Fri), 12.30-15.00 and 19.00-
21.30 (Sat-Sun)*
CREDIT CARDS *all major cards*
DRAUGHT BEERS *John Smith's Extra Smooth, Theakston XB, Foster's, Holsten
Export, Kronenbourg, Strongbow, Bass, Guinness*
Private room: 25 seated, 60 standing
NEAREST TUBE STATION *Sloane Square*

LAS FUENTES TAPAS BAR
36-40 High Street, Purley, CR8; 0181 763 1983
Tapas bars are springing up all over London, and in an area distinctly
short of any drinking venues it comes as something of a pleasant surprise
to stray across this busy, energetic example of the genre. Service is smart
and efficient, and the generous portions of all things tapas are reasonably
priced between £2 and £4. Bottled beers start at £1.30, spirits at £1.50
and wines at under £2. The room off the restaurant has a seating area
with plenty of space at the bar to grab a stool. The pleasant atmosphere
of Las Fuentes is due to the combined experience of eating and drinking
in an attractive space with an open kitchen. No surprises in the decor,
though – tiled walls, pictures of Spain, and the hackneyed use of wine
bottles around the walls. Nevertheless, the place has an exuberant kick to
it, and if you walk in on a busy night, you will be greeted with the rich
aroma of Hispanic delicacies wafting gently through the air.
OPEN *12.30-15.00 and 18.00-23.00 (Mon-Fri), 18.00-midnight (Sat)*
CREDIT CARDS *all major cards*
NEAREST RAILWAY STATION *Purley*

FULHAM TUP
268 Fulham Road, SW10; 0171 352 1859
Young, trendy Fulham and Chelsea Sloanes need a place to relax and get off
with each other. The Fulham Tup is actually in Chelsea, although as it's on the
Fulham Road it chooses to use that name. The pub is owned and operated by
Hugh Corbett, the man who created and sold the Slug and Lettuce chain, and
this latest venture is not a million miles away from that concept. The Fulham
Tup is a large, airy and bright one-roomed bar with stripped pine flooring and
half-panelled walls. The sizeable, well-spaced tables leave plenty of standing
room for the crowds who flock here in the evenings.

For the agriculturally challenged, a tup describes the process of a ram impregnating a ewe. Tupping is not particularly new on the Fulham Road, but if impregnating a ewe doesn't directly interest, then you could always eat one – whole legs of lamb are on offer at weekends, although you have to book in advance. The Tup is considering its own ale, Raddles (actually wax-covered harnesses worn by rams when copulating, which leave a deposit in the ewes' nether regions so the farmer can identify which ram did it with which ewe), and its own lager, Shear Delight. Should you spot a blue-bottomed ewe wandering raddled down the Fulham Road, you'll guess that she's been to the Tup for some Shear Delight and is no doubt on her way to bleat about it in the nearby Goat in Boots (qv).

OPEN *12.00-23.00 (Mon-Sat), 12.00-22.30 (Sun)*
FOOD *12.00-15.00 and 18.00-22.00 (Mon-Thurs), 12.00-15.00 and 18.00-21.00 (Fri), 12.00-21.00 (Sat-Sun)*
CREDIT CARDS *all major cards*
DRAUGHT BEERS *Courage Best, John Smith's Extra Smooth, Marston's Pedigree, Theakston XB, Foster's, Kronenbourg, Miller, Beamish, Scrumpy Jack, Old Speckled Hen*
Wheelchair access to venue
NEAREST TUBE STATIONS *Earls Court, Fulham Broadway*

Branches at:
CITY CITY TUP 66 Gresham Street, EC2; 0171 606 8176
   NEAREST TUBE STATION *Bank*
WEST END MARYLEBONE TUP 93 Marylebone High Street, W1; 0171 935 4373
   NEAREST TUBE STATIONS *Bond Street, Baker Street*

THE GATE

18-20 St John Street, EC1; 0171 336 6099
The Longroom, as was, has changed hands. It's had some high wooden wall-panels put in and seen the departure of Bitburger beer. Adnams, happily, has stayed on with the new owners. I can't understand why this place isn't busier. You could do much worse in this part of town.

OPEN *midday-23.00 (Mon-Fri), Saturday private parties only*
FOOD *midday-15.00 then 18.00-22.00 (Mon-Fri)*
CREDIT CARDS *all major cards, not Diners*
DRAUGHT BEERS *Stella Artois, Heineken, Hoegaarden, Guinness, Adnams, Wadworth 6X*
Private room seats 30, 50 standing or available for private parties on Saturdays of up to 200 people
NEAREST TUBE STATION *Farringdon*

THE GATEHOUSE

North Road, N6; 0181 340 8054
In Elizabethan times the Bishop of London built a toll house on the top of the hill, a high gate spanning the road. It gave the place its name, Highgate. There was an old tavern up there too, and when they pulled the toll gate down it stayed put.

Its successor is The Gatehouse, still there after many ups and downs. It was on a major down in 1993, standing empty and disconsolate. Then Wetherspoon's took it over and it seems to be enjoying life again. The Gatehouse has no music, gives non-smokers a big non-smoking bit, and serves good quick food all day (eight varieties of burger from £2.45). Its cask ales include the great Wetherspoon's bargain, a pint of Younger's Scotch Bitter for only 99p.

OPEN *11.00-23.00 (Mon-Sat), 12.00-22.30 (Sun)*
FOOD *11.00-22.00 (Mon-Sat), 12.00-21.30 (Sun)*
CREDIT CARDS *all major cards*

DRAUGHT BEERS *Courage Directors, Theakston Best, Sundance, Ridleys, Budweiser, two guest beers, Foster's, Kronenbourg, McEwan's, Guinness, Dry Blackthorn, two guest ales*
Wheelchair access to venue and loos
NEAREST TUBE STATIONS *Highgate, Archway*

THE GAZEBO

Kings Passage, Kingston, KT1; 0181 546 4495

There are two gazebos at The Gazebo, one on either side of it, and very nice they look too. This is an attractive modern pub, built in the Eighties in a lovely spot on the Thames, right next door to Young's Bishop out of Residence. Downstairs is the public bar, with wooden floors, a pinball machine and a pool table, and upstairs there's the saloon bar, with a big verandah overlooking the river and the green vistas beyond. There are steps down to moorings for customers who have come by boat, and picnic benches on the riverbank. The food is all right, too – good salads, a carvery on Sundays, a children's menu and good old-fashioned puds. And, of course, being a Sam Smith pub it's Sam Smith's beer, so that's reassuring.

OPEN *11.00-23.00 (Mon-Sat), 12.00-22.30 (Sun)*
FOOD *12.00-15.00 (Mon-Sun)*
CREDIT CARDS *Mastercard, Visa*
DRAUGHT BEERS *Old Brewery Bitter, Sovereign Bitter, Ayingerbräu, Ayingerbräu Pils, Ayingerbräu Prinz, Samuel Smith's Stout, Special Reserve, Dark Mild*
Wheelchair access to venue and loos. Private room seats 150
NEAREST RAILWAY STATION *Kingston*

GEORGE IV

185 High Road, W4; 0181 994 4624

Fuller, Smith and Turner has more than 200 pubs, and this is one of the eight in Chiswick, encircling the brewery. There's also The Mawson Arms on the corner of the brewery itself, The Bell and Crown (qv) and The Dove (qv) on the river, The Cross Keys, The Duke of York, The George and Devonshire and two in the High Street, The Old Packhorse and the George IV. They are all historic old pubs. Fuller's spent more than £460,000 recently bringing the George IV slap-bang up to date. Some of the changes belong entirely to this end of the 20th century – the new lavatories and kitchens, the air conditioning, the computerised tills operated by a touch on the screen and recording every aspect of every sale, and a big television screen for major sporting events. There is also a single open bar, low timber ceilings, bare floorboards, tongue-and-groove panelling, mahogany stairs leading to a gallery, drinking booths with old church pews and a cobbled yard with a fountain. It is, in short, an old English Ale and Pie house, Fuller's seventh. Within a matter of weeks of its reopening, trade had doubled. The house speciality is Georgie Porgie Pie – pork and apple in a creamy cider sauce.

OPEN *11.30-23.00 (Mon-Sat), 12.00-22.30 (Sun)*
FOOD *12.00-21.00 (Mon&Fri), 12.00-21.30 (Tue-Thur,Sat), 12.00-15.00 (Sun)*
CREDIT CARDS *all major cards, not AmEx and Diners*
DRAUGHT BEERS *Chiswick Bitter, ESB, London Pride, Carling Black Label, Grolsch, Heineken, Stella Artois, Guinness, Murphy's, Scrumpy Jack, Strongbow*
Wheelchair access to venue and loos
NEAREST TUBE STATION *Turnham Green*

THE GEORGE INN

77 Borough High Street, SE1; 0171 407 2056

To come across The George Inn for the first time is to meet an old friend. You feel you know it already from Christmas cards, Dickens and old movies. It is the archetypal coaching inn. You should really arrive in a stagecoach, but instead you park where you can, walk through the wrought-iron gateway on Borough High Street, and there it is – the cobbled yard, the overhanging galleries, the south front, all still in daily use. It is a moving sight.

We know a lot about The George. We know it was going strong in 1542, the year Henry VIII executed his fifth wife; we know it was rebuilt three times, emerging splendidly intact into the railway age, the same three-sided galleried building as before, with one big courtyard and a smaller one beyond it surrounded by stables. Then, humiliatingly, The George became a depot of the Great Northern Railway, which pulled down two of the fronts and built warehouses in their place. Luckily the south front survived and the warehouses did not – they were bombed in the war. What replaced them is pretty awful – two dreadful modern blocks – but you can keep your back to these as you sit at one of the picnic tables in the courtyard.

With only The George in view, you are in another age. The floorboards creak loudly as you pass from bar to bar in the old inn, twice as loudly as you go upstairs to the dark panelled restaurant and various function rooms. These upper storeys were, of course, bedchambers in The George's great days. You can't find a bed there now, but the food is good, the ale is better, old settles and chimney corners beckon, and in the summer there's the courtyard where Shakespeare, they say, once performed. It is a romantic place, safely in the hands of the National Trust, and never disappoints. It is, of course, an Evening Standard Pub of the Year.

OPEN *11.00-23.00 (Mon-Sat), 12.00-22.30 (Sun)*

FOOD *bar 11.00-23.00 (Mon-Sat); restaurant 18.00-21.30 (Wed-Fri)*

CREDIT CARDS *all major cards*

DRAUGHT BEERS *Bishop's Restoration, Boddingtons, London Pride, Heineken, Stella Artois, Guinness, Murphy's, Strongbow, Abbott's, Flowers Original, Old Speckled Hen, one guest ale*

Five private areas: 20-60 seated, 30-100 standing

NEAREST TUBE STATION *London Bridge*

THE GIPSY MOTH

60 Greenwich Church Street, SE10; 0181 858 0786

The magnificent *Cutty Sark* and the gallant little *Gipsy Moth*, both enjoying new careers as tourist attractions at Greenwich, get perhaps 300,000 visitors every year. It is thirsty work, looking at famous ships, and after seeing two of them, the whole family needs a drink and a snack and a loo. This large, efficient pub is right on the spot. A bit of luck all round, really. It used to be, unmemorably, The Wheatsheaf, but changed its name to The Gipsy Moth when Sir Francis Chichester's little boat, having gone round the world with only him on board, settled on its doorstep. So now, every summer, tourists arrive in a never-ending stream, have a meal and a drink, go to the loo and move on, letting someone else have the table. There are seats in the garden for 150 at a time.

OPEN *11.00-23.00 (Mon-Sat), 12.00-22.30 (Sun)*

FOOD *bar: 12.00-15.00 (Mon-Sat), 12.00-16.00 (Sun)*

CREDIT CARDS *all major cards*

DRAUGHT BEERS *Adnams, Burton Ale, Kilkenny, Tetley's, Carlsberg Export, Carlsberg Pilsner, Guinness, Dry Blackthorn*

Wheelchair access to venue and loos

NEAREST RAILWAY STATION *Greenwich*

THE GLASSBLOWER

Glasshouse Street, W1; 0171 734 8547

An everyday sort of pub two minutes from Piccadilly Circus. Gaming machines, juke box. Blokish is the word that comes to mind. It used to be

The Bodega. It was sort of Spanish in those days. Then Chef and Brewer got it and called it the Kilt and Celt and it became Celtic. Sort of. Now Scottish and Newcastle has gone for the Glassblower. Still that's easier to say after a few pints than Kilt and Celt.

OPEN *11.00-23.00 (Mon-Sat), 12.00-22.30 (Sun)*
FOOD *opening times*
CREDIT CARDS *all major cards*
DRAUGHT BEERS *Foster's, Beck's, Kronenbourg, Strongbow, Guinness, John Smith's Extra Smooth, a selection of real ales*
NEAREST TUBE STATION *Piccadilly Circus*

THE GLOBE TAVERN

83 Moorgate, EC2; 0171 606 4731

For more than 250 years two pubs stood side by side in Moorgate, a big one and a small one. The big one was The Globe Tavern. Next door was the more modest Swan and Hoop, later known as The Moorgate and later still as the John Keats at Moorgate (qv). The Globe's great strength has always been its site. It occupies the strategic corner of Moorgate and London Wall, a great place for a pub. It has had lots of owners, hundreds of landlords, countless customers. Waves of builders have come and gone. The latest of these has recently completed a renovation costing the best part of £500,000 and involving radical alterations. They have left it a big, boisterous pub with its upstairs restaurant twice the size it was. In the wide-open L-shaped bar the music is so loud that if it's your shout, you have to shout. There are driving machines, gaming machines, a tireless juke box, two television screens, all that sort of thing. It gets packed. All around brood the great City institutions. You think, perhaps, that the City is peopled by serious persons with tastes running to string quartets? Go to The Globe. 'It's a bit of a madhouse,' says the manager fondly, in the comparative hush of the pub next door. He manages that as well. Bass has ended up owning them both.

OPEN *11.00-23.00 (Mon-Fri)*
FOOD *12.00-15.00 (Mon-Fri)*
CREDIT CARDS *all major cards*
DRAUGHT BEERS *Bass, Caffrey's, London Pride, Carling Black Label, Carling Premier, Grolsch, Guinness, Red Rock*
Wheelchair access to venue. Two private rooms: 40-80 seated, 80-150 standing
NEAREST TUBE STATION *Moorgate*

THE GLOUCESTER

187 Sloane Street, SW1; 0171 235 0298

The Battle of Alexandria, 1801, is celebrated on the sign outside The Gloucester, a famous victory against Napoleon which earned the Gloucestershire Regiment the unique distinction of being permitted to wear a badge at the back of their headdress as well as the front. The Gloucester has been loyally marking this noted feat of arms ever since it was built 150 years ago, and the Gloucestershire Vets still meet in the back room there on the first Friday of the month. It is a small, comfortable pub in the heart of Knightsbridge, five minutes from Harrods and Harvey Nichols on the corner. It opens, remarkably enough, at 9am for breakfast, but, sorry, you'll have to wait until 11am to get a drink. I mean this isn't Smithfield Market; you can have a pint of bitter with your bacon and eggs there at 7am any weekday morning (see the Fox and Anchor).

OPEN *09.00-23.00 (Mon-Sat), 12.00-22.30 (Sun)*
FOOD *as opening hours*
CREDIT CARDS *all major cards*
DRAUGHT BEERS *Courage Best, Courage Directors, John Smith's Extra Smooth, Foster's, Holsten Export, Kronenbourg, Guinness, Strongbow*

Wheelchair access to venue. Private room: 20 seated, 35 standing
NEAREST TUBE STATION *Knightsbridge*

GOAT IN BOOTS

333 Fulham Road, SW10; 0171 352 1384

There is a small stretch of the Fulham Road that people refer to as The Beach. It is the Mediterranean atmosphere on summer evenings, the music, the drinks, the clothes. There has been a pub here for more than 400 years, and the original one enjoyed common rights for two cows and a heifer. The current building dates back to 1909 and has been at the epicentre of Chelsea nightlife for as long as anyone can remember. In 1994 Joel Cadbury, the son of Peter Cadbury, then an aspiring young 23 year old, wanted to buy the private drinking club upstairs, the King's Club. Courage didn't want to sell in piecemeal fashion, so Cadbury thought, what the hell, and bought the whole lot. The price he paid was a mere £140,000, and last year he sold it for a package worth £1.5 million while retaining the management contract.

The Goat in Boots is a decent-enough pub – stripped floors, wooden beams, not much furniture but plenty of places to lean. There's a downstairs cocktail bar, also loud and packed with people, and doormen on the door at weekends with the universal preference for the young and scantily dressed. The juke box gets turned up high and the crowd hops to the music. In somewhere like Pontefract, this would be a workaday pub, but on The Beach the up-market clientele use it as a rights-of-passage affair in a bid to get laid.

The King's Club upstairs is a more sedate affair. The music is quieter and there's a pool table. There is a bridge club here, where daily, afternoon and early-evening sessions are very well attended. On Mondays £20 buys you supper, half a bottle of wine and all the bridge companions you need. Cadbury also owns the nearby Vingt-Quatre, a 24-hour café, and promises more venues throughout London. Sadly, his venture into Battersea Square, and the much jinxed site that was recently SWXI, failed to appeal.

OPEN *11.30-23.00 (Mon-Sat), 12.00-22.30 (Sun)*
FOOD *12.00-15.00 (Mon-Sun)*
CREDIT CARDS *all major cards*
DRAUGHT BEERS *Courage Best, Courage Directors, John Smith's Extra Smooth, Beck's, Foster's, Kronenbourg, Miller, Guinness, Scrumpy Jack Wheelchair access to venue, not to loos*
NEAREST TUBE STATIONS *South Kensington, Gloucester Road*

THE GOLDENGROVE

146-148 The Grove, Stratford, E15; 0181 519 0750

The poet Gerald Manley Hopkins was born in this street in a handsome Georgian terrace house, lamentably bombed in 1941 and now covered by Newham Council's Finance and Housing Department. Stratford East was a sort of Hampstead in those days, but then the railways brought in the hoi polloi and the swanky Grove was never the same again. Still Nos 146 and 148 survived after a fashion and became briefly famous in the 1970s as one of Dicky Dirt's famous jeans emporia. It only took a year or two for poor Dicky Dirt to go bust and his big shop stood empty for ages, getting thoroughly depressed, not to say bashed up. Then Wetherspoon's bought it and put it to rights. They spent £800,000 on it and it is now a very nice pub. The traffic roars by, defying actors from Joan Littlewood's famous theatre to reach it, but they are nippy on their feet. None has been squashed flat yet. Goldengrove is light and comfortable and has as rural a beer garden as you could wish, the tables pleasantly placed under pergolas and everything blooming. I see Gerald Manley Hopkins under one of those pergolas, pen in hand. The Goldengrove is proud of him and has hung his poems, neatly framed, all over. One of them gave the pub its name. It begins:

'Margaret are you grieving

Over Goldengrove unleaving?'
This is a trying question. I don't know what poor Margaret's answer was.
OPEN *11.00-23.00 (Mon-Sat), midday-22.30 (Sun)*
FOOD *11.00-22.00 (Mon-Sat), midday-21.30 (Sun)*
CREDIT CARDS *all major cards on* **FOOD** *orders over £5*
DRAUGHT BEERS *Foster's, Kronenbourg, Holsten, McEwan's, Directors, Theakston,
London Pride, Spitfire, John Smith's Extra Smooth, Caffrey's, Guinness, Dry
Blackthorn, Webster's First Quality, many guest ales changed regularly
Wheelchair access to venue and disabled loos*
NEAREST RAILWAY STATION *Stratford, DLR*

GOLDEN LION

51 Dean Street, W1; 0171 434 0661
For years the Golden Lion in Dean Street was one of London's best-known gay
pubs, packed with solitary and, if they were wise, watchful drinkers. It was
one of the haunts of Dennis Nilsen, the serial killer. That, I'm afraid, is the most
interesting thing about the place. Nilsen would find it harder to find victims
there now. New managers and a new bar policy have wrought radical
change. There are two bars, gaming machines, satellite television and a juke
box, and traditional bar food upstairs (sausage, beans and chips, and pies).
OPEN *11.00-23.00 (Mon-Sat), 12.00-22.30 (Sun)*
FOOD *12.00-15.00 and 18.00-22.00 (Mon-Sat), 12.00-16.00 and 18.00-
22.00 (Sun)*
CREDIT CARDS *all major cards*
DRAUGHT BEERS *Courage Directors, John Smith's Extra Smooth, Theakston
Best, Beck's, Foster's, Kronenbourg, Guinness, Strongbow
Wheelchair access to venue
Private room: 25 seated, 40 standing*
NEAREST TUBE STATION *Piccadilly Circus*

THE GOLDEN LION

25 King Street, W1; 0171 930 7227
The Golden Lion, or Golden Lyon Tavern as it was in 1732, is a striking
sight in this rather uneventful street. It is five storeys high and has a mock-
Jacobean garret, black marble columns, projecting windows and a stucco
balustrade. It's also hemmed in by flat, modern office buildings, so you
certainly can't miss it. Something is missing, though. The lovely St James's
Theatre, The Golden Lion's old friend, which stood next to it for more than
a hundred years, was pulled down by developers in 1959. There were
furious objections. Laurence Olivier and Vivien Leigh led demonstrations
but the demolition men went in anyway. One of those office blocks
replaced it – the one on the right.... theatre and pub were unusually close.
A door led directly from the circle to The Golden Lion's upstairs bar,
which became the official theatre bar, with warning bells for the start of
performances and pre-ordered drinks waiting at the interval. Playgoers
flocked there, as did generations of actors, so it was a body blow for
The Golden Lion when the theatre was demolished. It went into rather a
depression for a while, but it has now had a much-needed face-lift and
seems to be feeling a lot better. Most of its customers work in neighbouring
offices. The offices close on Sunday. So does The Golden Lion.
OPEN *11.30-23.00 (Mon-Fri), 12.00-17.00 (Sat)*
FOOD *bar: 12.00-15.00 (Mon-Fri)*
CREDIT CARDS *all major cards*
DRAUGHT BEERS *Adnams, Tetley's, Carlsberg Export, Carlsberg Pils,
Castlemaine XXXX, Guinness, Addlestones, plus three guest ales
Wheelchair access to venue. Private room seats 50*
NEAREST TUBE STATION *Green Park*

THE GOOSE AND GRANITE

196 Clapham High Street, SW4; 0171 622 1543

A massive, cavernous pub owned by the Just So Pub Co., which cost Bass £250,000 to transform in 1996. Is there a bigger pub in London? Yes, there are several, actually, but you can't help asking yourself that question when you've turned up to meet a blind date on a Saturday evening just as a major event is throwing out from Clapham Common. The Goose and Granite is so big you might well get lost on the way back from the bar to your seat – it really wouldn't be out of place in a major railway terminus or an airport.

OPEN *11.00-23.00 (Mon-Sat), 12.00-22.30 (Sun)*
FOOD *12.00-22.00 (Mon-Sun)*
CREDIT CARDS all major cards, not AmEx
DRAUGHT BEERS Caffrey's, Just So Bitter, London Pride, Worthington Best, Carling Black Label, Carling Premier, Grolsch, Guinness, Cidermaster
Wheelchair access to venue and loos
NEAREST TUBE STATION *Clapham Common*

THE GOOSE AND GRANITE

264 Hoe Street, E17; 0181 520 8341

People who complain about things quite often complain about the new pub names. Mr Nicholas Winterton even raised the matter in the House. He called on Mr Michael Howard and Mr John Gummer to stop brewers using names that were detrimental to our heritage. Names like, he said, the Slug and Salad (sic). The Goose and Granite. Scruffy Murphy's...Well the only Goose and Granite around at the time was this one in Walthamstow. Take the Victoria Line to Walthamstow Central and you can't miss it. It is the big, good-looking pub on the corner with luxuriant baskets of flowers all the way round. It is a huge improvement on what went before.

The Goose and Granite started life as the Tower Hotel in the 1870s, when rural Walthamstow was expanding as you looked, factories going up, houses following. It had its ups and downs, mostly downs, with the usual name changes. By the 70s it was Flanagan's Tower and was doing quite well, a busy pub downstairs, bed and breakfast on the floors above, but this didn't last. By the 90s it was a sad sight, a broken-down old boozer, clearly on its last legs. There was then a spectacular dash to the rescue. Backed by Bass, a new young group called the Just So Pub Co. took it over and just about rebuilt it. The job took three months and cost well over £500,000 but the old pub has been transformed. It is now handsome, comfortable and popular, with lovely arched windows flooding the place with light. People who had lived in Walthamstow for years found themselves going in for the very first time.

OPEN *11.00-23.00 (Mon-Sat), 12.00-22.30 (Sun)*
FOOD *12.00-21.00 (Mon-Sat), 12.00-17.00 (Sun)*
CREDIT CARDS all major cards, not AmEx
DRAUGHT BEERS Bass, Caffrey's, London Pride, Ruddles County, Carling Black Label, Carling Premier, Grolsch, Guinness, Cidermaster
Wheelchair access to venue and loos. Private room: 60 seated, 100 standing
NEAREST TUBE STATION *Walthamstow Central*

THE GOOSE AND GRANITE

381 Lordship Lane, SE22; 0181 290 9401

For more than a hundred years London's horse-drawn buses and subsequent motor buses carried the destination blind 'Dulwich Plough' as the terminus of the number 12 bus route. Unbeknown to the buses, Bass had plans to convert this historic coaching inn to a Goose and Granite, part of their Just So Pub Co., and early one morning in 1997 Dulwich awoke to find the name suddenly changed. Bus drivers and little old ladies got into a panic – no one knew where they were going. The London Central Bus Company acted promptly, and new blinds were hastily ordered, this time, quite wisely, displaying Dulwich Library (across the road from the pub) as their destination.

OPEN *11.00-23.00 (Mon-Sat), 12.00-22.30 (Sun)*
FOOD *12.00-21.00 (Mon-Sat), 12.00-17.00 (Sun)*
CREDIT CARDS *all major cards, not AmEx*
DRAUGHT BEERS *Bass, Caffrey's, London Pride, Ruddles County, Carling Black Label, Carling Premier, Grolsch, Guinness, Cidermaster*
Wheelchair access to venue and loos. Private room: 60 seated, 100 standing
NEAREST RAILWAY STATION *East Dulwich*

GORDON'S WINE BAR

47 Villiers Street, WC2; 0171 930 1408

You either love it or hate it, but Gordon's is something of an institution in London's drinking circles. It is located in a tatty but enchanting basement near Charing Cross, and its charm lies in its unpretentious, no-nonsense approach to drinking. It feels like you've walked on to the set of a period drama. You sit in former wine cellars, with exposed brickwork and old wooden furniture – you'd half expect water to be dripping down the walls. Gordon's specialises in wines (it has a good range at modest prices) and a range of snack foods, including excellent cheese plates. The real boon, though, is the outside seating on Watergate Walk, which runs along the edge of Embankment Gardens. On summer evenings there are few places in this area that can provide a better resting spot. It remains a wonderful wine bar.

OPEN *11.00-23.00 (Mon-Fri), 17.00-23.00 (Sat)*
FOOD *12.00-21.00 (Mon-Sat)*
CREDIT CARDS *all major cards, not AmEx and Diners*
NEAREST TUBE STATIONS *Embankment, Charing Cross*

LA GRANDE MARQUE

47 Ludgate Hill, EC4; 0171 329 6709

This excellent bank conversion on Ludgate Hill is notable for its gentlemanly and understated atmosphere and its elegant, sophisticated decor – strictly for lovers of wine and champagne. The list, as supplied by Lay & Wheeler of Colchester, totals more than a hundred varieties and covers a broad range of prices, although those on a very tight budget shouldn't plan a long evening. There are 22 different champagnes from £20.95 and service can be a bit lacklustre, but all in all, this is an excellent bar.

OPEN *11.30-21.30 (Mon-Fri)*
FOOD *11.30-14.30 (Mon-Fri)*
CREDIT CARDS *all major cards*
DRAUGHT BEERS *Bitburger*
Wheelchair access to venue, not to loos
NEAREST TUBE STATIONS *Blackfriars, St Paul's*

THE GRAPES

76 Narrow Street, E14; 0171 987 4396

'The Six Jolly Fellowship-Porters, a tavern of a dropsical appearance, had long settled down into a state of hale infirmity', wrote Charles Dickens in *Our Mutual Friend*. 'In its whole constitution it had not a straight floor and hardly a straight line ... it was a bar to soften the human breast.'

The real name of the Six Jolly Fellowship-Porters was, and is, The Grapes. Dickens knew it well, describing it perfectly, and it is still there on the river at Limehouse. It hasn't changed all that much. It was old when Dickens knew it, with a history of press-gangs and dark doings. It is more than a hundred years older now and, not surprisingly, there is still not a straight floor and hardly a straight line. Happily, a recent renovation doesn't show too much, but the ancient deck, which until recently hung dropsically over the river, has been replaced with a robust new one, and a flight of new teak steps leads to a smaller deck outside the little first-floor dining room where fresh fish is served every day. The Grapes has a lively and charismatic licensee in Barbara Haig, a one-time Playboy bunny who has set her heart on becoming a Master Cellarman. Her Dickensian cellar may be just 4ft 3in high, but the beer, she says, is superb.

OPEN *12.00-15.00 and 17.30-23.00 (Mon-Fri), 19.00-23.00 (Sat), 12.00-15.00 and 19.00-22.30 (Sun)*

FOOD *bar 12.00-14.00 and 19.00-21.00 (Mon-Fri), 19.00-21.00 (Sat); restaurant 12.00-14.15 and 19.30-21.15 (Mon-Fri), 19.30-21.15 (Sat), 12.00-14.30 (Sun lunch)*

CREDIT CARDS *all major cards*

DRAUGHT BEERS *Burton, Tetley's, Carlsberg Export, Castlemaine XXXX, Guinness, Stella Artois, Adnams, plus a guest ale for winter only Wheelchair access to venue, not to loos. One private room: 28 seated, no standing*

NEAREST RAILWAY STATION *Westferry (DLR)*

YE GRAPES

16 Shepherd Market, W1; 0171 499 1563

When you're beating a merry path to the West End it's easy to forget that there are decent drinking venues in this part of Mayfair. It's worth stopping for a while at this popular pub, which is privately owned, a true free house. It is hard to see the walls for the objects in Ye Grapes. You might suppose that the contents of the attic of a grand country house had been generously scattered around – the heads of horned beasts, a pair of oars, a pair of guns, fish in glass cases, birds in glass cases. There is a restaurant upstairs, the Vinery, which also does cream teas in the afternoon. The pub has an impressive display of real ales, and you should really sample them all before you leave. I did, I think!

OPEN *11.00-23.00 (Mon-Sat), 12.00-22.30 (Sun)*

FOOD *12.00-14.30 (Mon-Sun)*

CREDIT CARDS *none taken*

DRAUGHT BEERS *Boddingtons, Flowers Original, Greene King IPA, London Pride, Manchester Gold, Marston's Pedigree, Wadworth 6X, Wexford Irish Ale, Heineken, Hoegaarden, Stella Artois, Guinness, Murphy's, Strongbow, Heineken Export, Labatt Blue Wheelchair access to venue, not to loos*

NEAREST TUBE STATION *Green Park*

THE GREEN MAN

Putney Heath, SW15; 0181 788 8096

In May 1798 the Prime Minister, William Pitt, rather fell out with the MP for Southwark so they rode to Putney Heath and fought a duel. Each fired twice, missed, agreed that honour was satisfied and rode home again. It was the talk of The Green Man that day. The Green Man was then a remote country inn on the edge of a notoriously dangerous bit of London. Putney had become a fashionable suburb but the Heath was not a place to walk at night. Highwaymen lurked, footpads abounded and rough justice was dispensed. Dick Turpin hid his guns in The Green Man and lived to rob another day, but Jerry Abbershaw, who used it as his base, was hanged on a gibbet outside it. Putney spread and prospered and respectable Victorians enjoyed a walk to The Green Man. Algernon Charles Swinburne, living with his friend Theodore Watts-Dunton at The Pines, 11 Putney Hill, always called in for a drink on his way to the Rose and Crown in Wimbledon Village. It was a warren of private bars and snugs then, but Swinburne would still know the pub today.

Take the number 14 bus out of town and your destination is assured. The pub is really two cottages back to back. There are two bars – the public bar on the right, the saloon bar on the left, linked by the counter. They are light and cheerful on summer days, snug and cosy after dark.

Outside, the old pub is flanked by two pretty courtyards with tables and benches and a big garden at the back, finely landscaped. Has anyone heard of Ringing the Bull? Of all old English pub games this one is thought to have the longest history of continuous play, and here it is in the bar of The Green Man, still being played, the ring suspended from the ceiling, the hook on the wall. The idea is to swing the ring on to the hook. It is harder than it looks.

OPEN *11.00-23.00 (Mon-Sat), 12.00-22.30 (Sun)*
FOOD *12.00-15.00 (Mon-Sun, winter); 12.00-15.00 and 19.00-21.00 (Mon-Sun, summer)*
CREDIT CARDS *none taken*
DRAUGHT BEERS *Young's Bitter, Young's Export, Young's Special, Guinness, Dry Blackthorn, Carling, Stella Artois, Young's Pilsner, plus a seasonal ale*
NEAREST TUBE STATION *Putney Bridge*
NEAREST RAILWAY STATION *Putney*

THE GRENADIER

Old Barrack Yard, Wilton Row, SW1; 0171 235 3074

A smart little pub, a well-bred little pub, tucked away in a quiet Knightsbridge mews and keeping up its standards. 'It is house policy', says the notice on the door, 'that customers should be suitably dressed ...' The Duke of Wellington is the presiding spirit in The Grenadier. His officers used it as their mess, he is said to have played cards here himself, his mounting block is outside and his patrician features look scornfully down at you from the walls.

The bar is tiny, but happily customers can spill out into the mews if it's fine, and there always seems to be room. The little restaurant at the back, candlelit at night, has crisp white linen cloths, crystal glassware and Beef Wellington on the menu. It can't seat more than 28, so it's best to book. The pewter bar counter has been scrubbed and polished daily since 1827, when the pub was built, and military memorabilia has steadily accumulated. They used to send a man from Wellington Barracks every week to groom the Guardsman's bearskin in the bar. It is made from the pelt of a female Canadian bear which, they say, like fingernails, goes on growing. A Sunday morning Bloody Mary bar is another tradition at The Grenadier. The Bloody Marys are made from a recipe passed from licensee to licensee, and the long-standing record for a single session is 276. I've half a mind to assemble my cronies and descend on the place one Sunday to see what we can do about it. The Grenadier is said to have a ghost who haunts only in September, the shade of an officer caught cheating at cards and flogged to death. Well, you can't have a fellow cheating. The pub has been investigated by mediums and visited by priests, and the ghost seems to be lying low for the moment.

OPEN *12.00-23.00 (Mon-Sat), 12.00-22.30 (Sun)*
FOOD *bar 12.00-14.30 and 18.00-22.00 (Mon-Fri), 12.00-22.00 (Sat-Sun); restaurant 12.00-14.00 and 18.00-21.45 (Mon-Sat), 12.00-22.00 (Sun)*
CREDIT CARDS *all major cards*
DRAUGHT BEERS *Courage Best, Theakston Best, Marston's Pedigree, Budweiser, Foster's, Kronenbourg, Guinness, Strongbow, John Smith's Extra Smooth, a monthly guest ale*
NEAREST TUBE STATION *Hyde Park Corner*

THE GREYHOUND

1 Kensington Square, W8; 0171 937 7140

Like many pubs The Greyhound has periodically reorganised itself to meet the changing needs of its local community. In The Greyhound's case, however, change has also been prompted by more dramatic events. It was built in 1899 and replaced an earlier pub on the site. At one time it became famous for billiards, with many leading players gracing the baize of its two full-size tables, including the late, great Joe Davis. In 1975 it became the *Evening Standard* Pub of the Year. In 1979 there was a major gas explosion and the place was all but destroyed. Luckily, it occurred at night and, as it happened, no one was sleeping there. The Greyhound today is a rather rakish workaday pub.

OPEN *11.00-23.00 (Mon-Sat), 12.00-22.30 (Sun)*

FOOD *12.00-21.00 (Mon-Sun)*

CREDIT CARDS *all major cards*

DRAUGHT BEERS *Courage Directors, John Smith's Extra Smooth, Theakston Best, Theakston XB, Beck's, Foster's, Kronenbourg, Guinness, Scrumpy Jack, plus a monthly guest ale*

Wheelchair access to venue, not to loos. Private room: 40 seated, 150 standing

NEAREST TUBE STATION *High Street Kensington*

THE GRID INN

22 Replingham Road, SW18; 0181 874 8460

'The day the heavens did not fall'

Southfields owes everything to the railway which arrived in 1889, planting a pretty little terracotta-red brick station among the fields. By 1907 a pleasant village-like community was comfortably established. There was a network of terraced streets known as the Southfields Grid, parades of shops, a church, a school and a stripped pine merchant, but as the years passed you could hardly fail to notice that something was missing. Southfields didn't have a pub. Newcomers were always given the same explanation. Some said it was the church, others the Spencer family, but someone had attached a covenant to the deeds of the land when selling it. No pub could ever be built there. The local council is puzzled by this. Indeed it has come to believe it to be a myth. Southfields, in short, may have been publess for 100 years for no good reason.

On 6 October 1994 it got a pub at last, The Grid Inn, a pleasant pub owned by J. D. Wetherspoon. This being Wetherspoon's, there is a large no-smoking area, a cheap pint and no music of any kind. Lots of local history is framed on the walls – pictures of local landmarks and notables. The Grid Inn serves snacks of crab cakes and nachos, main meals of chicken, ham and leek pie, and the famous JDW chilli con carne.

OPEN *11.00-23.00 (Mon-Sat), 12.00-22.30 (Sun)*

FOOD *11.00-22.00 (Mon-Sat), 12.00-21.30 (Sun)*

CREDIT CARDS *all major cards*

DRAUGHT BEERS *Courage Directors, London Pride, Theakston Best, Foster's, Kronenbourg, McEwan's, Guinness, Dry Blackthorn, Budweiser, Western First Quality Cider, four guest ales*

Wheelchair access to venue and loos

NEAREST TUBE STATION *Southfields*

THE GROUSE AND CLARET

Little Chester Street, SW1; 0171 235 3438

During the Blitz an entire row of the pretty mews houses in Little Chester Street was flattened, along with the two pubs at each end. The war over, houses and pubs were rebuilt in a decent neo-Georgian style. Some thought it a great improvement, and you could tell at a glance that The Pig and Whistle had gone up in the world, so much so that the old plebby name seemed quite inappropriate. So it got a name the owners thought would more befit its new station. It became The Grouse and Claret.

This is still a very swanky pub, with a grouse-moor mural over the front door, a public bar on the left and a big handsome saloon bar elaborately fitted with drinking booths on the right. Both are newly carpeted, and gleam with polish in case Her Majesty should call. She lives just round the corner. There is a flagged cellar bar mostly used for private parties and a handsome restaurant upstairs serving any amount of claret but no grouse at all. Well, the restaurant is called The Scandinavian. It goes in for smoked reindeer salad and poached kattfisk, with Artsoppa every Thursday. Artsoppa is Swedish pea soup with gammon, sausage and Swedish mustard. It is served with warm Swedish punch and followed by cakes with jam and cream.

OPEN *11.00-23.00 (Mon-Sat), 12.00-15.00 (Sun)*

FOOD *12.00-15.00 (Mon-Fri), food available all week for pre-booked parties, functions etc.*

CREDIT CARDS *all major cards*

DRAUGHT BEERS *Badger Bitter, Dempsey's, Tanglefoot, Hofbräu Export, Hofbräu Premium, M‚nchner Pilsner, Guinness, Dry Blackthorn, plus a guest ale*
Three private rooms: 55 seated, 50-120 standing

NEAREST TUBE STATIONS *Hyde Park Corner, Victoria*

THE GUINEA

30 Bruton Place, W1; 0171 409 1728

This exclusive little pub tucked down a Mayfair mews is small and dark, richly accoutred and gets packed at lunchtimes. Well, the beer is Young's, and the bar food is excellent. The licensee, Carl Smith, has won so many national steak and kidney pie contests that many competitions have asked him not to enter. He judges them now, but still continues to win a plateful of other food awards. His steaks and mixed grills are substantial, and worth the prices, which start at £14.35. Princess Margaret has dined here, as have Mel Gibson, Frank Sinatra, Sylvester Stallone, Jack Nicklaus and King Hussein. There's also a lighter menu for those with lighter appetites. This famous Mayfair pub-restaurant is worth any amount of trips.

OPEN *11.00-23.00 (Mon-Fri), 18.30-23.00 (Sat)*

FOOD *bar 12.00-14.30 (Mon-Fri); restaurant 12.30-14.30 and 18.30-23.00 (Mon-Fri), 18.30-23.00 (Sat)*

CREDIT CARDS *all major cards*

DRAUGHT BEERS *Ramrod Smooth, Young's Ordinary, Young's Special, Guinness, Young's Pilsner, Young's Export, Stella Artois, Carling Black Label, several seasonal ales*
Wheelchair access to venue. Private room: 30 seated, 50 standing

NEAREST TUBE STATIONS *Green Park, Bond Street*

THE GUN

27 Cold Harbour, E14; 0171 987 1692

This little riverside pub stands at the point where the Thames completes the deep loop enclosing the Isle of Dogs. The Gun may not have seen many admirals in its time, but seamen have always been its customers, as have lightermen and local dockers, river police and customs men. The world's navies still visit the docks, and The Gun always hoists its White Ensign to welcome them. Its three bars all have their mementos of visiting ships. Flags, crests, naval hat bands and paintings of ships hang everywhere. The Gun is a pub with an eventful past, and its future could be bright, too, with the Jubilee Line extension almost in its front garden and the Millennium exhibition directly across the water. The Lady Hamilton Room, now restored to its former elegance, will have an unrivalled view.

OPEN *11.00-23.00 (Mon-Sat), 12.00-22.30 (Sun)*

FOOD *bar 11.00-23.00 (Mon-Sat), 12.00-14.30 (Sun); restaurant 12.00-14.30 and 19.00-23.00 (Mon-Sat), 12.00-14.30 (Sun)*

CREDIT CARDS *all major cards*

DRAUGHT BEERS *Kilkenny, Nelson's Bitter, Tetley's, Carlsberg, Carlsberg Export, Castlemaine XXXX, Guinness, Strongbow, Marston's Pedigree, Double Diamond*
Wheelchair access to venue. Private room seats 40

NEAREST RAILWAY STATION *Crossharbour (DLR)*

THE HALF MOON

93 Lower Richmond Road, SW15; 0181 780 9383

This large Edwardian pub is a long-established music venue with live bands every night of the week. You could have seen the Rolling Stones here in their day, and Thin Lizzy. These days you can see their tribute counterparts, Stone Roses and Limehouse Lizzy. Status Quo, the Police and Dire Straits also played here, and still making history are the Hamsters, Nova, Boogie Brothers, Four Bills and a Ben, Wilko Johnson and Hank Wangford. Most styles of music are performed but they've stopped doing the Irish folk music. 'Nobody came,' says the new manager, Bob Brand. A recent quarter-of-a-million-pound refit has brought a dramatic transformation to the place, and they are keen to promote up and coming bands on the brink of stardom. You will find rock, blues, folk, R & B, ska, reggae...

OPEN *12.00-23.00 (Mon-Sat), 12.00-22.30 (Sun)*

FOOD *12.00-17.00 (Sat-Sun)*

CREDIT CARDS none

DRAUGHT BEERS *Young's Bitter, Young's Special, Guinness, Dry Blackthorn, Carling, Stella Artois, Young's Export, Young's Pilsner*
Venue room: 100 seated, 200 standing

NEAREST TUBE STATION *Putney Bridge*

HAMILTON HALL

Liverpool Street Station, EC2; 0171 247 3579

In 1901 the new Great Eastern Hotel built itself a ballroom. It set out to impress, and impress it did. From floor to ceiling it was three storeys high, and it had sumptuous decorations based on an apartment in the Palais Soubise in Paris – nymphs, garlands and cornucopias, marble fireplaces, soaring mirrors, fine paintings, all lit by chandeliers. When war broke out in 1939 it was closed. It stayed closed until the recent renovation of Liverpool Street Station, when J. D. Wetherspoon won the contract to take it over. The priceless fittings and decorations were found in a storeroom, and Hamilton Hall started a new life. It is now a remarkable pub, and it sometimes seems that everyone heading for the station is having a drink there first. The usual Wetherspoon's rules apply: no music, big no-smoking areas, cut-price beer.

OPEN *11.00-23.00 (Mon-Sat), 12.00-22.30 (Sun)*

FOOD *11.00-22.00 (Mon-Sat), 12.00-21.30 (Sun)*

CREDIT CARDS all major cards

DRAUGHT BEERS *Courage Directors, John Smith's Extra Smooth, London Pride, Theakston Best, Younger's Scotch Bitter, Foster's, Kronenbourg, Guinness, Dry Blackthorn, Sundance, Budweiser, two guest beers*
Wheelchair access to venue and loos

NEAREST TUBE STATION *Liverpool Street*

HAND AND SHEARS

1 Middle Street, EC1; 0171 600 0257

How nice to see this seemly old pub enjoying the autumn of its days in its placid little backwater off Smithfield. John Betjeman, who lived along the way in Cloth Fair, used to pop in sometimes, and overworked doctors and nurses from nearby Barts like it. There is no music or machines. It has kept its snug, the fire burns at the far end, the service is friendly, you can get doorstep sandwiches at the bar and a pubby lunch upstairs quite cheaply. Busy lunches lead in to sleepy afternoons and it's very quiet at weekends. It is closed at weekends. In the Middle Ages, though, it was absolutely buzzing. The Lord Mayor proclaimed Bartholomew Fair open from the inn doorway every year and the court of Pie Poudre (*Pieds Poudres*, dusty feet) met in the room above the bar to grant licences, test weights and measures, redress grievances and pursue fraud. Life swirled round it. For the Hand and Shears, those were the days.

OPEN *11.00-23.00 (Mon-Fri)*
FOOD *all day (Mon-Fri)*
CREDIT CARDS *all major cards*
DRAUGHT BEERS *Courage Best, Courage Directors, Foster's, Kronenbourg, Strongbow, Guinness, two weekly guest ales*
Private room: 35 seated, 50 standing
NEAREST TUBE STATION *Barbican*

THE HAND IN HAND

6 Crooked Billet, SW19; 0181 946 5720
A few doors along from the Crooked Billet (qv), facing the same small green, is the Hand in Hand, the Evening Standard Pub of the Year in 1982. What you see is four cottages run together with a pretty, south-facing courtyard in front, and a prize-winning riot of hanging baskets and window boxes. A horse chestnut gives shade to the tables, a vine crawls over one wall, and a wooden porch leads into the pub itself. You find yourself in a popular, busy inn, plainly decorated and simply furnished with carved wooden benches, stools and solid old tables. There is a family room for children, plus games machines and darts, and two television sets. People are very keen on the home-made pasta. Its biggest achievement, though, is in retaining the atmosphere of the simple beer house it was for a hundred years before Young's took it over in 1974. The Hand in Hand remains a lovely village pub.
OPEN *11.00-23.00 (Mon-Sat), 12.00-22.30 (Sun)*
FOOD *12.00-14.30 and 19.00-22.00 (Mon-Sat), 12.00-15.00 and 19.00-21.30 (Sun)*
CREDIT CARDS *Mastercard, Switch, Visa*
DRAUGHT BEERS *Young's Bitter, Young's Special, Young's Pilsner, Guinness, Scrumpy Jack, Young's seasonal ale, Carling Black Label, Stella Artois, Young's Export*
Wheelchair access to venue. Private room seats 20
NEAREST TUBE STATION *Wimbledon*

HANOVER SQUARE

25 Hanover Square, W1; 0171 408 0935
This is the sister bar to Cork and Bottle (qv); it is owned by Don Hewitson, whose name is clearly branded throughout the bar, should you be in doubt. The wine list is extensive, with descriptions written by the man himself, although it can be unwieldy if you're not a connoisseur. You have to decide the region you want first, followed by the colour. I suggested to my drinking partner of the evening that problems with the wine list might arise if you didn't agree with the Bacchus incarnate's opinions. His response was, 'Judging by the decor here you're unlikely to agree with anything he says.' He had a point. We couldn't work out what the hideous resting place was in the middle of the floor – a sort of freestanding shelf supported by champagne bottles. In any case, it didn't appear as though many of the clientele cared too much about the wines; most were drinking beers on our visit. Like Cork and Bottle, Hanover Square boasts air conditioning, but it needs turning up a few notches. Staff don't seem to like emptying ash-trays, even in quiet periods, and even when they've just served you food. It's a bar beneath the pavement, at the end of the day, and that's exactly what it feels like.
OPEN *11.00-23.00 (Mon-Sat)*
FOOD *as opening hours*
CREDIT CARDS *all major cards*
NEAREST TUBE STATION *Oxford Circus*

THE HARE AND BILLET

Hare and Billet Road, SE3; 0181 852 2352

There has been an ale house on this site under one name or another since the 17th century, which was not the best time to be out and about in Blackheath. It was just heath in those days, and rather nasty heath at that, with cut-purses lurking ready to cut your throat. The lights of the solitary old ale house must have been a welcome sight for travellers on the lonely London to Dover road. London is a mere half-hour away now, and The Hare and Billet is solitary no longer. Rumour has it that there is a ghost of a gentleman in a purple velvet suit in the cellar; maybe he was a victim of just such a cut-purse. It is one of Whitbread's Hogshead pubs and takes its beer very seriously. It has ten cask ales on draught and is gradually becoming more food-focused. Worth a visit.

OPEN *11.00-23.00 (Mon-Sat), 12.00-22.30 (Sun)*

FOOD *12.00-14.30 (Mon-Fri), 12.00-16.00 (Sat-Sun)*

CREDIT CARDS *all major cards, not AmEx*

DRAUGHT BEERS *Abroad Cooper, Adnams Southwold, Boddingtons, Flowers, London Pride, Marston's Pedigree, Young's Special, Heineken, Hoegaarden, Stella Artois, Guinness, Murphy's, Merrydown, nine real ales including guest ales changed regularly, Belgian beers*

NEAREST RAILWAY STATION *Blackheath*

THE HARE AND HOUNDS

216 Upper Richmond Road West, SW14; 0181 876 4304

The Hare and Hounds is a fine Georgian house of red brick on the Upper Richmond Road in East Sheen. Some punters were not best pleased when the faded, rather dingy charm of The Hare and Hounds was swept away in a major renovation a few years back. The newness wore off, and The Hare and Hounds has regained the comfortable, old-fashioned air we liked so much. It kept some of its best bits, anyway – the old bar, the panelling, the huge garden with its vast lawn and, most important, the full-sized snooker table. This being East Sheen, a golf society meets in the pub. They seem to appreciate the Young's ales though. The food, they say in The Hare and Hounds, is the cheapest in East Sheen. The pub has a menu that catches the essential spirit of the place – fish and chips, pie and mash, sizzling skillets. On Sundays it does a roast. Dogs are allowed in the public but not the main bar.

OPEN *11.00-23.00 (Mon-Sat), 12.00-22.30 (Sun)*

FOOD *12.00-15.00 and 17.00-21.30 (Mon-Sat), 12.00-15.00 (Sun)*

CREDIT CARDS *all major cards, not AmEx*

DRAUGHT BEERS *Young's Bitter, Young's London Lager, Young's Export, Young's Special, Young's Pilsner, Stella Artois, Carling Black Label, Guinness, Dry Blackthorn*

NEAREST RAILWAY STATION *Mortlake*

HARVEY FLOORBANGERS

1 Hammersmith Road, W14; 0171 371 4105

Harvey Floorbangers was started by one of the Slug and Lettuce founding fathers, Hugh Corbett. He sold this one to Regent Inns and very handsome it is, a substantial Victorian public house on the busy road opposite Olympia, the even more substantial Victorian exhibition hall. The pub used to be the Hand and Flower and all its days has found Olympia a most useful neighbour. A big exhibition there can double its trade. It is noted, locally, for its good ales and it sells big bold meals on 16-inch plates including scrummy burgers almost an inch thick. There's a particularly fine function room upstairs, a huge room with nine long windows. Above that there are ten rooms to let, all, as they say, *en suite*, with TV and continental breakfasts.

OPEN *11.00-23.00 (Mon-Sat), 12.00-22.30 (Sun)*

FOOD *12.00-14.30 and 18.30-21.30 (Mon-Sun)*
CREDIT CARDS *all major cards*
DRAUGHT BEERS *Bass, Brakspear, Caffrey's, Gale's IPA, Boddingtons,
Young's Special, Carling, Foster's, Holsten Export, Kronenbourg, Guinness,
Dry Blackthorn*
Wheelchair access to venue. Private room seats 120
NEAREST TUBE STATIONS *Olympia, High Street Kensington, Hammersmith*

HAVANA
490 Fulham Broadway, SW6; 0171 381 5005
Take your energy bags with you to this colourful, loud, vibrant Latin
American bar, which has helped to pump up the ever-increasing volume in
Fulham Broadway. Night after night the bar pulsates with Latin-influenced
jazz. There are DJs Tuesday and Wednesday, and live bands Thursday
through to Sunday. Every toe in the house taps away to the beat masters
of swing, salsa, jive, rumba, tango and acid jazz. There's room to dance,
and many do. Some come and dine first in the restaurant area, which
offers more than 20 appetisers and main courses, including two tapas for
£6.00 and a main course for around £10.00. Happy hour is from 6-8pm
and cocktails start at £4.25, so there are some bargains to be had. Our
man in Havana occasionally charges admission at the door: £3 after 11pm
on Thursday, £5 after 10pm Friday and Saturday. Fast, furious and fun.
OPEN *12.00-02.00 (Mon-Sat), 12.00-10.30 (Sun)*
FOOD *bar 12.00-02.00 (Mon-Sat), 12.00-10.30 (Sun); restaurant 1200-
10.30 (Mon-Sun)*
CREDIT CARDS *all major cards*
NEAREST TUBE STATION *Fulham Broadway*

HAVELOCK TAVERN
57 Masbro Road, W14; 0171 603 5374
In 1995 Peter Richnall bought a rather down-at-heel pub in West Kensington
called the Havelock Tavern. When he closed it to spruce it up, the place was
almost falling down around him. By April 1996 all had been sorted, and the
Havelock Tavern opened its doors as a well-designed, spacious bar with a
strong food focus. The Modern British menu boasts the likes of poached capon,
baked skate wing and char-grilled mushrooms (£5-£9), and the blackboard
specials display seasonal offerings and chef's favourites. The yard at the back is
decorated with trees and bedding plants. The West Ken trendies shouldn't think
of whooping it up here, though. In order to respect the peace of the neighbours,
the garden closes at 9.30pm, and they don't allow large gangs of people out
there. Wine is as popular as beer, but make sure you stuff your wallet full of
cash before you go; they don't take credit cards.
OPEN *11.00-23.00 (Mon-Sat), 12.00-22.30 (Sun)*
FOOD *12.30-14.30 and 19.00-22.00 (Mon-Sat), 12.30-15.00 and 19.00-
21.30 (Sun)*
CREDIT CARDS *none taken*
DRAUGHT BEERS *Courage Best, Courage Directors, Marston's Pedigree,
Budweiser, Foster's, Kronenbourg, Guinness, Strongbow*
Wheelchair access to venue
NEAREST TUBE STATION *Olympia, Shepherd's Bush*

THE HENRY ADDINGTON
22-28 Mackenzie Walk, E14; 0171 512 9022
Other bars and places where they sing have opened since this pub first
revealed its airy interior a few years back, and very welcome they must be
in this far flung outpost. The view from the Henry Addington is of Heron
Quays. 'It's like being on the deck of a luxury liner,' say the licensees,
Colin and Phyl Romney-Swallow, who have been in the business for more
than 30 years and pride themselves on their real ales and their food. The

pub has an airy interior, a 100-foot-long bar, and plenty of terrace seating where you can sip and enjoy the views. Henry Addington was Prime Minister from 1801 to 1804. In the course of time he became Viscount Sidmouth and gave the go-ahead for a wharf to be built on the Isle of Dogs to receive goodies from the Canary Islands. Hence Canary Wharf.
OPEN *11.00-23.00 (Mon-Fri), 11.00-17.00 (Sat), 12.00-17.00 (Sun)*
FOOD *11.00-21.00 (Mon-Fri), 11.00-16.00 (Sat), 12.00-16.00 (Sun)*
CREDIT CARDS *all major cards*
DRAUGHT BEERS *Bass, Caffrey's, London Pride, Carling Black Label, Grolsch, Staropramen, Guinness, Red Rock*
Wheelchair access to venue and loos. Private room seats 50
NEAREST RAILWAY STATION *Canary Wharf (DLR)*

THE HENRY HOLLAND
39 Duke Street, W1; 0171 629 4426
A lively bunch of shoppers and office workers gather in this pleasant old pub located down a side street opposite Selfridges. It has a good-looking bar downstairs, a fine panelled dining room upstairs, and a general air of having been built by the great 18th-century architect Henry Holland himself. Actually it was built, or anyway rebuilt, by Whitbreads in 1956. It was called The Red Lion before that.

This Henry Holland was quite a goer, but he had his setbacks. His new Drury Lane Theatre incorporated all the latest safety devices but burnt down all the same. By then, though, he had designed the first version of the Brighton Pavilion, quite a lot of Knightsbridge and – rather a stroke of luck – Southill Park in Bedfordshire for Mr Samuel Whitbread, the brewer. The present Samuel Whitbread, great-great-great-great-grandson of the founder, lives there still.
OPEN *11.00-23.00 (Mon-Sat), 13.00-21.00 (Sun)*
FOOD *12.00-15.00 (Mon-Sat)*
CREDIT CARDS *Mastercard, Switch, Visa*
DRAUGHT BEERS *Young's Special, Boddingtons, Flowers Original, Marston's Pedigree, Boston Beer, Heineken Export, Stella Artois, Guinness, Murphy's*
Wheelchair access to venue. Private room seats 36
NEAREST TUBE STATIONS *Marble Arch, Bond Street*

HENRY J BEANS
195 King's Road, SW3; 0171 352 9255
In the swinging 60s this was the swinging Six Bells. It swings today as Henry J Beans, an American vision of a London bar. It has about an acre of floor space, high pedestal tables with swivel-top stools, and wallfuls of enamelled ads, plus a vast paved garden with rows of picnic tables and benches. There's also wall-to-wall music, a video satellite system with 80 channels, and a high-speed kitchen producing burgers, hotdogs, deli sandwiches, Tex-Mex specials and French fries, for which there's a big demand. As for beers, there's Webster's and Foster's on keg, and these have to be among the most expensive keg beers around. They don't serve pints; halves or two-pint pitchers are what people drink, and they do a happy hour reduction which brings the prices into the realms of acceptibility. The big thing here is bottled beers, though – beers at the bar, beers out of vending machines – and many a cocktail. It always seems to be packed with young people who like their music loud. A party atmosphere prevails at the weekend, and the tuxedo-clad Rotweillers try to keep order at the door. Henry J Beans is a My Kinda Town venue now owned by the Capital Radio group.
OPEN *11.45-23.00 (Mon-Sat), 12.00-22.30 (Sun)*
FOOD *11.45-22.30 (Mon-Sat), 12.00-22.00 (Sun)*
CREDIT CARDS *all major cards*
DRAUGHT BEERS *Webster's, Foster's*
NEAREST TUBE STATION *Sloane Square*

THE HEREFORD ARMS

127 Gloucester Road, SW7; 0171 370 4988

This low William and Mary building got a bit of a spruce-up last year and is looking much the better for its new sunny exterior. Its sweep of tinted yellow windows the full length of the bar creates a sepia glow over the dim interior. The effect is deliberate, comparatively recent, and seems to work. The barmen are friendly and uniformed, the music is quiet and the food traditional and filling. One part is reserved for waitress service, though you can eat anywhere, and there are half a dozen picnic tables outside. This is a very popular, up-market pub. Rumour has it that Jack the Ripper drank here. During the war, American servicemen who played baseball in Hereford Square took a great shine to The Hereford Arms. The outstanding bill for broken windows has yet to be settled.

OPEN *11.00-23.00 (Mon-Sat), 12.00-22.30 (Sun)*

FOOD *12.00-22.00 (Mon-Sun), 12.00-21.30 (Sun)*

CREDIT CARDS *all major cards*

DRAUGHT BEERS *Courage Directors, Courage Best, Theakston Best, Kronenbourg, Beck's, Foster's, Guinness, Strongbow, one guest ale changed weekly*

NEAREST TUBE STATION *Gloucester RoadThe Hereford Arms*

HILLGATE ARMS

24 Hillgate Street, W8; 0171 727 8543

'Small but perfectly formed,' says a colleague of mine, regarding this very pleasant pub in a quiet backwater off Notting Hill. There is just room for tables and small benches along one outside wall, and it's hard enough getting a seat at any time, let alone when the sun comes out. The Hillgate Arms has luxuriant window boxes, hanging baskets and tubs, plus a cosy little restaurant at the back with very popular home cooking.

OPEN *11.00-23.00 (Mon-Sat), 12.00-22.30 (Sun)*

FOOD *bar 12.00-21.30 (Mon-Sat); restaurant (carvery) 12.00-14.45 (Mon-Sat), 12.00-14.45 (Sun lunch)*

CREDIT CARDS *all major cards, not AmEx*

DRAUGHT BEERS *Wadworth 6X, Webster's Yorkshire, Budweiser, Carlsberg, Foster's, Holsten, Guinness, Strongbow, Marston's Pedigree, Tetley's, Charles Wells Bombardier*

Wheelchair access to venue and loos. Private room: 20 seated, 40 standing

NEAREST TUBE STATION *Notting Hill Gate*

THE HOBGOBLIN

95 Effra Road, SW2; 0171 501 9671

The locals still call this substantial old pub The George Canning, which it was for 100 years or so but it is The Hobgoblin now. What would the serious-minded Mr Canning have made of that? In its later days The George Canning had become known for its country and western and funky Saturday nights, an unexpected fate for a pub named after a Prime Minister so sound on the corn laws, but would he have liked it any more now? It remains a popular venue with exceptional variety, techno, rap, and latin but occasional tap-dancing too and classical guitar and stand-up comedy every week. Prime Ministers rarely like stand-up comedy. The weekend discos remain a big hit. The old carpark of George Canning days is now a large beer garden from where you can drink the Wychwood real ales and watch the cars go by.

OPEN *midday-midnight (Mon-Sat), midday-23.00 (Sun)*

FOOD *midday-15.00 and 20.00-late (Mon-Sat), seasonal barbecues (Sat/Sun)*

CREDIT CARDS *none taken*

DRAUGHT BEERS *Courage Directors, Wychwood Special, Foster's, Kronenbourg, Guinness, Strongbow, Stella Artois*

Wheelchair access to venue. Private room: 150 seated, 300 standing

NEAREST TUBE STATION *Brixton*

HOGSHEADS

When the gloomy people complain about the branding or theming of pubs, they conveniently forget about this excellent chain from the House of Whitbread. Unfortunately for me, and ultimately you, this brewery giant doesn't like to talk about them. What I can tell you is that they are, for the most part, excellent venues and possibly the most important additions to the drinking scene in London. Excellent food is complemented by an enormous range of real ales in environments that are safe, comfortable and inviting. If there is one near you, I recommend you use it.

Branches at:

W1 GRAFTON ARMS 72 Grafton Way, W1; 0171 387 7923
  NEAREST TUBE STATION *Warren Street*

EPSOM ALBION 134 High Street, Epsom; 01372 744240

SOHO BLUE POSTS 28 Rupert Street, Soho, W1; 0171 437 1415

KINGSTON UPON THAMES DRUIDS HEAD Kingston Market, Kingston upon Thames; 0181 546 0723

WIMBLEDON HAND & RACKET 25-28 Wimbledon Hill Road, SW19; 0181 947 9391

SE3 HARE AND BILLET 1A Elliot Cottages, SE3; 0181 852 2352

CITY (EC3) 1 America Square, EC3; 0171 702 2381

CAMDEN 55 Parkway, Camden, NW1; 0171 284 1675

W4 30-34 High Road, W4; 0181 742 0021

WC2 23 Wellington Street, WC2; 0171 386 6930

CROUCH END 33-35 Crouch End Hill, N8; 0181 342 8465

CROYDON 60 High Street, Croydon; 0181 667 0684

EALING BROADWAY 46-47 The Mall, Ealing Broadway, W6; 0181 566 1417

CITY (EC3) 18 Fish Street Hill, Monument, EC3; 0171 929 5580

N1 77-78 Upper Street, N1; 0171 354 4367

SE13 344 High Street, SE13; 0181 690 2054

MAYFAIR 11 Dering Street, Mayfair, W1; 0171 629 0531

STREATHAM 68-70 Streatham High Road, SW16; 0181 696 7587

SURBITON 64-65 Victoria Road, Surbiton; 0181 399 4705

SUTTON 60-62 The High Street, Sutton; 0181 661 7430

TWICKENHAM 33-35 York Street, Twickenham; 0181 891 3940

SE1 OLD FATHER THAMES Albert Embankment, SE1; 0171 735 7004
  NEAREST TUBE STATION *Vauxhall*

CITY (EC4) OLD KING LUD 78 Ludgate Hill, EC4; 0171 329 8517
  NEAREST TUBE STATIONS *St. Paul's, Blackfriars*

CITY (EC1) ST PAULS TAVERN 53-56 Chiswell Street, EC1; 0171 606 3828
  NEAREST TUBE STATION *Barbican*

THE HOLLY BUSH

22 Holly Mount, NW3; 0171 435 2892

A long flight of steps up the hill from Heath Street and you reach one of Hampstead's oldest and most picturesque pubs. When it was built in 1643 it stood high and proud on its hill with wonderful views. Now the houses and cottages of old Hampstead crowd round it, no bad thing for a village pub like this one. Apart from that it has changed less than anyone could have expected. Well, it had seven bars in Victorian times but they must have been exceptionally small. There are four now, including one that used to be the landlord's living room. But the general look of the place can't have been much different in the days they hung a green branch over the door to announce that the beer was ready. The bare boards, the wood and plaster walls, the old wooden furniture are as they were, everything dark brown and nicotine. This is the effect that modern pub designers go for. The Holly Bush has always been like that.

Dr Johnson and Boswell both drank here. They must have caused a stir but nothing to the one made by Romney. In 1796 he gave up his grand house in Cavendish Square and bought a house behind the pub. He pulled down the stables, built a gallery for his pictures, enclosed half the garden for a riding house, got very miserable and went back to his wife in Kendal. Peace returned to The Holly Bush.

OPEN *midday-15.00 and 17.30-23.00 (Mon-Fri), midday-23.00 (Sat), midday-22.30 (Sun)*

FOOD *12.30-14.00 and 19.30-21.00 (Mon-Sat), 13.30-15.00 (Sun)*

CREDIT CARDS *none taken*

DRAUGHT BEERS *Benskins, Tetley's, Carlsberg Export, Castlemaine XXXX, Stella Artois, Carlsberg, Calder's Cream Ale, Guinness, Dry Blackthorn, two weekly guest ales*

NEAREST TUBE STATION *Hampstead*

HOLLYWOOD ARMS

Hollywood Road, SW10; 0171 349 9274

There must have been times in the last hundred years when this high-Victorian local would have exchanged its neo-Gothic arched windows for a little more passing trade. Life is not always easy so far from the Fulham Road. Happily, good little restaurants have opened on every side and The Hollywood Arms has now become a popular meeting place for young Chelsea.

The Hollywood Arms has a favourite historical figure, not one you may have come across. Jean-Pierre Blanchard, balloonist. In 1784 he took off from the field where the pub now stands and became the first man to cross the English Channel by air. So he and his balloon are on the pub sign and there are lots of pictures of hot air balloons inside.

The pub used to have day trips known as Hollywood Outings, but they have not survived. Possibly the name led to disappointments. There's a nice beer garden at the back with wooden picnic tables, much enjoyed by families in the summer. In the bar computer games and gambling machines compete with Sky Sports all the year round.

OPEN *11.00-23.00 (Mon-Sat), midday-22.30 (Sun)*

FOOD *midday-22.00 (Mon-Sun)*

CREDIT CARDS *Mastercard, Visa*

DRAUGHT BEERS *Courage Directors, John Smith's Extra Smooth, Theakston Best, Beck's, Foster's, Kronenbourg, Beamish, Strongbow*

Wheelchair access to venue. Private room: 60 seated, 100 standing

NEAREST TUBE STATION *Earls Court, South Kensington*

THE HOOP AND GRAPES

47 Aldgate High Street, EC3; 0171 480 5739

A remarkable thing happened to The Hoop and Grapes in 1666. It was NOT burned down in the Great Fire of London. It escaped by 50 yards and there it still is, the only surviving 17th-century timber-framed building in the City of London. Everyone used brick after the fire.

Until quite recently The Hoop and Grapes leaned, creaked, sloped to the east. Everyone liked it but it was getting a bit alarming, so the brewers spent more than one million pounds virtually rebuilding it. The two courtyards of its coaching inn days are are now part of the main bar, which is huge, all exposed timbers and brick with eating areas, drinking areas, standing-room-only chatting areas. It looks very old. Well it is very old and it has never been so popular. It is shoulder-to-shoulder time in all parts every lunchtime, and, totally underpinned, its old frame supported by steel, it is good for another 300 years.

OPEN *11.00-22.00 (Mon-Wed), 11.00-23.00 (Thurs-Sat)*

FOOD *midday-15.00 and 17.30-21.00 (Mon-Fri)*

CREDIT CARDS *all major cards*

DRAUGHT BEERS Adnams, Bass, Caffrey's, Hancock's HB, London Pride, Carling Black Label, Grolsch, Staropramen, Guinness, Cidermaster
NEAREST TUBE STATION Aldgate

THE HOPE

15 Tottenham Street, W1; 0171 637 0896

Big notices outside and in this busy little Whitbread pub announce that this is a Sausage and Ale House. The sausages certainly rule okay every lunchtime, a choice of 15 very different bangers supplied by the ingenious Simply Sausages. There's the Kentish hop sausage, for instance, made with pork, fuggles hops and porter, John Nott's sausage made from a 1720 recipe involving spinach, a beef and Guinness sausage, a Creole sausage from the States and four for vegetarians. Glamorgan sausage turns out to be made of Caerphilly and leeks. These, dished up with mash and baked beans and now reinforced with 13 different mustards, fill the little dining room upstairs from noon to 2.30pm and in the evening it returns to its role as second bar and function room. The Hope has a very lively landlord in Roger Fonseca from Portugal. The sausages were his idea. He thinks highly of this British delicacy. 'They are cheap and they fill you up,' he says. As for the ale, you get a choice of ten, eight on the handpumps and two served direct from barrels behind the bar.

OPEN 11.00-23.00 (Mon-Sat), midday-22.30 (Sun)
FOOD midday-14.30 (Mon-Fri)
CREDIT CARDS all major cards, not AmEx or Diners
DRAUGHT BEERS Boddingtons, Flowers Original, Marston's Pedigree, Wadworth 6X, Heineken, Heineken Export, Stella Artois, Guinness, Murphy's, Strongbow, Hoegaarden, plus four guest ales
Wheelchair access to venue. Private room: 24 seated, 40-50 standing
NEAREST TUBE STATION Goodge Street

HOPE AND ANCHOR

207 Upper Street, N1; 0171 354 1312

This big Victorian pub on the corner of Upper Street had more than its 15 minutes of fame in the late-70s. It became nationally famous as the leading venue of punk rock, the shock-horror sensation of the day. Just about anyone who was anyone played here. The Clash, The Damned, The Stranglers. The Sex Pistols were here twice. Live at The Hope and Anchor L.P.'s were brought out to prove it. They are great documents of the rough-and-ready quality of the bands and the crowds who came along to cheer them. It all became too much for the neighbours and the Environmental Health Authority closed the music room down and the pub was squatted. By punks, naturally. They moved on after a while and the pub reopened, but it was not until this year that the council finally relented and granted another music licence. So, great news, live music can once again be enjoyed at The Hope and Anchor. The music room downstairs has had plenty of money spent on it. It looks good, the sound system is very loud, and six nights a week you can watch indie and rock bands playing until midnight. When they really get going the floorboards in the room above vibrate. There is a big split-level bar on the ground floor with a modicum of charm, and on the first floor is a pool room with three tables and a rough-and-ready finish reminiscent of the old days when the bands could only play two chords and bin liners held together with safety pins were the height of fashion.

OPEN midday-23.00 (Mon-Sat), midday-22.30 (Sun); music room 21.00-midnight (Mon-Thurs), 21.00-01.00 (Fri-Sat)
FOOD midday-15.00 and 17.30-20.30 (Mon-Fri)
CREDIT CARDS none taken
DRAUGHT BEERS Abbot Ale, Greene King IPA, Carling Black Label, Kronenbourg, Stella Artois, Guinness, Strongbow
NEAREST TUBE STATION Highbury & Islington

THE HOP POLES

17 King Street, W6; 0181 748 1411

What impresses you most about this Victorian pub is its size. It is enormous. Those Victorians must have drunk a lot. Filling it seems to have been a problem of late. Way back in 1986 brewery, tenant and council agreed that the best thing to do was pull it down and build a new town on the site. Instead they closed it for six months and spent £400,000 on putting the old building right. They saved all the listed bits – elaborate front, handsome ceilings, etched mirrors – put a new roof on and got Mrs Holloway, a one time hop-picker, to reopen it. She was 96 at the time and very chipper.

It became clear to someone that what The Hop Poles needed was a REALLY big bar so in 1995 Scottish and Newcastle spent another £400,000 on it, knocking all the bars through on the ground floor. When it reopened customers found that if they took the afternoon off they could walk all the way round the vast island counter.

There used to be several hop poles on show at The Hop Poles, also bunches of hops above the bar, but they have gone now. I'm pleased to see that Mrs Holloway's picture is still on the wall.

OPEN *10.00-23.00 (Mon-Sat), midday-22.30 (Sun)*
FOOD *10.00-22.45 (Mon-Sat), midday-22.15 (Sun)*
CREDIT CARDS *Visa, Mastercard, Connect*
DRAUGHT BEERS *Greene King IPA, John Smith's Extra Smooth, Theakston Best, Foster's, Holsten, Kronenbourg, Miller, Guinness, Strongbow, Pilsner, Directors*
Wheelchair access to venue and loos. Private room seats 100
NEAREST TUBE STATION *Hammersmith, Piccadilly*

HORNIMAN AT HAY'S

Hay's Galleria, Tooley Street, SE1; 0171 407 3611

Hay's Galleria with its soaring atrium, its shops and galleries and cafés is a great place for a pub. *HMS Belfast* lies romantically off shore, Tower Bridge with its extraordinary power to cheer you up is just down river, and if you have been doing the riverbank walk you will be in need of a drink at just this point. You will be pleased, then, to find Horniman's waiting, expansive, confident and glossy, the long polished mahogany counter with its choice of five real ales, not to mention all the lagers, turning into a tea bar that also sells coffee and chilled milk. Then there's the big wide-open café, good fast food with children welcome, special portions, special prices. Part of the gallery upstairs is kept busy with private functions and there's a no-smoking bit somewhere. The Horniman in question was Mr F. J. Horniman, the Victorian tea importer and this used to be the wharf where his tea was landed. He seems to have been a charismatic character, a great traveller and collector. You can see his collections at the Horniman Museum in Forest Hill where he lived, and now there is this pub on his quay with lots of reminders of his life's work and the set of clocks from his office showing the time in foreign parts.The pub is 12 years old now, the style Victorian. This is the style, we are told, that beer drinkers prefer above all others.

OPEN *10.00-23.00 (Mon-Fri), 11.00-18.00 (Sat), midday-18.00 (Sun)*
FOOD *midday-15.00 (Mon-Sun)*
CREDIT CARDS *AmEx, Mastercard, Switch, Visa*
DRAUGHT BEERS *Adnams, Brakspear, Calder's Cream Ale, Marston's Pedigree, Old Speckled Hen, Tetley's, Carlsberg, Carlsberg Export, Castlemaine XXXX, Stella Artois, Guinness, Dry Blackthorn*
Wheelchair access to venue. Two private rooms: 60 and 70 seated
NEAREST TUBE STATION *London Bridge*

THE HORSE AND GROOM
68 Heath Street, NW3; 0171 435 3140

The original Horse and Groom seems to have been just the sort of old pub we now most admire. It was an 18th century tavern, the kind of old inn we put on Christmas cards but it must have seemed very rural to the newly fashionable Hampstead. So in 1899 Young's replaced it with something bang up to date. This was it, an imposing five-storey public house with a modish striped brick and stone façade and a high decorated gable, the height of late-Victorian taste. It was then the tallest building in Heath Street. It still is. The rich Victorian interior has been largely dismantled over the years but bits of it remain. Today there is one long open room. The front half is where the counter is, the back half where most of the tables are.

It is a friendly local with pleasant girls who bring your lunch to your table and chat to regulars spending happy, ruminative afternoons on their bar stools. It remains a genuinely Victorian pub. Convincing replicas of Charles I's death warrant and the Act of Union, 1707, are to be found tucked behind a gaming machine.

OPEN *midday-23.00 (Mon-Sat), midday-22.30 (Sun)*
FOOD *midday-16.00 (Mon-Sun)*
CREDIT CARDS *none taken*
DRAUGHT BEERS *Young's Bitter, Young's Special, Castlemaine XXXX, Young's Pilsner, Young's Export, Guinness, Dry Blackthorn*
Wheelchair access to venue. Private room: 30 seated, 70 standing
NEAREST TUBE STATION *Hampstead*

THE HOUSE THEY LEFT BEHIND
27 Ropemaker's Fields, E14; 0171 538 5102

Looking at Limehouse now it is hard to imagine it as it used to be – the boatyards, the docks, the maze of tenements. One day in 1871 Alexander II, Tsar of Russia, visited a ropeworks here. Could this have been in Ropemaker's Fields where, at No. 27, The Black Horse stood?

The Black Horse was a small inner-city pub built in 1856, part of a terrace in the heart of this teeming bit of the East End. It is still there but there is nothing else left of Ropemaker's Fields, not a single house, just this solitary pub. It is now called The House They Left Behind.

For years, public works went on all around the solitary House They Left Behind, a long trial by noise, mess and dust, but the crystal starts to clear. The dump at one side is a park now and the empty space at the front door is a piazza with benches, young trees and a sculpture of a seagull on a coil of rope. People play boules there all summer. The pub itself has new owners and new managers. It has been painted up and refurbished and, most important of all, a development of 11 flats has brought new neighbours at last. Not that they didn't have neighbours. Beyond the new piazza you see the tall terraced houses of Narrow Street, where David Owen is famously in residence.

OPEN *midday-23.00 (Mon-Sat) midday-22.30 (Sun)*
FOOD *midday-21.00 (Mon-Sun)*
CREDIT CARDS *none taken*
DRAUGHT BEERS *Worthington Bitter, Caffrey's Smooth, Carling, Bass Traditional, Grolsch, Staropramen, Guinness, Hancock's HB*
Wheelchair access to venue
NEAREST RAILWAY STATION *Westferry (DLR)*

HUNG, DRAWN AND QUARTERED
26-27 Great Tower Street, EC3; 0171 626 6123

Yes, I know it should be Hanged, Drawn and Quartered, so don't write to me, write to Fuller's, who insist that this is the common usage. Common it may be, but if you look on the outside of this building, I think you might find the answer – there isn't enough room for the word Hanged. This pub was opened in 1996 as a result of yet another conversion from a bank. For those who stray towards Tower Bridge after work, it is now a single-roomed banking hall with a bar in it and, like a bank, just a few places to sit down. Very creditable.

OPEN *11.00-22.00 (Mon-Tues), 11.00-23.00 (Wed-Fri) 12.00-15.30 (Sat)*
FOOD *12.00-15.00 (Mon-Fri), 12.00-14.30 (Sat)*
CREDIT CARDS *all major cards*
DRAUGHT BEERS *Chiswick Bitter, ESB, London Pride, Carling Black Label, Grolsch, Heineken, Stella Artois, Guinness, Murphy's, Scrumpy Jack, a guest ale*
Wheelchair access to venue and loo
NEAREST TUBE STATIONS *Monument, Tower Gateway (DLR)*

THE IMPERIAL

5 Leicester Street, WC2; 0171 437 6573
Leicester Street takes you from the hoopla of Leicester Square to the Chinese restaurants of Lisle Street, and half way up you find this lively West End local, much invigorated by the £150,000 that Scottish and Newcastle recently spent on it. Among other things it got a new kitchen so it opens for breakfast at 8am now. You have to wait till 11am for a drink, of course. Lots do. The street is pedestrianised now like the square itself, and the cluster of small tables outside is an oasis on a fine day. Queen Victoria, at her most grandmotherly, gazes down as the new juke box gets the old pub rocking.

OPEN *11.00-23.00 (Mon-Sat), midday-22.30 (Sun)*
FOOD *all day*
CREDIT CARDS *all major cards*
DRAUGHT BEERS *Theakston XB, Theakston Best, Courage Best, Directors, Guinness, Scrumpy Jack*
Wheelchair access to venue, not to loos
NEAREST TUBE STATIONS *Piccadilly or Leicester Square*

THE INTREPID FOX

99 Wardour Street, W1; 0171 287 8359
Like Soho itself The Intrepid Fox is old and battered and has seen a thing or two. In its young days its passion was politics, the Whig leader Charles James Fox its hero. It is he who is the Intrepid Fox, he the stout party in the beaver hat on the pub-sign. In the 1784 election there was free beer for anyone who would vote for him, and a bas-relief on the outside wall showing Fox waving a banner saying 'Champion of the People' is still there. The old pub has hit some rough patches along the way since then but it has new heroes today. It is now a leading rock, alternative and indie pub, so popular that you sometimes have to queue to get in. It is black leather jackets, pony tails and half-shaved heads in the big downstairs bar these days and the walls are covered with icons of more recent champions of the people – Jimi Hendrix, the Rolling Stones, The Who. They too have been overtaken by a whole new generation of intrepid foxes whose music plays all day, getting louder, ever louder – Oasis and Black Grape, Green Day and Offspring, Prodigy, Terrorvision, Rancid, Jane's Addiction, White Zombie, Beastie Boys...They don't do food now at the Intrepid Fox. This is not music you eat to.

OPEN *midday-23.00 (Mon-Sat), 15.00-22.30 (Sun)*
CREDIT CARDS *none taken*
DRAUGHT BEERS *Abbot Ale, Old Speckled Hen, Carlsberg Export, Carlsberg, Stella Artois, Guinness, Cidermaster, Murphy's*
NEAREST TUBE STATION *Piccadilly Circus*

THE ISLAND QUEEN

87 Noel Road, N1; 0171 359 4037

Life-sized wooden puppets of pirates hang from the ceiling over the horseshoe bar in this agreeably eccentric Islington local. One climbs a net, two fight, one lights a cannon. Bare floorboards, ceiling-high Victorian mirrors, a small pool room at the back – people who drink there like it just as it is. For years the original juke box played the magic music of the Sixties, thus ensuring a clientele of discrimination and allure. Alas, it became unwell and was pronounced beyond repair. A modern all-singing CD version took its place. Island Queen regulars reluctantly concede that it keeps true to the music but enough is enough. The thirtysomethings, says manager Garth Foster, would turn in their ashtrays if modernisation went one step further. There is a nice restaurant upstairs.

OPEN *midday-15.00 and 17.30-23.00 (Mon-Thurs), 11.00-23.00 (Fri), midday-23.00 (Sat), midday-22.30 (Sun)*

FOOD *bar 12.20-14.30 (Mon-Fri); restaurant 18.00-midnight (Fri-Sat), midday-16.00 (Sun)*

CREDIT CARDS *Mastercard, Visa*

DRAUGHT BEERS *Bass, Caffrey's, London Pride, Carling Black Label, Grolsch, Guinness, Dry Blackthorn*

Private room: 50 seated, 100 standing

NEAREST TUBE STATION *Angel*

JACK HORNER

236 Tottenham Court Road, W1; 0171 636 2868

Fuller's press on with their admirable campaign to change all of London's banks into pubs. In the living memory of anyone born in 1994 this was a branch of Martins'. It is now a useful new pub called the Jack Horner named after Little Jack Horner, one of the great heroes of English Literature. Horner's is a moving story. He was sitting in his corner eating his Christmas pie when, in a dramatic scene, he stuck in his thumb and pulled out a plum. 'What a good boy am I' he said. I see Robbie Coltraine in the part. You get a very nice pie in the Jack Horner, this being one of Fuller's Ale and Pie Pubs but it does get very busy. I put this down to the choice of opener, me actually. I made a speech, pulled the first pint and haven't been able to reach the bar since.

OPEN *11.00-23.00 (Mon-Sat)*

FOOD *11.00-20.00 (Mon-Sat)*

CREDIT CARDS *all major cards*

DRAUGHT BEERS *Chiswick Bitter, ESB, London Pride, Carling Black Label, Grolsch, Heineken, Stella Artois, Guinness, Scrumpy Jack, one seasonal ale and one guest ale*

Wheelchair access to venue and loos

NEAREST TUBE STATIONS *Warren Street, Goodge Street, Tottenham Court Road*

JACK STRAW'S CASTLE

North End Way, NW3; 0171 435 8885

This famous old coaching inn has a swashbuckling past and quite a showy present. Its past first though.... Jack Straw was Wat Tyler's right-hand man, a fiery leader of the Peasant's Revolt. He burned down the priory in Clerkenwell, addressed the peasants from a hay waggon on Hampstead Heath and hid in the inn. He was caught there and executed outside the front door.

The old inn was known as Jack Straw's Castle after that and kept the name when it was replaced by a coaching inn in 1721 after which it was all coaches arriving and coaches leaving and horses to water and travellers to feed and bustle and drama. Meanwhile Hampstead got fashionable and Jack Straw's Castle was discovered by literary London. Wilkie Collins started riding over and Thackeray and Dickens (of course), after which nothing much happened until the Second World War when it was banged about by a landmine. It was rebuilt in the early 1960s. A leading architect, Raymond C. Erith, was engaged and London got a spectacular new pub. Georgian-Gothic, said Mr Erith. Grounded Mississippi showboat, said the *Evening Standard*. It was three storeys high with a long weatherboard frontage, a parade of bay windows, arched Gothic windows from end to end and battlements on top. It got another major going-over in 1993. Just painting the weatherboarding cream and white took three men six weeks, but it is looking very spruce now as do the refurbished bars, function rooms and à la carte restaurant. There's lots going on. There are coach-loads of tour groups, lots of wedding receptions, a barbecue most summer evenings in the big courtyard at the back, a pleasant place with brick paving and cobbles, a tree with a tree seat and lots of wooden tables and benches. The first floor is private parties and the top floor is the restaurant. Jack Straw's Castle occupies one of the highest points in London and the restaurant has fine views over the Heath. If he had got a good table, Jack Straw would have seen them coming.

OPEN *11.00-23.00 (Mon-Sat), midday-22.30 (Sun)*
FOOD *bar midday-15.00 (Mon-Sun)*
CREDIT CARDS *all major cards*
DRAUGHT BEERS *Caffrey's, London Pride, Carling Black Label, Grolsch, Guinness, Dry Blackthorn, Worthington*
Wheelchair access to venue. Private rooms – two with own bars
NEAREST TUBE STATION *Hampstead*

JACOMOS

88-89 Cowcross Street, EC1; 0171 553 7641
Is this London's only lesbian bar? I am told so. I don't understand why there aren't more of them. Puts a new slant on the female-friendly label bars are trying to push, but more power to its elbow. I peeked in, and there wasn't a single dungaree or donkey jacket in sight.

OPEN *midday-23.00 (Mon-Fri), 18.00-23.00 (Sat), 17.00-22.30 (Sun) (Mon-Thurs and Friday lunchtime males allowed as guests, Friday evening, Saturday and Sunday no males allowed)*
FOOD *as opening hours*
CREDIT CARDS *all major cards, not AmEx*
DRAUGHT BEERS *Caffrey's, Grolsch, Red Rock Cider*
Wheelchair access to venue and loos
NEAREST TUBE STATION *Farringdon*

JACS

48 Lonsdale Road, W11; 0171 792 2838
Jacs's sign hangs in aged, cut-out metal outside this 1930s stone-fronted building close to the Portobello Road and the trendy, well-established drinking dens Beach Blanket Babylon and the Walmer Castle (qqv) on Ledbury Road. You enter through a series of double doors, first wooden then brass, with a tiny porthole window. You need to pause for a moment to absorb the extraordinary decor, which has such an impact on the eye it almost steals your breath. The wall on the left is painted deep red, and softly lit recesses display *objets d'art*. Walk past the large, circular island bar – note the aquarium, and two more, one on each side of the entrance to the back room, which is also painted deep red and has a massive skylight. Back in the main bar, the opposite wall has pictures interspersed with what looks like a series of book shelves. These are actually *trompe-l'oeils*. You are now at the front of the candlelit bar, with its velvet-draped armchairs, couches and wooden armchairs, and massive old wooden table. This is where you sit to watch the fractal video sequences on the large screen next to the VJ booth. Rising above you, almost cathedral-like, is a striking and effective mirrored gallery.

Jacs is beauty by design, an eclectic blend, visually stimulating. There is almost too much to look at, and I hope that this doesn't become its downfall. The music seems to be a mix of everything, but it returns to the R & B theme after a few excursions into the surreal. It attracts a quite varied, unpretentious Notting Hill crowd, but if the word gets out quick enough, this could be spoilt by the masses from other parts of town who find it trendy to hang out in alternative, ethnic bars. The air conditioning could do with a little help, and there was a poor choice in the white wine range – two to be exact.

OPEN 18.00-23.00 (Mon-Sat), 19.00-22.30 (Sun)
CREDIT CARDS all major cards, not AmEx or Diners
DRAUGHT BEERS John Smith's Extra Smooth, Foster's, Kronenbourg, Scrumpy Jack
Wheelchair access to venue. Private room holds 60 standing
NEAREST TUBE STATIONS Ladbroke Grove, Notting Hill Gate

JIMMIES WINE BAR

18 Kensington Church Street, W8; 0171 937 9988
Bare boards, wooden tables and church pews: you don't get pampered in this archetypal 70s-style wine bar. *Evening Standard* reporters know it well – this is where they have their farewell binges when they leave. There's live music most nights and anyone going in nightly has very catholic tastes: indie on Tuesdays, Brit-pop Wednesdays, blues Thursdays, acoustic funk Fridays and jazz Saturdays. Sundays are for recovering, so Jimmies doesn't bother opening.

OPEN 12.00-23.00 (Mon), 12.00-01.00 (Tues-Sat)
FOOD 12.00-22.30 (Mon-Sat)
CREDIT CARDS all major cards
NEAREST TUBE STATION High Street Kensington

JJ'S

105-109 The Broadway, SW19; 0181 540 8339
If you've ever been to the Wimbledon Theatre, you'll no doubt be familiar with this bar. Small and intimate, and covered with theatre posters, it is a good way from the top of Wimbledon Hill both in terms of geography and prices. Bottled beers start at £2.10, draughts at £1.80 and wines at £6.95. If you're going to the theatre, it's worth knowing that they cut 40p off the price of a pint between 5pm and 7pm. Don't expect to eat in the evenings, though; food is currently served only at lunchtimes. Main courses start at £4 and include an interesting range of stir-fries, omelettes, salads and pies with mashed potato.

OPEN 11.00-23.00 (Mon-Fri), 16.30-23.00 (Sat), 18.00-22.30 (Sun)
FOOD 11.30-15.30 (Mon-Fri), 12.00-15.00 (Sat)
CREDIT CARDS all major cards
DRAUGHT BEERS Young's, Young's Original, Young's Ramrod Smooth, Young's Special, Fuller's, London Pride, Castlemaine XXXX, Carling Black Label, Stella Artois, Young's Pilsner, Guinness, Dry Blackthorn
NEAREST TUBE STATION South Wimbledon
NEAREST RAILWAY STATION Wimbledon

JOE'S WINE BAR AND RESTAURANT

33 Lavender Hill, SW11; 0171 228 2960
Joe's is a place for wine-drinkers. Spirits are not served, and bottled beers are available as support rather than playing the leading role. The Ashby family, who own Joe's, are dedicated wine professionals, and that's the whole point of the place. The decor is simple and comfortable, with exposed brick walls and an unfussy seating arrangement. The menu, which changes every couple of weeks, is reassuringly short. I have been reliably informed that the food is rather good and house wines are reasonably priced.

OPEN *18.00-23.00 (Tues-Sat), 12.00-22.30 (Sun)*
FOOD *as opening hours*
CREDIT CARDS *all major cards*
Wheelchair access to venue
NEAREST RAILWAY STATION *Clapham Junction*

JOHN KEATS AT MOORGATE
83 Moorgate, EC2; 0171 606 4731

In 1795 John Keats was born here. The pub has changed beyond
recognition, but never mind, his father was its chief ostler and somewhere
in this building John Keats was born. This explains the unfamiliar new
name, the inn-sign, the portraits inside, the framed manuscripts and the
snatches of his poetry painted on the walls: 'I met a lady in the meads, Full
beautiful – a fairy's child...' In those days the pub was called the Swan
and Hoop. By the 1830s it had become the Moorgate Coffee House and
then it settled down for long years as the Moorgate. Now it is John Keats
at the Moorgate. All this chopping and changing! What hasn't changed
is that for all its long life it has lived flank to flank with a bigger, noisier
pub, The Globe Tavern. It still does. Today Bass owns them both and they
operate under a single licence. All the same, the John Keats at Moorgate
does its best to hold on to a separate identity. It shares a manager and a
cellar, it has even lost its separate street number, but it has its own restaurant
and kitchen, its own regulars, its own personality. No music for instance.
Conversation instead.

It gets frequent reminders of its position though. When the two pubs got
their shared licence in 1990 an interior door was inserted between them.
It is constantly in use and whenever anyone opens it you get a short sharp
blast of noise from its more assertive next door neighbour.

OPEN *11.00-23.00 (Mon-Fri) Closed Sat & Sun*
FOOD *bar midday-20.00 (Mon-Fri); restaurant midday-15.00 (Mon-Fri)*
CREDIT CARDS *all major cards*
DRAUGHT BEERS *Bass, Caffrey's, London Pride, Carling Black Label, Carling
Premier, Grolsch, Guinness, Red Rock*
Wheelchair access to venue
NEAREST TUBE STATION *Moorgate*

K BAR
84-86 Wardour Street, W1; 0171 439 4393

Bouncers, or door whores as they are commonly referred to, are the
welcome mat of any institution and you can usually suss out the style of the
venue by the cut of their jib. Skeletal clipboard girls guard the aspirational
joints, smartly dressed good-looking guys guide you into the fashionable
joints, and tuxedo-clad thuggish brutes push you around in the tacky venues.
K Bar belongs to the latter, which comes as some surprise because when
it burst on to the scene a couple of months ago it was widely reported as
being one of the most exclusive members' bars in town, with membership
'by invitation only'. The owners, Piers Adam and his cronies, issue the
invites to mates and they in turn can nominate their mates. Well, even rents
in Soho have to be paid, and it now appears that things have changed to
the extent that even if we're not friends of Piers we can apply to the bar for
membership. How exciting. They won't specify the criteria for acceptance
but I reckon if you're the sort of person who likes holidaying in Ibiza,
you're in. Non-members can go with a member but late-night admission
charges range from £5 to a staggering £10 at weekends. It's a fairly big
venue with none of the intimacies of a decent members' bar and the food,
which I couldn't bring myself to try, is provided by Spiga, the restaurant
above. I hear tell that the K concept is to be rolled out throughout the
country so I suspect that the people of Kettering, Kidderminster and
Keighley can barely contain themselves.

OPEN: *20.00-02.00 (Tues-Wed), 20.00-03.00 (Thurs-Fri), 21.00-03.00 (Sat)*
FOOD *same as opening times*
CREDIT CARDS *all major cards*
Available for private hire for up to 500 people
NEAREST TUBE STATIONS *Leicester Square, Picadilly Circus*

KEMIA BAR AT MOMO

25 Heddon Street, W1; 0171 434 4040
A truly beautiful re-creation of a Bedouin tent with all the furnishings brought in from Morocco. It is tremendously popular but the small basement limits the number of people they can allow in. Membership is free but by invitation only. You could try begging but your bowl will likely be tossed aside by the clip-board on the door. Bribery is the only other thing I can think of.
OPEN *19.00-01.00 (Mon-Sun)*
FOOD *as opening hours*
CREDIT CARDS *all major cards*
NEAREST TUBE STATION *Piccadilly Circus*

KETTNER'S CHAMPAGNE BAR

29 Romilly Street, W1; 0171 437 6437
The champagne bar at Kettner's is an elegant drawing room where, as the name suggests, they serve champagne only. City suits and Soho media darlings with expense accounts seem to occupy most of the bar. The conservatory bar at the back – white walls, white tiled floors, views of the kitchen, and a desperate need for air conditioning – serves normal drinks for the smaller budget, i.e., those of us not on expense accounts. Kettner's always seems busy, but it is an uncomfortable place to wait on your own for a friend – you don't want to buy a bottle of champagne in the lounge or occupy a table in the bar à la Billy-no-mates, and there are few comfortable spots in which to lose yourself. Publicity material states that the bar was '... established in 1867 by Auguste Kettner, chef to Napoleon III, and [has been] renowned ever since for superb food and wine'. I'll bet Mr Kettner never thought he'd end up owned by the same people who own the Pizza Express chain.
OPEN *12.00-midnight (Mon-Sun)*
FOOD *12.00-midnight (Mon-Sun)*
CREDIT CARDS *all major cards*
Private rooms: four rooms: 10-80 seated, up to 100 standing
NEAREST TUBE STATIONS *Tottenham Court Road, Leicester Square*

KING OF BOHEMIA

10 Hampstead High Street, NW3; 0171 435 6513
The young Elector Palatine should have left well alone but no, he would become King of Bohemia. You could see what was going to happen – he lost both Bohemia and his Palatinate and Europe got the 30 Years War. What Hampstead got was this pub on the High Street. Not this one exactly, you understand, but one on the same site, built in 1613, the year the would-be King of Bohemia married James I's daughter. This is more or less the one that replaced it in 1935, bow-fronted, neo-Georgian, just the thing for a neo-king. It has just emerged from its latest Whitbread renovation, which closed it for four weeks.

It is very smart and perky again, its glass doors opening the whole frontage to the street in fine weather and parquet flooring stretching into the distance. People tend to eat in the furthest room, which has a lower ceiling and a fireplace though they can, and do, eat anywhere in the pub. It is an attractive, popular pub which gets very lively in the evening and if there's ever a quiet moment it can reflect with pleasure that it is the only pub in the land to be called King of Bohemia.
OPEN *11.00-23.00 (Mon-Sat), midday-22.30 (Sun)*

FOOD *11.00-20.00 (Mon-Thurs), 11.00-16.00 (Fri), 11.00-18.00 (Sat), midday-18.00 (Sun)*
CREDIT CARDS *all major cards, not AmEx*
DRAUGHT BEERS *Boddingtons, Boston Beer, Flowers IPA, Flowers Original, London Pride, Wadworth 6X, Marston's Pedigree, Heineken, Heineken Export, Stella Artois, Guinness, Murphy's, Merrydown*
Wheelchair access to venue
NEAREST TUBE STATION *Hampstead*

THE KING'S HEAD

4 Fulham High Street, SW6; 0171 736 1413
Drive the full length of the New King's Road in a car without brakes without turning right or left and this is what you would eventually hit. It is an enormous five-storey Edwardian pub with a fairytale tower in the middle and a banner with a bold claim: 'London's Premier Live Music Venue'. There may be something in that. A new stage and lighting system recently installed has taken it a long way. Bands of many sorts play seven nights of the week and it is now, No. 1 for secret gigs. Regular record launches and album previews are held there. It has made a place for itself. There is always a clue to something special going on. A sign reads 'Bar closed to public'. This need not apply to you. At secret gigs, as at any other, they need an audience so leave your name, address and telephone number in the book at the door and you will be told about it. The admission price varies and the place itself remains as uncheery as before. A large black room with a bar leads to a smaller black room with a stage and sophisticated equipment. The music is anything from middle-of-the-road to heavy rock, each style with its own audience but all tolerant of strangers wearing the wrong clothes.

If this is not your scene, you can go through the unlabelled connecting door, past the ladies and into the comparatively bright lights of the public bar. This has its own customers. You will find them drinking at a massive U-shaped bar, playing pool, feeding coins into machines, watching music, sport and films on big-screen television and listening to a major juke box in constant use. The bar has its own entrance from the street and one to the beer garden, which seems to have grown. On sunny days 250 people can and do find a seat. A new barbecue has been installed and people bring their own sausages and burgers and cook them themselves. It is big enough for two sheep at once.
OPEN *Bar: 11.00-midnight (Mon-Sat), midday-22.30 (Sun); Music room 20.30-midnight (Mon-Sat)*
FOOD *barbecue available – bring your own* **FOOD**
CREDIT CARDS *none taken*
DRAUGHT BEERS *Caffrey's, Carling Black Label, Tennent's Pilsner, Tennent's Extra, Guinness, Dry Blackthorn*
Wheelchair access to venue. Private room seats 150
NEAREST TUBE STATION *Putney Bridge*

THE KING'S HEAD

115 Upper Street, N1; 0171 226 1916
There are now at least a dozen theatre pubs in London. This particular example is a substantial Victorian pile with a busy and in some ways eccentric life of its own. When the nation went decimal in 1971, the manager, Dan Crawford, was reluctant to replace his noble Victorian till, so he didn't. The King's Head continued with the old currency, and it still does. The theatre is at the back. The productions staged here get brilliant casts and national reviews. Many have transferred to the West End. One transferred to Broadway and won four Tony awards. There is a fair-sized apron stage and a decent view from just about anywhere. Supper is served at tables in the theatre before the performance – you don't have to

eat there but most people do. A three-course meal costs £8-10s-0d, and you stay on at your table to watch the play. Tickets for this cost £10 during the week and £11 on Saturday. The capacity is 125 with 90 able to eat. Meanwhile the pub will have been filling up and, the play over, departing theatregoers have to squeeze through a crowded bar to reach the street. Some stay on for the Adnams and the music which follows the show – there is folk, rock or jazz until midnight.

OPEN *11.00-midnight (Mon-Thurs), 11.00-01.00 (Fri-Sat), 12.00-midnight (Sun)*

FOOD *bar as opening hours; pre-theatre dinner 19.00-20.00 (Tues-Sat)*

CREDIT CARDS *all major cards for theatre bookings only, not AmEx or Switch*

DRAUGHT BEERS *Adnams, Benskins, Burton Ale, Carlsberg, Löwenbräu, Guinness, Olde English*

Wheelchair access to venue and loos

NEAREST TUBE STATIONS *Highbury & Islington, Angel*

KING'S HEAD AND EIGHT BELLS

50 Cheyne Walk, SW3; 0171 352 1820

For years this much-loved pub was the heart of bohemian Chelsea. Generations of painters, craftsmen and writers drank there – Whistler, Turner, Walter Greaves, Augustus John. It is still a pleasant, good-looking pub and while successive modern improvements have lessened its old romantic appeal they will certainly have increased its turnover. Another £80,000 has just been spent on it, largely to help it look its age. The King's Head and Eight Bells had modest beginnings, starting life as two small 15th-century seamen's pubs side by side on the riverbank. The King's Head was for officers, the Eight Bells for the crews. Eight bells were rung to summon the men back to their ships. The two pubs merged in 1580 and it became the local river boatmen's pub. Then the artists made it their own and by the 1960s the old stucco building, much changed, had become a tourist attraction. Yet more changes lay ahead.

Tourists come in greater numbers than ever. What they see may not be the pub that Whistler knew, but it is comfortable and, goodness knows, well-appointed with its big bar at the front offering its customers a choice of eight cask ales. The bar opens on to a busy restaurant at the back. Both have a wealth of modern period features. It is sad but no one's fault that it is no longer on the river bank. The original riverside Cheyne Walk still passes the door but Chelsea Embankment long since came between river and pub. The embankment gardens have also intervened. Today customers must be content with just a glimpse of distant ships and pleasure boats at high tide while the traffic of modern London thunders past in between.

OPEN *11.00-23.00 (Mon-Sat), midday-22.30 (Sun)*

FOOD *midday-22.00 (Mon-Sat), 12.30-14.00 and 19.00-22.00 (Sun)*

CREDIT CARDS *Delta, Mastercard, Switch, Visa*

DRAUGHT BEERS *Boddingtons, Flowers Original, Old Speckled Hen, Heineken, Heineken Export, Stella Artois, Murphy's, Strongbow, Wadworth 6X, Adnams*

Wheelchair access to venue

NEAREST TUBE STATION *Sloane Square*

THE KING WILLIAM IV

77 Hampstead High Street, NW3; 0171 435 5747

Near the top of Hampstead's steep leafy High Street is one of north London's principal gay pubs, prosperous, respectable and middle class, mirroring, as pubs do, the community it serves. The King William IV stands four-square on its corner. It is built of yellow London brick and has black shutters, window boxes and hanging baskets bright with flowers. The interior is very smart, the ceiling lincrustaed, the walls sponged, stippled, papered and panelled. There is a substantial island counter and a team of cheerful barmen dealing with four separate drinking areas. Seasoned regulars gather in the small bar at the front. Some have hardly budged in 25 years. Younger customers stick to the big open space at the other end. The upstairs bar is used for functions and a set Sunday lunch (£4.95). The food, which is good, is lunchtime only, but you don't have to go far to find restaurants at other times. The garden – large, pleasant and filled with tables – can always count on a busy and sociable summer.

OPEN 12.00-23.00 (Mon-Sat), 12.00-22.30 (Sun)

FOOD 12.00-18.00 (Mon-Sun)

CREDIT CARDS all major cards, not AmEx and Diners

DRAUGHT BEERS Brakspear, Courage Best, Courage Directors, John Smith's Extra Smooth, Budweiser, Foster's, Kronenbourg, Beck's, Guinness, Dry Blackthorn

Wheelchair access to venue

NEAREST TUBE STATION Hampstead

KUDOS

10 Adelaide Street, WC2; 0171 379 4573

A glass fronted, modern-designed, un-closeted gay café bar, which is fairly quiet during the day and buzzes in the evenings when the suits finish work. Downstairs there is a cruiser room with occasional DJs. Call in to get your queue-jump tickets for Heaven, GAY and The Fridge.

OPEN 11.00-23.00 (Mon-Sat) 12.00-22.30 (Sun)

FOOD 11.00-17.00 (Mon-Sat), 12.00-17.00 (Sun)

CREDIT CARDS all major cards

DRAUGHT BEERS Bombardier, Foster's, Q Lager, Red Stripe

NEAREST TUBE STATION Charing Cross

THE LADBROKE ARMS

54 Ladbroke Road, W11; 0171 727 6648

The Ladbroke is a handsome early-Victorian pub that was noticeably unshining when Ian MacKenzie took it over. He gave it a good clean, of course, and did a bit of the old refurbishing, but the key to its renaissance was bright, friendly new staff and a radical change in the kitchen, astonishing the customers with food you actually wanted to eat. There are good cask ales, and the wine list isn't bad either. Classical music or light jazz plays quietly in the background, and the raised terrace outside is famously crowded all summer.

OPEN 11.00-15.00 and 17.30-23.00 (Mon-Fri), 11.00-23.00 (Sat-Sun)

FOOD bar 12.00-14.30 and 19.00-22.00 (Mon-Fri), 12.00-22.00 (Sat-Sun)

CREDIT CARDS Mastercard, Visa

DRAUGHT BEERS Courage Best, Courage Directors, John Smith's Extra Smooth, Theakston XB, Guinness, Strongbow, Abbot Ale, Everard's, Beck's, Kronenbourg, five real ales

Wheelchair access to venue, not to loos

NEAREST TUBE STATION Holland Park and Notting Hill

THE LAMB

94 Lamb's Conduit Street, WC1; 0171 405 0713

The Lamb was built in the 1720s and twice improved almost beyond recognition by the Victorians, who despised anything 18th century. There were alterations in our own time, too, but thankfully the 1959 restorers left the handsome façade, the etched windows and the splendid U-shaped bar counter, which is ringed by brilliant-cut hinged snob screens. Open them and you are face to face with the barman. Close them and your drink will slide discreetly towards you under the screens. It is all convincingly Victorian – the Spy cartoons, the musical comedy stars, the leather sofas and the splendid Polyphone, great-grandfather of the CD player, with discs going back to 1830. The Lamb belongs to John Young, chairman of the brewery and quite a celeb, making movies and starring in the Antiques

Roadshow. Put £1 in the charity box and the staff will wind up the Polyphone and let it play. There is a little patio at the back but, whenever they can, regulars at The Lamb like to drink outside in Lamb's Conduit Street. It was here, in 1577, that a conduit was laid to bring water to the houses. It was designed and paid for by William Lamb, an Elizabethan engineer with a good heart who also provided 120 pails for poor women to carry the water in. The name of the pub and the name of the street ensure that this good deed is still remembered 400 years later. It has long been one of the most admired pubs in London.

OPEN *11.00-23.00 (Mon-Sat), 12.00-22.30 (Sun)*
FOOD *12.00-17.00 (Mon-Sat), 12.00-15.30 (Sun)*
CREDIT CARDS *Mastercard, Visa*
DRAUGHT BEERS *Young's Ordinary, Young's Special, Young's seasonal ales, Carling Black Label, Stella Artois, Young's Export, Young's Pilsner, Guinness, Oatmeal Stout, Scrumpy Jack*
NEAREST TUBE STATIONS *Russell Square, Holborn*

THE LAMB AND FLAG

33 Rose Street, WC2; 0171 497 9504

Half of Covent Garden seem to go to this small, charming, much-loved pub, tucked away up an alley between Garrick Street and Floral Street. If they can't get in, they drink on the pavement and in the summer when everyone drinks outside you can hardly see the pub for the people. It is easily the oldest pub in the area and it is proud of its hairy youth. The back room was called the Bucket of Blood after the bare knuckle fights held there, and John Dryden was badly beaten up in the alley in 1679. They call the upstairs room the Dryden Room – you get a good straightforward lunch up there, and Dixieland jazz on Sunday nights. Once you've been drinking here for a hundred years or so, they'll mount a brass plaque on the bar in recognition of your service. There are hundreds of them now; some faded, some sparklingly new.

OPEN *11.00-23.00 (Mon-Thurs), 11.00-22.45 (Fri-Sat), 12.00-22.30 (Sun)*
FOOD *12.00-15.00 hot meals (Mon-Sat), 12.00-17.00 bar snacks (Mon-Sat)*
CREDIT CARDS *none taken*
DRAUGHT BEERS *Courage Best, John Smith's Extra Smooth, John Smith's Yorkshire, Marston's Pedigree, Foster's, Kronenbourg, Guinness, Dry Blackthorn, Scrumpy Jack, Young's Bitter, Young's Special*
NEAREST TUBE STATION *Covent Garden*

THE LAMB TAVERN

ADDRESS Leadenhall Market, EC3
PHONE 0171 626 2454

Sir Horace Jones, the Victorian architect, gave London three magnificent markets, Smithfield, Billingsgate and Leadenhall. The grandest of these was Leadenhall, the game, fish and poultry market in the heart of the City. It is still a fine sight with its great stone arches, lofty arcades and stunning cast-ironwork, and it includes one of London's stateliest pubs, The Lamb Tavern. Every weekday The Lamb fills up with energetic, talkative men in suits. Many work at Lloyds and seem to take every opportunity to get out of their spectacular new building and into the pubs and winebars of Sir Horace's market. The Lamb has never been busier, and Young's has sought to ease the crush by slotting a new mezzanine floor into the once soaring saloon bar. Then there was the most helpful decision to pedestrianise the market between 11am and 3pm so The Lamb can now offer the new market traders four floors to drink in and a wide stretch of pavement to drink on. They arrive in ever larger numbers around lunchtime, and The Lamb is then busy until the last City gent makes for home around 9pm. Now that the marble pillars disappear into a ceiling of modest height the main bar is nowhere near as impressive, but the cavernous smoking room in the basement keeps its old style and so does the top floor with its tall windows and fine view of the market. This is a no-smoking bar. It was the City's first and has proved very popular. Each level of The Lamb serves food but this high elegant room is the place to eat. The market closes at weekends and quite often film crews move in. John Wayne spent days at The Lamb when scenes for *Brannigan* were being shot. Robert Mitchum was there for *The Winds of War* and Tom Selleck for *Magnum*. The BBC shot some of *Bleak House* in The Lamb, and both the landlord's children got parts.

OPEN *11.00-21.00 (Mon-Fri)*

FOOD *11.00-14.30; toasted sandwiches until 21.00*

CREDIT CARDS all major cards, not Switch

DRAUGHT BEERS Young's Bitter, Young's Special, Carling Black Label, Young's Export, Stella Artois, Young's Pilsner, Guinness, Oatmeal, Scrumpy Jack *Private room seats 50*

NEAREST TUBE STATION Bank

THE LATCHMERE

503 Battersea Park Road, SW11; 0171 223 3549

The most imposing Victorian pubs can have their ups and their downs. I have to report that The Latchmere, always a powerful presence, is having an up. The big shabby bar has been thoroughly refurbished. The battered kicked-in counter has been replaced by a smart new one and the walled garden, not long ago a dump, is lovely, its picnic tables encircled by climbing roses, vines and ivy.

Lots goes on at The Latchmere. Well, it has an energetic and ambitious lessee now, the one-time paratrooper Alan Grace. It was Grace who started the Canal Café Theatre in a Little Venice pub called the Bridge House. Taking over the Latchmere meant he had one of London's leading pub theatres on his first floor. It had a high reputation then and it still has. It seats 90 and has a new production every month, good modern plays as a rule with excellent casts. Susannah York has played there and Kate O'Mara and familiar television faces often appear. It is called the Grace Theatre at The Latchmere now after Alan Grace, not the present Alan Grace but his father. He was a rising young actor at the beginning of a promising career when the war broke out. He was killed in action three months before the birth of his son.

OPEN *11.00-23.00 (Mon-Sat), midday-22.30 (Sun)*

FOOD *midday-16.00 (Mon), midday-15.00 and 17.30-20.00 (Tues-Fri), midday-20.00 (Sat)*

CREDIT CARDS Mastercard, Switch, Visa

DRAUGHT BEERS Greene King IPA, Foster's, Kronenbourg, Guinness, Abbot, Tetley's, Boddingtons, Stella Artois, Strongbow

NEAREST RAILWAY STATION Clapham Junction

THE LAVENDER

171 Lavender Hill, SW11; 0171 978 5242

The Lavender is a home from home for the mixed clientele of young Clapham professionals and street-trendy types. It seems to do very good business as both a restaurant and a bar. It has been around long enough to feel well used, and it's all the better for that. Enormous windows at the front contribute greatly to the feeling of space, and the ceiling fans, spinning alarmingly fast, keep the air circulating on those balmy Battersea evenings. It's £2-£2.50 for bottled beers and £8.50 for the house wines.

OPEN *10.00-23.00 (Mon-Sat), 10.00-22.30 (Sun)*

FOOD *12.00-15.30 and 19.00-23.00 (Mon-Thurs), 12.00-15.30 and 19.00-23.30 (Fri), 12.00-16.00 and 19.00-23.30 (Sat), 12.00-16.00 and 19.00-22.30 (Sun)*

CREDIT CARDS all major cards

NEAREST RAILWAY STATION Clapham Junction

LEGLESS LADDER

339 Battersea Park Road, SW11; 0171 622 2112

This was the first of the two Legless Ladders in London – the one-time Prince of Wales in Battersea Park Road. It had got tired and dusty, and Jeremy Hampton bought the lease. He turned the three Victorian bars into a big, open-plan space, scrapped the massive old bar counter and brought in lots of pine tables with numbered pews. The new Legless Ladder has become a popular drinking hole for young and sporty Battersea settlers, who go for the big helpings of hearty British food and pints of lager, and also for the big matches prominently featured on screens specially installed for the occasion. Major rugby internationals pack the place with cheering fans. Sunday lunch is the busiest day in a sport-free week, although you have to be on the ball – they still chuck you out at 3pm.

OPEN *12.00-23.00 (Mon-Sat), 12.00-22.30 (Sun)*

FOOD *12.00-14.30 and 19.00-22.00 (Mon-Fri), 12.00-21.00 (Sat-Sun)*

CREDIT CARDS *all major cards, not AmEx*

DRAUGHT BEERS *Bass, Courage Directors, John Smith's Extra Smooth, Theakston Best, Stella Artois, Foster's, Kronenbourg, Guinness, Strongbow Wheelchair access to venue. Private room seats 50, 100 standing*

NEAREST TUBE STATION *Battersea Park*

LEGLESS LADDER

1 Harwood Terrace, SW6; 0171 610 6131

Sister-pub of the original Battersea version, this modern, almost circular pub has a central island bar, large wooden tables, stripped pine floors, big windows, and French doors which open out to a large beer garden. The owner is Jeremy Hampton, whose wife Tammy supervises the blackboard-driven menu of sumptuous burgers with real chips, plus pastas, roasts and salads. The pub is slightly difficult to find, being tucked away off the King's Road, but the rather well-heeled folk of Fulham consider it worth hunting down. No doubt there will be more Legless Ladders in the future.

OPEN *12.00-23.00 (Mon-Sat), 12.00-22.30 (Sun)*

FOOD *12.00-15.00 and 19.00-22.00 (Mon-Thurs), 12.00-21.00 (Fri-Sat), 12.00-18.00 (Sun)*

CREDIT CARDS *all major cards, not AmEx*

DRAUGHT BEERS *Bass, Courage Directors, Theakston Best, John Smith's Extra Smooth, Budweiser, Foster's, Kronenbourg, Guinness, Strongbow Wheelchair access to venue*

NEAREST TUBE STATION *Fulham Broadway*

THE LEICESTER ARMS

44 Glasshouse Street, W1; 0171 734 7641

Many a tourist, footsore in Piccadilly Circus, looks up Glasshouse Street, sees the Leicester Arms and that's it. 'A real traditional London pub,' they tell their friends back home and they're right. Doing up pubs is one of the traditions of our day and Scottish and Newcastle, whose pub this is, has just spent a vast sum on the Leicester Arms, putting new windows in, clearing out the residue of past improvements and generally making more space. Miss Sarah Miles who manages it is very pleased. She had already doubled the takings in the upstairs dining room. She is sure she will redouble them now. In any case it's best to book. The Leicester Arms is one of three pubs that gaze challengingly at each other across this little junction. They could hardly be more different. This is the up-market one with new air conditioning, a handsome staircase and a wine list, not to mention a chef and a roomy beer cellar.

OPEN *11.00-23.00 (Mon-Sat), midday-22.30 (Sun)*

FOOD *opening times*

CREDIT CARDS *all major cards*

DRAUGHT BEERS *Foster's, Kronenbourg, Beck's, Holsten Export, Guinness, John Smith, Scrumpy Jack, Theakston Best Bitter, Theakston XB, Directors*
Wheelchair access to venue, not to loos
NEAREST TUBE STATION *Piccadilly*

THE LEINSTER ARMS

17 Leinster Terrace, W2; 0171 723 5757

The Leinster Arms is the home of a Burton Ale Grand Master Cellarman, a notable personage. Her name is Olive McCarthy and she was the first woman Grand Master Cellarman ever. Mrs McCarthy, disconcertingly youthful-looking mother of two sons both at college, has run the Leinster Arms herself since her husband left. She took over from him as manager and she has been a conspicuous success. The pub has blossomed and she has been heaped with prizes. Every year it seems there is a new trophy for being puller of the perfect pint. This has always been an attractive pub. It is an old coaching house in Bayswater with a big, cheerful, comfortable bar, good plain food served all day, Olive herself behind the bar and, you will not be surprised to hear, fine cask ales that rise from an immaculate cellar in perfect condition.

OPEN *11.00-23.00 (Mon-Sat), midday-22.30 (Sun)*
FOOD *11.00-20.00 (Mon-Sat), midday-20.00 (Sun)*
CREDIT CARDS *all major cards*
DRAUGHT BEERS *Marston's Pedigree, Old Speckled Hen, Tetley's, Carlsberg, Castlemaine XXXX, Stella Artois, Guinness, Dry Blackthorn, several guest ales*
Wheelchair access to venue and loos
NEAREST TUBE STATIONS *Lancaster Gate, Paddington, Queensway, Bayswater*

THE LONDON APPRENTICE

62 Church Street, Isleworth, TW7; 0181 560 1915

Here's a sports report. In 1828 Luke Walker, the Colliers' Champion, met Ned Donnelly, the Colossal Coal Heaver in a sensational fist fight. It went for 37 rounds and left both men covered in blood. Luke Walker won. What he won was The London Apprentice. The idiotic owner had bet it on the other chap. The London Apprentice was famous even then. It was, and indeed is, a fine old pub on the river at Old Isleworth. Syon House, the Duke of Northumberland's London home, is next door and lots of people come to see it but The London Apprentice considers itself every bit as historic. Lots of people come to see it as well. It is agreeably old. It dates back to Tudor times and they would have us believe that Henry VIII drank here. Goodness me, and Charles I AND Oliver Cromwell, but perhaps not at the same time, and every familiar pub story is claimed: the secret tunnel, the smugglers, the ghost, even poor Dick Turpin who must have been exhausted. Still how nice that it has survived in such good nick to tell the tale, picking up a fine 18th-century façade and much historic luggage on the way. So there it stands with its terrace over the river, its conservatory, its ground floor dining room and the grand à la carte restaurant upstairs, a lovely room with hand-printed wallpaper, huge oriel window and plaster reliefs more than 300 years old. This is where the ghost lurks.

More importantly, the two bars seem to have hardly changed at all. Regulars still play darts and shove-ha'penny and bar billiards in the old bar at the back, and the main bar remains the heart of the pub with two huge oak posts that keep the whole building up. Try not to lean on them too hard.

OPEN *11.00-23.00 (Mon-Sat), midday-22.30 (Sun)*
FOOD *Bar: 11.00-14.30 and 18.00-21.30 (Mon-Sat), midday-16.00 (Sun); Restaurant: midday-15.00 and 18.00-21.30 (Mon-Sat), midday-17.30 (Sun)*
CREDIT CARDS *all major cards*
DRAUGHT BEERS *Courage Best, Courage Directors, Old Speckled Hen, John Smith, Wadworth 6X, Kronenbourg, Foster's, Holsten, Guinness, Strongbow*
NEAREST RAILWAY STATION *Isleworth*

THE LORD MOON OF THE MALL
16-18 Whitehall, SW1; 0171 839 7701

The imposing Victorian building next to the Whitehall Theatre was built in 1872 by a favourite pupil of Sir Gilbert Scott to house one of London's grandest banks. Cocks, Biddulph and Co. were bankers not just to Prime Ministers and Lord Chancellors but also to Thomas Chippendale and John Constable. Edward VII had an account there from the age of three. Much later it became the most prestigious branch of Martins Bank and then of Barclays.

Barclays moved out in 1992 and in came J. D. Wetherspoon's with a million pounds to spend on one of the most distinguished buildings on the market. What had been a most superior bank became a most superior public house. Early customers lowered their voices as they entered. The building is used to that sort of thing. It is much jollier than it used to be of course. Widely spaced tables occupy the one-time banking hall with its high coffered ceiling and magnificent arched windows. More arches lead from here to the main bar with its polished granite counter and to what was once the partners' room where dukes awaited an invitation to sit. It is all opened up now and there are lots of comfortable chairs for us, I'm happy to say.

The Lord Moon of the Mall was Wetherspoon's 106th pub. It shares with the others the well-known Wetherspoon's characteristics, no music, a big no-smoking area, and a 99p pint of Younger's Scotch Bitter. It is open all the hours permitted and does food all day. Look carefully at the neo-Gainsborough facing you as you go in. The 18th-century blade leaning on the garden urn is the chairman and founder of Wetherspoon's, Tim Martin. Through the glass doors, at the head of what used to be the stairs down to the vaults, stands an elegant man in a dinner jacket. That is Tim Martin too, a statue this time.

OPEN *11.00-23.00 (Mon-Sat), midday-22.30 (Sun)*
FOOD *11.00-22.00 (Mon-Sat), midday-21.30 (Sun)*
CREDIT CARDS *all major cards, not Diners*
DRAUGHT BEERS *Caffrey's, Courage Directors, London Pride, Theakston Best, Guinness, Dry Blackthorn, Weston's, John Smith, Foster's, Kronenbourg, McEwan's, Miller, two daily guest ales*
Wheelchair access to venue and loo
NEAREST TUBE STATION *Charing Cross*

LORD'S TAVERN
The Grace Gates, St John's Wood Road, NW8; 0171 266 5980

Front Page pubs took over this historic tavern in 1997 and converted it into one of their up-market foodie pubs. Old taverners won't recognise the Front Page-ified inn, with its bright woodwork, big tables, real ales and champagnes, and its Modern British menu. The tried-and-tested reputation of the new owners means that the residents of St John's Wood Road now have a real gem on their doorstep. They might want to avoid it when England play at Lord's, as half the stadium seems to pop in for one.

OPEN *11.00-23.00 (Mon-Sat), 12.00-22.30 (Sun)*
FOOD *12.00-14.30 and 18.30-22.00 (Mon-Sat), 12.00-17.00 (Sun)*
CREDIT CARDS *all major cards*
DRAUGHT BEERS *Caffrey's, Foster's, Kronenbourg, Miller Pilsner, Guinness, Strongbow*
NEAREST TUBE STATIONS *Maida Vale, St John's Wood, Warwick Avenue*

LUPO
50 Dean Street, W1; 0171 434 3399

The bar staff at Lupo are a handsome, trendy bunch of youngsters with hairstyles so fashionable that if my mother were to go in she would whip out her scissors and give them all a good seeing-to. They seem to have developed their own dialect in this Estuary English-free zone, sort of public school meets ageing hippy: 'Hey Juss-tin, more beeas, yaah?' The owner, Paul-Jean Foster, tells me he would only employ someone who would be happy to drink here. The Soho-media types seem to rub along quite happily with the serious modes and artistically bent. Lupo has wonderful late opening hours, and to control the numbers they charge £5 admission after 11pm from Thursday to Saturday.

Three bar areas and two private rooms provide plenty of pocketed places to sit, and the two main bars have a bit of hanging-around space. Concertina walls open up in the summer, when the crowds spill on to the pavement clutching their bottled beers (£2.50) or glasses of wine (from £2.20) and sway to the beat of the acid jazz and dance music. The restaurant serves surprisingly decent food but isn't especially cheap (tuna steak £10.75, duck or lamb £11). The bar gets busy with the after-work crowd and then again with the late-night revellers. As for the name Lupo? 'Latin for wolf,' they told me. I looked it up and found lupor, which is something to do with lewd women. I think I prefer that definition.

OPEN *12.00-01.00 (Mon-Wed), 12.00-02.00 (Thurs), 12.00-03.00 (Fri), 15.00-03.00 (Sat)*
FOOD *12.00-15.00 and 18.00-23.30 (Mon-Sat)*
CREDIT CARDS *all major cards*
Two private rooms: 90 and 100 seated
NEAREST TUBE STATION *Leicester Square*

THE LYCEUM TAVERN
354 Strand, WC2; 0171 836 7155
In the days when Henry Irving's great Lyceum Theatre was alive and well, the little Lyceum Tavern was part of theatrical London. The pub backed on to the theatre and actors and singers and backstage staff were in and out all the time. They will surely be again and quite soon. A huge £14-million restoration is bringing the Lyceum to life again. Meanwhile the Lyceum Tavern couldn't sit around and wait. It long since made another life for itself. Samuel Smith got it with five others when it bought Hennekey's in 1980 and has done it over very nicely with cosy drinking booths in the main bar and a pleasant panelled bar overlooking the Strand upstairs. There are plans for a thorough refurbishment soon and when the new Lyceum reopens at last it should find its old friend in very good shape.
OPEN *11.30-23.30 (Mon-Sat), 12.00-22.30 (Sun)*
FOOD *12.00-15.00, 17.00-21.00 (Mon-Sun), snacks all day everyday*
CREDIT CARDS *all major* **CREDIT CARDS**, *not AmEx or Diners*
DRAUGHT BEERS *Samuel Smith's*
Wheelchair access to venue, not to loos
NEAREST TUBE STATIONS *Covent Garden, Embankment*

THE MAD HATTER
3-7 Stamford Street, SE1; 0171 401 9222
So named because this very building was constructed as a hat factory in late Victorian times. After years of neglect, our friendly local brewer, Fuller's, bought the place and converted it into one of their Ale & Pie houses. It seems to be going down rather well with the local businesses – IPC Magazines is just across the way and there are numerous other local businesses available to prop this place up. They've chucked a few hats into glass cases to remind us of its millinery connections, and I rather approve of the line of booths along the right-hand wall. But Fuller's need to sharpen up on this brand in terms of design and staff uniforms (poor buggers are all dressed up like bus conductors) to make it ready for the 21st century. I have to say the food is good, and the beers are Fuller's, of course, so that's pleasing. Should you have too much pop, you'll be happy to know that this is a hotel. Rooms are £72.50 per night. Cheaper at weekends.
OPEN *11.00-23.00 (Mon-Sat), midday-22.30 (Sun)*

FOOD *midday-15.00 then 18.00-21.15, no food served Friday evening*
CREDIT CARDS *all major cards*
DRAUGHT BEERS *Heineken, Stella Artois, Carling, London Pride, Fuller's ESB, Chiswick, Storm*
Wheelchair access to venue
NEAREST TUBE STATION *Blackfriars (also near Waterloo Station)*

THE MAGDALA TAVERN
2a South Hill Park, NW3; 0171 435 2503

There are three bullet holes in the cream tiled frontage and a notice explaining how they came to be there. It was here, it says, that Ruth Ellis shot and killed her lover, David Blakeley, on 10 April 1955. She stood over him putting three more bullets into his body as he lay on the pavement, then quietly waited for the police to come. She was the last woman to be hanged in Britain and she gave this otherwise unmemorable local a sort of macabre glamour.

There is a theatrical gloss to it now, with photographs of Alan Bates, John Gielgud and others, but the star, quite rightly, is Ruth Ellis. She stares bleakly from the frame, blonde, ashen, heavily made-up in an open-neck shirt blouse with a silk scarf and a broad belt tightly fastened. With the photograph is a letter she wrote from Holloway and two miniature certificates, the official declaration of execution and the death certificate, signed by the prison surgeon on 13 July 1955.

OPEN *11.00-23.00 (Mon-Sat), 12.00-22.30 (Sun)*
CREDIT CARDS *all major cards, not AmEx and Diners*
DRAUGHT BEERS *Caffrey's, Bass, London Pride, Carling Black Label, Guinness, Dry Blackthorn, three guest ales*
NEAREST TUBE STATION *Hampstead*
NEAREST RAILWAY STATION *Hampstead Heath*

THE MAGPIE AND STUMP
442 King's Road, SW10; 0171 352 5017

A few years ago this rather down-at-heel pub was given a new lease of life when Allied Domecq completely gutted the place and transformed it into what they saw as an up-market bar. It is now a handsome building – large windows, tables outside in the summer and two rooms inside where you can eat all day. It is fair to say that The Magpie has struggled somewhat with its new identity as a bar rather than a pub. The amusement-arcade features in the downstairs bar were largely to blame for this; a new manager, Tim Brown has removed the majority of them. There are discos now instead. The bar is conveniently situated directly opposite the World's End estate.

OPEN *12.00-23.00 (Mon-Sat), 12.00-22.30 (Sun)*
FOOD *12.00-16.00 (Mon-Fri), 12.00-17.00 (Sat-Sun)*
CREDIT CARDS *all major cards*
DRAUGHT BEERS *Tetley's, Carlsberg, Carlsberg Export, Stella Artois, Guinness, Dry Blackthorn*
NEAREST TUBE STATIONS *Sloane Square, South Kensington*

THE MAGPIE AND STUMP
218 Old Bailey, EC4; 0171 248 5085

Few London pubs have a more macabre past than this one. It stood facing the gallows of Newgate Jail and would rent out its upper floors for all-night parties before an execution. Vast crowds whooped it up below while the nobs drank, played cards and at dawn watched the wretched prisoner slowly strangling on the gibbet while his relations hung on his legs to hasten his end. The sight gave them a good appetite for The Magpie and Stump's large execution breakfast.

After being remodelled in 1931 the pub settled down to a respectable old age as a tourist attraction, and all was well until 1988 when it was sold to a developer and demolished. The deal was that a new Magpie and Stump should be part of the new building. This is it. The only hint that there might be a pub in Old Bailey is an inn-sign oddly attached to what looks like an office wall. The fascia and entrance are hidden away round the corner in an alley called Bishop's Court. Inside, you find a large modern pub on three levels. There's the main bar, a younger, louder bar with big-screen TV on the floor below, and a bar for private hire under that. If you are peckish you can have anything you want as long as it's baguettes or pizzas. The pub is handsomely equipped and fully air-conditioned. There is even a lift. But nothing, not even the inn-sign, was saved from the historic old tavern.

OPEN *11.00-22.00 (Mon-Wed), 11.00-23.00 (Thurs-Fri)*
FOOD *as opening hours*
CREDIT CARDS *all major cards*
DRAUGHT BEERS *Bass, Caffrey's, London Pride, Carling Black Label, Staropramen, Guinness, Red Rock*
Wheelchair access to venue and loos
NEAREST TUBE STATION *St Paul's*

THE MAPLE LEAF

41 Maiden Lane, WC2; 0171 240 2843
Canadian flags catching the breeze in Maiden Lane proclaim that here is the Canadian pub. It used to be a rackety English one called the Bedford Head but it's been The Maple Leaf for years now and is known to Canadians everywhere – the London pub where you find Canadian beer, Canadian food and, most importantly, other Canadians. It got a major refit recently and re-opened on Canada Day with all sorts of Canadian hoopla. Everyone agreed it was hugely improved. For one thing it seemed about twice the size and there were reminders of Canada everywhere, also six carefully placed television screens so no one need lose a moment of the ice hockey. There is a strong Canadian accent at the bar too. It is, boasts The Maple Leaf, the only pub in the world outside North America to have draught Molson. Then there is the excellent Canadian food, the burgers and the steaks and the home-made meatloaf and brunch served all day with fresh juice, ham, griddled eggs, hash browns with pancakes and maple syrup.

There's always a big street party on Canada Day and ice hockey. Did I mention ice hockey? Videos of every big match are flown over straight away. Big baseball videos come too and matches are shown every Tuesday and Thursday, so you can sit round the TV with your mates in Covent Garden, England, watching the drama with one bucket of chicken wings and one of ice cold beer. It's almost like being at home.

OPEN *11.00-23.00 (Mon-Sat), midday-22.30 (Sun)*
FOOD *midday-22.00 (Mon-Sun)*
CREDIT CARDS *all major cards*
DRAUGHT BEERS *Theakston Best, Kronenbourg, Foster's, Molson Canadian, Guinness, Scrumpy Jack*
NEAREST TUBE STATIONS *Covent Garden, Charing Cross*

MARKET BAR

240a Portobello Road, W11; 0171 229 6472
Very mixed, young and trendy bar with large draped curtains, candles that have been burning for years, and a serious sound system.

OPEN *12.00-23.00 (Mon-Fri), 12.00-midnight (Sat), 12.00-22.30 (Sun)*
FOOD *12.00-15.30 and 18.00-22.30 (Mon-Sat)*
CREDIT CARDS *Visa, Mastercard, Switch*
Wheelchair access to venue
NEAREST TUBE STATIONS *Westbourne Park, Ladbroke Grove*

MARKET CAFÉ BAR

21 The Market, Covent Garden, WC2; 0171 836 2137

Located above the Market Café on the south-west side of the market, this bar has a rather unimpressive interior but a spectacular terrace which is worth the fight for a space. From here you can watch the buskers on the west piazza, safe in the knowledge that you won't have to pay.

OPEN *ground floor 10.00-24.30 (Mon-Sun), upstairs 12.00-02.00 (Mon-Sun)*
FOOD *ground floor 10.00-24.00 (Mon-Sun), upstairs 12.00-02.00 (Mon-Sun)*
CREDIT CARDS *all major cards*
Wheelchair access to ground level
NEAREST TUBE STATION *Covent Garden*

THE MARLBOROUGH

46 Friar Stile Road, Richmond; 0181 940 0572

This is a particularly good find. Friar Stile Road, off Richmond Hill, is slightly off the beaten track, but it's worth making a detour to visit The Marlborough. The pub begins long and narrow, dividing evenly into three – first the public bar, with wooden floors and high-backed settles; then the saloon, carpeted, curtained and set about with green leather chesterfields; and beyond that a servery with an open grill selling steaks, chops and burgers. What is impressive about the pub is its wonderful walled garden, which seemingly goes on for miles. Children play on the garden furniture far enough away from the drinking area for them not to bother anyone. Picnic tables fill the lawns, and there is an undercover terrace with its own heating system so you can enjoy the garden through the changing seasons. The Marlborough is efficiently run by an erudite Dublin lad named Oisin Rogers, who could win an Olympic gold for talking. If you ask, he will undoubtedly talk you into having a home-made beefburger, swordfish or tuna loin steak, or a mixed charcuterie of European meats, all washed down, of course, with a drop of the black stuff.

OPEN *12.00-23.00 (Mon-Fri), 11.00-23.00 (Sat), 12.00-22.30 (Sun)*
FOOD *12.00-15.00 and 18.30-21.00 (Mon-Sun)*
CREDIT CARDS *all major cards*
DRAUGHT BEERS *Everards Tiger, Adnams, Tetley's, Stella Artois, Carlsberg Export, Castlemaine XXXX, Guinness, Dry Blackthorn*
Wheelchair access to venue
NEAREST TUBE STATION *Richmond*

MARQUESS TAVERN

32 Canonbury Street, N1; 0171 354 2975

See this high-Victorian pub standing proudly by the New River Walk, Corinthian pillars reaching from first floor to balustraded roof, every inch a listed building and a credit to the Marquesses of Northampton whose pub it used to be. The present Marquess has hung on to a lot of Canonbury, his substantial birthright, but for some reason his father sold The Marquess. Young's has it now. They bought it in 1979 and, as they say, restored it to its former glory, adding two ancestral portraits of their own. They look very much at home in the big high-ceilinged saloon bar. The adjoining room is impressive, a bar-cum-dining room with a fine arched ceiling, booths and big mirrors. It was a pool room in its misspent youth. This is truly a fine pub and well placed. The New River, originally designed to bring drinking water to the 17th-century City of London, now brings ducks and river walkers to its door. Picnic tables await them. The Marquess rightly prides itself on its beer and serves hearty traditional food. In keeping with the times, it provides unhearty food as well. There's a good salad bar.

OPEN *11.00-23.00 (Mon-Sat), midday-22.30 (Sun)*
FOOD *midday-15.00 (Mon-Sun), cold buffet from 11.00*
CREDIT CARDS *none taken*

DRAUGHT BEERS *Young's Bitter, Young's Export, Young's Special, Carling Black Label, Stella Artois, Young's Pilsner, Guinness, Dry Blackthorn, one seasonal ale*
Wheelchair access to venue and loos. Private room seats 80
NEAREST TUBE STATION *Highbury & Islington*
NEAREST RAILWAY STATION *Essex Road*

THE MARQUIS OF GRANBY

51 Chandos Place, WC2; 0171 836 7657
The Marquis of Granby at the back of Coliseum has a long imposing frontage that makes you expect a large imposing pub, but it is a sliver of a pub, a wedge, all length and no width.
Still, nothing wrong with wedges. At the thin end of the wedge is a very small snug. At the thick end of the wedge is a rather larger bar parlour. The main bar, getting gradually wider, is in between and the whole thing has been elaborately refitted. Back bar, bar counter, furniture, everything was replaced. It has been carefully done, with a Gothic screen rescued from a demolished church put to good use. The pub's rush hour is the Coliseum interval when opera-goers, cast and orchestra erupt in the bar for a very quick one indeed. This is the answer given if anyone asks why there is no music. The orchestra, explains the landlord, won't have it.
There was a pub on this site in Charles II's day, the Hole in the Wall. Was it this shape? It was where Claude Duval the highwayman was caught sleeping it off. After his execution he was buried in St Paul's Church under a stone that reads:
Here lies Duval. Reader, if male thou art
Look to thy purse; if female to thy heart.
OPEN *11.00-23.00 (Mon-Sat), midday-22.30 (Sun)*
FOOD *11.00-19.00 (Mon-Sun)*
CREDIT CARDS *all major cards*
DRAUGHT BEERS *Pedigree, Tetley's, Adnams, Guinness, Dry Blackthorn, Stella Artois, Castlemaine XXXX, Carlsberg, guest ale*
Wheelchair access to venue, not to loos. Private room: 40 seated, 100 standing
NEAREST TUBE STATIONS *Charing Cross, Covent Garden*

MASH

19-21 Great Portland Street, W1; 0171 637 5555
This is a 1998 vision of a 21st-century bar. OK, not much foresight there, but Mash may well be the harbinger for a new generation of eating and drinking venues in London. Unlike many other restaurant and bar cohabitations, Oliver Peyton (the man from Atlantic) has succeeded here, and at his original London venue, in recognising the importance of the bar as an integral part of the visitor experience. With the restaurant discreetly tucked away on the upper level, the ground floor combines the minimalist yet comfortable aesthetics of the modern genre with the coppers and kettles which comprise the essential industry of a working brewhouse. It is refreshing to find quality ales in such a bar, and the brewmaster, Alastair Hook, has been developing some wonderful beers during his time at Mash & Air, the Manchester sister bar, for the past year or so. The results bring us four highly credible ales – sampling is a must and respect for their alcohol content is desirable: the malty-sweet Mash (5.4%), the fruity Peach beer (5%), the Wheat beer (5.6%) and the very palatable Abbey ale (6.5%). Not to be outdone, the almost encyclopaedic wine list includes 195 wines (£12.50-£150), of which 22 are available by the glass (from £4.50). Mash will likely become an instant success, and so long as the ludicrous door policies are not transferred from the Atlantic, it is worth the effort to visit. It's still early days so they haven't got the service side of things sorted out, but I didn't mind, I was really only here for the beer.

OPEN *20.00-23.00 (Mon-Fri), 10.00-23.00 (Sat), 11.00-22.30 (Sun)*
FOOD *during opening hours*
CREDIT CARDS *all major cards*
DRAUGHT BEERS *own brews*
Wheelchair access to venue and loos
NEAREST TUBE STATION *Oxford Circus*

MASONS ARMS

169 Battersea Park Road, SW8; 0171 622 2007

There appears to be a new trend in the licensed sector for the offspring of rather well-to-do families to set themselves up in the pub business. Joel Cadbury started out with the Goat in Boots (qv) on the Fulham Road, Lord Fermoy followed a more conventional route into pub management with a Bass training scheme at the Windsor Castle (qv) and now Ewan Guinness, heir to the Guinness empire, has bought himself a pub or two. Three years ago, the Masons Arms was a burnt-out shell of a building near the Dogs' Home on the Battersea Park Road. Guinness and his business partner Matt Jacomb have made a splendid job of bringing the building to life again. It now has one very large, L-shaped room with big, well-spaced tables and a lounge area with chesterfields by the fireplace. The clientele is young but not childish – more Eagles fans than Boy Zone followers. Food is very much the thing here, as the open kitchen near the door suggests. The menu changes every few weeks, but on our most recent visit we had char-grilled calamari, chorizo and blackened tomato pancake (£6.50), pan-fried Scottish salmon on rocket and pimento frittata (£7) and a char-grilled beefburger with big chips (£5.80). This was Guinness's first pub. He has another one now, the Stonemasons (qv) in Hammersmith. They serve Guinness in both pubs.

OPEN *11.00-23.00 (Mon-Sat), 12.00-22.30 (Sun)*
FOOD *12.00-22.00 (Mon-Sun)*
CREDIT CARDS *all major cards*
DRAUGHT BEERS *Boddingtons, Brakspear, Bostons Beer, Wadworth 6X, Heineken Export, Hoegaarden, Stella Artois, Guinness, Merrydown, Strongbow*
Wheelchair access to venue
NEAREST RAILWAY STATION *Battersea Park*
NEAREST TUBE STATION *Vauxhall*

THE MASONS ARMS

51 Upper Berkeley Street, W1; 0171 723 2131

The plaque on the wall of this nice corner pub in W1 tells a romantic though gory tale, not one everybody believes. The story is that the pub cellars were originally dungeons where unfortunate persons about to be hanged at Tyburn languished, chained to the walls. A tunnel, it is said, led directly from the cellars to Tyburn just round the corner at Marble Arch. They were particularly ghastly executions, much enjoyed by the charming populace, and they went on until 1783. As the pub was built around 1780 the dungeon story could be true and the bright new manager, Sarah Grant, joins in the spirit of the thing by taking occasional parties down there, a candle casting horrid shadows. She points out the old iron fittings on the walls. For the manacles she says. The Masons Arms is in all other respects a cheerful and agreeable old pub. Its wooden floor is dressed several times a week with fresh sawdust. This is not popular with the cleaners who say it gets everywhere, but visitors like it.

OPEN *11.00-23.00 (Mon-Sat), midday-22.30 (Sun)*
FOOD *as opening hours*
CREDIT CARDS *all major cards*
DRAUGHT BEERS *Tanglefoot, HP Export, Pilsner Premium, IPA, Dorset Best, Guiness, Dempsey's, Blackthorn*
Wheelchair access to venue and loos
NEAREST TUBE STATION *Marble Arch*

MATCH

45-47 Clerkenwell Road, EC1; 0171 250 4002

A quality cocktail bar of considerable substance. Novices can train by buying into the mini marathon package of 5 for £10, or the match marathon of 10 for £20. I went through the big one twice, I think, and supplemented it with some excellent grub.

OPEN *11.00-midnight (Mon-Fri), 18.00-midnight (Sat)*

FOOD *midday-23.30 (Mon-Sat)*

CREDIT CARDS *all major cards*

DRAUGHT BEERS *Stella Artois, Hoegaarden*

Wheelchair access to venue and loos

NEAREST TUBE STATION *Farringdon*

THE MAYFLOWER

117 Rotherhithe Street, SE16; 0171 237 4088

In the spring of 1620 the *Mayflower* up-anchored at Rotherhithe and sailed down the Thames on the first lap of her historic journey to the New World. She had been moored next to a riverside tavern called The Shippe. It would be nice to think that its customers cheered and waved as she started her great adventure. The *Mayflower* was back at Rotherhithe eight months later, anchoring near The Shippe again. Surely the crew bowled into the bar that night, but her glory days were over. Within a year her captain was dead. They buried him in the graveyard of St Mary's Church, hard by The Shippe, and the *Mayflower* lay rotting at her old moorings. The Shippe stood another 100 years or so and was then rebuilt. They called the new pub The Spread Eagle and Crown, a serviceable name but The Shippe had been better and its new name is better still. It changed to The Mayflower in the 1960s when, all patched up after the war – its top floor had been blown off in the blitz – it set its cap at American visitors who were understandably thrilled to find it still tucked away by the church among the wharfs and warehouses.

I must say the dark little bar with its old black settles and tables casts a powerful spell. You can buy British and American stamps there under a curious long-standing licensing arrangement and you get a good view of the river from the restaurant upstairs, newly refurbished after a change of owner. The best view is from the jetty at the back of the old pub. It juts out over the river and you see the water slapping the timbers through the gaps. Just over there, where the old Thames barges wallow, is more or less where the *Mayflower* was anchored. This is the place to drink to a gallant ship, a great voyage and the captain in the graveyard behind you.

OPEN *midday-23.00 (Mon-Sat), midday-22.00 (Sun)*

FOOD *midday-22.00 (Mon-Sat), midday-19.00 (Sun)*

CREDIT CARDS *all major cards*

DRAUGHT BEERS *Greene King IPA, Abbot Ale, John Smith's Extra Smooth, Guinness, Strongbow, Kronenbourg, Stella, Carling Black Label, Irish Harp, seasonal beer, 1 guest ale (weekly)*

Restaurant available to groups of more than 15, seats maximum 35

NEAREST TUBE STATION *Rotherhithe*

THE MELTON MOWBRAY

18 Holborn, EC1; 0171 405 7077

The Melton Mowbray is a medium-sized modern pub in Holborn with no history to speak of or ambience you would notice. It opens only five days a week. But on the day it first opened it went from nothing to being the highest trader in the company and it is now taking almost £1 million a year. It used to be a sports shop. Then in 1993 Fuller's spent £407,000 making it one of their first Ale and Pie houses and its immediate success took everyone aback. Middle management from every office in sight converged on it, a highly-desirable clientele, good mannered, free spending and, as a rule, quick eating. It became a big place for lunch and within a year Fuller's was spending another £120,000 winning more league tables by opening up a bar downstairs. It too was an instant success and tables outside gave them more seats still. Almost a thousand people a week are having lunch there now, the pub gets packed every day and people arrive at 12.30pm to make sure of a table. So how is it done? Well they use the space well and it is all state of the art in the big cellars, with electronic hoists for the beer and amazing computerised ovens in the kitchens. The pies rotate behind glass doors and cook in 2 minutes 45 seconds. It is an arresting bit of kitchen theatre. The office workers who pack The Melton Mowbray every day from Monday to Friday don't care about that though. My theory is they just seem to like having lunch there, that's all.

OPEN *11.00-23.00 (Mon-Fri)*
FOOD *11.00-20.00 (Mon-Fri)*
CREDIT CARDS *all major cards, not Diners*
DRAUGHT BEERS *Chiswick Bitter, Fuller's ESB, London Pride, Carling, Grolsch, Heineken, Stella Artois, Guinness, Scrumpy Jack, seasonal ale*
Wheelchair access to venue and loos. Private room: 70 seated, 100 standing, or Gallery (overlooking bar – not private) 25 seated, 35 standing
NEAREST TUBE STATION *Chancery Lane*

METBAR

Metropolitan Hotel, 19 Old Park Lane, W1; 0171 447 5757
Another venue where the driving machine of publicity has manufactured the element of exclusivity. They will tell you that there are 2,000 people on the waiting list, which doesn't appear to have changed since it opened to an already full membership list a year or so back. How can a place have a full membership before it opens? They sent out unsolicited memberships to almost everyone I know, that's how, and none of them get used. Which is not surprising, as it rivals only a motorway service station café for design, and I can match the atmosphere by standing at a bus stop in the rain. Membership is free so you could pander to them and apply, but the best way to get in is to sport a Donna Karan coat and say you've come to tidy up. Alternatively, try the I'm-a-resident-of-the-hotel trick.

OPEN *08.30-03.00 (Mon-Sat), 08.30-22.30 (Sun)*
FOOD *as opening hours*
CREDIT CARDS *all major cards*
Wheelchair access to venue
NEAREST TUBE STATION *Hyde Park Corner*

MIN'S

31 Beauchamp Place, SW3; 0171 589 5080
There are too few drinking places in Knightsbridge and even fewer worthy of any report, so I was quite sanguine when I heard of the opening of this new bar and restaurant, which comes to us courtesy of the owners of the nearby Enterprise, a long-established haunt of the Sloane set. There is only one beer, Rebel, a mildly sweet lager from the Czech Republic, bittered by the price tag of £4.50 (plus 45p service) per bottle. I opted for the wine list and the prices (£11.50-£150) reflect the rent for the property rather than the quality of wines. It's a small venue and, of the five of us present, four complained about the high-volume music. 'It has been levelled,' we were told. For this I read, 'Bog off, the staff like it'. Our waitress, fresh from the East Beirut School of Gerrymandering & Sorcery, told me off for scribbling notes on the drinks list. Well done, that girl, for being so assertive, I thought, and now get lost please. When the bill arrived, service was included. When the credit card slip arrived it was left open to tip again. The tactic of accidentally double charging often works when you've drunk too much, are on expenses or simply don't check properly, so how should you respond? I call the manager, explain that not only am I not prepared

to tip on the credit card but want the original service deleted for trying to trick me. It works every time, and quite rightly causes them a lot of hassle. This might be Knightsbridge, but I'm not paying for it.
OPEN *midday-23.00 (Mon-Sat)*
FOOD *midday-15.00 then 19.00-midnight (Mon-Sat)*
CREDIT CARDS *all major cards, not AmEx and Diners*
Wheelchair access possible to first floor only. Private room seats 10-14, 20 standing
NEAREST TUBE STATION *Knightbridge*

MIRO
3-4 Mile End Road, SW6; 0171 610 3457
The former Chapel Lafayette re-emerged last year as a badly re-designed bar and restaurant. It has bottled beers, cocktails and wines. Weekends are popular, when the bar fills up with a young, happy Fulham crowd, but they charge £3 admission after 10pm. Good for a late-night drink earlier in the week when admission is free.
OPEN *18.00-midnight (Tues-Wed), 18.00-01.30 (Thurs-Sat)*
FOOD *during opening hours*
CREDIT CARDS *all major cards*
Wheelchair access to venue
NEAREST TUBE STATION *Fulham Broadway*

THE MITRE
24 Craven Terrace, W2; 0171 262 5240
Whitbread's are great refurbishers of pubs. Each Whitbread pub gets a turn every five years and if it waits long enough it may get a REAL going over. The Mitre, a much admired pub in Bayswater, a Grade II listed building, emerged from one such recently. It took 11 weeks. It always was Victorian and it is sort of Victorian still, brand new, pastiche Victorian, a perfect example of this popular modern pub style. There are three bars, plus a family room and a function room, all beautifully decorated and handsomely furnished in the Victorian manner, hung with portraits and pretty clocks. Two have marble fireplaces, one has a stag's head, one a charming skylight formerly boarded up. The smallest at the back has a portrait of Disraeli, the coming man they say, and there is no smoking in the family room which has its own entrance to the hall and so to the street. Down worn stone stairs, an original feature, to the piano bar which has a maze of little drinking areas tucked under low ceilings and arches with flagged floors, big barrels, an old kitchen range and its own entrance to the little cobbled mews at the side. It is full of atmosphere and is thought to have a friendly ghost. 'It is still there,' says Helen Watts who runs The Mitre with her husband, Terry. 'When we are in bed we can hear it banging doors in the basement.'
OPEN *11.00-23.30 (Mon-Sat), midday-22.30 (Sun)*
FOOD *midday-21.30 (Daily)*
CREDIT CARDS *all major cards, not AmEx and Diners*
DRAUGHT BEERS *Boddingtons, Marston's Pedigree, Whitbread, Wadworth 6X, Heineken, Heineken Export, Stella Artois, Murphy's, Guinness, Strongbow*
Wheelchair access to venue. Two private rooms: seat 30 and 70
NEAREST TUBE STATION *Lancaster Gate*

THE MONARCH
45 Chalk Farm Road, NW1; 0171 916 1049
Drastic things have been happening in The Monarch. This small, intimate and unobtrusive music pub opposite the Roundhouse has had the builders in. Capacity has been doubled. You can get 400 in now. The loos have been trebled. The live music has been moved into a new home upstairs and the ground floor bar has been redesigned. You can get a lot more in there as well. Despite the changes the spirit of the old Monarch is intact

and it continues to be a leading showcase for up-and-coming bands. Music industry movers and shakers regularly drop by to check out the latest happening band. Recent discoveries include Marion, Space and Kula Shuker who have all been in the charts since then.

The new upstairs room, complete with its own bar, its decent-sized stage and high ceiling make this venue just about unbeatable for this kind of gig. You can usually expect a crush. After all you just may catch the new Rolling Stones here... Recommended.

OPEN *20.00-midnight (Mon-Thurs), 20.00-2.00 (Fri-Sat)*
FOOD *none served*
CREDIT CARDS *all major cards*
DRAUGHT BEERS *Stella, Boddingtons, Hoegaarden, Heineken Export, Dry Blackthorn*
Wheelchair access to venue, not to loos. Venue or upstairs room available for hire
NEAREST TUBE STATIONS *Chalk Farm, Camden*

THE MONKEY PUZZLE
30 Southwick Street, W2; 0171 723 0143

A very annoying thing happened to The Monkey Puzzle on the night of 16 October 1987. The great gale blew its monkey puzzle tree down. It was a large, handsome and impossible-to-climb monkey puzzle tree, pride of the garden and the pub had been named after it. Now look.

Well, life in The Monkey Puzzle goes on. It is a modern pub built into the ground floor of an apartment block and lots of cheery red signs guide you in saying 'Welcome' in a dozen different languages. Private hotels abound in these parts and there are lots of tourists on the streets. New owners have changed the beers and have redesigned and replanted the garden which now looks very nice with its new tables and handsome awning. A young monkey puzzle tree in a sheltered corner keeps its fingers crossed.

OPEN *11.00-23.00 (Mon-Sat), midday-22.30 (Sun)*
FOOD *midday-21.00 (Mon-Sun)*
CREDIT CARDS *all major cards*
DRAUGHT BEERS *Badger, Dempsey's, Dorset IPA, Tanglefoot, Hofbräu, Guinness, Dry Blackthorn*
Wheelchair access to venue
NEAREST TUBE STATIONS *Edgware Road, Paddington*

THE MOON UNDER WATER
28 Leicester Square, WC2; 0171 839 2837

The Moon under Water used to be an Angus Steak House until 1992 when Wetherspoon's took it over. From being a long thin restaurant with steaks it became a long thin pub with food all day. It specialises in good cask ales, cheaper than most, but Wetherspoon's famous cut-price pint of Younger's Scotch bitter is not quite so cheap here. This being Leicester Square, it is £1.50 a pint – still one of the cheapest pints in the West End, however. The Moon under Water has a strong character, won't have music and won't have smoking round the bar. Far from putting anyone off, all this seems to bring more people in, and Wetherspoon's have recently been making a bit more room inside by moving the bar and losing some of the booths. The fickle Westminster Council sometimes allows drinking outside and sometimes won't. At the moment they will, so 12 people can enjoy refreshments in one of the biggest pedestrianised areas in central London. Very good of you, Westminster.

OPEN *11.00-23.00 (Mon-Sat), 12.00-22.30 (Sun)*
FOOD *11.00-22.00 (Mon-Sat), 12.00-21.30 (Sun)*
CREDIT CARDS *Visa, Mastercard, AmEx*

DRAUGHT BEERS *Courage Directors, Theakston Best, Foster's, Kronenbourg, Guinness, Dry Blackthorn, Old Rosie Cider, Spitfire Ale, two weekly guest ales*
Wheelchair access to venue and loos
NEAREST TUBE STATION *Leicester Square*

MORPETH ARMS

58 Millbank, SW1; 0171 834 6442

The Tate Gallery delights some, sends others reeling down Millbank. They should reel to the right. In minutes they will find comfort and reassurance in this trusty and dependable Victorian pub. All is traditional and familiar in The Morpeth Arms and will stay so. It is a listed building now, admired and popular. The summer is particularly busy with stout tables and wooden benches right across the front and down the side. These are regularly filled, particularly at lunchtime. The traffic roars by and you can hardly hear yourself speak, but they do a decent lunch and it's a Young's pub so the beer is good too. Don't venture into the cellars though. They say that soon after the pub was built in 1845 a convict on the run hid in the labyrinth of vaults beneath the pub, lost himself and was never seen again. Visitors to the vaults though have felt a hand on their shoulder and have been chilled by an unseen presence dripping water. It has sent them dashing back to the Tate. Stand with your back to the pub and look across the river. The extraordinary building facing you is the new headquarters of MI5.

OPEN *11.00-23.00 (Mon-Sat), midday-22.30 (Sun)*
FOOD *11.00-20.00 (Mon-Sun)*
CREDIT CARDS *all major cards, not AmEx*
DRAUGHT BEERS *Young's Bitter, Young's Special, Guinness, Dry Blackthorn, Stella Artois, Carling Black Label, Young's Pilsner, Young's Export, one seasonal ale*
Wheelchair access to venue. Private room: 36 seated, 60 standing
NEAREST TUBE STATION *Pimlico*

THE MUCKY DUCK

108 Fetter Lane, EC4; 0171 242 9518

Scene: Two ladies chatting outside a factory bearing the sign, Sid Brown's Tool Works. One is saying to the other: 'You're a very lucky woman Mrs Brown'. Partners Gareth Stones and Tony Crowe are proud of the framed seaside postcards at the Mucky Duck. All those bathing belles, landladies, red-nosed drunks, vicars and fat ladies in stripes with all their doubles entendres are worth the detour from Holborn or Fleet Street. The Mucky Duck has been so named only since July 1993 before which it was The Swan, a Fleet Street haunt with a strong presence from the neighbouring and now deserted Daily Mirror building. Gone are the hacks and also the stuffed swan that used to look down on the assembly at the bar. Upstairs is Annie's Bar. Annie was a previous incumbent. It is a bright room with a busy lunch crowd. Parties are held here. The speciality upstairs as well as down is the Mucky Duck Doorstep, a sandwich measuring two inches thick. With the Mucky Duck going strong, Stones and Crowe formed The Mucky Pub Co. and looked around for a second pub. They found The Devonshire Arms in Duke Street and are usually there these days, leaving The Mucky Duck in the safe hands of Maurice Daley, the one-time Stoke City goalkeeper. A third pub is in the offing.

OPEN *11.00-23.00 (Mon-Fri)*
FOOD *midday-14.30 (Mon-Fri)*
CREDIT CARDS *Mastercard, Visa*
DRAUGHT BEERS *Caffrey's, Greene King, London Pride, Tiger, Carling Black Label, Carling Premier, Guinness, Dry Blackthorn, Staropramen*
Private room: 35 seated, 60-70 standing, **OPEN** *for evening functions*
NEAREST TUBE STATION *Chancery Lane*

THE MULBERRY BUSH

Upper Ground, SE1; 0171 928 7940

After 50 years of furious dispute the new Coin Street is emerging. One redevelopment scheme after another has grappled with these 16 prime acres on the South Bank. There were two public inquiries, countless court actions, constant protests and demonstrations but now the first groups of new houses and flats are finished and occupied. They have cafés, restaurants and shops, a riverside walkway, a park and a market. They also have a fine modern pub. The Mulberry Bush sits on the outer rim of the Mulberry Co-op, which was the first of the housing co-operatives to be completed. The National Theatre and LWT are to the left, IPC Magazines and the *Daily Express* to the right and very stylish developments lie straight ahead. Something tells me that The Mulberry Bush won't be short of customers. It is a Young's pub and very pleasant. Its big bar has a whole wall of glass doors which fold back completely, the conservatory at the back is a no-smoking area with air-conditioning and its own entrance, and a broad spiral staircase takes you to the restaurant on the first floor. You can stand on the balcony there and wave to the Oxo tower which is coming to spectacular life again. How great that after all the alarums and excursions it has survived.

OPEN *11.00-23.00 (Mon-Sat)*

FOOD *Restaurant: midday-21.00; Bistro/Bar: 11.00-23.00*

CREDIT CARDS *all major cards*

DRAUGHT BEERS *Young's: Pilsner, Export, Best Bitter, Special, First Gold; Dirty Dick's, Winter Warmer, Ramrod Smooth, Carling Black Label, Stella, Guinness, Strongbow*

Wheelchair access to venue, disabled loo on ground floor. Private room seats 40, 80 standing

NEAREST TUBE STATIONS *Waterloo, Embankment, Blackfriars*

MULLINS COFFEE HOUSE

27 The Market, Covent Garden, WC2; 0171 379 7724

A tiny little coffee shop sits on the south-eastern corner of the market. The entrepreneurial owners concentrate on wines in the evening and have some of the most perfect outside seats on the piazza. Sit for a while, sip on your wine, and the entire world will wander by. There are few better locations in London.

OPEN *11.30-23.00 (Mon-Sat) 12.00-18.00 (Sun)*

FOOD *12.00-14.30 and 17.30-22.00 (Mon-Fri), 12.00-15.00 and 17.30-10.00 (Sat), 12.00-15.00 (Sun)*

Pastries available during opening times

CREDIT CARDS *all major cards*

NEAREST TUBE STATION *Covent Garden*

J. J. MURPHY'S

43-45 Beauchamp Place, SW3; 0171 581 8886

There are bigger Irish theme pubs and noisier and possibly more Irish but none, I think, with a better address than the new J. J. Murphy's. Beauchamp Place. Knightsbridge. Directly opposite the famously fashionable San Lorenzo's. A simple home-town pub could hardly do better than that. The pub that was here before was called the Grove Tavern. Do you remember it? No, few do. Anyway Whitbread's, whose pub it was, closed it and in its place put J. J. Murphy's, London's first. Others will follow in more modest places. Apparently there really was a J.J. Murphy. It was his brewery in County Cork that made the Murphy's stout which is still sold all over London. J. J. Murphy's in Knightsbridge sells Murphy's of course, and Guinness and Hurley's, an Irish ale. It is an agreeable pub filled with nooks and crannies, snugs and booths. It has taped Irish music all day and live Irish music on Sunday afternoons – a violin and someone singing as a rule. The food is

Irish too of course, bacon and cabbage, Dublin Coddle and the like, cooked daily by Mohammed, the resident chef. I'm told he makes the soda bread every morning too.

OPEN *11.00-23.00 (Mon-Sat), midday-22.30 (Sun)*
FOOD *11.00-21.00 (Mon-Thurs), 11.00-17.00 (Fri), 11.00-16.00 (Sat)*
CREDIT CARDS *all major cards, not AmEx*
DRAUGHT BEERS *Boddingtons, Hurley's, Wadworth 6X, London Pride, Heineken, Heineken Export, Stella Artois, Guinness, Murphy's, Strongbow*
NEAREST TUBE STATION *Knightsbridge*

THE MUSEUM TAVERN

49 Great Russell Street, WC1; 0171 242 8987

The pub that first occupied this commanding corner in Bloomsbury was called the Dog and Duck. Well that wouldn't do once the British Museum opened on the other side of the road and in 1761 it chose a daring new name. It became the British Museum Tavern.

It seems to have been a homely place. You could take your own pork or lamb and have it cooked for a penny. Clearly something grander was required and it was rebuilt in 1798 and again, grander yet and grander, in 1855. This time William Finch Hill, the theatre architect, was the designer. His building, renamed the Museum Tavern, had four entrances to five bars, with pool and billiards and rooms for lodgers upstairs. He suspended huge globes from ornate iron fittings above the doors and gas lamps in every window. It is this building, the outside hardly changed, that you see today. Generations of scholars have crossed the road from the British Museum to drink here. Among them was the museum's most famous student, Karl Marx, who is still suspected by the pub of having broken one of the mirrors in the bar's back fitting. Marx would presumably have approved of what has since happened to the pub interior – all divisions between public bar, private bar, jug bar and bar parlour abolished. No juke boxes or taped music lurks to alarm shy denizens of the British Museum who still come in. It remains a gentlemanly, scholarly pub surrounded by academic bookshops, and in nearby Coptic Street is what some people, i.e. me, consider the best pizza house in London.

OPEN *11.00-23.00 (Mon-Sat), midday-22.30 (Sun)*
FOOD *11.00-22.00 (Mon-Sat), midday-22.00 (Sun)*
CREDIT CARDS *all major cards*
DRAUGHT BEERS *Courage Best, Courage Directors, Theakston Best, Theakston Old Peculier, John Smith's, Beck's, Foster's, Kronenbourg, Guinness, Strongbow, one monthly guest ale*
Wheelchair access to venue
NEAREST TUBE STATIONS *Tottenham Court Road, Russell Square*

THE NAG'S HEAD

53 Kinnerton Street, SW1; 0171 235 1135

The Nag's Head, tucked away in this little mews in the most expensive part of town, is a very chatty pub. It isn't very big and the bar counter is a chatty sort of height, as high as your average kitchen table. The stools round it the height of kitchen chairs. Then there's the landlord, Kevin Moran, and his son Peter. They chat to everyone. Kevin was a successful stunt man before he hurt his back, and Peter describes himself as a jobbing actor though he is mostly at the The Nag's Head. Still, he says, a pub IS acting and this is an extrovert and entertaining place. Conversation is general with much laughter and newcomers are soon part of it. Kinnerton Street is smart now but it was mostly stables when it started in the 1820s. The Nag's Head was the ostlers' pub. It was tiny, a single bar not much bigger than a horse's stall and this is how it stayed into the 1960s. Len Cole, the formidable landlord of the day, would say that The Nag's Head was the smallest pub in London and that was how he liked it. His successors saw no point in unused space at the back and it is a bit bigger now and the Morans have made it a lot more comfortable. Pictures and photographs and mementos of times past now cover the panelled walls, fires are lit in winter and in the summer people take their drinks into the mews. The front bar is for drinking and talking and the back bar is for eating and talking with food from noon to 10 pm. Unless they sell out first...

OPEN *11.00-23.00 (Mon-Sat), midday-22.30 (Sun)*
FOOD *midday-21.30 (Mon-Sun)*
CREDIT CARDS *none taken*
DRAUGHT BEERS *Adnams, Benskins, Kilkenny, Tetley's, Carlsberg, Castlemaine XXXX, Lowenbräu, Guinness, Olde English*
NEAREST TUBE STATIONS *Hyde Park Corner, Knightsbridge*

THE NARROW BOAT

119 St Peter Street, N1; 0171 226 3906

There was a time when The Narrow Boat looked liked a narrow boat, outside and in. But one June night in 1993 fire broke out on board. It was spotted in the early hours by the landlord of the day, Michael Basson, who called the fire brigade. Firemen did their best but there wasn't much left of The Narrow Boat in the morning. Rebuilding it took the rest of the summer and while they were about it Bass made the pub bigger and more publike. It would never be mistaken for a real narrow boat again. It still has a lovely site on the bank of the Regents Canal in Islington, though. A small deck overlooking the water, a spiral staircase going down to the towpath and a bit of the old boatlike saloon remain. Nautical objects still abound and the new Narrow Boat attracts a youngish crowd as it always did. There's bar billiards and gaming machines and a Wurlitzer juke box playing everything from Elvis to Oasis and the food is youthful and reasonably priced. Live bands play on Fridays, there's a regular quiz night and in the basin beyond, as they always did, narrow boats gather.

OPEN *midday-23.00 (Mon-Sat), midday-22.30 (Sun)*
FOOD *midday-15.00 (Mon-Sun)*
CREDIT CARDS *all major cards, not AmEx*
DRAUGHT BEERS *Bass, Caffrey's, London Pride, Carling Black Label, Carling Premier, Grolsch, Guinness, Red Rock*
Wheelchair access to venue. Private room seats 40
NEAREST TUBE STATION *Angel*

NAVAJO JOE

34 King Street, WC2; 0171 240 4008

Navajo Joe! Who he? He might be the man the press release describes as a person 'deprived of his ancestral hunting grounds, dignity and way of life who took comfort in the white man's laughing waters' before earning huge amounts of money through compensation from the US government. Alternatively, he might simply be a waiter at this bar who served me far too many of their wide range of tequilas during several unmemorable visits I deigned to make.

It is the height of modernism: a long modern bar with a galleried upper level and a basement that many people have yet to discover. It promises much, but you have to practically beg the staff for a drinks list and then they don't seem to be so knowledgeable about the encyclopaedic and expensive range of drinks on offer. A South West American menu is hinted at, but I can't even contemplate as to where or how people would eat comfortably here; the sheer enormity of the crowds means that even forcing down the odd dozen or so tequilas is taxing enough. On the subject of crowds, the group which owns this bar prides itself on having the longest queues in London. This is no selling point, and regular readers will know that I plead with you not to stand in line to part with your hard-earned cash. Another boast is that the owners have previously won the

Evening Standard Bar of the Year competition three years running. This, I can tell you, is as true as I am sober after a long night chasing the worm in Covent Garden.

OPEN *12.00-23.00 (Mon-Sat); closed Sun*
FOOD *12.00-midnight (Mon-Sat)*
CREDIT CARDS *all major cards*
Wheelchair access. Private room seats 40, 60 standing
NEAREST TUBE STATIONS *Covent Garden, Leicester Square*

NEW MOON

88 Gracechurch Street, EC3; 0171 626 3625

This handsome, dignified City pub occupies a commanding position in Leadenhall Market, the lofty arcade in the heart of the money market, where you can still find butchers, bakers and candlestick makers. The high Victorian hall with its long counter fills with brokers when the markets close, and the long downstairs bar gets busy at lunchtimes. This is where the food is served. During the pub's most recent refurbishment John Hall, the licensee, found an old menu dated 18 August 1900. In those days the pub was called The Half Moon and boasted the sort of restaurant that has printed, dated menus. You did well in this one: rump steak 1 shilling, potatoes (boiled) 2d... . Lunch in the New Moon costs rather more nowadays.

OPEN *11.00-23.00 (Mon-Fri)*
FOOD *11.30-14.30 (Mon-Fri) – Pizzas*
CREDIT CARDS *all major cards, not AmEx and Diners*
DRAUGHT BEERS *Boddingtons, Brakspear, London Pride, Marston's Pedigree, Wadworth 6X, Heineken Export, Stella Artois, Guinness, Murphy's, Strongbow, one seasonal ale*
NEAREST TUBE STATIONS *Monument, Liverpool Street, Bank*

THE NIGHTINGALE

97 Nightingale Lane, SW12; 0181 673 1637

You may not hear a nightingale at The Nightingale but other birds carol away. The pub has a delightful and secluded paved garden, the perfect place for a quiet drink on a summer's evening. Borders, window boxes and hanging baskets are all luxuriant. It wins prizes for its flowers. It has had a prize from Camra for the quality of its beer too and recently won one for the quality of its customers. The Association of London Brewers and Licensed Retailers had a contest to find which pub inside the M25 had raised most money for charity. It turned out to be The Nightingale. The pub itself is comfortable and welcoming, with homemade soups, cottage pie and real sausages at lunchtime, and has an impressive wine list, ten reds, nine whites, two sparkling and a good house claret. It is packed in the evening.

OPEN *11.00-23.00 (Mon-Sat), 12.00-22.30 (Sun)*
FOOD *12.00-14.15 and 19.00-21.15 (Mon-Sat), 12.00-22.30 (Sun)*
CREDIT CARDS *all major cards*
DRAUGHT BEERS *All Young's range, including seasonal ales, Stella Artois, Carling Black Label, Guinness, Dry Blackthorn*
Wheelchair access to venue
NEAREST TUBE STATION *Clapham South*

NOTTING HILL ARTS CLUB

21 Notting Hill Gate, W11; 0171 460 4459

This is a club (of sorts) where you can expect almost anything to happen. It is located in a decent-sized air-conditioned basement, where you may well find people playing board games, watching cult movies on a big screen, having dance nights or parties, or reading a book from the Penguin selection available. There are two rooms: one with a large circular island bar, seating booths and some stray 60s and 70s plastic-coated settees. The other room is where the events take place. The Club is a novel idea, well thought-out, and fills a much-needed gap in the market for a young, fashionable clientele. It is helping to make Notting Hill a destination for drinking. Another point to its credit is that it doesn't have any of those silly dress codes that so many decent places appear to be adopting.

OPEN *18.00-01.00 (Mon-Sat), 18.00-23.00 (Sun)*
FOOD *as opening hours*
CREDIT CARDS *all major cards, not AmEx*
NEAREST TUBE STATION *Notting Hill Gate*

O BAR

83 Wardour Street, W1; 0171 437 3490
The Round House, built in 1892 on a fine corner site in Soho, large, dignified, five-storied, personified Victorian virtues. It was an alderman among pubs. Ah, the sigh of the pumps as the careful pints were drawn, the top hats in the private bar, the corsets in the snug. It has undergone an astonishing transformation. It is now the O Bar, a glittering glam arena fuelled by Costa cocktails, strutting its stuff through the 90's with music thudding, disco, acid jazz, funk, and every table taken, queues outside and doormen with headsets and intercoms. It doesn't open until mid-afternoon. It doesn't close until the early hours – 3am on Fridays and Saturdays It gets bigger as you look. There are three bars now. Downstairs is a grey and silver basement where DJs rule at weekends. This opens only in the evening and its juke box takes over during the week. The first floor is now a lounge bar with easy chairs and chesterfields and views right up Wardour Street from floor to ceiling windows. The main bar on the ground floor is where the action is though, absolutely packed, music belting, barmen tossing glasses and bottles around like Tom Cruise in Cocktail. It never happened at the Round House in all its days.

OPEN *14.00-03.00 (Mon-Sat), 14.00-22.30 (Sun)*
FOOD *18.00-02.00 (Mon-Sat), none on Sun*
CREDIT CARDS *all major cards, not AmEx*
Wheelchair access to venue. Private room seats 43
NEAREST TUBE STATIONS *Piccadilly Circus, Leicester Square, Tottenham Court Road*

OFFICE BAR

3-5 Rathbone Place, W1; 0171 636 1598
We all like to feel and look the part in preparation for a night on the tiles. When I went to Office recently, the prefectly lit, fully-mirrored stairwell provided a stark reminder of those parts of my body I'd hoped weren't as public as the mirrors reflected. It was quite a relief to get inside the large colourful, air-conditioned bar, and plonk myself down at one of the well-spaced tables to begin the slow alcoholic descent into memory loss. A pitcher of Alabama Slammer (£11.95) helped, even though I had just missed the half-price happy hour (5-7pm). Wednesday is games night (£5), and from the list of over 100 I found Ker-Plunk and Connect 4 taxing enough, and decided to steer well clear of a rather intimate young group playing Twister. Office has club nights Thursday to Saturday (prices vary), with live bands, soul, ska and 60s classics. I returned for lunch one day and found it a surprisingly sedate affair – but I'd forgotten about those bloody mirrors.

OPEN *12.00-03.00 (Mon-Sat)*
FOOD *as opening hours*
CREDIT CARDS *all major cards*
NEAREST TUBE STATION *Tottenham Court Road*

O'HANLON'S

8 Tysoe Street, EC1; 0171 837 4112
There can't be a more Irish pub in London. This has nothing to do with any ersatz sub-genre of Irish theme pubs popping up all over the place. This

is an Irish pub that just happens to be in London. John O'Hanlon from County Kerry bought it some five years ago, named it after himself, moved his family in to run the place – and soon had a resounding success on his hands. Inside this little corner pub in Clerkenwell there's a big plain bar where you'll find the man himself pouring out the pints and presiding over the craic. His mother can be found in the kitchen preparing all the home-cooked dishes and baking the soda bread. The beers? Well, they come from a new brewery in London called O'Hanlon's – he brews them himself underneath the arches in Vauxhall. The standard bearer is O'Hanlon's Dry Stout, then there's a wheatbeer he calls Malster's Weiss, an English light ale called Blakelyes No. 1, and Myrica Ale, an Irish ale brewed with bog myrtle and honey. So succesful are these brews that many London free houses are now stocking them.

OPEN *12.00-23.00 (Mon-Sat), 18.00-22.30 (Sun)*
FOOD *12.00-14.30 (Mon-Sat) and 18.00-21.00 (Mon-Fri)*
CREDIT CARDS *none taken*
DRAUGHT BEERS *Blakeley's No. 1, Malster's Weiss, Myrica Ale, O'Hanlon's Red Ale, Carling Black Label, Staropramen, Guinness, O'Hanlon's Dry Stout, O'Hanlon's Smooth Dry Stout, O'Hanlon's seasonal ale Wheelchair access to venue. Private room seats 30-40*
NEAREST TUBE STATION *Farringdon, Angel*

OLD BANK OF ENGLAND

194 Fleet Street, EC4; 0171 430 2055
Fuller's, which likes to turn banks into pubs, has excelled itself with this one. It is a magnificent Grade I listed building which for 87 years was the Law Courts' branch of the Bank of England. Now it is one of the most imposing pubs in London. It was put up here next to the Law Courts in 1888 at the suggestion of the Treasury. 'Sombre and opulent,' wrote Sir Nikolaus Pevsner. It replaced The Cock, one of London's most historic inns, which was obliged to move across the road. How ironic that, 100 years later, the grand usurper should have become a pub itself.

Outside nothing has changed; inside there has been an adjustment or two but high Victorian it remains and great heavens the Banking Hall! Noble columns, high Italianate windows, a magnificent ceiling with chandeliers that have to be winched down from the floor above when a bulb goes. Confidently centre stage middle reigns its splendid new bar. The floor above, now occupied by solicitors, was once part of the 27-room apartment provided for the bank manager, such a personage was he. His one time office is now a club room, the office next to it a restaurant. There is less formal food too. You place an order at the bar and it is brought to you or, anyway, to the lawyers and bankers who crowd in at lunchtime. They are back in force on their way home in the early evening. Bank vaults always give builders headaches but the vaults in this one beat anything. Impenetrable strongrooms. Vast walk-in safes. A bullion room with steel-reinforced walls four feet thick, armour plated ceilings and mammoth steel doors. To get pipes from the new cellar to the bar took thermal lances and diamond drills. The bullion room is the wine and spirit store now. It must be the safest wine and spirits store in history.

OPEN *11.00-23.00 (Mon-Fri)*
FOOD *midday-20.00 (Mon-Fri)*
CREDIT CARDS *all major cards*
DRAUGHT BEERS *Chiswick Bitter, ESB, Fuller's seasonal ale, London, Carling Black Label, Grolsch, Stella Artois, Guinness, Murphy's, Scrumpy Jack Pride, one guest ale*
Private room: 20-50 seated, 20-80 standing
NEAREST TUBE STATION *Temple*

THE OLD BELL TAVERN

95 Fleet Street, EC4; 0171 583 0070

What happened to Fleet Street's busy pubs when the newspapers left? We are nettled to report that this trauma had less effect on them than was expected. The newish Popinjay closed and the King and Keys, scene of much dramatic confrontation, was transformed into a scruffy Murphy's, but the rest seem much as they were. Rather more so if anything. Here is The Old Bell Tavern, a senior Fleet Street pub, built in 1678 by Sir Christopher Wren as a hostel for his masons. He was rebuilding St Bride's Church, which had been burned out in the Great Fire, and he needed somewhere to lodge them so up went The Old Bell. You know St Bride's? It is a beautiful church and for all these years The Old Bell has been its nearest neighbour, just a lathe and plaster job, nothing very special but getting steadily more interesting with age. It has been a licensed tavern for 300 years and it, too, is now a listed building. In the great days of Fleet Street The Old Bell was a printers' pub, small but cosy, its bar tucked away behind its off-licence. After the newspaper diaspora in the late 80s it had to find an entirely new clientele, as did all the pubs in Fleet Street. It is now a lawyers', and bankers', pub and is doing well again. There have been changes. The off-licence has gone altogether making the pub a little bigger. In its place is a comfortable snug, and a handsome stained-glass window faces the street. Printers taking a trip down memory lane will notice such things and will be pleased to see that the triangular oak stools, a feature of the pub since its early days, are still there. These according to The Old Bell, are unique to The Old Bell.

OPEN *11.00-23.00 (Mon-Fri)*

FOOD *midday-15.00 (Mon-Fri)*

CREDIT CARDS all major cards

DRAUGHT BEERS Brakspear, Marston's Pedigree, Pope's Original, Tetley's, Carlsberg, Castlemaine XXXX, Stella Artois, Guinness, Dry Blackthorn, a weekly guest ale

Wheelchair access to venue through back doors

NEAREST TUBE STATION Blackfriars

THE OLD BULL AND BUSH

North End Road, NW3; 0181 455 3685

The Old Bull and Bush, declares The Old Bull and Bush, is probably the most famous pub in the world. It's right. It probably is. It was the song that did it, of course. Florrie Forde, the great Victorian music hall star, 15 stone and swathed in mauve brocade, sang it the length and breadth of the land. It made her a fortune and The Old Bull and Bush a household name, and 100 years later we can still join in. Extraordinary. Oh well, here we go:

  Come, come, come and make eyes at me
  Down at the Old Bull and Bush (ta ra ra ra ra)
  Come, come, drink some port wine with me
  Down at the Old Bull and Bush

The Bull and Bush had a long history before that. Booklets on the bar tell the story. Old farmhouse. Charles I. Medicinal springs. Hogarth, William Pitt, Gainsborough making his helpful remark - 'What a delightful little snuggery is this said Bull and Bush...' Then the pleasure garden and the music licence and concerts and sing-songs and half the East End heading for a day in the country and a good old knees-up down at the old Bull and Bush. With Florrie Forde's smash hit they had the perfect song for it. The Old Bull and Bush is still going great guns. There were huge changes to it in the 20s and again in the 80s when it closed for three months for a major rebuilding job. The pub was changed from top to toe with new bars, new kitchens, new places to eat, jolly bits and quiet bits. One of the new bars might be a country house library.

They use this one for private parties now. It is the one that has the piano and every now and then one of the guests will sit down at it and bang out the only possible song all over again...

Hear the little German band
Just let me hold your hand
Do do have a little drink or two
Down at the Old Bull and Bush. Bush Bush.

OPEN *midday-23.00 (Mon-Sat), midday-22.30 (Sun)*
FOOD *midday-22.00 (Mon-Sat), midday-21.30 (Sun)*
CREDIT CARDS *all major cards*
DRAUGHT BEERS *Calder's Cream Ale, Tetley's, Carlsberg, Castlemaine XXXX, Guinness, Dry Blackthorn, Addlestones, a weekly guest beer*
Wheelchair access to venue and loo
NEAREST TUBE STATION *Golders Green*

YE OLD COCK TAVERN

22 Fleet Street, EC4; 0171 353 8570

Ask not why the chicken crossed the road. The Olde Cock crossed the road in 1887 to make way for a bank, uncommonly civil. It was, then as now, a famous old tavern. Pepys, Goldsmith, Sheridan and Dickens all knew it well and Tennyson had written a poem about it, not perhaps his best but its first verse is hard to beat:

'Oh plump headwaiter at the Cock
To which I most resort
How goes the time?' 'Tis five o'clock'
'Go fetch a pint of port.'

The Olde Cock rescued as much as it could from the old building – pictures, furniture, the fireplace and its overmantel (Grinling Gibbons they say), and resumed its role in life which was filling poets with port and others with strong ale.

It was comfortably past the 100th anniversary of its great move when, in April 1990, a disastrous fire broke out in the bar and most of the things that had been rescued from the old tavern were destroyed. Still the building itself, a copy of the old one and a landmark in Fleet Street, was saved. So, happily, was the old fireplace and, after eight months in the hands of the builders and restorers, Ye Olde Cock reopened looking every bit itself again. Some in Fleet Street even reported improvements. The upstairs restaurant was lighter, they said, and in some ways nicer and still had its excellent carvery at lunchtime. As for the Dickens Room on the second floor, with its old panelling and Dickens mementos, this was untouched by the fire. It is a pleasant period room used for special occasions. Take with a pinch of salt tales of Dickens dining there. He died before the olde cock crossed the road.

OPEN *11.00-23.00 (Mon-Fri) (Functions only at weekends)*
FOOD *Bar: 11.00-15.00; cold buffet and hot stock pot all day*
CREDIT CARDS *all major cards*
DRAUGHT BEERS *John Smith's Extra Smooth, Directors Bitter, Guinness, Strongbow, Theakston Best Bitter and Old Peculier, Foster's, Kronenbourg*
Wheelchair access to venue. Private rooms, two, both seat 60
NEAREST TUBE STATION *Temple Gate*

THE OLD COFFEE HOUSE

49 Beak Street, W1; 0171 437 2197

It is a pub, but The Old Coffee House was a coffee house in the 18th century and didn't see the need to change its name when its primary purpose changed to selling alcohol. The bar is filled with stuffed animals, brass things hanging from the ceiling, and such rare and curious items as the boxing gloves used by Dave Charnley to knock out David 'Darkie' Hughes when defending his lightweight title in 1961. It was the shortest-ever British title fight and lasted 40 seconds. The Old Coffee House is proud of its range of lunches – 20 main courses on offer every day, plus trad pub grub. You can still get coffee in The Old Coffee House. Filter only.

OPEN 11.00-23.00 (Mon-Sat), 12.00-15.00 and 19.00-22.30 (Sun)
FOOD 12.00-15.00 (Mon-Sat)
CREDIT CARDS none taken
DRAUGHT BEERS Courage Best, Courage Directors, Marston's Pedigree, John Smith's Extra Smooth, Budweiser, Foster's, Holsten, Kronenbourg, Guinness, Strongbow
Wheelchair access to venue, not to loos. Private room: 30 seated, 40 standing
NEAREST TUBE STATIONS Piccadilly Circus, Oxford Circus

OLD DR BUTLERS HEAD

Masons Avenue, EC2; 0171 606 3504

Masons Avenue gives you a good idea of how things would have looked in 17th century London after a miracle clean-up. Add piles of horses' dung and emptied chamber pots, don't look too closely and you could almost be in the London of James I. It is a narrow flagstoned alley, a black and white five-storey half-timbered mansion on one side and the Old Dr Butlers Head a few feet away on the other. The pub has one big bar with old timbers, bare floorboards, ancient-looking panelling up to the ceiling, old barrels and stout wooden furniture. Every lunchtime the bar is full of smartly dressed City men and women. Up two steps at the back there are tables and chairs, and girls making goodlooking sandwiches, and upstairs are two floors of restaurants, with roasts and Dr Butler's Daily Specialities. Dr Butler was a dreadful old quack who fired off pistols inches away from the ears of his patients to cure epilepsy and dropped poor souls with ague into the river. The great cure that got him in with King James I was his medicinal ale – good for your tum, he said. He bought several alehouses to sell it in, and got this one in 1616. It is the last remaining of Dr Butler's pubs, but it hasn't sold his ale for 300 years.

OPEN 11.00-23.00 (Mon-Fri)
FOOD 11.00-15.00 (Mon-Fri)
CREDIT CARDS all major cards
DRAUGHT BEERS Boddingtons, Brakspear, Flowers, Marston's Pedigree, Wadworth 6X, Heineken, Stella Artois, Guinness, Strongbow, London Pride
Private room seats 120
NEAREST TUBE STATION Moorgate

YE OLDE CHESHIRE CHEESE

Wine Office Court, 145 Fleet Street, EC4; 0171 353 6170

The Cheshire Cheese is one of London's most celebrated taverns. It is the archetypal 17th-century chophouse – small, cosy rooms, black settles, sawdust-covered floors, creaking stairs, open fires and good old boys in the chimney corner. The original tavern burnt down in the Great Fire of London but was rebuilt the following year, and there were no major changes for the next 300 years. The Yorkshire brewers Samuel Smith bought it in 1986 and found it distinctly unsteady on its pins. In 1990 the pub was underpinned and tightened up, totally refurbished and effectively extended. By the time it reopened it had just about doubled in size. The old tavern now has six separate bars, three restaurants and a private dining room. A modern kitchen on the top floor supplies food to them all, sending it down by dumb waiters. By and large the restoration has been a mannerly one. The pub seems hardly to have changed at all, even keeping the faded gilt notice above the door saying 'Gentlemen Only'. The management hope women customers will ignore this. The building itself has stopped leaning and groaning. The floorboards, still swept and freshly scattered with sawdust twice a day, have lost their creak. It is now ready for the millennium.

OPEN *11.30-23.00 (Mon-Sat), 12.00-17.00 (Sun)*
FOOD *bar 12.00-14.30 (Mon-Fri); restaurant 12.00-21.30 (Mon-Sat), 12.00-16.00 (Sun)*
CREDIT CARDS *all major cards*
DRAUGHT BEERS *Old Brewery, Samuel Smith's Dark Mild, Ayingerbräu, Ayingerbräu Pils, Samuel Smith's Stout, Samuel Smith's Reserve Cider*
Private room: five function rooms catering for 15-120
NEAREST TUBE STATIONS *Blackfriars, Chancery Lane*

YE OLDE MITRE TAVERN

1 Ely Court, Ely Place, just off Hatton Gardens, EC1; 0171 405 4751
Few pubs have had closer brushes with great events than Ye Olde Mitre Tavern. The medieval Bishops of Ely were vastly rich and powerful. Their palace was hereabouts and in 1547 one of them, the well-named Bishop Goddrich, built this little tavern for his servants. It was all go in the bishops' palace. The Black Prince stayed there, John of Gaunt died there, Henry VIII feasted there and Elizabeth I danced round its cherry tree and gave most of the estate to her favourite, Sir Christopher Hatton.

Things went from great to disastrous for the bishops and in 1772 their palace was pulled down. The little tavern came down too but it was speedily rebuilt to the original plan and here it is, one of London's most picturesque pubs with a stone mitre from the bishops' gatehouse in the wall and the trunk of the cherry tree in a corner of the bar. The two small dark panelled rooms with their high settles and old prints are as they have always been. They share a counter and sometimes a shoe horn would be needed to get in one more City gent. Up the narrow winding stairs is the Bishop's Room, rather larger. You have a good chance of getting a seat there, or poke about outside. There's a narrow yard with barrels for tables if you don't mind standing.

It is well tucked away, this old pub. Ely Court, a narrow covered alley off Hatton Gardens, is the best way to it. Leave by the even narrower alley which will take you to Ely Place and there, turning left, you will find The Mitre's most distinguished neighbour, St Etheldreda's, the 13th century bishops' church. You used to have sanctuary in both church and pub. Until quite recently the police could not enter either. Note for villains: they can now. Note for everyone else: it closes at weekends.

OPEN *11.00-23.00 (Mon-Fri)*
FOOD *11.00-21.45 (Mon-Fri)*
CREDIT CARDS *none taken*
DRAUGHT BEERS *Burton, Friary Meux, Tetley's, Carlsberg, Castlemaine XXXX, Guinness, Dry Blackthorn*
Private room seats 25
NEAREST TUBE STATION *Chancery Lane*

YE OLDE SURGEON

183 Tottenham Court Road, W1; 0171 631 3618
A theme pub and what do you suppose the theme is? An operating theatre. Honestly. It's all Spitting Image type surgeons and patients at Ye Olde Surgeon, jokes involving cutting bits off and sewing bits on, humorous skulls, funny bandaged bits, real life ads for Ex-Lax. They used to do a cocktail called Lop It Off and a bar snack called Double Hernia but they've lopped these off now.

OPEN *11.00-23.00 (Mon-Fri), midday-22.30 (Sun)*
FOOD *as opening hours*
CREDIT CARDS *all major cards, not AmEx*
DRAUGHT BEERS *Courage Directors, Theakston Best, Beck's, Foster's, Kronenbourg, Guinness, Strongbow, one guest ale*
Wheelchair access to venue, not to loos
NEAREST TUBE STATIONS *Goodge Street, Warren Street*

YE OLDE SWISS COTTAGE
98 Finchley Road, NW3; 0171 722 3487

'Ye Olde' is the new bit in the name of this curious pseudo-Swiss chalet on the extraordinarily busy Finchley Road, which gave its original name to the new bus terminus, then to the Metropolitan Line station, and soon to the entire district. It is an enormous pub with four bars, a private pool club, a terrace with picnic tables, and a deep wooden balcony around three of its sides. Samuel Smith bought it in 1986, and there has been a lot of refurbishing since then. The Victoria Bar (with music) and the Albert Bar (without) are now big, comfortable rooms with sofas, armchairs, wing chairs and button-backed chairs, grouped around widely spaced coffee tables. The Tap Room is plain and pleasant, and you could give a ball in the vast upstairs bar, now used as a function room.

OPEN *11.00-23.00 (Mon-Sat), 12.00-22.30 (Sun)*
FOOD *12.00-15.00 and 18.00-20.30 (Mon-Sat), 12.00-15.00 (Sun)*
CREDIT CARDS *none taken*
DRAUGHT BEERS *Old Brewery Bitter, Sovereign Bitter, Ayingerbräu Pils, Ayingerbräu Prinz, Samuel Smith's Extra Stout, Special Reserve*
Wheelchair access to venue, not to loos. Private function room: 150 people standing
NEAREST TUBE STATION *Swiss Cottage*

THE OLDE WINE SHADES
6 Martin Lane, EC4; 0171 626 6876

One of only two taverns to have survived the Great Fire (see The Hoop and Grapes), The Olde Wine Shades almost didn't survive at the hands of the developers. A furious battle erupted, but this fine pub lives on to tell the tale. It has been in continual use as a pub since 1663, and is owned by El Vino these days. It no longer sells draught beer, but it asks its gentlemen customers to wear jackets and ties, as it has always done, and retains its genteel shabbiness, with its old carpet runner and assorted tables and chairs. The substantial City people who eat and drink here find this all very agreeable. Things don't change much at The Olde Wine Shades. The wine list is as sound, and the food as good, as ever. Victor Little, who runs the pub, has been there since 1961. He is silver-haired and courteous, and an unmistakable figure of authority.

OPEN *11.30-20.00 (Mon-Fri)*
FOOD *12.00-15.00 (Mon-Fri)*
CREDIT CARDS *all major cards, not Diners*
Private room seats: 40 people (evenings)
NEAREST TUBE STATION *Cannon Street*

THE OLD KING LUD
78 Ludgate Hill, EC4; 0171 329 8517

The great cataclysm that changed the face of Ludgate Circus for ever is but a folk memory now. The great railway bridge, my son, the ancient office blocks, where are they now? Well, The Old King Lud is still there or anyway its façade is, as decorative and swanky as ever, still five storeys high, though it seems sunk a few feet. You actually go down steps to get in now. Behind all the mid-Victorian swagger, though, is a brand new pub. It looks old enough. Whitbread's have made the rebuilt King Lud into the most spectacular of their Hoghead pubs, so it is all ancient timbers and old flagstones. There are country benches and old wooden tables, a great gantry is loaded with barrels and in the far reaches of the vast bar a huge vat labelled Fermenting Vessel No. 1 which seems wedged into the corner. The customers have changed too. Youthful machismo is the style of the day. A minimum of 20 different cask ales are on tap every day and vast quantities are downed, customers using two-pint tankards and four-pint jugs to save time. The staff is young and lively too and throws itself into the spirit of the thing, particularly on Friday nights when the place is jumping. On Sundays a deep peace descends on the King Lud. Sunday papers are on offer. The four-pint jugs doze behind the bar counter. You might almost think this was one of those quiet sleepy old pubs you hear about.

OPEN *11.00-23.00 (Mon-Fri)*

FOOD *midday-22.30 (Mon-Fri)*

CREDIT CARDS *all major cards*

DRAUGHT BEERS *Heineken, Stella Artois, Guinness, Murphy's, Strongbow, Hoegaarden, 18-20 real ales which are changed on a weekly basis*
Wheelchair access to venue and loos

NEAREST TUBE STATION *Blackfriars, St Paul's*

THE OLD RED LION

72 High Holborn, WC1; 0171 405 1748

This Red Lion has a rather grisly claim to fame. After the restoration of Charles II it was felt necessary to punish the three men considered most responsible for his father's execution – Oliver Cromwell, his son-in-law Henry Ireton and the judge who sentenced Charles I to death, John Bradshaw. They were dead already as it happened, buried in Westminster Abbey, but they were punished all the same. They were disinterred, taken to Tyburn and strung up. On the way there the cart stopped off at the Red Lion where the three bodies lay overnight. They can hardly have been very welcome guests. Ireton, the youngest of the three, had been dead ten years.

The old pub has been rebuilt, restored and refurbished any number of times since then. The latest renovation closed the pub for six weeks. In the saloon bar they kept the good looking Victorian back bar but everything else was replaced. It is still Victorian after a fashion and very comfortable but brand new. The first floor got a restaurant, lost it and now has a bar with a pool table. The ghosts of the Lord Protector and his cronies, should they have chosen to hang round, won't know where they are.

OPEN *11.00-23.00 (Mon-Fri)*

FOOD *as opening nours (hot sandwiches only)*

CREDIT CARDS *all major cards*

DRAUGHT BEERS *Abbot Ale, Greene King IPA, Wexford Irish Cream, Harp, Kronenbourg, Stella Artois, Carling Black Label, Guinness, Dry Blackthorn, Greene King seasonal ales*
Wheelchair access to venue

NEAREST TUBE STATIONS *Holborn, Chancery Lane*

OLD RED LION

418 St John Street, EC1; 0171 837 7816

Lively Islington pub with a theatre upstairs that can sit 50 comfortably, 60 if everyone breathes in. Actors, directors and designers perform miracles on a stage the size of an in-tray.

Downstairs one set of the original Victorian partitions has survived to give two big bars. Both get packed. Not so long ago there was a small and sunless beer garden in the alley at the back. Derelict buildings on either side have been demolished and now daylight pours in and sometimes the sun. For two years the managers, Joanne and Paul Pavitt, have been dreaming of a beer garden there with grass and flowers and lots more tables. After all this time permissions, as I write, are still anxiously awaited. Joanne's parents used to manage the Old Red Lion and she has lived there since she was seven. Paul worked in a bank down the road and would come into the Red Lion at lunchtime. So they met and fell in love and married and they are running the place now. You never know where romance will bloom.

OPEN *11.00-23.00 (Mon-Fri), 11.00-15.00 then 19.00-23.00 (Sat), 12.30-15.00 then 19.00-22.30 (Sun)*

FOOD *midday-15.00 (Mon-Fri) hot **FOOD**; cold buffet all day*

CREDIT CARDS *all major cards, not AmEx or Switch*

DRAUGHT BEERS *Bass, London Pride, Worthington E, Carling Black Label, Grolsch, Tennent's Extra, Pilsner, Staropramen, Guinness, Caffrey's, Dry Blackthorn*
Wheelchair access to venue, not to loos. Private room upstairs is a theatre.
OPEN *Tues-Sun evenings*
NEAREST TUBE STATION *Angel (Islington)*

THE OLD SHADES
37 Whitehall, SW1; 0171 930 4019
Walk up Whitehall from Trafalgar Square and you pass three interesting pubs almost next door to each other, The Silver Cross, The Old Shades and The Clarence. The Old Shades is the one in the middle. It is a Grade II listed building, which means that you get told off if you pull it down. It is Flemish-Gothic with carved spandrels, cross-mullioned leaded casements and an elongated gable, a long thin pub put up in 1898. Yes, it seems older and there was, in fact, a tavern on the spot long before that. I dare say that the crowd that watched the execution of Charles I just up the road came in for a drink afterwards but The Old Shades believes in letting bygones be bygones and there is a nice portrait of the Queen on a horse over the mantlepiece at the far end. Old Shades gets a lot of tourists and welcomes Big Occasions. Almost any parade down Whitehall does wonders for trade. Riots of the poll tax sort don't.
OPEN *11.00-23.00 (Mon-Sat), midday-18.00 (Sun)*
FOOD *midday-15.00 and 17.00-20.30 (Mon-Fri), midday-16.00 and 17.00-20.00 (Sat), midday-17.00 (Sun)*
CREDIT CARDS *not AmEx*
DRAUGHT BEERS *Bass, Caffrey's, London Pride, Carling Black Label, Carling Premier, Grolsch, Guinness, Cidermaster*
Wheelchair access to venue. Private room: 30 seated, 60 standing
NEAREST TUBE STATION *Embankment*

THE OLD SHIP
25 Upper Mall, W6; 0181 748 2593
The Old Ship is probably the oldest pub in Hammersmith. It is a 17th-century riverside hostelry and at one time it was steeped in history and tradition. In the last three years though new lessees, Paul and Lionel Bann-Murray, have changed just about everything – character, appearance, customers, name. Some changes met with fierce local opposition and the Bann-Murrays have made compromises lately. They have returned the old pub to its original colours, cream and black, and dropped their new name for it, The Ranger on the River. It is The Old Ship again now and the music has been turned down a bit. It remains a radically altered pub with a big new modern kitchen, new lavatories and a powerful new sound system. The wide first-floor balcony, once the landlord's private domain, is still crowded with lunchers whenever the sun shines and the manager's old sitting room and the old kitchen upstairs are both public dining rooms now, one the Quarter Deck, the other the Mess Room. Both can be hired. Music remains a major part of life in the new Old Ship with pop videos and a busy juke box, and there are all the major sporting fixtures on satellite TV. Olive branches having been offered and largely accepted, this venerable old tavern is now established as the most youthful of the five pubs on Hammersmith's riverside.
OPEN *11.00-23.00 (Mon-Sat), midday-22.30 (Sun)*
FOOD *10.00 (for breakfast)-22.30 (Mon-Sat), 09.00 (for breakfast) -22.00 (Sun)*
CREDIT CARDS *all major cards*
DRAUGHT BEERS *John Smith's Extra Smooth, Old Speckled Hen, Wadworth 6X, Foster's, Kronenbourg, Guinness, Adnams, Morrells, Stella Artois, Strongbow*
Wheelchair access to venue and loos. Two private rooms.
NEAREST TUBE STATION *Hammersmith*

OLD THAMESIDE INN

2 Clink Street, SE1; 0171 403 4243

The Old Thameside Inn has just had a great stroke of luck. A major tourist attraction has moved next door, the *Golden Hinde* no less, the remarkable replica of the 16th-century warship in which Sir Francis Drake sailed round the world. The new *Golden Hinde* has been round the world herself, sailing more than 100,000 miles since her launch in 1973. Now she has found a fine berth in a dry dock next to the Old Thameside. The new Globe Theatre is a near neighbour too. They are both brilliant news for the pub.

In spite of its name and ancient appearance, The Old Thameside is one of London's newer pubs. It opened in 1985. So much for the Old. The Thameside bit is right enough though. There is just the new riverside walk between it and the river. Riverside walkers are the more pleased to see it because the stretch between London Bridge and Cannon Street railway bridge is rather uneventful. Beer and sandwiches wait inside, there's hot food at lunchtime, and the picnic tables along its front have a fine view of Fishmonger's Hall. The Old Thameside used to be a spice warehouse, busy and prosperous at first, apparently abandoned later on. Then it was cleverly converted, the designers keeping the heavy timbers and the old flagstone floor. It could hardly have a more interesting site. There's the remains of the Clink prison, too, just round the back. This is now a museum. I guarantee you will come thankfully away.

OPEN *11.00-23.00 (Mon-Fri), midday-16.00 (Sat-Sun)*
FOOD *midday-14.30 (Mon-Fri), midday-14.30 (Sat-Sun)*
CREDIT CARDS *all major cards*
DRAUGHT BEERS *Adnams, Calder's Cream Ale, Marston's Pedigree, Tetley's, Carlsberg Export, Castlemaine XXXX, Guinness, Dry Blackthorn, five guest ales*
Private room: 20-60 seated, 60-150 standing
NEAREST TUBE STATION *London Bridge*

O'NEILL'S

The O'Neill's chain is probably one of the best examples of the new generation of Irish theme pubs. In 1994 the Irish Pub Company approached Bass with ideas and designs, and Bass agreed to try them out on one of their struggling pubs, the Tap and Hen in Aberdeen. It was an instant success, and Bass were so pleased they developed O'Neill's as one of their brands. There are now more than 100 up and down the country, 30 of them within the M25 area. People argue that we have enough of them; the matter has even been raised in Parliament. What we might well have enough of are the poorer versions of this ersatz genre, but O'Neill's pubs are certainly not among them. OK, so maybe they don't all look like that in Ireland, but we mustn't rubbish their attempts at authenticity (see the Earl's Court Road O'Neill's, below). We don't live in Ireland for one thing, so I see nothing wrong with the tailoring of a theme to meet the demands of a discerning London market. A representative from the Irish Tourist Board told me, 'If it sells Cork dry gin, Bushmills whiskey and Ballygowan mineral water, it's Irish all right.'

O'Neill's sells them all – in fact the pubs stock a rather good range of Irish whiskeys, plus Carrolls and Major cigarettes and Tayto crisps. The menu changes regularly but they retain old favourites such as Irish lamb stew with soda bread, sausage and onion with colcannon (potatoes mixed with cabbage and spring onions and lashings of butter), beef and stout pie, and boxty, a traditional Irish potato pancake. The main meals are usually served at lunchtimes only, with the lite-bite menu of snacks until 7pm.

O'Neill's employ a high proportion of Irish staff, who take the business of not being very serious, very seriously. Don't be surprised if you find them singing or dancing away during their shift – they're encouraged to have fun, and it can be quite contagious. They are generally also quite knowledgeable about the drinks they serve, so don't be afraid to ask, particularly when there are so many whiskeys to choose from. If you're still not convinced about theme bars, bear in mind that with 102 O'Neill's in the country, 102 pubs have been saved from possible closure, creating jobs, stimulating the economy, and most important of all, providing us with choice.

Branches at

BECKENHAM 9 High Street, BR3; 0181 663 1001
   NEAREST RAILWAY STATION *Beckenham Junction*

BLACKHEATH 52 Tranquil Vale, SE3; 0181 297 5901
   NEAREST RAILWAY STATION *Blackheath*

CAMDEN 55 Camden High Street, NW1; 0171 255 9851
   NEAREST TUBE STATION *Camden Town*

CITY 31-36 Houndsditch, EC3; 0171 397 9841
   NEAREST TUBE STATION *Liverpool Street*

CITY 64 London Wall, EC2; 0171 786 9232
   NEAREST TUBE STATION *Moorgate*

CITY 65 Cannon Street, EC4; 0171 653 9951
   NEAREST TUBE STATION *Mansion House*

COVENT GARDEN 40 Great Queen Street, WC2; 0171 269 5911
   NEAREST TUBE STATIONS *Covent Garden, Holborn*

COVENT GARDEN 14 New Row, WC2; 0171 557 9831
   NEAREST TUBE STATION *Leicester Square*

CROYDON 1 South End, CR0; 0181 760 0141
   NEAREST RAILWAY STATIONS *East Croydon, South Croydon*

EARLS COURT 326 Earls Court Road, SW5; 0171 244 5921
   NEAREST TUBE STATION *Earls Court*

FINCHLEY 744 High Road, N12; 0181 343 6951
   NEAREST TUBE STATION *Woodside Park*

ILFORD 109 Station Road, IG2; 0181 514 9931
   NEAREST RAILWAY STATION *Ilford*

KINGSTON-UPON-THAMES 3 Eden Street, KT1; 0181 481 0131
   NEAREST RAILWAY STATION *Kingston-upon-Thames*

LEYTONSTONE 762 Leytonstone High Road, E11; 0181 532 2411
   NEAREST TUBE STATION *Leytonstone*

MARYLEBONE 56 Blandford Street, W1; 0171 467 3821
   NEAREST TUBE STATION *Baker Street*

MARYLEBONE 4 Conway Street, W1; 0171 307 9941
   NEAREST TUBE STATION *Great Portland Street*

MARYLEBONE 73-77 Euston Road, NW1; 0171 255 9861
   NEAREST TUBE STATION *King's Cross*

MAYFAIR 21 Old Burlington Street, W1; 0171 479 7621
   NEAREST TUBE STATION *Oxford Circus*

MAYFAIR 7 Shepherd Street, W1; 0171 408 9281
   NEAREST TUBE STATION *Green Park*

MAYFAIR 22-23 Woodstock Street, W1; 0171 647 8931
   NEAREST TUBE STATION *Bond Street*

MUSWELL HILL 291-293 Broadway, N10; 0181 365 2390
   NEAREST TUBE STATION *Highgate*

RICHMOND 28 The Quadrant, TW9; 0181 334 0111
   NEAREST TUBE STATION *Richmond*

STREATHAM 78a Streatham High Road, SW16; 0181 696 5941
   NEAREST RAILWAY STATION *Streatham*

SUTTON 37 High Street, SM1; 0181 770 9821
   NEAREST RAILWAY STATION *Sutton*

UPPER HOLLOWAY 456 Holloway Road, N7; 0171 607 2855
   NEAREST TUBE STATIONS *Holloway Road, Finsbury Park*

UPPER NORWOOD 96-98 Church Road, SE19; 0181 768 1001
   NEAREST RAILWAY STATION *Crystal Palace, Gypsy Hill*

WALLINGTON 89 Manor Road, SM6; 0181 773 9132

NEAREST RAILWAY STATION *Wallington*
WEST END 34-37 Wardour Street, W1; 0171 479 7941
NEAREST TUBE STATIONS *Leicester Square, Piccadilly Circus*
WIMBLEDON 66 The Broadway, SW19; 0181 545 9931
NEAREST TUBE STATION *Wimbledon*
EARLS COURT 326 Earls Court Road, SW5; 0171 244 5921
NEAREST TUBE STATION *Earls Court*

ORANGE BREWERY
37 Pimlico Road, SW1; 0171 730 5984
A head of Bacchus looks down from the arch over the corner doorway to the bar of The Orange Brewery, a fine four-storey Victorian pub in the bit of London where Chelsea meets Pimlico. The Orange Brewery makes all its own ale in a brewhouse directly underneath the bar. It is a most satisfactory arrangement, leading, as you can see, to a big saving in brewer's drays. Three main house ales are brewed there, SW1, the pub's best-selling bitter, SW2 which is rather stronger and Pimlico Porter, a revival of the rich dark ale that was the principal beer drunk in London in the 18th- and 19th-centuries. John Horne, the young brewer, has now added a lager, Victoria Lager 5% ABV, the only house-brewed lager in the country, he says. He regularly takes parties round.

As for the pub itself, this has just emerged from a root-and-branch improvement which has actually improved the place, not always the case. The bar itself seems hardly to have changed since Victorian times. It even has gas light. The dark old dining room though is now a comfortable second bar with a glass-topped platform looking down on big vats in which SW1 and SW2 slowly ferment. It is a spectacle that lacks drama but always has a happy ending. Mozart composed his first symphony round the corner in Ebury Street. No. 180. He was eight years old.
OPEN *11.00-23.00 (Mon-Sat), midday-22.30 (Sun)*
FOOD *midday-22.00 (Mon-Sun)*
CREDIT CARDS *all major cards*
DRAUGHT BEERS *SW1, SW2, Leffe Blonde, Victoria Lager, Pimlico Porter, Scrumpy Jack*
Wheelchair access to venue
NEAREST TUBE STATION *Sloane Square*

ORANGE TREE
45 Kew Road, Richmond; 0181 940 0944
The Orange Tree that stood here in the 18th century got its name from the first orange tree to be brought to Britain, a superstar in Kew Gardens. It is a friendly name for the large dignified Victorian public house that replaced it in the 1890s. A man might raise his hat if he had one to this imposing pub with its fine brick and terracotta façade obligingly standing so near Richmond Station. It is very Victorian inside with red walls covered in pictures, a very large L-shaped bar and big bulbous mahogany pillars, but everything is big about this pub. Indeed in 1971 they found there was any amount of room on the first floor for a theatre seating 80 people.

For the next 20 years the Orange Tree Theatre staged plays and sometimes musicals there. Some got transferred to the West End and it became quite famous. It dreamed of more space though and in 1989 converted a little school nearby into a theatre-in-the-round. It still uses the theatre in the pub a lot too, new writers, experimental productions, that sort of thing. They now call it The Room. The wine bar and restaurant in the cellars seem to flourish and a new terrace with a trellis pergola opened at the back in the heatwave of the summer of 1997. The eight tables there and the ten at the front, were a smash hit as the days got increasingly tropical. It is very enterprising, the Orange Tree, as befits a former *Evening Standard* Pub of the Year.

OPEN *11.00-23.00 (Mon-Sat), midday-22.30 (Sun)*
FOOD *bar midday-15.00 and 18.00-22.00 (Mon-Sat); restaurant midday-15.00 and 18.00-22.00 (Mon-Sat), midday-15.00 (Sun lunch)*
CREDIT CARDS *all major cards*
DRAUGHT BEERS *Ramrod Smooth, Young's Bitter, Young's Export, Young's Pilsner, Young's London Lager, Stella Artois, Carling Black Label, Oatmeal Stout, Guinness, Scrumpy Jack*
Wheelchair access to venue. Private room: 60-70 seated, 100 standing
NEAREST TUBE STATION *Richmond*

ORIEL
50-51 Sloane Square, SW1; 0171 730 2804
The perfect meeting point for Sloane Square tube and the Royal Court Theatre is as popular as ever, and the ladies who lunch here flock to their regular nesting spot at the terrace bar. As for the remaining space, the Sloane set who once pervaded the ground-floor bar have been relegated below stairs. The downstairs bar is actually quite comfortable and is still very popular with after-work drinkers and cappuccino sippers. People have been known to travel from the far-flung fields of Putney to take breakfast here at weekends in the belief that this is what Chelsea people do. Chelsea people will probably be in a greasy spoon.
OPEN *11.00-23.00 (Mon-Sat), 12.00-22.30 (Sun)*
FOOD *bar as opening hours; restaurant upstairs 08.30-22.45, downstairs 11.00-16.00 (Mon-Sun)*
CREDIT CARDS *all major cards*
DRAUGHT BEERS *Stella Artois*
Wheelchair access to venue and loos, not downstairs. Private room: 50-60 seated, 120 standing
NEAREST TUBE STATION *Sloane Square*

OXO TOWER BAR
8th Floor, Oxo Tower Wharf, Barge House Street, SE1; 0171 803 3888
The success of the Oxo Tower Bar is down to the happy combination of the Harvey Nicks elegance and the wonderful panoramic view of London's skyline. It isn't cheap, and certainly isn't easy to get to, but worth a punt on a special occasion.
OPEN *11.00-23.00 (Mon-Sat), 12.00-22.30 (Sun)*
CREDIT CARDS *all major cards*
Wheelchair access to venue and loos
NEAREST TUBE STATIONS *Blackfriars, Waterloo*

PARADISE
19 Kilburn Lane, W10; 0181 969 0098
The Paradise by way of Kensal Green is the full title of this bar, which has been has been quietly beavering away for the past five years, establishing itself as the stamping ground for urban, street trendies in this otherwise venue-desolate part of north-west London. The bar is owned by Frank Ormonde, whose Portobello Road gallery supplies the interior furnishings. The upstairs Oriental room holds artefacts from his shop, and a pair of Indonesian pillars seemingly supports the entire building. This is where you might find the live music, the DJs, the poetry readings or the comedy nights. Everything But The Girl's Ben Watt is a regular, and is known to DJ and jam here occasionally. The restaurant room opens out to a garden patio with space enough for 30 people. Although the Modern British fare is of good quality, I hear the service can be quite slow. As I write, the Paradise is only open in the evenings (apart from Sundays when roast lunches are on offer at £5.80), but plans are afoot to make it an all-day venue. It's a real find, a good starting point for the Cobden Club, and worth any number of detours for a buzzing night out.

OPEN *17.00-23.00 (Mon-Sat), 17.00-22.30 (Sun)*
FOOD *19.30-midnight (Mon-Sat), 19.30-23.30 (Sun)*
CREDIT CARDS *all major cards, not AmEx*
DRAUGHT BEERS *John Smith's Extra Smooth, London Pride, Holsten, Kronenbourg, Miller, Guinness*
Wheelchair access to venue. Private room: caters for 100
NEAREST TUBE STATION *Kensal Green*

PAXTON'S HEAD
153 Knightsbridge, SW1; 0171 589 6627
Sir Joseph Paxton was the Victorian landscape gardener who designed and built the Crystal Palace. He would surely have approved of the brilliant decorated mirrors that cover the walls of the bar here. Some have had to be replaced with plain glass, but most of the originals have survived and sparkle as they always did. The polished mahogany bar counter and the listed ceiling are terrific too. It remains one of Nicholson's ale houses.
OPEN *11.00-23.00 (Mon-Sat), 12.00-22.30 (Sun)*
FOOD *12.00-21.00 (Mon-Sun)*
CREDIT CARDS *all major cards*
DRAUGHT BEERS *Tetley's, Carlsberg Export, Adnams, Wadworth 6X, Old Speckled Hen, Stella Artois, Castlemaine XXXX, Guinness, Dry Blackthorn, two guest ales*
Wheelchair access to venue; Private room: 50 seated, 100 standing
NEAREST TUBE STATION *Knightsbridge*

LA PERLA
28 Maiden Lane, WC2; 0171 240 7400
You might be surprised to discover that La Perla is part of a chain – the newest addition from the Cafè Pacifico Group – as it bears none of the corporate hallmarks of some other theme bars. La Perla is as authentically Mexican as you're likely to get in London, and it is worth any number of visits to get through its comprehensive menu of drinks and food. It has 16 beers, nine of which are imported from Mexico – including the wonderful Negra Modela, an exotic Hispanic rendition of Guinness, only lighter. It also has an eclectic range of 16 wines, but that isn't the point here – you should really tackle the tequilas, margaritas, daiquiris and cocktails. The food is excellent, and you can choose from the botanas (appetisers) or the main meals of platillos exquisitos. Over the course of several visits, I tried, and recommend, the fajitas chiquitas with chicken (£6.50) or prawns (£6.95); the buritto especial, which includes a flour tortilla filled with beans, cheese, onions and peppers, covered in a mild tomato sauce, and served with refried beans and rice; the vegetarian dish of the day; and the sirloin, chicken and honey roast pork (to £8.95). I could go on for ever! If you call in on a hot summer's day, sit with a margarita and a plate of quesadillas and close your eyes – you could almost be in Mexico. Did I mention the service? It is extraordinarily efficient and friendly, and given the number of bars I've been to this year, I ought to know.
OPEN *12.00-23.45 (Mon-Sat), 12.00-22.30 (Sun)*
FOOD *bar 12.00-22.45 (Mon-Sat), 12.00-22.00 (Sun); restaurant 12.00-23.45 (Mon-Sat), 12.00-22.30 (Sun)*
CREDIT CARDS *all major cards, not Diners*
DRAUGHT BEERS *Red Stripe*
Wheelchair access to venue
NEAREST TUBE STATIONS *Covent Garden, Charing Cross*

THE PHENE ARMS
9 Phene Street, SW3; 0171 352 3294
When Dr Samuel Phene built this pub and the streets around it back in 1851 he couldn't possibly have imagined that they would sit so unhappily

side by side. Recent years have seen The Phene being dragged through the courts by its neighbours on the grounds of noise pollution. Is this a disco pub? Does it have heavy rock nights? It doesn't have any music at all, and not even a gaming machine. The problem was people chattering in the garden. This otherwise unimpressive local in the quiet backwaters of Chelsea has a wonderful, well-used, well-liked (for the most part) garden, which people flock to on a warm summer's evening. The neighbours revolted, are still revolting, and the latest thing is that the garden must be cleared by 10.40pm. Happily, this doesn't apply to the roof terrace, where 14 people can while away the evening to their hearts' content, telling people to shush! in the garden below.

OPEN *11.00-23.00 (Mon-Sat), 12.00-22.30 (Sun)*

FOOD *bar 11.00-23.00 (Mon-Sat), 12.30-22.30 (Sun); restaurant 12.00-15.00 and 19.00-22.30 (Mon-Fri), 12.00-16.00 (Sat-Sun)*

CREDIT CARDS *all major cards, not Switch*

DRAUGHT BEERS *Adnams, Courage Best, Courage Directors, Old Speckled Hen, Webster's, Budweiser, Carlsberg, Coors, Foster's, Holsten, Kronenbourg, Guinness, Scrumpy Jack, Strongbow*

Wheelchair access to venue. Two private room seat 20 and 80

NEAREST TUBE STATION *Sloane Square, South Kensington*

PICKLED PELICAN

22 Waterford Road, SW6; 0171 736 1023

This was perhaps the first of the modern-day breed of bars to arrive in Fulham. It opened in 1989 as a result of a conversion and buy-out from the Waterford Arms. The Pickled Pelican consists of one bright room, with a raised seating area with large windows, and a floor area with plenty of space for people to crowd into in the evenings. It was an immediate success, and it is still going strong as a popular meeting place for young boozers and wine tipplers, who like the loud music, social intercourse and burger and snack menu. In the words of the manager, 'You don't get a big bill at the Pelican.' Yes, I know, and it's well worth a try. A very decent, trouble-free bar which is ever-so-slightly starting to look its age.

OPEN *11.00-15.30 and 17.30-23.00 (Mon and Thurs), 11.00-23.00 (Tues, Wed, Fri and Sat), 12.00-22.30 (Sun)*

FOOD *11.00-15.00 and 17.00-22.00 (Mon-Sun)*

CREDIT CARDS *all major cards*

DRAUGHT BEERS *Boddingtons, Marston's Pedigree, Old Speckled Hen, Wadworth 6X, Budweiser, Foster's, Holsten Export, Guinness, Strongbow*

NEAREST TUBE STATION *Fulham Broadway*

PJS

52 Fulham Road, SW3; 0171 581 0025

An extraordinarily popular bar-brasserie in an area of South Kensington full of boutiques and restaurants, PJs looks like a rather up-market pub, with its big, imposing bar. It was formerly a pub. You may remember it as The Cranley Arms. The white linen-covered tables are reserved for people eating, but you can perch at the bar and wonder why they have a huge aeroplane propeller suspended from the gallery above. PJs is on the expensive side of drinking, but the Kensington and Chelsea darlings who go here don't worry about that. They occasionally put a menacing person on the door. Menacing people in South Kensington are rather snotty, actually.

OPEN *12.00-23.45 (Mon-Sat), 12.00-23.00 (Sun)*

FOOD *as opening hours (Mon-Sat), 12.00-22.30 (Sun)*

CREDIT CARDS *all major cards*

Wheelchair access to venue. Private room: 40 seated, 80 standing

NEAREST TUBE STATION *South Kensington*

PLUMBERS ARMS

14 Lower Belgrave Street, SW1; 0171 730 4067

The Plumbers Arms, despite its robust tradesman's name, is distinctly above stairs. Not too many plumbers live in Lower Belgrave Street these days, although they were once part of an army of builders constructing Belgravia and the pub was one of the first buildings to go up. Today it is a pleasant single-bar pub with a lincrusta ceiling, a splendid mahogany bar counter, old plates and prints and smart barmen in white shirts and grey waistcoats polishing up the gleaming beer pulls. It has well-kept cask ales, and denizens of Lower Belgrave Street find it a very good place for lunch.

But it is not its cellar nor its kitchen that has given the Plumbers Arms its celebrity. This stems from the melodramatic events of the rainswept November night in 1974 when, bleeding and soaked to the skin, Lady Lucan stumbled in. She had a shocking story to relay. An intruder had murdered her nanny, Sandra Rivett, and had then attacked her. He was still in the house. The police were called and the body of the nanny was discovered in the Lucan family home on the other side of the street. Later that night Lord Lucan turned up briefly at a friend's house in Sussex before disappearing. He has never been seen since. The murder has still not been resolved. The episode has left a lasting mark on The Plumbers Arms, which obliquely refers to it in a brief history of Belgravia in its menu. 'In more recent years,' it writes, 'Belgravia has had its share of horror and mystery, not only Belgravia but also the Plumbers Arms.' It certainly has.

OPEN *11.00-23.00 (Mon-Fri), 12.00-15.00 (Sat)*

FOOD *as opening hours*

CREDIT CARDS *all major cards*

DRAUGHT BEERS *Courage Directors, John Smith's Extra Smooth, Theakston Best, Foster's, Beamish, Kronenbourg, Scrumpy Jack, one guest ale Wheelchair access to venue. Private room: 25 seated, 30-40 standing*

NEAREST TUBE STATION *Victoria*

THE POLAR BEAR

30 Lisle Street, WC2; 0171 437 3048

In New Zealand, The Polar Bear is the one London pub everyone has heard of, and young New Zealanders arriving in London head straight for it. There is a Kiwi advice centre upstairs, with a noticeboard offering accommodation and information on all kinds of activities. The pub has three bars nowadays: the main bar on the ground floor, which gets very lively, the quieter upstairs bar and the late-night cellar bar. New Zealanders seem to like late-night cellar bars. Almost anything goes in this place so long as it's rugby and drinking related. They wouldn't want you to miss a moment of rugger, so there are six TV screens in the main bar, two big screens and four small ones in the cellar bar, and another big screen and a small one in the quieter bar upstairs. There's also a papier mâché figure of Jonah Lomu. He hasn't been here yet, but I'm sure he will.

OPEN *main bar 11.00-23.00 (Mon-Sat), 12.00-22.30 (Sun); upstairs bar 16.00-23.00 (Mon-Sat); basement bar 20.00-03.00 (Mon-Sat)*

FOOD *12.00-15.00 and 18.00-21.00 (Mon-Sun)*

CREDIT CARDS *all major cards, not AmEx*

DRAUGHT BEERS *Caffrey's, Carling Black Label, Grolsch, Guinness, Red Rock Wheelchair access to venue*

NEAREST TUBE STATION *Leicester Square*

PO NA NA

316 King's Road, SW3; 0171 352 4552

This funky, friendly pleasure basement on the happening end of the King's Road is known essentially as a late-night drinking venue which gets packed with Sloanes and other interesting types eager to make new acquaintances. The name Po Na Na is made up, but the design is apparently that of a

Moroccan souk bar. The trendy people who come here are more intent on having a good time, getting it on with the opposite sex and sinking a few drinks. Bottled beers, wines and Champagne are staple drinks, but the house speciality is a vodka Red Bull, a caffeine-loaded cocktail to keep you going. There's no charge for admission but the scary doorman frightens off unruly gangs and, when the place is full, controls entry on a one-out, one-in basis. To get the best tables and avoid the queues, you should arrive before the pubs shut.

OPEN *19.00-01.00 (Mon-Sat)*
FOOD *during opening hours*
CREDIT CARDS *all major cards*
NEAREST TUBE STATIONS *Sloane Square, Fulham Broadway*

Branches at:
CHELSEA THE FEZ CLUB 222-224 Fulham Road, SW10; 0171 352 5978
    NEAREST TUBE STATION *South Kensington*
KENSINGTON 20 Kensington Church Street, London, W8; 0171 795 6656
    NEAREST TUBE STATION *Kensington High Street*
CROYDON 32-34 High Street, Croydon; 0181 681 1066
    NEAREST RAILWAY STATION *Norwood Junction*
ISLINGTON 259 Upper Street, N1; 0171 359 6191
    NEAREST TUBE STATION *Angel*

PORTERS

16 Henrietta Street, WC2; 0171 836 6466
Lord Bradford opened this bar next to his much-celebrated restaurant in the summer of 1997 with the explicit aim of providing customers with a better quality bar. In design terms it is of the modern genre: two air-conditioned rooms painted purple and white. The ground floor fills up quickly with the after-work crowd, but if you fight your way through you might find a space in the much bigger basement bar which has plenty of seating space. It's pleasing to find there are so many ales on tap, a wide range of bottled beers and all wines are available by the glass. I've always had problems with the food though. I find it expensive and rather poor quality from a restaurateur. The last time I had a chicken sandwich there (£6.95 with chips an extra £1.50), I was hard pushed to find the meat which, when I did, had clearly been cooked a long time ahead of service.

OPEN *11.00-23.00 (Mon-Sat), 12.00-22.30 (Sun)*
FOOD *11.00-22.30 (Mon-Sat), 12.00-22.00 (Sun)*
CREDIT CARDS *all major cards*
DRAUGHT BEERS *Boddingtons, Bombardier, Eagle, Manchester Gold, Marston's Pedigree, Old Speckled Hen, Wadworth 6X, Heineken, Stella Artois, Guinness, Strongbow, Red Stripe*
Wheelchair access to venue
NEAREST TUBE STATIONS *Covent Garden, Leicester Square*

THE PRINCE ALFRED

Formosa Street, W9; 0171 286 3027
One of the most splendid examples of a Victorian pub in London, The Prince Alfred has barely changed since it opened its various doors in 1862. They have kept everything – the beautiful curved and etched glass, the towering centrepiece, the massive mahogany counter and, best of all, the splendid carved and glazed partitions. These divide the space into five separate bars: the Public, the Gentlemen's, the Ladies', the Private and the Snug, into which one has to duck. There are little doors in the partitions, but once in there you are assured of perfect privacy. Rotating snob screens hide you from even the bar staff. The Prince Alfred has a sixth bar now, bigger than all the others, open-plan in the modern way, and kitted out with a pool table and gaming machines. It is an incongruous mix, but this is a much loved pub nevertheless.

OPEN *12.00-23.00 (Mon-Sat), 12.00-22.30 (Sun)*
FOOD *12.00-15.00 and 18.00-21.00 (Mon-Sun)*
CREDIT CARDS *none taken*
DRAUGHT BEERS *Marston's Pedigree, Prince Alfred's House Bitter, Tetley's, Carlsberg Export, Carlsberg, Stella Artois, Guinness, Murphy's*
NEAREST TUBE STATION *Warwick Avenue*

THE PRINCE BONAPARTE
80 Chepstow Road, W2; 0171 229 5912
There used to be a local in Notting Hill Gate called The Artesian. It was a very bad neighbour. Rough. Beth Coventry and Phillip Wright bought it a few years ago and have succeeded in bringing it immeasurably up-market. It is now well established as a foody pub of the 90s. The two old bars are as one, light floods through the restored conservatory roof, and a splendid open kitchen offers dishes such as aubergine tagine, roast duck leg and grilled tuna (from £3.75 to £9.50). They serve five reasonably priced white wines and seven reds; two of each by the glass. The Prince Bonaparte has a growing reputation for quality food, but declines to call itself a bar or a bistro. It remains a pub. There is draught ale and draught lager on the hand pumps, you can't book a table, they don't take credit cards, and you order your food at the bar.
OPEN *12.00-23.00 (Mon and Wed-Sat), 18.30-22.30 (Tues), 12.00-22.30 (Sun)*
FOOD *12.00-22.30 (Mon-Sat), 12.00-22.00 (Sun)*
CREDIT CARDS *none taken*
DRAUGHT BEERS *Boddingtons, IPA, Caffrey's, London Pride, Tennent's Extra, Bass Ale, Carling Black Label, Grolsch, Staropramen, Guinness, Scrumpy Jack*
Wheelchair access to venue
NEAREST TUBE STATION *Notting Hill Gate*

THE PRINCE OF TECK
161 Earls Court Road, SW5; 0171 373 3107
Earls Court has long been the stamping ground for travelling Australians. Parts of it are so Australian you wonder why they bothered to leave home at all. Here in the centre of their community, as a pub should be, is The Prince of Teck. It is a handsome pub with gargoyles on the outside. Inside, there's a map and boomerangs, and a stuffed and very male kangaroo. For those who've been away from home too long, there's also a handy glossary of the language – gidday, cow's hoof, djavagidweegend? There are no carpets and there is very little furniture. The lager is cold. Upstairs is the Princess Lounge, a complete contrast to the rest of the pub. It has a fitted carpet, comfy seats and swagged curtains. Curtains? You're sure this bit isn't for cow's hoofs, Bruce?
OPEN *11.00-23.00 (Mon-Sat), 12.00-22.30 (Sun)*
FOOD *11.00-15.00 and 17.00-21.00 (Mon-Sat), 12.00-20.00 (Sun)*
CREDIT CARDS *none taken*
DRAUGHT BEERS *Courage Best, Young's Bitter, Young's Special, Beck's, Foster's, Kronenbourg*
Wheelchair access to venue, bottom level only
NEAREST TUBE STATION *Earls Court*

THE PRINCE OF WALES
38 Clapham Old Town, SW4; 0171 622 4789
You can't miss The Prince of Wales. 'POW POW POW' is painted in large letters on the parapet, the Union Jack flies from the flagpole and there's the jaunty figure of a sailor sitting on the roof. It is just as extrovert inside with a vast collection of curios and *objets* collected around the world by the landlord in his seafaring days. They hang from the ceilings and cover every inch of the walls. Happily there remains some room for the customers, though not a lot.

The Prince of Wales is a small, cosy sort of place with a loyal following. Musicians, actors, artists and students crowd in and lots goes on – regular pub outings to the Derby, Wimbledon and such, Saturday cabaret once a month, pancake races on Shrove Tuesday and at closing time they play 'Land of Hope and Glory'. You don't meet jollier pubs.

OPEN *midday-23.00 (Mon-Sat), midday-22.30 (Sun)*
FOOD *sandwiches midday-19.00 (Mon-Sat); hot **FOOD** midday-16.00 (Sun)*
CREDIT CARDS *none taken*
DRAUGHT BEERS *Boddingtons Gold, Flowers, Heineken, Heineken Export, Stella Artois, Guinness, Murphy's, Scrumpy Jack, one guest ale*
Wheelchair access to venue
NEAREST TUBE STATION *Clapham Common*

THE PRINCE OF WALES
48 Cleaver Square, SE11; 0171 735 9916

Cleaver Square is an agreeable place to live, a backwater of nice houses, Georgian mainly, near enough to the City and House of Commons to be popular with both. Lambeth Council intends to restore the garden in the centre and will be including a pitch for boules. The little pub in the corner is getting a facelift too. The Prince of Wales is a comely Edwardian local named for the Prince who became George IV. It is a small, intimate pub, the first in London to have all its small bars knocked into one. It seems a peaceful and friendly place but you would hardly believe the troubles it has seen. For years it had a dire reputation. It was where the hard men drank, where the Richardson gang met the Krays for summit meetings and successive landlords had a bad time of it. The last one arrived to find the pub with no furniture at all, people sitting on the floor and the caretaker manager armed with a stick with a hook on it. She herself was threatened, bullied and attacked.

In recent years, happily, peace has broken out and a new owner has arrived. Roger Jensen, a young man who has never had a pub before, bought the freehold and is now learning as he goes along. He has already decorated the outside and now he is about to start on the bar. The counter will be moved and the back garden redesigned with tables, chairs, a pergola and a barbecue. His main job though is getting to know his neighbours in Cleaver Square and the streets roundabout. They have already taken to George, his English bulldog, a connoisseur of Marston's Pedigree Bitter, who spends his evenings in the bar. George was a little poorly recently. Jensen was surprised by all the get well cards.

OPEN *12.00-15.00 then 17.30-23.00 (Mon-Fri), 12.00-16.00 then 19.00-22.30 (Sat-Sun)*
FOOD *midday-15.00 (Mon-Fri); Sunday roast during winter*
CREDIT CARDS *all major cards*
DRAUGHT BEERS *Guinness, Stella, Carlsberg, Abbot, Marston's Pedigree, Rayments, IPA, Carling, Scrumpy Jack, 2 guest ales*
Wheelchair access to venue
NEAREST TUBE STATION *Kennington*

THE PRINCE OF WALES
150 Drury Lane, WC1; 0171 240 9935

The Prince of Wales rather boasts of its proletarian background. It was, says the potted history on the outside wall, formerly a potato warehouse. In 1852 though it went up in the world, became a pub. Well appointed, good position, heart of theatreland. It was nothing if not socially upward mobile. The one-time warehouse went for it and boldly assumed the rank of the Queen's eldest son. Time passes. It is 1982 and The Prince of Wales, now full of stuffed animals and cobwebs, is looking tired and down at heel. What's this? A gang of revolutionary persons is taking it apart. Farewell Victoriana, farewell respect of rank. It re-opens as a trendy bar-café with lowered ceilings, red walls, chrome fittings, a juke box and a cheeky new name. It is now Charley's. The kids pour in. A hit, a palpable hit. Another decade and Charley's has dated badly too so it gets another new personality. It closes for six weeks, reopens and, good lord, it is the Prince of Wales again. Once more it is in the style of the moment. It has become one of Scottish and Newcastle's modish T. and J. Barnard pubs so it is 1990s early ale house, wooden floors and plain wooden furniture, pies with meat, potatoes and veg all under the same puff pastry lids, seven English ales on tap and a rack of 20 different bottled beers, some quite exotic, behind the counter. Barbara Fitzgerald, the extremely experienced landlady, thought they would never sell, not at that price, but they go well. Fruity bottled ale brewed by Trappist monks in a remote monastery is the height of fashion. As always the Prince of Wales is moving with the times.

OPEN *11.00-23.00 (Mon-Sat), midday-22.30 (Sun)*
FOOD *all day until 22.00*
CREDIT CARDS *all major cards*
DRAUGHT BEERS *Courage Best, Directors, Theakson Best, Theakston XB, John Smith's Extra Smooth, John Smith Best, Guinness, Foster's, Beck's Export, 2 guest ales weekly*
Wheelchair access to venue. Private rooms, one seats 96, standing 150 the other seats 40, standing 60
NEAREST TUBE STATIONS *Covent Garden, Holborn*

THE PRINCESS OF WALES

1a Montpelier Row, Blackheath, SE3; 0181 297 5911
The heath that gives Blackheath its name has seen some rare goings on. Henry V arriving in triumph from Agincourt, Henry VIII with a face of thunder meeting poor Anne of Cleves, Wat Tyler and Jack Cade inciting revolution. Samuel Pepys, appalled by a bloated body on a gibbet, would have liked the heath much better now with its fairs, folk walking their dogs and lovers entwined in the grass. There are good pubs all round its borders with The Princess of Wales standing out, a hugely popular Georgian pub with three bars that get so crowded that they have given up on food in the evening. You do very well earlier in the day though with hearty pub lunches in the stylish conservatory and the beer garden at the back. All summer the heath on the other side of the road is dotted with its customers. What could be nicer on a sunny day than to take your drink on to this agreeable common? There are rules. Plastic glasses only on the grass. Heath must be cleared 20 minutes after last orders.

Which Princess of Wales was this then? It was Caroline of Brunswick, Queen Caroline for a while, the one who was married to George IV. The nation watched agog as their marriage spectacularly collapsed. Caroline is said to have been fat, coarse and unwashed but the people took her side, waving, cheering, shouting 'The Queen! The Queen!' whenever she appeared. They named pubs after her. That shows how much they liked her.

OPEN *midday-23.00 (Mon-Sat), midday-22.30 (Sun)*
FOOD *midday-15.00 and 17.00-21.00 (Mon-Thurs), midday-21.00 (Fri-Sun)*
CREDIT CARDS *all major cards, not AmEx*
DRAUGHT BEERS *Bass, Caffrey's, London Pride, Carling Premier, Grolsch, Guinness, Dry Blackthorn, guest ales*
Wheelchair access to venue; disabled loos to be installed in October '98
NEAREST RAILWAY STATION *Blackheath*

PROSPECT OF WHITBY

57 Wapping Wall, E1; 0171 481 1095
The Prospect of Whitby has seen some changes over the years. Wapping has been transformed by the massive riverside redevelopment projects and this charming pub sits neatly in the conversions. It is the oldest riverside pub in London and probably the most famous. Its flagstoned bar, with its

pewter-topped counter sitting on old barrels, must have been used by half London in its long day. There's a separate section for bar snacks now, a good restaurant up creaking stairs, and a jolly riverside terrace with picnic tables under an old weeping willow. The inn was built around 1520 and was, from the start, a haunt of smugglers, thieves and other low lifers. Indeed, it boldly called itself the Devil's Tavern. Misbehaving sailors were hanged along the low-water mark, a popular entertainment drawing big crowds. The pub was burnt down, rebuilt, changed its name – the *Prospect* (from Whitby) was a merchant ship which moored nearby – and, slowly, slowly, it started to get respectable. It is very respectable now, as you can see from the two chairs by the dining-room door. A notice on one of them reads: 'This chair was occupied by HRH Princess Margaret when dining here on June 26, 1949'.

It was as well she was not dining here on 14 January 1953, when Robert Harrington 'Scarface' Sanders and his Red Scarf Gang raided the Prospect of Whitby, where a certain Captain John Cunningham was giving a small dinner party. He and his guests were relieved of their watches, jewellery and money at pistol point. Scarface was caught soon afterwards when, doing another job, he shot at a policeman. He got life. He could have fared worse. He could have been hanged at low water mark just below the nice old Prospect of Whitby and left there while the tide rose and fell three times.

OPEN *11.30-15.00 and 17.30-23.00 (Mon-Fri), 11.30-23.00 (Sat), 12.00-22.30 (Sun)*

FOOD *bar 12.00-14.30 and 18.00-21.00 (Sat), 12.00-15.00 and 19.00-21.00 (Sun); restaurant 19.00-22.00 (Mon-Sat), 12.00-14.30 (Sun lunch)*

CREDIT CARDS *all major cards*

DRAUGHT BEERS *Courage Directors, John Smith's Extra Smooth, Marston's Pedigree, Foster's, Kronenbourg, Guinness, Strongbow*

Wheelchair access to venue. Private room: 50 seated, 80 standing

NEAREST TUBE STATION *Wapping*

PUNCH AND JUDY

40 The Market, Covent Garden, WC2; 0171 379 0923

The Punch and Judy in Covent Garden has been renamed. It is The World Famous Punch and Judy now. Well, the Quite Well Known Punch and Judy doesn't have quite the same ring, I see that. It is the modern pub at the piazza end of Charles Fowler's elegant market hall, a brilliant place to be. A section of the old overnight vegetable store with its flagged floor and vaulted arches makes a perfect cellar bar and opens into a courtyard in the glass-roofed arcade. You can sit and drink there whatever the weather and still think you are in the open air. Someone else got the ground floor but the Punch and Judy re-emerges on the floor above with a light modern bar opening on to a balcony of royal proportions. It stretches the whole width of the building with a shelf for drinks-in-progress all the way along. Below is the West Piazza, London's first square originally designed by Inigo Jones. Now street entertainers perform there to big crowds all summer long and, lining the balcony, customers of The Punch and Judy, The World Famous Punch and Judy, have the front row in the circle. The Punch and Judy was one of many prizes in Scottish and Newcastle's purchase of the big Chef and Brewer chain. It was showing signs of wear but the new owners have spent £200,000 on it lately, a lot of it, as the pub says, to improve customer flow. The staff has lots of languages and needs them, the food remains hearty and traditional, the lager sales are phenomenal. Business at The World Famous Punch and Judy is booming.

OPEN *11.00-23.00 (Mon-Sat), midday-22.30 (Sun)*

FOOD *11.00-22.30 (Mon-Sat), 11.00-22.00 (Sun); sandwiches available till closing time*

CREDIT CARDS *all major cards, not AmEx*

DRAUGHT BEERS *Beamish Black, Courage Best, Courage Directors, Theakston Best, Theakston XB, Foster's, Kronenbourg, Beamish, Strongbow*
NEAREST TUBE STATION *Covent Garden*

PUZZLE

90-92 Balham High Rd, SW12; 0181 265 7243

A small empire of modern pubs is breaking the market, and the man behind the empire is Jamie Dutton-Forshaw, he of the family who own and run the Burtonwood brewery in Warrington. With such a background, it was probably inevitable that he should enter the industry, and his current total of five pubs throughout London is continuing to expand. I'm not in love with the style (a hybrid of Slug & Lettuce and a hotel foyer with a smattering of kitsch thrown in for good measure), but they are adding useful foody pubs in areas which desperately need them and are clearly proving popular with their local communities (the late license in Balham helps, and woe that other venues don't follow suit). The puzzling thing about all of them is that, while they are all described as Free Houses, there is an absence of any top-quality ales.

I might well use these venues again for eating. The menu includes many creative dishes alongside the comfort foods of bangers and mash, fish and chips, all-day breakfasts and a good range of salads and sandwiches. Most dishes can be had for under a fiver, and although the food won't win any catering awards, it is really rather good quality pub grub. These are suburban venues which wouldn't work in central London but, with a bit of fine-tuning, I wouldn't be too unhappy to find one at the end of my street.

OPEN *noon-23.00 (Mon-Tues), noon-midnight (Wed-Thurs), noon-1.00 (Fri-Sat), noon-22.30pm (Sun)*

FOOD *12.00-14.30 & 19.00-22.00 (Mon-Fri), 12.00-18.00 (Sat), 12.00-20.00 (Sun)*

CREDIT CARDS *all major cards, not Switch*

DRAUGHT BEERS *Directors, Tetley's, Theakston XB, John Smith's*
Wheelchair access

NEAREST TUBE STATION *Balham*

Branches at:
PUZZLE 188-190 New North Road, N1; 0171 226 6307
PRINCE'S PUZZLE 151 St John's Hill, SW11; 0181 265 7265
PUZZLE 1 St James's Road, Kingston-upon-Thames; 0181 549 7366
PUZZLE 47-49 Lavender Hill, SW11; 0171 978 5004

THE QUEENS

49 Regent's Park Road, NW1; 0171 586 0408

Rather an upheaval at The Queens, the pleasant Victorian pub on Primrose Hill. This is a prosperous London village, home over the years to writers, actors, musicians and artists, and the old pub was rather going to sleep some thought. The young entrepreneurs who have made the Chelsea Ram such a pleasant place recently took it over. They closed it for a fortnight while the decorators moved in and when it opened again not all the regulars were best pleased. They found that the bar was now cream and dark blue for one thing and had lost its old fitted carpet for another. There were modish old-fashioned floorboards instead. Upstairs, where few ever ventured, there was now a very agreeable balcony bar with a modern open kitchen, and Adam Baldwin from The Ram fruitfully installed. That meant delicious salads and fresh fish and pasta and Aberdeen Angus steaks and puddings and some very good wine. I wonder what Kingsley Amis would have made of all this? It was his local, he had a drink there every Saturday and he was not a man who liked change of any sort. He liked good food though, and good wine even more, and even he would surely have welcomed the reopening of the first-floor balcony with four

tables under a large white umbrella and bosky views of Primrose Hill. On balance ructions may have been avoided.

OPEN *11.00-23.00 (Mon-Sat), midday-22.30 (Sun)*

FOOD *bar 12.30-14.30 and 19.00-21.45 (Mon-Sat), midday-15.00 and 19.00-21.30 (Sun)*

CREDIT CARDS all major cards, not AmEx or Diners

DRAUGHT BEERS Ramrod Smooth, Young's Bitter, Young's Special, Castlemaine XXXX, Grolsch, Young's Export, Young's Pilsner, Stella Artois, Guinness, Oatmeal Stout, Strongbow

Wheelchair access to venue, not to loos

NEAREST TUBE STATION Chalk Farm

QUEENS HEAD

25-27 Tryon Street, SW3; 0171 589 0262

Long-established gay local with Dolly Daydream staff. There's nothing threatening or heavy about the pub, which is in fact hetero-friendly.

OPEN *11.00-23.00 (Mon-Sat), 12.00-22.30 (Sun)*

FOOD *bar all day*

CREDIT CARDS none taken

DRAUGHT BEERS Courage Best, Courage Directors, John Smith's Smooth, Foster's, Holsten Export, Kronenbourg, Guinness, Scrumpy Jack, Strongbow

NEAREST TUBE STATION Sloane Square

QUO VADIS

26-29 Dean Street, W1; 0171 437 9585

The entrance to Quo Vadis bar and restaurant scores about zero on my design scale. It is as welcoming as a government building for illegal immigrants, and the staff who greet you contribute little to the warmth. The bar upstairs is spacious while having hardly anywhere to sit. Too much of the space has been given over to the art (if we can call it that) of Damien Hirst, and even if you're standing (which you inevitably will be), there isn't a single place to rest your drink. Frankly, it's not my idea of fun to pay for expensive drinks only to have to look at some decomposing animal's head in a glass case. There are skeletons in the cupboard (literally) at Quo Vadis – you might mistake them for the waiting staff.

OPEN *11.00-23.00 (Mon-Sat))*

FOOD *Restaurant 12.00-15.00 and 18.00-11.30 (Mon-Sun)*

CREDIT CARDS all major cards

NEAREST TUBE STATION Tottenham Court Road

THE RACING PAGE

2 Duke Street, Richmond; 0181 940 1257

This big sporty pub in Richmond has a racing scene across the top of the bar, with cantering horses, led by Desert Orchid. Below is a fine selection of beers, wines and champagne. The Racing Page is owned by Front Page Pubs, which means a few things. Stylewise it has highly varnished wood, well-spaced tables and chairs, and plenty of room for milling about in. Most of the major sporting events are broadcast on a large-screen TV, and quality bar food is available at inexpensive prices.

OPEN *11.00-23.00 (Mon-Sat), 12.00-22.30 (Sun)*

FOOD *12.00-14.30 and 18.00-21.00 (Mon-Fri), 12.00-19.00 (Sat-Sun)*

Live music Sunday nights, big screen for live sports

CREDIT CARDS Mastercard, Visa

DRAUGHT BEERS Theakston XB, Foster's, Holsten Export, Bass, Kronenbourg, Guinness, Strongbow

Wheelchair access to venue

NEAREST TUBE STATION Richmond

RAILWAY

18 Clapham High Street, SW4; 0171 622 4077

A bright, airy, spacious and colourful bar which is just a little bit too convenient for Clapham North tube or Clapham High Street railway station. The youngish clientele spill out on to the pavement, proving that there is life outside the Old Town. To walk past the Railway would be something of a missed opportunity, as they know what they're doing in Clapham these days. The bar is owned by Ann and Tom Halpin – creators of The Sun and The Falcon (qqv) – who are almost entirely responsible for the renaissance of Clapham as an eating and drinking destination. Here, you can opt for a range of baguettes (£3), and a number of small but interesting main courses, which include boiled bacon and cabbage (£4.95), chicken with tarragon (£5.50), and Japanese beef with ratatouille (£6.50). Japanese beef? I never heard the like...

OPEN *11.00-23.00 (Mon-Sat), 12.00-22.30 (Sun)*
FOOD *12.00-16.00 and 18.00-21.30 (Mon-Sun)*
CREDIT CARDS *all major cards*
DRAUGHT BEERS *Caffrey's, Worthington's Best, Grolsch, Staropramen, Tennent's Extra, Tennent's Pilsner, Guinness, Dry Blackthorn*
NEAREST TUBE STATION *Clapham North*

THE RAILWAY TAVERN

15 Liverpool Street, EC2; 0171 283 3598

Is there a self-respecting town in all the land that does not have a Railway Tavern? London has 18. This and the one that follows can stand for them all. First the grand Railway Tavern of the main line terminus. This one is opposite Liverpool Street, a big, impressive high-ceilinged bar with recent Victorian fittings, an island of booths in the middle and partitions around the outside walls. There is a roomy games room upstairs – pool table, pin ball machines, fruit machines and a loud juke box and pizzas to eat here or take away, a Pizza Hut franchise. There is also a small wine bar with Moulin Rouge murals. You generally get served quickly. The staff know that customers either have a job to go to or a train to catch. This Railway Tavern has been so much a part of Liverpool Street Station for so many years that it has become known as Platform 19. 'Meet you on Platform 19,' say older commuters, showing they know a thing or two. Liverpool Street, you will gather, has 18 platforms. Trains run at weekends, the City of London doesn't. The City's Railway Tavern compromises. It opens on Saturdays, closes on Sundays.

OPEN *11.00-23.00 (Mon-Fri), midday-17.00 (Sat)*
FOOD *11.00-21.00 (Mon-Fri)*
CREDIT CARDS *all major cards*
DRAUGHT BEERS *Boddingtons, Boston Beer, Flowers Original, London Pride, Manchester Gold, Heineken, Heineken Export, Stella Artois, Guinness, Murphy's, Scrumpy Jack, Strongbow*
Wheelchair access to venue, not to loos. Two private rooms
NEAREST TUBE STATION *Liverpool Street*

THE RAT AND CARROT

60 Chelsea Manor Street, SW3; 0171 352 0725

Mel and Irene Barnett (see The Admiral Codrington) took over The Rat and Carrot early in 1996, and this once sleepy, gloomy pub seemed to come to life again almost overnight. There has barely been a quiet night since, as the young 'uns of Chelsea hang around the pool table smacking gum, chatting each other up and arranging dates in trendy clubs for later on. There is an attractive garden at the back which draws them out in the summer, but Mel draws them back in again at 9.30pm – must respect the neighbours. Do they do food? I do believe they do, but with all those young people there, the thought of food didn't cross my mind.

OPEN *11.00-23.00 (Mon-Sat), 12.00-22.30 (Sun)*
FOOD *12.00-15.00 (Mon-Sat)*
CREDIT CARDS *all major cards, not AmEx*
DRAUGHT BEERS *Abbot Ale, Boddingtons, Courage Directors, Greene King IPA, London Pride, Wexford Irish Cream Ale, Budvar, Carlsberg, Foster's, Kronenbourg, Stella Artois, Guinness, Strongbow*
Wheelchair access to venue, not to loos
NEAREST TUBE STATIONS *Sloane Square, South Kensington*

RAT AND PARROT PUBS

The PR people who handle this Scottish & Newcastle exercise in pub branding accused me of biased reporting following my comments in last year's Guide. Biased, *moi*? I don't think so. But the PR girlies do get a bit hot under the collar when I refuse to print their ideas and opt for the safer method of going out, investigating for myself and reporting my findings here. I complained last year that the food was, how do I say this?, overpriced crap. Happily the rest of London is improving in leaps and bounds in the quality of its food in pubs so now there is no reason to go to Rats anymore. But hang on a second, maybe you should go for the rather fine quality ales? No. Then what about the friendly, attentive bar staff? No. The fun, games and camaraderie of a decent local? Don't even think about it. To admire the swirly patterned carpets? Go to your grandmother's house – she'll be pleased to see you. But there must be some reason for going here; after all, the PR girlies said the brand worked well? Making money on over-priced rubbish doesn't mean it's working well. It means they are making a profit, and there is a subtle difference. So I guess you shouldn't bother then? You should never be seen knowingly drinking in a Rat and Parrot.

Branches at:
BAYSWATER 99 Queensway, W2; 0171 727 0259
    NEAREST TUBE STATION *Bayswater*
BECKENHAM 157 High Street, BR3; 0181 658 9618
    NEAREST RAILWAY STATION *Beckenham Junction*
BELGRAVIA 4 Elizabeth Street, SW1; 0171 730 3952
    NEAREST TUBE STATION *Victoria*
CAMDEN 25 Parkway, NW1; 0171 482 2309
    NEAREST TUBE STATION *Camden Town*
CHISWICK 122 High Road, W4; 0181 995 4392
    NEAREST TUBE STATION *Stamford Brook, Turnham Green*
COVENT GARDEN 63-66 St Martin's Lane, WC2; 0171 836 2990
    NEAREST TUBE STATION *Leicester Square*
CROYDON 24 Park Street, CR0; 0181 688 2607
    NEAREST RAILWAY STATION *East Croydon*
EALING 23 High Street, W5; 0181 567 3228
    NEAREST TUBE STATION *Ealing Broadway*
EARLS COURT 123 Earls Court Road, SW5; 0171 370 2760
    NEAREST TUBE STATION *Earls Court*
FULHAM 704 Fulham Road, SW6; 0171 736 3014
    NEAREST TUBE STATION *Parsons Green*
HAMPSTEAD 250 Haverstock Hill, NW3; 0171 431 0889
    NEAREST TUBE STATION *Belsize Park*
HARROW 84 St Ann's Road, Harrow, HA1; 0181 427 0552
    NEAREST TUBE STATION *Harrow-on-the-Hill*
NOTTING HILL 206 Kensington Church Street, W8; 0171 229 8421
    NEAREST TUBE STATION *Notting Hill Gate*
PUTNEY 160 Putney High Street, SW15; 0181 780 1282
    NEAREST TUBE STATION *East Putney*
SOHO 77 Wardour Street, W1; 0171 439 1274
    NEAREST TUBE STATION *Piccadilly Circus*
SUTTON 33-35 High Street, SM1; 0181 642 4930

NEAREST RAILWAY STATION *Sutton*
WEST HAMPSTEAD 100 West End Lane, NW6; 0171 624 7611
NEAREST TUBE STATION *West Hampstead*

RED LION

Crown Passage, SW1; 0171 930 4141

Crown Passage is a narrow alley just opposite St James's Palace. It is lined with useful little shops. Some go up it for the ironmonger or the cobbler, others use it as a shortcut from Pall Mall to King Street. Quite a few never get past the Red Lion. This tiny black timber-fronted pub with its leaded glass windows, hanging baskets and antique lanterns looks too picturesque to be true but it is every bit as old as it seems. It has been there for more than 400 years, has the second oldest beer licence in London and is still very much in business. The small, panelled bar is open all day and fills up quickly at lunchtime and again when people finish work. There is a small pleasant room upstairs that serves good plain pub food, and on the last Saturday of every January the pub is packed with splendidly attired Cavaliers. They come together to mark the execution of their hero, King Charles I, on 30 January 1649. The Red Lion remembers this well but it knew King Charles II better, or so legend has it. He lived in St James's Palace over the road and his lively mistress Nell Gwynne lived round the corner at 79 Pall Mall. Some discretion seemed appropriate so Nell would slip into the Red Lion, go down the cellar steps and through a tunnel. At the other end the King would be waiting. Is this true? Unromantic surveyors doubt it. They have had a good poke round in the cellar and there's no tunnel there, they say.

OPEN *11.00-23.00 (Mon-Sat), midday-22.30 (Sun)*
FOOD *midday-14.30 (Mon-Sat)*
CREDIT CARDS *all major cards, not AmEx*
DRAUGHT BEERS *John Smith's, Directors, Adnams, Ruddles County, Carlsberg, Foster's, Kronenbourg, Guinness, Strongbow*
Restaurant for hire: 24 seated, 40 standing
NEAREST TUBE STATIONS *Piccadilly Circus, Green Park*

RED LION

Duke of York Street, SW1; 0171 930 2030

This is the most glittering of Red Lions. On all sides brilliant cut and bevelled glass flashes and sparkles. It is a real star, a small Victorian gin palace of a most superior kind, almost totally unspoiled. 'Uncommonly well preserved', wrote Sir Nikolaus Pevsner. That was high praise from him. Did I mention it was small? It is small. There are just 300 square feet of it, not a lot. In summer it spills on to the pavement, but the rest of the year sees Londoners reverting to one of their most profoundly held beliefs: there's always room for one more inside. Mr Michael Browne who has run the pub for 11 years likes to see it really full. He will tell you that he sells more beer per square foot than any other pub in Piccadilly. In its bohemian past Jermyn Street flower girls would offer their services for 2d a time in the private bar. The Red Lion, robbed of its private bar, is the height of respectability these days and you see unexpected people pushing through the crush. Clint Eastwood. Andrew Lloyd Webber. Mr Lloyd Webber is said to like it because there is never any music of any sort. You can eat here too. Well, you can get a sandwich – oh and home-made fish and chips on Fridays and Saturdays.

OPEN *11.30-23.00 (Mon-Sat)*
FOOD *midday-14.30 (Mon-Sat)*
CREDIT CARDS *none taken*
DRAUGHT BEERS *Burton, Tetley's, Carlsberg Export, Castlemaine XXXX, Stella Artois, Murphy's, Guinness, Dry Blackthorn, four regular guest ales*
NEAREST TUBE STATIONS *Green Park, Piccadilly Circus*

RED LION

48 Parliament Street, SW1; 0171 930 5826

Of all the Red Lions this one lies nearest to the corridors of power. Around it are great ministries of state. Across the road is the Prime Minister. Round the corner are the Houses of Parliament themselves. This is the MPs' pub, the one they nip into before some brisk legislating. It is a handsome pub, Eclectic Flemish Baroque, as you can see, a Grade II listed building and historical in spades. The original Red Lion was built on this site in 1733 and was nervously visited by Charles Dickens when he was only 11. The adventure appears in *David Copperfield*: 'What is your best – your VERY best – ale a glass?' 'Twopence-halfpenny,' says the landlord 'is the price of the Genuine Stunning ale.' 'Then,' says I, producing the money, 'just draw me a glass of the Genuine Stunning if you please...' They pulled that Red Lion down in 1899 during the great pub boom and built this one in its place, a superior pub, no cost spared. It has changed hardly at all since then. Most of the original fittings are still in place and it's pretty well full all day, the bar walls covered in drawings, cartoons and photographs of famous politicians, mostly long departed. There's a nice old-fashioned dining room upstairs with old-fashioned English food and a cable television set tuned into the Parliamentary channel, letting Members keep an eye on their colleagues at work. There's another screen in the bar. Bar and restaurant also have division bells. There's a comfortable cellar bar too. The Parachute Regiment has reunions here and it was much liked by demonstrating miners. The licensee liked them right back. 'Top quality customers,' he says. The pit banners they presented to the pub are now part of its history.

OPEN *11.00-23.00 (Mon-Sat), midday-22.30 (Sun)*

FOOD *Bar 11.00-15.00 (Mon-Sun); Restaurant midday-14.30 (Mon-Sun)*

CREDIT CARDS *all major cards, not AmEx*

DRAUGHT BEERS *Adnams, Broadside, Calder's Cream Ale, Murphy's, Red Lion Bitter, Tetley's, Carlsberg, Castlemaine XXXX, Stella Artois, Guinness, Dry Blackthorn*

Wheelchair access to venue, main bar only. Private room seats 35

NEAREST TUBE STATION *Westminster*

THE RED LION

1 Waverton Street, W1; 0171 499 1307

There's a proud pride of red lions in London, at least 24 of them, but socially this is surely the one that has done best. It is the Mayfair Red Lion and it is very smart these days. To see it now with its quiet restaurant, its old prints, its panelled walls and its well-heeled regulars it is hard to imagine its ragged-trousered beginnings. In those days – it is the 17th century we are talking about now – it stood on a muddy unmade road just by the boundary of Chesterfield House, lordly seat of the Earls of Chesterfield. Its customers were toughs from the notorious May Fair, street traders from Shepherds Market, grooms from the big house. Then the workmen building Berkeley Square, Hill Street and Chorley Street made it their own. That was a step up all right and, as the exclusive Mayfair of the 19th century took shape, it was the great army of domestic servants that kept the place going. Now, of course, the basements they worked in and the attics they slept in are expensive Mayfair apartments and it is the occupants of these who fill today's totally gentrified Red Lion with a hum of quiet conversation. It is a charming pub the year round. In winter the seats to get are the winged settles near the fire, in summer people crowd the forecourt and the food is a cut above at any time. How lucky to have such a local. 'Quite unspoiled,' people say. That's not it. Vastly improved is what it is. Chesterfield House, though, is nowhere to be seen. They pulled it down in 1937.

OPEN *11.00-23.00 (Mon-Fri), midday-15.00 then 18.00-23.00 (Sat), midday-15.00 then 18.00-22.30 (Sun)*

FOOD Bar: *midday-14.45 then 18.00-21.30 (Mon-Sun); Restaurant: midday-14.30 then 18.00-21.30 (Mon-Sun)*
CREDIT CARDS *all major cards*
DRAUGHT BEERS *Courage Best, Directors, Theakston, Greene King IPA, Guinness, Strongbow, Beck's, Kronenbourg, Foster's*
Wheelchair access to venue
NEAREST TUBE STATION *Green Park*

RIKI TIK

23-24 Bateman Street, W1; 0171 437 1977
Exceptionally modish lounge bar where suits are certainly not *de rigueur*. The strict door policy enforces this, as Quentin Tarantino was to discover. Such a policy is most irritating when you want to meet up with a group of friends, but can't co-ordinate your wardrobes to the liking of the Door Whores (the rather unkind name given to bouncers these days). If you make it inside, you'll find the atmosphere very laid back.
OPEN *12.00-01.00 (Mon-Sat)*
FOOD *12.00-18.00 (Mon-Sat)*
CREDIT CARDS *all major cards, not AmEx*
NEAREST TUBE STATIONS *Tottenham Court Road, Leicester Square*

THE RISING SUN

38 Cloth Fair, EC1; 0171 726 6671
This old Smithfield pub used to be picturesque to the point of almost falling over. Now it is very chipper, having been given a thorough going over by Samuel Smith, the Yorkshire brewers. The general feeling in the bar is now modishly Victorian, beefed up with non-stop music and flashing fruit machines. There is a quieter room above where you can have lunch. You feel you could almost touch St-Bartholomew-the-Great, the oldest church in the City outside the Tower, from the upstairs windows. The Rising Sun had a rapscallionly youth with body-snatchers slipping laudanum into drinks at the bar. This would not be allowed today. Sam Smith won't have people putting stuff into his beer.
OPEN *11.30-23.00 (Mon-Fri), midday-15.00 then 19.00-23.00 (Sat), midday-15.00 then 19.00-22.30 (Sun)*
FOOD *midday-14.00 (Mon-Sat)*
CREDIT CARDS *Visa, Mastercard*
DRAUGHT BEERS *Sam Smith's Old Brewery Bitter, Ayingerbräu Lager and Pilsner, Sam Smith's cider, stout and mild*
Wheelchair access to venue. Private room seats 50
NEAREST TUBE STATION *Barbican*

THE RISING SUN

46 Tottenham Court Road, W1; 0171 636 6530
Next time you are in Tottenham Court Road have a look at The Rising Sun. It is feeling a lot better now, thank you. The Rising Sun was designed by two much admired Victorian architects called Treadwell and Martin and is said to be their masterpiece, elaborate art nouveau Gothic, delicate mouldings, heraldic beasts, rising suns, decorative gables, an elegant bartizan. A bartizan is an overhanging turret. In the early 80s the owners of the day made a bizarre decision. They changed its name to The Presley, lowered the ceiling by about two yards, anointed it with pictures of Elvis and turned it into a rock 'n' roll bozo. It was an eccentric interlude which the next owners, Scottish and Newcastle, speedily put behind them. It is now The Rising Sun again, or almost. The extravagant Victorian interior is irretrievably gone. It is now what they call Ale House, bare boards, real ales and speedy pies. The façade, though, has been meticulously restored. So good news from this generally ill-favoured thoroughfare. Outside, a minor masterpiece rescued. Inside, well, at least the ceiling is back where it belongs.

OPEN *11.00-23.00 (Mon-Sat), midday-22.30 (Sun)*
FOOD *all day for sandwiches and snacks; 18.00-23.00 for main meals and specials*
CREDIT CARDS *all major cards*
DRAUGHT BEERS *Beck's, Foster's, Guinness, John Smith's Extra Smooth, Theakston Best and XB, Abbot Ale, Scrumpy Jack, 3 guest ales*
Wheelchair access to venue
NEAREST TUBE STATIONS *Tottenham Court Road, Goodge Street*

ROBERT BROWNING

15 Clifton Road, W9; 0171 286 2732
On one of his sorties from his Yorkshire stronghold seven years ago Sam Smith bagged a down-at-heel Victorian pub called The Eagle. He refurbished it from top to toe, as he does, and here it is now, a glossy Sam Smith pub called The Robert Browning. Locals still call it The Eagle.

As a young man Browning lived briefly nearby overlooking the canal, and he would have been astonished to hear that pictures of him and his beloved would one day cover the upstairs bar of the boisterous new pub down the way, not to mention his passionate love letters and some of the passionate poems he wrote for her. His marriage certificate too. 'Age: of full age. Rank or Profession: Gentleman.' It is a nice pub, this reborn Robert Browning. The main bar downstairs is where the serious drinking is but the first floor bar is where I see Robert and Elizabeth, a comfortable Victorian sitting room with long windows, button-backed leather sofas, mahogany tables, lamps, mirrors, portraits.
He wrote:
> There you stand
> Warm too and white too;
> Would this wine
> Had washed all over that body of yours
> Ere I drank it.

Is this what goes on at the Robert Browning?
OPEN *11.30-23.00 (Mon-Sat), midday-22.30 (Sun)*
FOOD *midday-14.30 (Mon-Sat), 17.30-21.00 (Sun)*
CREDIT CARDS *Mastercard, Visa*
DRAUGHT BEERS *Old Brewery Bitter, Sovereign, Ayingerbräu Pils, Ayingerbräu Prinz, Samuel Smith's Extra Stout, Special Reserve*
Wheelchair access to venue. Private room seats 30
NEAREST TUBE STATION *Warwick Avenue*

ROSE AND CROWN

2 The Polygon, Clapham Old Town, SW4; 0171 720 8265
Together with The Sun and The Prince of Wales (qqv), the Rose and Crown makes up a triangle of pubs in Clapham Old Town, and it would be churlish not to mention it in this Guide. It is a traditional Victorian pub with one room and a couple of snugs. Should you want to get away from the madding crowds of the Old Town, then this pub will offer you the necessary respite.
OPEN *11.00-23.00 (Mon-Sat), 12.00-22.30 (Sun)*
FOOD *12.00-14.30 (Mon-Sat), 12.00-16.00 (Sun)*
CREDIT CARDS *none taken*
DRAUGHT BEERS *Abbot Ale, Greene King IPA, Wexford Irish Cream Ale, Harp, Kronenbourg, Stella Artois, Guinness, Strongbow, three guest ales*
NEAREST TUBE STATION *Clapham Common*

THE ROSE AND CROWN

55 High Street, SW19; 0181 947 4713
The Rose and Crown in Wimbledon Village is one of south London's great pubs. The *Evening Standard* Pub of the Year judges thought so and gave it

the crown in 1970. It is an old pub, 1640 is old. Charles I still had his throne and his head in 1640 and it is as pretty a pub as you could hope to find, a beautiful house of old brick, lovely in its proportions inside and out. It keeps its powerful appeal for generation after generation. In its days as a coaching inn the London coach began and finished here. It was as popular then as it is now. Inside, old maps of Wimbledon and a complete set of Hogarth's *Idle Prentice* add to the pub's historical feel but nothing does this more than the benign, ghostly presence of its two most famous regulars. Leigh Hunt and Swinburne were leading figures in bohemian London. Swinburne was actually famous. He was not only a poet but a notoriously dissipated poet. Such was the life he led, it was whispered, that his health had broken down. That is why he lodged at 2 The Pines, Putney, and walked across heath and common to The Rose and Crown. Celebrity was ever a predicament and sightseers started gathering at The Rose and Crown to see the dying poet. His solution was to move his chair upstairs. The chair is still upstairs, though his table continues to do service in the bar. He lived to 72. The bar still draws crowds. There is a small no-smoking area now, a light, plain lounge and a buttery serving hot and cold food. A conservatory leads to a little garden, paved, ivy-walled and thoroughly charming, where families recuperate after constitutionals on the common, young lovers seek a quiet table, people read papers and chat. Poets, their health ruined by dissipation, may also take their chances.

OPEN *11.00-23.00 (Mon-Sat), midday-22.30 (Sun)*

FOOD *11.00-22.00 (Mon-Sat), midday-16.30 (Sun)*

CREDIT CARDS *none taken*

DRAUGHT BEERS *Young's Bitter, Young's Special, Castlemaine XXXX, Grolsch, Young's London Lager, Young's Premium Lager, Guinness, Dry Blackthorn Wheelchair access to venue*

NEAREST TUBE STATION *Wimbledon*

THE ROSE OF YORK

Petersham Road, Richmond, TW10; 0181 948 5867

When Samuel Smith, the Yorkshire brewers, set its cap on London its first pub was this one. It was an old cavalry barracks which had been made into a pub called Tudor Close, and Sam Smith really went to town on it. The Tudor fakery was stripped away, new cellars were excavated and a team of craftsmen from Yorkshire worked on it for 16 months. The Rose of York emerged as from a chrysalis and almost at once became the *Evening Standard* Pub of the Year. Sixteen years later it is still a most appealing country pub with its big comfortable bar, its good traditional food, its lovely sheltered courtyard and a view of Petersham meadows and the bend in the Thames so beautiful that it has been painted by Turner and Reynolds and thousands of times by the rest of us. There was quite a lot of space in the old barracks and The Rose of York has been letting a few rooms for bed and breakfast as old inns used to. It has been adding to them and now has 12 bedrooms with en suite bathrooms. En suite bathrooms? You would have done well to get a bowl and a jug of hot water in the old inns of England.

OPEN *11.00-23.00 (Mon-Sat), midday-22.30 (Sun)*

FOOD *midday-15.00 and 18.30-21.30 (Mon-Sat), midday-15.30 (Sun)*

CREDIT CARDS *none taken*

DRAUGHT BEERS *Old Brewery Bitter, Ayingerbräu, Ayingerbräu Pils, Ayingerbräu Prinz, Samuel Smith's Extra Stout, Special Reserve Wheelchair access to venue*

NEAREST TUBE STATION *Richmond*

THE ROUND HOUSE

1 Garrick Street, WC2; 0171 836 9838

The Round House, the substantial Victorian pub on the corner of Garrick Street, had got distinctly rowdy, not to say rough. It can happen. So what do you do? Scottish and Newcastle closed it down. They then gave it a new interior and reopened it as the first of their new real ale houses. This meant a nice wooden floor, plain wooden furniture, eight draught ales on the hand-pumps and pies with puff pastry tops floating up from the kitchen. It also meant short shrift for troublesome customers. Troublesome customers weren't keen on any of this, particularly the short shrift, and agreeable new customers replaced them.

A potted history on the front has a theory about the name. For its first 75 years, it says, the pub was called Petters Hotel. It was then renamed The Round House because of its shape. But it isn't round, it's elbow-shaped. It should be called The Elbow. Please note: This is the pub. The Garrick Club is further down.

OPEN *11.00-23.00 (Mon-Sat), midday-22.30 (Sun)*

FOOD *midday-21.00 (Mon-Sun)*

CREDIT CARDS *all major cards, not AmEx*

DRAUGHT BEERS *Abbot Ale, John Smith's, Marston's Pedigree, Old Speckled Hen, Theakston Best, Theakston Hogshead, Theakston Old Peculier, Beck's, Bombardier, Foster's, Guinness, Strongbow*

Wheelchair access to venue

NEAREST TUBE STATIONS *Leicester Square, Covent Garden*

THE ROUND TABLE

St Martin's Court, WC2; 0171 836 6436

St Martin's Court, the little pedestrians-only cut between St Martin's Lane and Charing Cross Road, has old book shops, Sheekey's, the restaurant and oyster bar, the stage doors of the Albery and Wyndham's and this extremely pleasant Victorian pub. There is a history of it on the outside wall, rather rumbustious apparently. These parts were the resort of 'horsy and fighting men' and prize fights were arranged in local taverns. The original Round Table put up the American champion John C. Heenan to contest the belt with the valiant Tom Sayers. It doesn't say who won. Those days finished with the Queensberry Rules and anyway The Round Table was rebuilt in 1877 and with theatres on all sides it became more theatrical than sporting. So it is today, a civil, good-looking pub with downstairs and upstairs bars, both very busy at times, and the landlord, Norman Gregory from Manchester, uses a doorman to discourage such horsy and fighting men as may pass by. It has become known for its cask ales. Big blackboards have lists of the guest beers coming soon. Knowledgeable barmen wear grandfather shirts and aprons and happily guide you through the ales on tap and serious beer drinkers can have two- or four-pint jugs. There are beer festivals four times a year during which The Round Table has been known to get through 50 guest ales in 14 days. It is a reasonable place to eat too. Good pies.

OPEN *11.00-23.00 (Mon-Sat), midday-22.30 (Sun)*

FOOD *midday-21.00 (Mon-Sun)*

CREDIT CARDS *all major cards*

DRAUGHT BEERS *Theakston Best, Theakston Old Peculier, John Smith's Extra Smooth, Kronenbourg 1664, Beck's, Foster's, Guinness, Strongbow, four guest ales*

Private room: 30 seated, 40 standing

NEAREST TUBE STATION *Leicester Square*

THE RUNNING FOOTMAN

5 Charles Street, W1; 0171 499 2988

This interesting Mayfair pub, properly called I Am The Only Running Footman, commemorates a job no longer on offer in the Job Centres of the nation. In the 18th century seriously grand persons employed footmen to run before their carriages, lighting the way, paying tolls, preventing collisions and generally showing what fine fellows their masters were. The running footmen and indeed footmen of all kinds met in this old Mayfair pub. It was originally the Running Horse but it was renamed by the 4th Duke of Queensberry, the one they called Old Q. He was a great swell, infamous, wrote his biographer, for his shameless debaucheries. A footman always ran ahead of his carriage.

The new name has served the pub well for 200 years and it still brings people in. The pub itself is totally changed. It was almost entirely rebuilt in the 1930s but it looks as old as you could wish with its dark panelling and bottle glass windows. Tourists love it. The pub sign shows a running footman of course. He seems most unsuitably dressed. He wears a powdered wig, a feathered hat, knee breeches and buckled shoes. The running footman in the big painting inside is even more encumbered. He carries a tall cane topped with a silver ball containing a little something to keep him going and blows a horn as he lopes along. The painting used to be over the fireplace in the saloon bar, but you could easily miss it now. In the last redecoration they stuck it on the ceiling.

OPEN *11.00-23.00 (Mon-Sat); midday-15.00, 19.00-22.00 (Sun)*
FOOD *all day*
CREDIT CARDS *all major cards*
DRAUGHT BEERS *Theakston, Directors, Kronenbourg, Beck's, Foster's, John Smith, Strongbow, Guinness, one guest ale*
Wheelchair access to venue
NEAREST TUBE STATION *Green Park*

RUPERT STREET

50 Rupert Street, W1; 0171 292 7141
One of the most recent and positive additions to the gay scene is this well-designed, bright and cheery, air-conditioned bar. It has a large hanging-around bit, a comfort zone at the back furnished with comfortable sofas and armchairs, and a constant flow of traffic between the two. Food here ranges from moules (£5.50) through a wide range of Modern British fare to a Mediterranean puff of cheeses and vegetables (£6.95). They would serve all evening if they could, but the sheer enormity of the night-time crowds means last orders are at 7pm. Did I mention the loos? Here are some of the most dramatic loos of any pub or bar in London. Ladies' cubicles have their own washbasins, men's have plenty of sprucing-up space, and there is an extra communal washing area with a water fountain. Little backpacks seem to be the essential accoutrements and, thanks to the air conditioning, you won't leave with your clothes smelling of cigarette smoke. The hefty aroma of aftershaves, however, can linger for days after a visit.

OPEN *09.00-23.00 (Mon-Sat), 12.00-22.30 (Sun)*
FOOD *12.00-19.00 (Mon-Sun)*
CREDIT CARDS *all major cards, not AmEx or Diners*
DRAUGHT BEERS *Caffrey's, Carling Black Label, Carling Premier, Grolsch, Red Rock*
Wheelchair access to venue and loos. Private room: 32 seated, 300 standing
NEAREST TUBE STATION *Piccadilly Circus*

THE RUTLAND

Lower Mall, W6; 0181 746 5586
The Rutland, a big lively pub on Hammersmith's riverside, was an early recruit to the olde English alehouse look. It has been bare boards and ancient timbers there for some years. The regulars like it, so do tourists. It has a great position with a double rank of tables along the river wall. The sun has just to shine for ten minutes and every table is occupied and like all five pubs along this short stretch of river it does brilliantly on Boat Race days. This is just half way along the course and the crowds are prodigious. Oriel College, Oxford, bags the wide balcony on the first floor, a big marquee goes up at the side and half

London seems to be there waving, cheering and trying to drink the Rutland dry. A bout of refurbishing is in the offing. There will be a longer bar, a wall will be knocked through, alcoves and more seating installed and the upstairs thoroughly smartened up. That will be nice for Oriel. The coat of arms on the side wall, motto 'Pour Y Parvenir' ('In Order to Accomplish') is the Duke of Rutland's. There are clearer messages.

OPEN *11.00-23.00 (Mon-Sat), midday-22.30 (Sun)*
FOOD *all day*
CREDIT CARDS *all major cards*
DRAUGHT BEERS *Foster's, Kronenbourg, Greene King IPA, Directors, Courage Best, John Smith's Extra Smooth, Guinness, Strongbow*
Wheelchair access to venue, not to loos. Private room seats 50/60, standing 120
NEAREST TUBE STATION *Hammersmith*

SAINT

8 Great Newport Street, WC2; 0171 240 1551

A sexy, opportunistic atmosphere in a futuristic basement bar which, incidentally, has a jolly good if expensive restaurant area. The clientele tend to be young fashion victims with great bodies and people who like to wear shades in the dark. It isn't difficult to join. Telephone for an application form and you should hear the result within a couple of weeks. Costs are £20 joining fee plus £50 per year. Tends to close private functions rather too often for my liking. Glam girls should be able to blag their way in easily enough.

OPEN *17.30-01.00 (Mon-Thurs), 17.30-02.00 (Fri-Sat)*
FOOD *bar as opening hours; restaurant 19.30-23.00 (Mon-Thurs), 17.30-02.00 (Fri -Sat)*
CREDIT CARDS *all major cards*
Wheelchair access to venue and loos
NEAREST TUBE STATION *Leicester Square*

ST JOHN

26 St John Street, EC1; 0171 251 0848

A bit like a covered street-walkway but seems to attract an erudite bunch. Quite a cold atmosphere meant that I opted for a couple of vodka shots from the freezer. Friendly staff.

OPEN *11.00-23.00 (Mon-Fri), 18.00-23.00 (Sat)*
FOOD *restaurant: 12.00-15.00 and 18.00-23.30 (Mon-Fri), 18.00-23.30 (Sat) food bar: 11.00-23.00 (Mon-Fri), 18.00-23.00 (Sat)*
CREDIT CARDS *all major cards*
DRAUGHT BEERS *Wadworth 6X, Budvar, Heineken, Hoegaarden, Stella Artois, Guinness*
Wheelchair access to venue and loos. Private room seats 20
NEAREST TUBE STATION *Farringdon*

ST PAUL'S WINE VAULTS

29-33 Knightrider Street, EC4; 0171 236 1013

This wine bar was until recently known as The Horn Tavern. Eldridge Pope spent a lot of money doing it up, and the long, narrow ground-floor bar is now looking very smart, with its varnished wood furniture. There's a basement bar too – great for private parties or just to dine by candlelight in the evenings. Although beers are brewed by Eldridge Pope, they're no longer sold here. The emphasis is very much on good wine, with over 100 on the list, starting at £6.95.

OPEN *12.00-23.00 (Mon-Fri)*
FOOD *12.00-14.00 (Mon-Fri)*
CREDIT CARDS *all major cards*

DRAUGHT BEERS *Hardy Country, Royal Oak, Courage Best, Tetley's Smooth, Carlsberg, Beck's, Guinness, Dry Blackthorn*
Private room seats 16
NEAREST TUBE STATION *Mansion House*

THE SALISBURY

90 St Martin's Lane, WC2; 0171 836 5863

The Salisbury is sometimes said to be the most beautifully preserved Victorian public house in London. It has lovely windows, brilliant-cut, acid etched, delicately engraved and Sir Nikolaus Pevsner admired its Lincrusta ceiling, the art nouveau bronze figures of alluring maidens, the flower stalks and flowers out of which electric bulbs grow. You have to go early to get a proper look at this famous pub as it is packed to the doors a lot of the time. Every evening and often lunchtimes doormen check who comes in and on occasion who goes out, an anti riff-raff move apparently. Well you can't get everyone in. The surprising thing is that anyone can get a drink at all in a pub so popular and so populated. In the thick of the crush, however, with theatregoers talking ten to the dozen all round you, a path to the bar mysteriously opens before you when the need is greatest. Some very patient customers actually find seats – there are curved banquettes with copper-topped tables – but it is noticeable that all the famous ones stand. There are usually some of these, exactly who depending on what is playing in the West End at that moment. There is a rather dull room at the far end, often partitioned off for private parties. This is no fun at all.

OPEN *11.00-23.00 (Mon-Sat), midday-22.30 (Sun)*
FOOD *all day, midday-closing (Mon-Sun)*
CREDIT CARDS *all major cards*
DRAUGHT BEERS *Calder's Cream Ale, Kilkenny, Marston's Pedigree, Theakston Best, Carlsberg, Carlsberg Export, Lˆwenbräu, Guinness, Dry Blackthorn*
Wheelchair access to venue
NEAREST TUBE STATION *Leicester Square*

THE SALUTATION INN

154 King Street, W6; 0181 748 2365

Walk far enough along King Street in Hammersmith and you will come to this agreeable pub. Old coaching inn, rebuilt 1909, listed building. Go in. I think it will surprise you. First the bar, all polished and gleaming, an excellent bar, and the home-cooked meals are good and I expect you'll like the conservatory. What is so unexpected, though, lies beyond. It is a beautiful walled garden, colourful, tranquil, the perfect place for a quiet bosky drink on a warm afternoon away from the workaday reality of Hammersmith. It has earned The Salutation Inn umpteen accolades. It has been Fuller's Garden of the Year seven times and has won London in Bloom contests time and again. So much admired is this garden that the Queen Mother, patron of the Royal Horticultural Society, came to see it in 1989, congratulated everyone in sight and pulled a few pints. A nice pub with a lovely garden. If you work in King Street or live nearby, what luck.

OPEN *11.00-23.00 (Mon-Sat), midday-22.30 (Sun)*
FOOD *midday-22.00 (Mon-Sun)*
Beer garden – seasonal barbecues
CREDIT CARDS *none taken*
DRAUGHT BEERS *Chiswick Bitter, Fuller's ESB, London Pride, Fuller's Seasonal Ales, Carling Black Label, Stella Artois, Grolsch, Tennent's Extra, Heineken, Stella Artois, Guinness, Strongbow*
Wheelchair access to venue
NEAREST TUBE STATIONS *Ravenscourt Park, Hammersmith*

THE SCARSDALE

23a Edwardes Square, W8; 0171 937 1811
You need to look carefully for this pub as it is tucked away in a corner of
Edwardes Square to the south of Kensington High Street. People warm to
the pub as soon as they see it. Its impeccable Georgian façade is covered
in flowers and greenery, and it is just as attractive inside, with high ceilings,
wooden fans, a rich gleam of mahogany and brass, and the original etched
glass. The Scarsdale's traditional pub food is very popular, and people
travel for miles to sample it. It is one of London's most admired pubs, has
no music at all and has been an *Evening Standard* Pub of the Year.
OPEN *12.00-23.00 (Mon-Sat), 12.00-22.30 (Sun)*
FOOD *12.00-14.30 and 18.30-21.45 (Mon-Sat), 12.30-15.30 (Sun)*
CREDIT CARDS *Mastercard, Visa*
DRAUGHT BEERS *Courage Directors, Theakston Best, Theakston XB, Beamish
Red, Beck's, Foster's, Kronenbourg, Guinness, Strongbow, three weekly
guest ales*
NEAREST TUBE STATIONS *High Street Kensington, Earls Court*

SCOTTS

20 Mount Street, W1; 0171 629 5248
Scotts has been given a new lease of life, is fully refurbished and stylishly
redesigned by its new owners, Chez Gerard. It looks the business: slick
and sophisticated. On my visit, the clientele included a group of Japanese
businessmen, a City gathering quaffing champagne, a genteel elderly
couple drinking wine and a rather glamorous foursome meeting for what
appeared to be pre-supper drinks. Then there was yours truly, markedly
under-dressed, having a bad-face day and looking like a character from
Manon des Sources. Do you know what? They didn't mind in the slightest.
The ultra-efficient bar staff have many years' experience behind them –
and it showed. They know how to put someone at their ease, how to chat,
what to say, what not to say, and most of all, how to pour a decent drink.
I ordered a G & T, and it was among the best presented I've had in
London – not too much ice, a large gin, a slice of freshly cut lemon, and a
premium tonic from an individual bottle with only a little added to the drink.
   The surroundings are similar to those of The Savoy, but with the addition
of booths with drapes which can be drawn. Before you ask, people do
actually draw them. A 25-foot frieze behind the bar depicts the glamour,
opulence and decadence of 30s London. Scotts is not without its modernity
– a large, bubbling, water-filled tubular glass obelisk acts as the core of
the spiral staircase which leads up to the restaurant. There is the most
wonderful private room for dining, plus lavatories I'd be happy to see
anywhere (no menacing staff demanding money). If any of you have been
wondering whatever happened to the pianist Bobby Crush, I think I've found
him (or a lookalike, at least) – he tinkles the ivories here most evenings.
OPEN *17.30-23.00 (Mon-Sat)*
FOOD *12.00-15.00 and 18.00-23.00 (Mon-Sat), 12.00-15.00 and 19.00-
22.00 (Sun)*
CREDIT CARDS *all major cards*
Two private rooms: 14 and 22 seated, up to 40 standing
NEAREST TUBE STATIONS *Green Park, Bond Street*

SCRUFFY MURPHY'S

Scruffy Murphy's is Allied Domecq's vision of an Irish theme pub; the
Denman Street branch is perhaps the most Irish in the chain. You see them
all over town – there's often an old grocer's bicycle leaning against the
outside wall. While many people criticise such pubs, they certainly inject
a new lease of life into tired old venues. There are currently 10 Scruffy
Murphy's in London, and we probably won't be seeing any more for the
time being. You may well spot one on your foreign travels, however. There's

a Scruffy Murphy's in Norway, one in Poland and three in Sweden! There's even one in Dublin, where they converted The Hive, a pub in the heart of the fair city, into an Irish theme bar. The cheek of it! London Scruffys all serve Irish food, English cider and Danish lager brewed in England. They're not particularly good examples of the genre, and with so many Irish theme bars saturating the market, such places need to be a little bit special to become a venue of choice.

Branches at:
BROMLEY 10 Widmore Road, BR1; 0181 460 4828
    NEAREST RAILWAY STATION *Bromley North*
CHELSEA 451 Fulham Road, SW10; 0171 352 8636
    NEAREST TUBE STATION *Earls Court*
CITY 142 Fleet Street, EC4; 0171 353 2451
    NEAREST TUBE STATIONS *Temple, Blackfriars, Chancery Lane*
SOHO 15 Denman Street, W1; 0171 437 1540
    NEAREST TUBE STATION *Piccadilly Circus*
SUTTON 67 High Street, SM1; 0181 770 0009
    NEAREST RAILWAY STATION *Sutton*
WEST HAMPSTEAD 283-285 West End Lane, NW6; 0171 794 7817
    NEAREST TUBE STATION *West Hampstead*
WHETSTONE 1262 High Road, N20; 0181 445 1110
    NEAREST TUBE STATIONS *Totteridge and Whetstone*

SECRETS

62 Glenthorne Road, W6; 0181 563 7974
Table dancing, I am reliably informed, is about to take Britain by storm. This is not your average strip-joint but more of an upmarket eating and drinking venue where people take their clothes off to dance. There are plenty of rules to follow: no jeans or trainers, over 21s only, remain seated, £10 for every dance they do especially for you, £5 for each track when they sit at your table, no physical contact (except to place money in their garters) and no propositioning, shouting or profane language. Your £10 admission gives you a £5 discount on food and drinks. Plans are afoot for a ladies' night on Mondays with male dancers going the full monty.
OPEN *19.00-02.00 (Tues-Fri), 20.00-02.00 (Sat)*
FOOD *19.00-01.00 (Tues-Fri), 20.00-01.00 (Sat)*
CREDIT CARDS *all major cards*
Wheelchair access to venue
NEAREST TUBE STATION *Hammersmith*

THE SEKFORDE ARMS

34 Sekforde Street, EC1; 0171 253 3251
This is a pleasant street-corner local in Clerkenwell, a bit of London that has had more than its share of ups and downs. It is having a distinct up at the moment. The surrounding streets have never seemed more prosperous and The Sekforde wears a confident air with window boxes and fresh paint and new tables on the pavement. It is a real village pub and it plays a central part in local life. The local Rotarians meet in the first floor restaurant and the staff and students from the City University seek daily inspiration in its comfortable bar.

There is a Sekforde Arms in the little Suffolk town of Woodbridge too. Thomas Sekforde, a 16th-century worthy, was a lawyer there, then retired to Clerkenwell, a thing that sometimes surprises people. They assume it would be the other way round. Many years later the two pubs, so many miles apart, quite independently took his name.
OPEN *11.00-23.00 (Mon-Sat), midday-16.00 (Sun)*
FOOD *bar midday-21.00 (Mon-Sat), 12.30-14.30 (Sun); restaurant midday-15.00 (Mon-Sat), midday-14.30 (Sun)*
CREDIT CARDS *all major cards, not AmEx*

DRAUGHT BEERS *Young's Bitter, Young's Special, all Young's ales, Stella Artois, Carling Black Label, Young's Pilsner, Young's Extra, Young's Export, Guinness, Dry Blackthorn*
Private room: 38 seated, 50 standing
NEAREST TUBE STATION *Farringdon*

THE SEVEN STARS
53 Carey Street, WC2; 0171 242 8521
You're not doing too well? You're heading for Carey Street. This little back street is where the bankruptcy courts are and many a man facing financial disaster has slipped into The Seven Stars to buck himself up. It is a charming little wooden-fronted old pub, built in 1602, one of the smallest in London with two small bars and nowhere to sit. It is much used by lawyers who apparently don't mind standing. It was recently taken over by Mr and Mrs Geoff Turner who continue the pub's ancient practices, no music, no TV, no games, closed at weekends.
OPEN *11.00-21.00 (Mon-Fri)*
FOOD *11.00-21.00 (Mon-Fri)*
CREDIT CARDS *all major cards*
DRAUGHT BEERS *Foster's, Kronenbourg, Theakston Best, Directors, Guinness, Blackthorn, Strongbow*
Wheelchair access to venue
NEAREST TUBE STATIONS *Holborn, Chancery*

LE SHAKER
159 Old Brompton Road, SW5; 0171 373 1926/7
The unusual combination of serious cocktail drinking with fine Vietnamese dining can be found on this unlikely stretch of the Old Brompton Road as you head away from Chelsea towards Earls Court. The cocktails might well be expensive at around £8, but they're very strong, very large (without the tacky accoutrements of fiddly umbrellas and plastic sticks), and when they're shaken under the professional eye of Mark Boccard Schuster – many times a world-champion cocktail shaker – you might feel that your money is well spent. Le Shaker has one long bar, where you can sit (if you get there early enough) and watch the theatre of the cocktail making. The barmen seem to enjoy their work, although they appear slightly miffed when asked the predictable question, 'Ooh! What's in that one, then?' The clientele don't generally care about the prices – serious money earners and sun-bed-tanned lottery winners don't worry about such things.
OPEN *18.30-23.30 (Mon-Sat)*
FOOD *as opening hours*
CREDIT CARDS *all major cards*
NEAREST TUBE STATIONS *South Kensington, Earls Court*

SHAKESPEARE'S HEAD
29 Great Marlborough Street, W1; 0171 734 2911
There is something very appealing about this picturesque Tudor pub built in the 1920s with the figure of the bard himself leaning thoughtfully from a window and gazing down Carnaby Street. His hand is still missing. He lost it in the war. The Shakespeare's Head had a thorough face-lift recently but is still as Tudor as you could wish and very keen on Shakespeare. There are quotes all round the bar. 'We'll teach you to drink deep ere you depart' and 'Et tu Brute?' as Marc Antony said when getting in a round. The bard might well have approved of the dining room upstairs, a sombre rather noble room where you can have a roast beef dinner at a very moderate price. After a quiet start this has taken off and is doing very well now. A rather careless ghost has recently surfaced, knocking glasses off shelves and bottles too but only out of hours. Out-of-hours hours are fewer than they used to be. The bar opens for breakfast at 9am and the

restaurant stays open until midnight. This is one of the pubs that English Heritage is currently thinking of listing.

OPEN *11.00-23.00 (Mon-Sat), midday-22.30 (Sun)*
FOOD *midday-21.00 (Mon-Sun)*
CREDIT CARDS *all major cards*
DRAUGHT BEERS *Foster's, Kronenbourg, Directors, Theakston, John Smith's Extra Smooth, Beck's, Strongbow, Guinness*
Wheelchair access to venue, not to loos
NEAREST TUBE STATION *Oxford Circus*

THE SHED BAR

Chelsea Village, Fulham Road, SW6; 0171 565 1440

I'd like to give The Shed Bar an award. It's the worst bar in Fulham and has no excuses as it's part of the new complex in Chelsea Village. Food seems to be a high priority but I didn't dare try the Shed Bar burger (£5.50) or the Fat Boys Chips. I was sufficiently put off by the Kronenbourg at £2.70 a pint. This isn't worth the short walk from the Fulham Road.

OPEN *11.00-23.00 (Mon-Sat), midday-22.30 (Sun)*
FOOD *midday-22.00 every day*
CREDIT CARDS *all major cards*
DRAUGHT BEERS *Foster's, John Smith's Extra Smooth, Kronenbourg, Courage Best*
Wheelchair access
NEAREST TUBE STATION *Fulham Broadway*

SHEILA'S BAR BARBIE

41 King Street, WC2; 0171 240 8282

Walking through Covent Garden one day I couldn't resist popping into this bar. It pretends to be everything Australian and, judging by the audible accents, it is. What I can't work out is why people fly halfway round the world and go somewhere that reminds them of home. This bar is surely poking fun at the Australian culture, implying that life down under is macho-orientated and trashy. Sheila's has fake corrugated-steel walls, Aussie flags and pictures, and – what a surprise – a boomerang directing you into the barbie. Beer can be sunk in pitchers – they like that. Food includes baguettes called husband-beaters, plus bushman's brekkie (bacon, egg, beans, tomato, mushrooms, lamb chop, a kind of sausage called a snagette and toast and coffee) for £4.95 and a bushman's veggie brekkie. Veggie brekkie? For bushmen? I don't think so. They advertise a five-course meal: four tinnies and a waggle pie – now that's more like a bushman's brekkie. As for a waggle pie, don't ask the staff, they're not really sure, but I am reliably informed that it contains diced lamb in puff pastry. If this is authentically Australian, I think an Australian might be a little embarrassed.

OPEN *11.30-23.00 (Mon-Sat), 12.00-22.30 (Sun)*
FOOD *as opening hours*
CREDIT CARDS *all major cards*
DRAUGHT BEERS *Castlemaine XXXX, Foster's*
Wheelchair access to venue and loos
NEAREST TUBE STATION *Covent Garden*

SHELLEY'S

10 Stafford Street, W1; 0171 493 0337

This most tasteful and prosperous public house is named, you might well suppose, after Percy Bysshe Shelley, poet and good egg. His likenesses are all over, also pictures of his wife, his holiday home, his tomb. Several of his poems are on the walls too, his portrait in oils hangs above the fireplace in the panelled doubles bar and there he is, at his most romantic, on the inn sign outside. Shelley's was a private house in his day. Did he live here? No, but he must have passed it a few times because he stayed at Cooke's Hotel round the corner, and here's a funny thing. Years after Percy Bysshe drowned in Italy the house became a pub, The King John's Head, and in 1862 someone called Fred Shelley (no kin) bought it. Then a J. Shelley had it and when HE sold it the new owner changed the name to The Shelley Hotel. Did he call it after Percy Bysshe or Fred? Fred has a strong claim, but there you are. Percy Bysshe gets the glory and how nice to have a pub named after a poet, and such a poet. Shelley was a sociable chap. I think he might have liked Shelley's, all those pictures of him and his poems over the fireplace and it has quite a swagger about it. Sir Nikolaus Pevsner included it in his great book on London. He called it 'a pub in a thoroughly debased style.' Sir Nikolaus! Language!

OPEN *11.00-23.00 (Mon-Wed), 11.00-24.00 (Thurs), 11.00-1.00 (Fri-Sat), midday-22.30 (Sun)*

FOOD *9.00-24.00 (Mon-Sat), 9.00-22.00 (Sun)*

CREDIT CARDS *all major cards, not Diners*

DRAUGHT BEERS *Adnams, Southwold, Tetley's, Marston's Pedigree, Adnams Broadside, Stella, Carlsberg Export, Castlemaine XXXX, Guinness, Dry Blackthorn, 2 guest ales*

Wheelchair access to venue, not to loos. Private room seats 80, standing 100

NEAREST TUBE STATION *Green Park*

SHERLOCK HOLMES

10-11 Northumberland Street, WC2; 0171 930 2644

Sherlock Holmes has us in thrall. The stories sell around the world and members of far-flung Sherlock Holmes societies arrive all summer to pay their tribute. They all end up with notebooks and cameras at the Sherlock Holmes in Northumberland Street to find the bar filled with other Sherlock Holmes tours, locals on Sherlock Holmes walks and television crews interviewing everyone. Robert Davie, the licensee, and his family are no longer surprised to be woken at 3am by someone in the street taking pictures. 'This must be the most photographed pub in London,' he says.

The Sherlock Holmes is a smartly turned out pub in the modern Victorian style with a comfortable restaurant, a hidden verandah and a unique tourist attraction: Holmes' study as it appeared one foggy night in *The Empty House*, every item supplied by the Conan Doyle family. There it is, the cosy room and Holmes by the window shot through the head by the vile Colonel Moran. But of course Holmes had foreseen it all. Moran had shot a mannequin. He was no match for Holmes. In Sir Arthur Conan Doyle's day, the pub was part of the Northumberland Hotel, which you may remember from *The Hound of the Baskervilles*. It has been The Sherlock Holmes since 1957, a brilliant stroke. It ensured customers in droves. Holmes, not a modest man, would have approved of all the hoopla, the brisk sale of specially made Holmes' memorabilia, specialities in the restaurant like 'Moriarty's grilled mushrooms' and the usually glowing comments in the visitor's books. You will recognise the lean hawk-nosed figure on the sign in the street, smoking a curved pipe. Peter Cushing of course!

OPEN *11.00-23.00 (Mon-Sat), midday-22.30 (Sun)*

FOOD *bar midday-22.30 (Mon-Sun); restaurant midday-15.00 and 17.30-22.45 (Mon-Thurs), midday-22.30 (Fri-Sun)*

CREDIT CARDS *all major cards*

DRAUGHT BEERS *Boddingtons, Flowers Original, Old Speckled Hen, Sherlock Holmes Ale, Heineken, Heineken Export, Stella Artois, Murphy's, Wadworth 6X, Hoegaarden, Strongbow, a weekly guest ale*

Wheelchair access to venue, ground floor only. Private room seats 40

NEAREST TUBE STATION *Embankment*

THE SHIP

10 Thames Bank, SW14; 0181 876 1439

From the saloon bar of The Ship at Mortlake you get a fine view of a yellow pole sticking out of the river. This is the finishing post for the Oxford and Cambridge Boat Race and for one moment on Boat Race day it becomes the most important post sticking out of any river anywhere. Boat Race day is when it all happens at The Ship. By the time it opens its doors there's a wall of people on both sides of the river and right across Chiswick bridge and the pub is under siege. Boat Race watchers get through a lake of lager and an ocean of bitter beer and keep a team of cooks working flat out at the barbecue long after the two crews have collapsed over their oars. The Ship closes early that night and a huge clear-up begins. By the time everyone gets to bed The Ship is ship-shape again. It is a handsome pub on the Surrey side of the river with deep bay windows and balustrading right round the eaves. The Ship has plenty of big occasions through the year. The river overflows. Summer pig roasts draw the crowds. There's St Patrick's Day with Irish session musicians and Burns Night with the haggis, the ode to the haggis and David Morgan from Limerick in a kilt. There are ale festivals and quiz nights. But it's the Boat Race that has made The Ship famous, the Boat Race that gets the adrenalin going. It is the day of days in Mortlake.

OPEN *11.00-23.00 (Mon-Sat), midday-22.30 (Sun)*
FOOD *midday-14.30 and 18.00-21.30 (Mon-Sat), midday-21.00 (Sun)*
CREDIT CARDS *all major cards*
DRAUGHT BEERS *Courage Best, Courage Directors, John Smith's Extra Smooth, Foster's, Budweiser, Kronenbourg, Guinness, Strongbow, one guest ale*
Wheelchair access to venue
NEAREST RAILWAY STATION *Mortlake*

SHIP INN

41 Jews Row, SW18; 0181 870 9667

The one problem presented by this remarkable pub is finding it. This is not easy. It is set back from the river, hemmed in by a cement works, a bus depot and a car park and no one lives in Jews Row or has any idea where it is. The faint-hearted have been known to give up. All the same, on a sunny summer's afternoon there might be fully 600 customers in and around The Ship Inn at Wandsworth, so it can be reached. Try this. Drive across Wandsworth Bridge, go round the roundabout and just before you reach the bridge again take the little slip road on the left. That's The Ship on your right with the figurehead. On the other hand you could parachute in.

There's a public bar at the front, a big conservatory overlooking the garden, an attractive restaurant with a long open kitchen in which chefs toil away in full view producing modish holiday food – asparagus frittata, spaghetti puttanesca, mussel and squid stew, that sort of thing. You have this either in the restaurant or in the riverside garden. Sunday lunch on a summer's day is when it all comes together, outside in the sun, the river slipping by, the barbecue producing prodigious quantities of steaks and burgers. The garden has its own bar and a riverside marquee, green and white stripes, lovely. This garden is a great place for parties and you get an extraordinary number of people there. More than a thousand have been known to mill round the 12-foot television screen which is put up for the last night of the proms. Thousands come for the fireworks show on Guy Fawkes' Night. The beer is Young's which shares the credit with Charles and Linda Gotto who rescued the place from what seemed like certain oblivion. The Gottos are now tenants of four Young's pubs and have their own farm which provides their pubs with much of the meat they need. An *Evening Standard* Pub of the Year.

OPEN *11.00-23.00 (Mon-Sat), midday-22.30 (Sun)*

FOOD *bar as opening hours; restaurant midday-15.00 and 19.00-22.30 (Mon-Sun)*

CREDIT CARDS *all major cards*

DRAUGHT BEERS *Ramrod Smooth, Young's Bitter, Young's Special, Castlemaine XXXX, Young's Export, Young's Pilsner, Beamish, Guinness, Scrumpy Jack*

Wheelchair access to venue. Two private rooms: 10 seated, 30-150 standing

NEAREST RAILWAY STATION *Wandsworth Town*

SHOELESS JOE'S

555 King's Road, SW6; 0171 384 2333

On big sporting occasions, you must book your table at Shoeless Joe's a month in advance for the downstairs bar. Televised events can only be truly appreciated when you're watching the thing on a 16-foot video wall with an endless supply of chilled beers. The clue is to start early and order food to put a decent lining on your stomach before getting on with the unruly (but gentlemanly) behaviour of screaming your rocks off during the match. I had a sumptuous burger and fries (£7) but had to wait for ever for the limited-choice relish. My companions had a chicken tortilla sandwich (£6) and an 8oz New York strip with potatoes (£11). Try and book one of the raised booths (some have their own TV) or one of the row of tables on the balcony level. Those who don't book take their chances on the floor space, which can fill up very quickly. On Friday and Saturday nights there are fairly wild but fun discos, with screens displaying fractal videos (a sort of 90s high-tech lava lamp).

The ground-floor restaurant has recently been reorganised and is focusing on the bar more than the food these days. It's much quieter than the basement, but don't opt for the table on its own in the corner – the waiting staff can't see you, and it seems to be a case of 'can't see, won't serve'. Service is included in the final bill, but when we each threw in a credit card to divide up the bill, they told me they would be rounding each payment up to the nearest 10p. Call me mean, but if you multiply all those ten pences by the number of people who share their bills over the course of a year, then I think it's just a little too much in their pockets rather than ours. Anyway, I refused, and they gave in with just a little bit of a sulk. Having had my moan, I should add that I think Shoeless Joe's is one of the best additions to this stretch of the King's Road. It provides a complete mix of entertainment, from quiet drinks to full meals and a party atmosphere. And as the holiday-camp man Fred Pontin used to say, 'Remember, book early'.

OPEN *bar 12.00-midnight (Mon-Sat), 12.00-18.00 (Sun); club 21.00-01.00 (Thurs-Sat)*

FOOD *12.00-midnight (Mon-Sat), 12.00-22.30 (Sun)*

CREDIT CARDS *all major cards*

DRAUGHT BEERS *Freedom Ale, Marston's Smooth Ale, Kronenbourg, Labatt's, Guinness*

Wheelchair access to venue. Two private rooms: 30-70 seated, 60-200 standing

NEAREST TUBE STATION *Fulham Broadway*

SHUCKBURGH ARMS

47 Denyer Street, SW3; 0171 589 8382

When Scottish & Newcastle converted the Shuckburgh Arms into a Finnegan's Wake in October 1996, throwing the baronet's coat of arms into a skip, they hadn't bargained on the dramatic reaction. Sir Rupert Shuckburgh, whose ancestors occupied the building in the last century, was incensed: 'My family has been proud to be associated with this pub for more than a hundred years, and I have often visited it. I think its new name is a silly name, I will never go there again and I hope that no one else does.' As if to fulfil this aristocratic prophecy, the people of Chelsea stayed away, forcing S & N into an embarrassing U-turn. 'It just wasn't doing any business as a Finnegan's Wake, so the brewery decided to put things back as they were,' says manager Jason Gregory. When the *Evening Standard* informed Sir Rupert that the pub was to revert to its former name, complete with a new coat of arms which S & N claimed had been 'painstakingly recreated', he agreed to go along to the opening night. There were some nervous moments as Sir Rupert and Lady Shuckburgh inspected the premises before delivering their verdict. 'We like the pub, but they've used the wrong coat of arms.' The nice people at S & N are 'looking into the matter'.

OPEN *11.00-23.00 (Mon-Sat), 12.00-22.30 (Sun)*
FOOD *11.00-23.00 (Mon-Sun)*
CREDIT CARDS Visa, Mastercard
DRAUGHT BEERS *Greene King IPA, John Smith's Smooth, Theakston Best, Beck's, Foster's, Kronenbourg, Guinness, Scrumpy Jack*
Wheelchair access to venue. Private room seats 30
NEAREST TUBE STATION *South Kensington*

THE SILVER CROSS

33 Whitehall, SW1; 0171 930 8350
This lively old pub, a brothel in the reign of Charles I, a tavern since the reign of Charles II, is the repository of much myth and legend including, quite possibly, the brothel bit. Is it really haunted by the Tudor maid whose portrait hangs above the carved fireplace, murdered, they say, dumped in the Thames and not best pleased? 'We're still being haunted,' says Tony Whitehead, the Irish landlord cheerfully. There are three pubs in a row in this bit of Whitehall and this is the oldest, also the smallest. Now that the bar has been moved to the far end, though, there's room enough. Alterations of this sort can be made but preservation orders are in place to protect the important bits, the ceiling for instance. The ceiling is the great prize of The Silver Cross. It is a beautiful barrel-vaulted ceiling. Barrel vaulting is special. The barrels over the bar are just barrels.

OPEN *11.00-23.00 (Mon-Sat), midday-22.30 (Sun)*
FOOD *midday-22.00 (Mon-Sun)*
CREDIT CARDS all major cards
DRAUGHT BEERS *Theakston Best, John Smith's Extra Smooth, Directors, Kronenbourg, Foster's, Guinness, Strongbow*
Wheelchair access to venue
NEAREST TUBE STATION *Charing Cross*

SLAP HARRY'S

1-3 Warwick Street, W1; 0171 734 4409
Thirteen TV screens in the bar, one of them huge, all of them on: no one can accuse Slap Harry of under-doing things. They go on at midday the minute the pub opens and stay on in a companionable way until it closes in the early hours of the morning. Sport, music, films. Films, music, sport. Slap Harry's, a minute or so from Piccadilly Circus, is what is known as a late-night venue. It is comparatively quiet during the day, even light and airy in the summer with a wall of windows that concertinas back, entirely opening one side of the bar to the tables and chairs on the pavement. The transformation happens in the evening. Doors and windows close, down come the blinds to black the place out and in come the doormen. The sound inside starts to rise. At around 9pm a DJ takes over in the main bar and the volume rises with every record played. By 11pm when it costs £2 to get in, four giant Roboscans are producing sensational lighting effects and the place is thumping. It costs you more in the basement but then it's even louder down there, so fair dos. The basement bar DJs play soul, reggae and R and B and the music ricochets off the walls. It has Roboscans too and massive air conditioning and there's not a chair in sight. You don't come down those stairs to sit down.

OPEN *main bar midday-01.00 (Mon-Wed), midday-03.00 (Thurs-Sat), midday-22.30 (Sun); basement bar 20.00-01.00 (Wed), 21.00-03.00 (Thurs), 21.00-03.00 (Fri-Sat), 19.00-22.30 (Sun)*
FOOD *midday-15.30 (Mon-Sat)*
CREDIT CARDS *none taken*
DRAUGHT BEERS *Caffrey's, Carling Black Label, Carling Premier, Guinness Two private rooms: 60-80 seated, 60-200 standing*
NEAREST TUBE STATION *Piccadilly Circus*

SLUG AND LETTUCE

Slug and Lettuces have done a great job injecting new leases of life into some of London's fading pubs. There's a rather splendid one by the river in Richmond, a popular one in St Martin's Lane, a locals' local in Bayswater, and one for young Fulham on the pull. The good thing about Slug and Lettuces is that they don't seem to be afraid to change, and are constantly evolving. Only a few years ago they all got a bit of a spruce-up, and they are now looking lighter and brighter. They have a standard offering, which means similar ales and fare throughout the chain, and the staff have been trained, they tell me, to very high standards in customer service. In this Guide's experience, their politeness almost makes up for their sometimes indifferent attitude to table care. The menu looks and generally is very inviting. The Cajun spiced chicken burger got the thumbs-up, as did the linguini with bacon, peas, herbs, wine and cream (both £5.75). We all moaned about the fries, though, which, for some completely illogical reason, arrived coated with more than enough salt to put an end to any slug trail.

Branches at:
BATTERSEA 4 St John's Hill, SW11; 0171 924 1322
   NEAREST RAILWAY STATION *Clapham Junction*
BAYSWATER 47 Hereford Road, W2; 0171 229 1503
   NEAREST TUBE STATION *Bayswater*
COVENT GARDEN 114 Upper St Martin's Lane, WC2; 0171 379 4880
   NEAREST TUBE STATION *Leicester Square*
FULHAM 474 Fulham Road, SW6; 0171 385 3209
   NEAREST TUBE STATION *Fulham Broadway*
ISLINGTON 1 Islington Green, N1; 0171 226 3864
   NEAREST TUBE STATION *Angel*
KINGSTON-UPON-THAMES Turks Boatyard, Thameside, KT1; 0181 547 2323
   NEAREST RAILWAY STATION *Kingston-upon-Thames*
PIMLICO 11 Warwick Way, SW1; 0171 834 3313
   NEAREST TUBE STATION *Pimlico, Victoria*
RICHMOND Riverside House, Water Lane, TW9; 0181 948 7733
   NEAREST TUBE STATION *Richmond*
SOHO 80-82 Wardour Street, W1; 0171 437 1400
   NEAREST TUBE STATIONS *Oxford Circus, Piccadilly*
WALTON-ON-THAMES Thameside, KT12; 01932 223996
   NEAREST RAILWAY STATION *Walton-on-Thames*
WANDSWORTH 21 Alma Road, SW18; 0181 874 1833
   NEAREST RAILWAY STATION *Wandsworth Town*
PUTNEY 14 Putney High Street, SW15; 0181 785 3081
   NEAREST TUBE STATION *Putney Bridge*

SMITHFIELD FREE HOUSE

334 Central Market, EC1; 0171 248 5311
The Smithfield Free House occupies a prime site in the old Smithfields Market. What the market traders would make of the place now, I'm sure I can't say. This youthful pub has pool tables and non-stop music increasing in volume hour after hour. At 10pm the music takes over completely, and kids come from all over London for the nightly disco.

OPEN *pub 12.00-23.00 (Mon), 11.00-23.00 (Tues-Fri); club 22.00-02.00 (Tues-Thurs), 21.00-03.30 (Fri-Sat)*
FOOD *12.00-15.00 (Mon-Fri), 18.00-22.00 bar snacks*
CREDIT CARDS *all major cards, not Diners*
DRAUGHT BEERS *Bass, Caffrey's, Worthington, London Pride, Carling Black Label, Carling Premier, Grolsch, Staropramen, Guinness, Strongbow*
Wheelchair access to venue, not to loos
NEAREST TUBE STATIONS *Chancery Lane, Farringdon*

SOAP

116 Princedale Road, W11; 0171 792 9302

Why Soap? They tell me it's an acronym for Society of Alternative People. I wish they hadn't. Who are these alternative people? Are they the happy bunch of Christian Scientists? Are they a meeting group of the Holland Park Temperance Society? I was intrigued, especially by their invitation, which assured me I would enjoy 'the space and its clientele'. How dare they assume what I might enjoy. For all they know I might get my kicks from downloading animal porn from the internet. It turns out to be a cheap pub conversion aimed at Notting Hillbillies. It has no draught beers, just bottles and cocktails, and there's hardly anywhere to sit because the giant Jenga-constructed furniture leaves a long way to fall if you've had too much pop. The only food on offer was rice, peas and chicken (£7.50), which was described as 'wicked, man' by a woman drinking what she said was 'a Malibus and Cokes'. I reckon that this is a chill-out venue in terms of cool rather than a place to relax, and that late evenings will be quite energetic. This will be fun if you're pissed, but you must resist the temptation to steal the relishes from the eye-level glass shelf over the bar. I'm not sure this venue is going to wash.

OPEN *17.00-middnight*
FOOD *snacks available during opening times*
CREDIT CARDS *all major cards, not AmEx*
Wheelchair access to venue and loo. Private room due to open soon, 100 people seated
NEAREST TUBE STATION *Holland Park*

SOFA BAR AT THE DRAWING ROOM

103 Lavender Hill, SW11; 0171 350 2564

The Drawing Room is a restaurant, but if you go through the doors and turn right you'll find the Sofa Bar. No prizes for guessing what you'll be sitting on. It's small, cosy, and a perfect respite from the frenetic activity of the main road. Clocks feature largely, for no other reason than that the owner has a collection of them and this seemed an ideal place to display them. Low-level lighting, table service and plenty of foliage help to create a relaxed atmosphere. Drinks will be brought to your table. Very civilised.

OPEN *pub 17.00-midnight (Mon-Sat), 11.00-19.00 (Sun)*
FOOD *As opening hours*
CREDIT CARDS *All major cards, not AmEx*
Wheelchair access to venue
NEAREST RAILWAY STATION *Clapham Junction*

SOHO BREWING COMPANY

41 Earlham Street, WC2; 0171 240 0606

The growth of brew-pubs continues at a snail's pace in London but each new addition provides a very useful alternative on the drinking scene. Following fast on the heels of Mash, this new bar and restaurant (curiously named, as it is actually in Covent Garden) occupies a realistic-looking brewery cellar with its arched ceilings and exposed brickwork. The first, impressive sight as you descend the stairs is the gleaming copper of the vats and the pipeworks which draw the beers direct to the bar. Five beers are promised although only four were available on my visit: the Soho Pale (4.5%) is a refreshing beer but served so cold it disguises what should be a hoppy flavour; I enjoyed the Soho Red (4.6%), which was much more flavoursome; Soho Wheat (5%) is based on traditional wheat-beer recipes (cloudy appearance and rich, fruity aftertaste); and the Freedom Pilsener (5%) comes from the now-famous Fulham brewery. It's best to try these by the half pint (from £1.50) until you find the one you like.

The spacious bar has furniture that wouldn't look out of place in a children's nursery including a few – but not enough – leaning tables. When the crowds gather (and gather they surely will) this is going to be a noisy affair. I didn't care much for the three-strong greeting group at the door, which may be a hint that another dreary door policy is on the way. If you do have the slightest trouble getting in, spin on your heel and pop over the road to Belgo, which has an excellent range of Belgian beers.

OPEN *11.00-midnight (Mon-Sat)*

FOOD *midday-15.00 then 18.00-23.00 (Mon-Sat)*

CREDIT CARDS *all major cards*

DRAUGHT BEERS *own brew, Freedom lager*

Wheelchair access to venue, not to loos

NEAREST TUBE STATIONS *Covent Garden, Leicester Square*

SOHO SOHO

11-13 Frith Street, W1; 0171 494 3491

The ground floor of this noisy, busy brasserie has a bar with limited seating potential, but that doesn't seem to bother the crowds of after-work drinkers who happily squeeze together to allow a few more in. It's fun, young, and on a summer's eve you can sit and breathe in the air of traffic-ridden Frith Street.

OPEN *12.00-23.00 (Mon-Sun)*

FOOD *as opening hours*

CREDIT CARDS *all major cards*

Wheelchair access to venue and loos

NEAREST TUBE STATIONS *Tottenham Court Road, Leicester Square*

SOHO SPICE

124-126 Wardour Street, W1; 0171 434 0808

No, this is not a new member of the uniquely talented singing troupe. Soho Spice is a rather attractive bar beneath the restaurant of the same name. The heat and dust of an Indian bazaar may be missing, but the colourful decor, burning incense sticks, spicy snacks and khurta-clad staff help to evoke dreamy images from the subcontinent. You know you're in London, though – the modern, air-conditioned bar serves draught Kronenbourg (£1.75 for a half pint) and an Indian beer, Kingfisher (brewed in Kent). Thankfully, there is also an Indian-import beer, Cobra (£4 for 65cl), and they spice up the cocktails with aromatic infusions of cinnamon, cumin, fennel or ginger-stuffed apricot (£4.95). Bar snacks include the ones you might expect, but also chaat (chicken in a pepper sauce) and crisp mini-pooris with a yoghurt sauce (all £2.95). With most drinking joints in this part of town bursting at the seams, it made a pleasant change to find this under-used, perfectly agreeable bar that might be just a little too posh for Posh Spice.

OPEN *12.00-midnight (Mon-Thurs), 12.00-00.30 (Fri-Sat)*

FOOD *as opening hours*

CREDIT CARDS *all major cards*

DRAUGHT BEERS *Kingfisher, Kronenbourg*

NEAREST TUBE STATIONS *Piccadilly Circus, Tottenham Court Road*

THE SPANIARD'S INN

Spaniard's Road, NW3; 0181 731 6571

The Spanish Ambassador to the Court of James I is said to have lived here. That would explain the name. It is a 16th-century weatherboarded house on the road that cuts through Hampstead Heath and none of the many additions and alterations has spoiled it in any way. It has been a tavern for 400 years, most of that time deep in the countryside but life has not been without drama or glamour. Highwaymen, like modern New Yorkers, could be good company when not actually shooting you and were often there. Dick Turpin stabled Black Bess in the toll gate that still juts into the road causing daily traffic jams in both directions, and a musket ball he fired while holding up the Royal Mail is on show in the bar. They used to have his pistols too but they were pinched as were the rifles left behind by the Gordon rioters who were boozing in the bar when soldiers arrived and marched them off to Newgate Goal. Things are usually more peaceful in the Spaniard's Inn. Shelley, Keats and Byron all went there and so, you will not be surprised to hear, did Charles Dickens. In *The Pickwick Papers* this was where Mrs Bardell and her friends plotted Mr Pickwick's downfall. You can imagine Mr Pickwick in the saloon bar with its low ceilings, old panelling and cosy alcoves. Bar stools surround the old wooden bar and there is a charming panelled room upstairs with original beams and shutters and a splendidly sloping floor. There are real fires in winter and in the summer one of the best pub gardens you will ever see, with raised lawn and roses, a fine pergola and a big terrace of picnic tables. At the bottom of the garden more than 100 budgies lead busy lives in a big aviary. Children love them and are welcome here. It is a pub worth making any sort of detour to visit. Mind the toll gate.

OPEN *11.00-23.00 (Mon-Sat), 12.00-22.30 (Sun)*
FOOD *12.00-21.00 (Mon-Sat), 12.00-18.00 (Sun)*
CREDIT CARDS *all major cards*
DRAUGHT BEERS *London Pride, Bass, Hancock's, Adnams, Landlord, guest beers*
Wheelchair access to venue and loos. Private room seats 30
NEAREST TUBE STATIONS *Golder's Green, Hampstead*

THE SPORTING PAGE

6 Camera Place, SW10; 0171 376 3694

The Sporting Page sits happily tucked away in a quiet little side street, sheltered from the endless roar of the traffic on the King's Road and Fulham Road. It is a small, whitewashed pub with a rather smart interior of varnished pine and rosewood and murals depicting sporting scenes from yesteryear. Big red canopies featuring the Bollinger trademark hint at what goes on inside: this pub sells more Bollinger than any other pub in the country and is second only to The Lanesborough among retail outlets. The quaffing clientele pile in from the City after work, along with the old military brigade and public-school types, for evenings of antics and tomfoolery. On rugby occasions the big screen comes down and the crowds don their designer rugby attire to cheer on the action.

The Modern British menu, more adventurous than the usual pub fare, is very popular and includes traditional comfort foods such as bangers and mash. As The Sporting Page can be very busy in the evenings, the smart time to go is during the day and (unsurprisingly for this area) on Saturday evenings, when the locals pack up their picnic hampers and disappear off to the country for the weekend. Back to the Bolly: a bottle is remarkably good value at £30 (NV), a jeroboam is £135, and a Methuselah £300. They don't yet stock a Nebuchadnezzar, but should you want one, have a word with Kerry Ennis – the manager, who takes no prisoners – she'll sort you out. For those who like to know these things, the order of bottle sizes for champagne is as follows: quarter (20cl), half (37.5cl), bottle (75cl), magnum (2 bottles), jeroboam (4), rehoboam (6) Methuselah (8), Salmanazar (12), Balthazar (16) and Nebuchadnezzar (20).

OPEN *11.00-23.00 (Mon-Sat), 12.00-22.30 (Sun)*
FOOD *12.00-14.30 and 19.00-22.00 (Mon-Fri), 12.00-19.00 (Sun)*
CREDIT CARDS *all major cards*

DRAUGHT BEERS *John Smith's Extra Smooth, Bass, Courage Best, Foster's, Holsten Export, Kronenbourg, Miller, Guinness, Strongbow*
Wheelchair access to venue, not to loos
NEAREST TUBE STATION *Fulham Broadway*

SPORTS ACADEMY

24 King William Street, EC4; 0171 397 9861

I lured my friend Alex away from his high-powered City job with the promise of a free lunch. This two-bar venue has 24 TV monitors and one huge video-wall in the upstairs bar, perfect for watching the hectic schedule of sporting events upon us. I ordered a cola, only to receive a chemical arrangement dispensed from a gun over a glass of ice, for which I was charged £1.55. I wish I'd refused to pay, and will the next time I'm involved in a similar unarmed robbery. Alex ordered a pint of Carling (his choice but there was little else to choose from), which at £2.20 a pint works out cheaper than the cola. We went to the air-conditioned basement bar to eat and should have read the signs when the staff spent most of their time apologising for their slowness. We were eventually rewarded with table service by an attentive but ineffective young chap who looked like he might be on a day-release scheme from one of Her Majesty's institutions. Twenty-five minutes later, the food arrived. My warm ciabatta of ham and cheese (£3.95) had been nuked to cotton-wool softness, defeating the only point of ordering ciabatta, which is that you get a decent crusty sandwich. Alex's burger and fries (£5.95) partially made up in quantity for what it lacked in taste or nutritional value. This is not quality food – and it's good stodge only if you're going to have a bucketful of lager. As Alex pointed out to me on the way back to the office, 'There is no such thing as a free lunch'.

OPEN *11.00-23.00 (Mon-Fri), closed Sat and Sun for private hire*
FOOD *11.00-15.00 every day, snacks available until 21.00*
CREDIT CARDS *all major cards, not AmEx or Diners*
Wheelchair access to venue and loos. Two bars available for private hire to accommodate 125 and 200 respectively
NEAREST TUBE STATION *Monument*

J.D. SPORTS BAR

Lidlington Place, NW1; 0171 387 1495

J.D. Sports Bar is a pub for bikers run by bikers. That doesn't mean to the exclusion of everyone else – in fact, they depend on others, as bikers are not big drinkers. The kings of the road come and show off their equipment, which they proudly polish on the road outside. J. D. Sports Bar's bold claim is to be Camden's best rock pub. It doesn't open until 5pm on weekdays and it has two impossible biker video games. Why not go along for the ride?

OPEN *11.00-23.00 (Mon-Sat), 12.00-22.30 (Sun)*
FOOD *12.00-15.00 and 17.00-20.00 (Mon-Fri), 12.00-17.00 (Sun)*
CREDIT CARDS *none taken*
DRAUGHT BEERS *John Smith's Extra Smooth, Foster's, Budweiser, Kronenbourg, Guinness, Strongbow*
NEAREST TUBE STATIONS *Mornington Crescent, Euston, Camden Town*

SPORTS CAFÉ

80 Haymarket, SW1; 0171 839 8300

This is a much better example of a themed sports bar than its near neighbour Football. The Sports Café has been designed in the American big-bar style, with the large spaces broken up carefully so you don't quite feel like you're in a scrum. There are two bars downstairs and one bar upstairs, where they hold sports-related promotional events. Drinks are not cheap (£2.65 for a pint of Foster's), but then they never are in places like this. There are plenty of TV screens and a large screen visible from the restaurant area.

OPEN *12.00-02.00 (Mon-Thurs), 12.00-03.00 (Fri-Sat), 12.00-23.00 (Sun)*
FOOD *12.00-23.30 (Mon-Sun); bar snacks after midnight (Mon-Thurs and Sun), 12.00-01.00 (Fri-Sat)*
CREDIT CARDS *all major cards*
DRAUGHT BEERS *Boston Beer, Foster's, Heineken, Miller, Stella Artois, Murphy's, Max Dry, Strongbow*
Wheelchair access to venue and loos. Private room: 50 seated, 70 standing
NEAREST TUBE STATION *Piccadilly Circus*

THE SPOT
29 Maiden Lane, WC2; 0171 379 5900
The Spot is a collection of bars occupying a prime position in growing-ever-popular Maiden Lane. There's a couple of bars on the ground floor, a tatty one on the right and the main bar on the left. You go up to the Oval Room, which is kind of oval. This is where the serious action is – it has a large screen, a party atmosphere, and loud music, an eclectic mix of soul, R & B, house and garage. Monday night is comedy night (£4 or £8 including dinner). The Spot is open late but they charge £4 admission after 11pm on Fridays and Saturdays.
OPEN *11.30-midnight (Mon-Sun)*
FOOD *as opening hours*
CREDIT CARDS *Mastercard, Switch, Visa*
DRAUGHT BEERS *Caffrey's, Carling Black Label, Carling Premier, Grolsch, Guinness, Dry Blackthorn*
Wheelchair access to venue
NEAREST TUBE STATIONS *Covent Garden, Charing Cross*

THE SPOTTED DOG
15 Longbridge Road, Barking; 0181 507 7155
A most untoward thing happened to The Spotted Dog, Barking, in 1994. The Barking Dog opened right next door. You can understand how it felt. I mean it had been there on its spacious corner since 1870, a handsome, dignified sort of pub, mock Tudor, genuine Victorian and now here was this brash newcomer, this Barking Dog, undercutting its prices and taking its customers in droves. It was not best pleased. After some initial dismay The Spotted Dog pulled itself together and did something it had never before had to do. It started competing. It knocked two of its various bars together, opened everything out a bit, redecorated, lightened things up and gradually new customers arrived and old customers returned. Now, says The Spotted Dog, it is doing better than it was before. There is, it seems, room for two dogs, one spotted, one barking in Barking.
OPEN *midday-16.00 (Mon-Fri), 18.00-23.00 (Wed-Thurs), 19.00-23.00 (Sat), midday-17.00 (Sun) and 17.30-23.00 (Fri)*
FOOD *same as opening, stops serving 1 hour before closing*
CREDIT CARDS *all major cards*
DRAUGHT BEERS *Davys Old Wallop*
Wheelchair access to venue, not to loos. Private room: 50 seated, 80 standing
NEAREST TUBE STATION *Barking*

THE SPREAD EAGLE
71 Wandworth High Street, SW18; 0181 877 9809
The Wandsworth one-way system is the heart of the Young's empire. At its centre is the old Ram Brewery itself and around it orbits a solar system of attendant planets making up a mighty pub crawl. The Brewery Tap, The Brewers Inn which used to be the vast Two Brewers but which is now a substantial pub and a 16-room hotel, The Kings Arms with its big garden running down to the river, smaller satellites like The Crane and The Grapes, the comfortable Queen Adelaide, The Old Sergeant, built and

owned, would you believe it, by John Nash, The Alma and The Ship. The Spread Eagle stands four square in the heart of the High Street. There has been a Spread Eagle there for almost 300 years but the first one was rebuilt at great cost in 1892 and there it is, a temple of Victoriana. The mahogany bar counter, backed by a fine display of etched mirrors and ornate woodwork, curves over the bare boards of the public bar, through the upholstered comforts of the saloon bar and into the old dining room. Each area is separated from its neighbour by splendid etched glass partitions and doors. Brass lamps and chandeliers abound and old prints cover the walls.

The Spread Eagle has played a central part in Wandsworth life. It was a coaching inn, provided stables and a ballroom, served as a magistrates court, hosted town meetings without number. Lord Spencer's agent met tenants and collected rents here and the pub's general usefulness continues with wedding receptions and meetings. A new landlord is doing good things with the food, there's a Friday night disco and there has been a big influx of students from the nearby South Thames College lately. The square building at the back used to be Assembly Rooms for dances, concerts and music hall, then, sensationally, it became a bioscope. Alas bioscopes everywhere were killed off by the new fangled cinema and the Spread Eagle's has lain idle since. There are always plans for it. Next year perhaps.

OPEN *11.00-23.00 (Mon-Sat), midday-22.30 (Sun)*

FOOD *midday-14.30 (Mon-Sat)*

CREDIT CARDS *all major cards*

DRAUGHT BEERS *Young's Special and Bitter, Young's Pilsner and Export, Carling Black Label, Stella, Guinness, Ramrod Smooth, Dry Blackthorn, seasonal ale*

Wheelchair access to venue and loos. Private rooms, one seats 60, standing 100 the other seats 40, standing 80

NEAREST RAILWAY STATION *Wandsworth Town*

SPRINGBOK

20 Bedford Street, WC2; 0171 379 1734

Here's a zoological piece. A springbok is a graceful, strikingly marked gazelle-like antelope of the Bovidae family. It is native to the open, tree-less plains of southern Africa and once roamed in such dense masses it destroyed the area over which it passed. When alarmed or excited it makes a series of stiff-legged vertical leaps more than 3 metres off the ground, known as pronking. A certain amount of pronking goes on in this basement bar. The phenomenon of global grouping continues unabated in London, and most of the punters here have some connection with South Africa. It's high energy, loud music, TV screens and video games, with loud talking, fast-living boozers downing the Castle lager. There's a quieter bar, the Tunnel Bar, at the back; it has tables and chairs where you can relax – a little – and think of home.

OPEN *12.00-23.00 (Mon-Sat), 12.00-midnight (Thurs-Sat), 12.00-22.30 (Sun)*

FOOD *12.00-21.00 (Mon-Sun)*

CREDIT CARDS *all major cards, not AmEx*

DRAUGHT BEERS *John Smith's Extra Smooth, Foster's, Kronenbourg, Guinness, Dry Blackthorn*

NEAREST TUBE STATIONS *Covent Garden, Charing Cross, Leicester Square*

THE STAR TAVERN

6 Belgrave Mews West, SW1; 0171 235 3019

The Star Tavern was built for the household servants of the nobility. There were plenty of both in 19th-century Belgravia. Four dukes lived round the corner in the newly built Belgrave Square and the local servant population was enormous. The Star Tavern had to be big and it was every bit as hierarchical as the great town houses around it. Saloon bar, private bar, public bar or snug, the butlers, valets, footmen and coachmen understood exactly which was for them and which was not. A couple of wars and the partitions came down and after that you didn't know whose shoulder your shoulder might be rubbing. Actors, gangsters, the Gaekwar of Baroda, it was a rich mix in the saloon bar of The Star Tavern and you were never sure if Paddy Kennedy would even let you in. He ruled The Star Tavern in the 1950s and 60s and would not serve you if he did not like the cut of your jib. He was particularly particular about who used the upstairs bar where, they say, the Great Train Robbers planned their deed. Kennedy made a few bob in his day, lived well, spent freely but the horses were his undoing. Sadly he died broke in the licensed trade's home. On winter evenings you still look for a table near one of the open fires and on a summer evening customers like to take their drinks into the mews where there are tubs of geraniums, hanging baskets of lobelia and very little traffic. The Star Tavern's food is a draw, and this is a Fuller's house so the beer is a big plus. Like the ESB it sells, the Star Tavern is a pub of Extra Strong Character. It was the *Evening Standard* Pub of the Year in 1992.

OPEN *11.30-23.00 (Mon-Fri), 11.00-23.00 (Sat), midday-15.00 and 19.00-22.30 (Sun)*

FOOD *midday-14.30 and 18.00-21.00 (Mon-Fri), 11.30-15.00 and 18.30-23.00 (Sat), midday-14.30 and 19.00-22.30 (Sun)*

CREDIT CARDS *Visa, Mastercard, Delta*

DRAUGHT BEERS *Chiswick Bitter, Fuller's ESB, London Pride, Carling Black Label, Grolsch, Heineken, Guinness, one seasonal ale*
Private room: 45-50 seated, 90-100 standing

NEAREST TUBE STATION *Knightsbridge*

STONEMASONS

54 Cambridge Grove, W6; 0181 748 1397

Located just off Glenthorne Road in Hammersmith, this is a new, well-designed bar with a strong food focus. It has probably been saved by the intervention of Ewan Guinness and Matt Jacomb (see Masons Arms), who came across a rather gloomy saloon bar, The Cambridge Arms, bought it, all but demolished the interior, added a room at the back, gave it a skylight, big windows, bare-board flooring and big tables to eat at, and installed an open kitchen. It's early days yet but the Stonemasons seems to have lost itself somewhere in the dictionary between a bar and a restaurant. It is clearly a bar where you can go for a pint, but it also serves up some reasonable quality food according to a barely legible handwritten, badly photocopied menu. This includes crocodile with New Zealand mussels in a Thai red curry (£7.50), pan-fried calves' liver in sage and onion mash (£6.50), Cumberland sausages with mash and gravy (£5.10) and plenty of vegetarian alternatives. The problem with open kitchens is that they should be a spectacle in themselves, a form of theatre. This one lacked drama, and the chefs busying away in the middle of it all looked like suitably cast extras from *Trainspotting*, so it came as something of a surprise when we got our food and discovered how delicious it all was. The bar service is painfully slow, tables are often littered with the debris of previous occupants, and if you ask the rarely-to-be-found waitress, who might just happen to stray by, for more drinks, she'll reiterate the house policy, 'Please order at the bar'.

OPEN *12.00-23.00 (Mon-Sat), 12.00-22.30 (Sun)*

FOOD *12.00-22.15 (Mon-Sat), 12.00-21.45 (Sun)*

CREDIT CARDS *all major cards*

DRAUGHT BEERS *Boddingtons, Boston Beer, Wadworth 6X, Heineken, Hoegaarden, Stella Artois, Guinness, Strongbow*

NEAREST TUBE STATION *Hammersmith*

THE SUN

47 Clapham Old Town, SW4; 0171 622 4980

A rather fine Victorian building takes pride of place in the Old Town and is one of the most popular meeting points in Clapham. It seems that you don't need the might of a giant brewer behind you to transform an old pub into the kind of venue the public clearly wants. Ann and Tom Halpin, a couple who were weaned on the pub scene in Ireland, bought the lease of The Sun from Bass. After such an extravagant purchase, they needed to get the place up and running as soon as they could. They all but gutted the building and let loose a couple of artists, Caroline Ward and John Hammond, to create an effective and handsome interior of distressed green and yellow paintwork, spruced-up woodwork and bizarre, rain-forest-decorated loos.

There is ample space for relaxed lunching and good quality, well-presented food. The 'lunch for a fiver' deal offers an ever-changing selection of dishes, includes a glass of wine or beer, and is available until the late afternoon, when the place fills up with Clapham's twenty- and thirtysomethings returning from work. The evening crowds occupy every available inch of floor space, and the large garden at the side, which now has its own bar, is as likely to be packed in February as it is in August (they use garden heaters). You needn't be put off by the vast numbers who congregate here – they are fun, friendly and street-fashionable, and the fast and efficient bartenders ensure that getting a drink is an easy trip.

OPEN 11.00-23.00 (Mon-Sat), 12.00-22.30 (Sun)

FOOD 12.30-16.00 and 18.00-21.30 (Mon-Fri, all day (Sat-Sun)

CREDIT CARDS all major cards, not AmEx

DRAUGHT BEERS Caffrey's, Grolsch, Staropramen, Tennent's Extra, Tennent's Pilsner, Guinness, Dry Blackthorn

Wheelchair access to venue. Private room seats 50

NEAREST TUBE STATION Clapham Common

THE SUN AND DOVES

61-63 Coldharbour Lane, SE5; 0171 733 1525

A ray of hope now shines in Camberwell, whose residents have for far too long been denied any decent drinking venues. In September 1995 Mark Dodds, then a landscape gardener but with considerable experience in the food and drink industry, negotiated with Inntrepreneur to obtain the lease of this sleepy little local just a few hundred yards from Camberwell Green. His vision was to retain the pub as the focal point of the community while providing a modern bar in line with contemporary expectations. He closed the old place down, gutted it, refurnished and redecorated it on a very tight budget, and three months later opened the doors to the people of Camberwell. As if to illustrate the dictum that nature abhors a vacuum, it filled up quickly, becoming an almost instant success and proof positive that you don't need to spend the fantastic sums now being sloshed around by the big breweries on refurbishment projects to give the punters what they want.

The Sun and Doves has one large, brightly coloured room with painted floorboards scratched almost clear again with wear. Rickety old furniture provides plenty of seating space, and there's a raised area where the leopard-skin seats are – that's the sexy corner! A simple curtain partitions the restaurant area, which leads on to a rather handsome patio garden at the back. The bohemian atmosphere is supported with works of art on the walls, which change monthly, providing a showcase for new artists. Two years on and the place is thriving, nearly all the profits have been put back into the pub, enabling them to update the furniture, add a smoke-extraction system, and so forth. There are clearly some very good-looking people in Camberwell, and it seems they are more than happy to spend their leisure time in The Sun and Doves.

OPEN *11.00-23.00 (Mon-Fri), 12.00-23.00 (Sat), 12.00-22.30 (Sun)*
FOOD *bar 11.00-15.00 and 18.00-23.00 (Mon-Fri), 12.00-15.00 (Sat-Sun); restaurant 12.00-15.00 and 18.30-22.00 (Mon-Thurs), 12.00-15.00 and 18.30-22.30 (Fri-Sat), 12.00-21.30 (Sun)*
Beer garden
CREDIT CARDS *all major cards, not AmEx*
DRAUGHT BEERS *Courage Directors, John Smith's Extra Smooth, Foster's, Kronenbourg, Guinness, Scrumpy Jack*
Wheelchair access to venue. Private room: 40 seated, 50-80 standing
NEAREST TUBE STATION *Oval*
NEAREST RAILWAY STATION *Denmark Hill*

SUN AND THIRTEEN CANTONS

21 Great Pulteney Street, W1; 0171 734 0934
There has been a pub on this site for more than 300 years, and the first of these started life simply as The Sun. In the late 1600s many Soho pubs adopted the name Thirteen Cantons to recognise the mostly Protestant Swiss community that had settled in the area. In Switzerland a canton is a political division, and at the end of the Thirty Years War in 1648, thirteen cantons were declared free from the rule of the Holy Roman Emperor. A further religious war in Switzerland in 1656 resulted in victory for the Catholics, leading to the oppression of the Protestant communities. Many Protestants made their way to London and congregated in Soho, still expressing their allegiance to their cantons.

The old Sun and Thirteen Cantons survived until 1882, when it was demolished and rebuilt as the pub we see today standing square on the corner of Great Pulteney Street and Beak Street. Goldcrest Films bought the building about five years ago, as well as the brasserie next door. They gutted everything and created a much bigger pub with a comforting green and cream decor. On warm days the first thing you notice is the crowds of people spilling out on to the pavement; on colder days they all snuggle into the small main bar. There is a much bigger room, which was the brasserie, with wooden wall panels, framed mirrors, marble-topped tables and a very discreet large-screen TV which rolls down from the ceiling for major sporting events. By day this room is used as a restaurant serving a constantly changing menu of pastas, salads and chef's specials (the Toulouse sausages are a good bet). In the evenings the local businesses release their media executives, and they all seem to come to this pub. You're likely to overhear conversations about media awards and web sites, and find the clientele dressed in designer suits rather than City suits, and carrying portfolios rather than attaché cases. You can tell they're media people, as even the over-35s are trendy. Go downstairs, past the loos, and you'll find another big room with its own bar – much darker than upstairs, and illuminated with red lights. Fuller's bought it just over a year ago, but they have left everything just as it should be.
OPEN *12.00-23.00 (Mon-Fri), 16.00-22.30 (Sun)*
FOOD *12.00-15.00 (Mon-Fri)*
CREDIT CARDS *all major cards*
DRAUGHT BEERS *Carling Black Label, Guinness, London Pride, Heineken, Stella Artois, Murphy's, Strongbow*
Wheelchair access to venue. Private room: 60-70 standing
NEAREST TUBE STATION *Piccadilly Circus*

THE SUN INN

Church Road, SW13; 0181 876 5256
First find Barnes Green. Note the willow which grows aslant the brook, the avenue of horse chestnuts, the house, on the left, where Henry Fielding lived. Take a turn round the pond and there's The Sun, a pretty Georgian building with a mansard roof, a pergola, windows boxes and hanging

gardens. Before you go in, though, go round the back and have a look at Barnes Bowling Club, still owned by the brewers. It has a very rare, old fashioned green, a sort of inverse crown with the centre lower than the sides. Here, so the story goes, Elizabeth I was taught to play by Drake and Walsingham. Inside, The Sun little seems to have changed since its days as an 18th-century coaching inn. There is a charming warren of little rooms, a jumble of nooks and snugs divided by rails, pillars, stained-glass panels and curious sliding leaded windows. There are wooden floors on different levels, beams, low ceilings, stuffed owls, a piano, a huge stuffed pike, old prints, old bottles, old rugs, bric à brac of all sorts and a ghost. This fussy spirit, thought to be a former landlord, used to move the plates around but seems satisfied with their new positions. He still alters the clocks but no one minds and during opening hours The Sun couldn't be livelier. Barnes is awash with celebrated persons of a musical and theatrical sort and this is where they drink. The Sun is really a country pub, the perfect object of a walk. The dog will be welcomed, many are counted among the regulars. They are happy to see children too, at lunchtime anyway. It gets very crowded, of course, but that is what you would expect. Sunday lunch, traditional roast, is particularly popular.

OPEN *11.00-23.00 (Mon-Sat), midday-22.30 (Sun)*

FOOD *midday-14.45 (Mon-Sat), 18.00-21.00 (Mon-Fri), midday-16.00 (Sun)*

CREDIT CARDS *all major cards*

DRAUGHT BEERS *Adnams, Burton Ale, Calder's Cream Ale, Marston's Pedigree, Tetley's, Carlsberg, Castlemaine XXXX, Old Speckled Hen, Stella Artois, Guinness, Taunton*

NEAREST RAILWAY STATION *Barnes Bridge, Barnes*

THE SURPRISE

6 Christchurch Terrace, SW3; 0171 352 4699

The Surprise was the name of the frigate that took Charles II to safety in France, a voyage celebrated on the pub sign. There is the frigate heaving to, there the king being rowed out to board her. He stands heroically in the prow, his wig understandably askew. This happened in Falmouth 200 years before this handsome Victorian pub was built, but The Surprise remains properly grateful to its namesake and there are lots of pictures of the graceful fighting ship or others like it in the bar, lots of pictures of old Chelsea too and the surprise about The Surprise is to find so little changed by the years. The black oak bar with its painted frieze still serves the public bar with its bare floorboards, its dart board and shove-ha'penny board on one side and the saloon bar. Change would be met with outrage. There were even some grumbles when they brought the gents in from the yard. There is no music, ever.

OPEN *midday-23.00 (Mon-Sat), midday-22.30 (Sun)*

FOOD *midday-14.30 (Mon-Sat)*

CREDIT CARDS *all major cards, not AmEx*

DRAUGHT BEERS *Bass, Caffrey's, Hancock's HB, Worthington Best, Carling Black Label, Grolsch, Guinness, Red Rock*

Wheelchair access to venue

NEAREST TUBE STATION *Sloane Square*

THE SUSSEX

20 Upper St Martin's Lane, WC2; 0171 836 1834

On 12 October 1992 the IRA planted a bomb in this pub, in the men's lavatory. Five customers were injured, one died days later. The Sussex replaced its windows, mended its shattered bar and got on with it. The pub has just emerged from a £250,000 refit which has given it a bright new interior, new windows, new most things. There it is in the heart of the West End, everywhere just a short walk away. Tourists love this pub. So do Londoners.

OPEN *11.00-23.00 (Mon-Sat), 12.00-22.30 (Sun)*
FOOD *11.00-23.00 (Mon-Fri), 11.00-18.30 (Sat), 12.00-18.30 (Sun)*
CREDIT CARDS *all major cards*
DRAUGHT BEERS *Courage Best, Courage Directors, John Smith's Extra Smooth, Foster's, Miller, Kronenbourg, Guinness, Strongbow*
NEAREST TUBE STATIONS *Leicester Square, Covent Garden*

THE SWAN

66 Bayswater Road, W2; 0171 262 5204

Tourists love The Swan. They come in time and again during their holiday here and years later come back and tell the barmen about it. They were staying in a hotel just round the corner, they will say, and on their very first day they found The Swan. The Swan is genuinely pretty and genuinely old. It was there in the 18th century, or anyway some of it was, and it takes care to look its age. A major refurbishing last winter closed the whole pub for nine weeks but, to general relief, it looked much the same when it reopened. The Swan was a built as a coaching inn, then became the Floral Tea Gardens, then happily it went back to being a tavern and today, though bigger, it is still a nice domestic size, just two storeys, with a handsome swan painted on the stucco and lanterns and hanging baskets and tables and chairs on a deep terrace. This terrace is a tremendous asset. It stretches to the pavement, much of it sheltered by a glass canopy, so let it rain, and the traffic roars by, but let it roar. This is London after all. Until the big refurb they lit the gas lamps on the terrace every night and you could almost be back a hundred years. The big old lamps are still there but they are electric now.

The food is comfortably English. You can get a hearty English breakfast from 10am every morning, there's a roast on the menu every lunchtime, and have a look at the big old painting in the room at the back, a typically English scene. There is The Swan and there is Bayswater Road and those kindly redcoats are allowing felons one last drink before hanging them at Tyburn. The locals used to enjoy that and entertainment is still provided at The Swan. There's a typical English singsong in the back room every night and everyone, whether they are from Tokyo, Texas or Tottenham Court Road, ends up joining in.

OPEN *10.00-23.00 (Mon-Sat), 10.00-22.30 (Sun)*
FOOD *10.00-22.00 (Mon-Sat), 10.00-21.30 (Sun)*
CREDIT CARDS *all major cards*
DRAUGHT BEERS *Courage Directors, John Smith's Extra Smooth, Theakston Best, Beck's, Foster's, Kronenbourg, Beamish, Strongbow*
Wheelchair access to venue
NEAREST TUBE STATION *Lancaster Gate*

THE SWAN

77-80 Gracechurch Street, EC3; 0171 283 7712

For 23 years Franco and Maria Ferrer ran the Rossetti in St John's Wood. It was big, sunny and Mediterranean and all seemed well but Franco, Mario and the Rossetti all came to a crossroads together. The pub was being sold and Franco and Maria were homesick for Barcelona. They went home and new owners took over the Rossetti and pulled it down. Franco and Maria's retirement did not last long. They had a nice house, the beach was nearby and the sun shone but they were homesick again, this time for London. So it is that Franco and Maria are running a London pub again. It is The Swan, cosy, Dickensian and probably the smallest pub in the City of London. If a chap of moderate girth stands at the downstairs bar another chap of moderate girth can hardly squeeze by. One has a strange urge to shout 'Move right down the bus please'. Nevertheless substantial City gents line this bar every lunchtime, eating, drinking and breathing in whenever a newcomer arrives. There's a nice little upstairs bar, too, and a tiny cellar crammed high with barrels delivered once a week at 6am, and the Ferrers, living above the pub again, say how lovely it is to get so much time off.

OPEN *11.00-23.00 (Mon-Fri)*
FOOD *midday-14.30 (Mon-Fri)*
CREDIT CARDS *AmEx, Mastercard, Visa*
DRAUGHT BEERS *Chiswick Bitter, ESB, London Pride, Grolsch, Heineken, Stella Artois, Guinness, Scrumpy Jack, one guest ale*
Wheelchair access to venue, ground floor only
NEAREST TUBE STATIONS *Monument, Bank*

TACTICAL CAFÉ

27 D'Arblay Street, W1; 0171 287 2823

Two shops knocked together have realised a student's fantasy: poetry and book readings, specialist jazz nights, light shows and DJs with visuals. The decor is a complete mix from the two old shops – a granite-tiled floor and metal tables and chairs in one half, wooden floors and coloured plastic in the other. Bookcases separate the two halves – the books are for sale, by the way. When I was a student I wanted to open a bar that did everything. I didn't, of course, but the Tactical Café is trying to do just that.

OPEN *09.00-23.00 (Mon-Fri), 12.00-23.00 (Sat), 12.00-22.30 (Sun)*
FOOD *as opening hours*
CREDIT CARDS *none taken*
NEAREST TUBE STATION *Oxford Circus*

THE TALBOT TAVERN

Little Chester Street, SW1; 0171 235 1639

The nearer the Palace the better the address. If this is so then Little Chester Street is a very grand address indeed. It is just a stone's throw from the Queen's garden wall though I do hope you aren't thinking of doing any such thing. It is a mews, originally built to house Chester Street's horses for whom nothing but the best was good enough, and there was a pub at either end for the vast army of people working in the grand houses on every side. An air raid in the Second World War got them both and much of the mews as well. All was rebuilt in time and Little Chester Street still has two pubs, the renamed Grouse and Claret at one end, The Talbot Tavern at the other.

The Talbot is a big, jolly sort of pub with a lively young crowd from the local offices at lunchtime and in the evening. The one-time car park is now a terrace with lots of tables and chairs, very popular in the summer. At weekends the offices are empty and the locals depart for their second homes so The Talbot takes the weekend off. People sometimes hire the whole pub for weddings on Saturdays. The Talbot likes to claim kinship with the talbot, a hunting dog brought to England by William the Conqueror. The nearest thing to a talbot now, says the Kennel Club, is the bloodhound. The one on the pub sign doesn't look anything like a bloodhound. More like a beagle, if you ask me. Mr Edward Heath lives round the corner.

OPEN *11.00-23.00 (Mon-Fri)*
FOOD *11.00-22.00 (Mon-Fri)*
CREDIT CARDS *AmEx, Mastercard, Visa*
DRAUGHT BEERS *Brakspear, Courage Best, Courage Directors, John Smith's Extra Smooth, Theakston Best, Beck's, Foster's, Holsten, Guinness, Strongbow*
Wheelchair access to venue
NEAREST TUBE STATION *Hyde Park Corner (exit 5)*

THE TATTERSHALL CASTLE

King's Reach, Victoria Embankment, SW1; 0171 839 6548

The *Tattershall Castle*, a coal-fired paddle steamer, used to make eight trips a day between Hull and New Holland, carrying up to 1,000 people plus cars and livestock. A million pounds was spent on her by Scottish & Newcastle to make her ship-shape and ready for a new career as a floating pub. Her taste for nightlife has not gone unnoticed. The nightclub in the stern is open Thursday (until 2am), Friday and Saturday (3am) and Sunday (midnight). The pub can't keep traditional ales, but two lagers and a bitter are piped into ten big tanks in the barge moored alongside. These have to be refilled twice a week in the summer when the decks are crowded and the demand for lager seems insatiable. There is a buffet downstairs, snacks in the bar, a barbecue on deck (weather permitting), and in the afternoons they do teas. The Tattershall is moored at Victoria Embankment near Waterloo Bridge.

OPEN *11.00-23.00 (Mon and Tues), 11.00-02.00 (Wed and Thurs), 11.00-03.00 (Fri and Sat) 12.00-22.30 (Sun)*

FOOD *11.00-22.00 (Mon-Sat), 12.00-22.00 (Sun)*

CREDIT CARDS *AmEx, Mastercard, Visa, Switch*

DRAUGHT BEERS *John Smith's Extra Smooth, Foster's, Kronenbourg, Beamish, Strongbow*

NEAREST TUBE STATION *Embankment*

TEATRO

93-107 Shaftesbury Avenue, W1; 0171 494 3040

Has the look of an executive airport lounge. Owned by ex-footballer Lee Chapman and his wife, Leslie Ash. There's a cosy snogging booth which is good for assignations, and there seemed to be many on my last visit. Your £150 joining fee and £300 a year thereafter doesn't guarantee acceptance. They won't say who can join, but call for an application form, complete the direct debit mandate and return it for consideration by a secret committee. Retired footballers and aspiring actresses should be able to blag their way in.

OPEN *10.00-02.00 (Mon-Wed), 10.00-03.00 (Thurs-Fri), 18.00-03.00 (Sat)*

FOOD *during opening hours*

CREDIT CARDS *all major cards*

Wheelchair access to venue and loos

NEAREST TUBE STATIONS *Leicester Square, Picadilly Circus*

THREE GREYHOUNDS

25 Greek Street, W1; 0171 287 0754

The Three Greyhounds is the Tudor-looking building on the corner of Greek Street and Old Compton Street, a genuinely old pub with half-timbering that was added in the 20s. The interior was faked up a few years ago to recreate Ye Olde England, but that doesn't matter either. What matters is the romantically named Roxy Beaujolais, who took over the place in 1992, bringing a touch of glamour and style previously lacking at this fine Soho watering hole. Nobody misbehaves in the Three Greyhounds any more now that this is Roxy's place – she won't have any music or gangs of lads. She's a very good cook, too, and if you go there, you'll find out for yourself. If you can't make it in person, you can still find out what I mean, as she recently published her own cookbook, *Home from the Inn Contented*. So if you go there, have a few real ales, sample the food and chat to Roxy, you too will be able to go home from the inn contented.

OPEN *11.00-23.00 (Mon-Sat), 12.00-22.30 (Sun)*

FOOD *12.00-16.00 (Mon-Sat)*

CREDIT CARDS *none taken*

DRAUGHT BEERS *Adnams Bitter, Adnams Broadside, Marston's Pedigree, Tetley's, Carlsberg, Castlemaine XXXX, Guinness, Addlestones, Stella Artois, Murphy's, one guest ale*

Wheelchair access to venue

NEAREST TUBE STATION *Leicester Square*

THE TOTTENHAM

6 Oxford Street, W1; 0171 636 7201

London's pub population has been going down for years. Oxford Street used to have 20, now it has only one. This one. Its Victorian architect wanted the best for it and bits of its birthright survive – some decorated mirrors and carved mahogany, three tapestry panels representing the seasons, a skylight. It is busy enough. By day it gets tourists and shoppers. By night young bloods heading for the clubs cram the two bars, take over the pinball and gaming machines and rock along with the music. The Tottenham is just opposite Tottenham Court Road Underground. Some prefer the Central Line.

OPEN *11.00-23.00 (Mon-Sat), midday-22.30 (Sun)*
FOOD *bar midday-15.00 (Mon-Sun); sandwiches and baked potatoes available until closing time*
CREDIT CARDS *all major cards*
DRAUGHT BEERS *Stella Artois, Calder's Cream Ale, Murphy's, Carlsberg, Carlsberg Export, Castlemaine XXXX, Guinness, Dry Blackthorn, 5 guest ales Wheelchair access to venue. Private room seats 50*
NEAREST TUBE STATION *Tottenham Court Road*

THE TOWNHOUSE

3 Green Street, W1; 0171 499 4489

Very smart bar on the ground floor with an even smarter basement bar and restaurant for gay men of all ages. It seems to be frequented by gay celebrities, smart business men and pretty young boys. It is quite easy to join. Call for an application form and pay your fee (£50 for 18-21 year olds, other memberships from £175). The only criteria is that you have to be gay. As far as I'm aware, you don't have to prove it. The door is open to non-members who are guests of members, but you could try saying you are joining George Michael (not literally, you understand).

OPEN *18.00-01.30 (Mon-Sat)*
FOOD *18.30-midnight (Mon-Sat)*
CREDIT CARDS *all major cards, not Diners*
Private room seats 20, 35 standing
NEAREST TUBE STATIONS *Marble Arch, Bond Street*

THE TOWN OF RAMSGATE

62 Wapping High Street, E1; 0171 264 0001

This dark little pub, the scene of many grisly events, still stands its corner in this narrow cobbled street, pinioned between the mass of Oliver's Wharf and the dank alley known as Wapping Old Stairs. Many terrified men in chains went down those old stone steps to be tarred and hung from a post in the river while three tides washed over them. This was the fate of the dashing privateer Captain Kidd. The disgraced Judge Jeffreys, caught in the bar trying to get away to Hamburg, was almost lynched and dragged to his death in the Tower. Captain Bligh drank here with Fletcher Christian before the *Bounty* sailed, and press gangs kept their unwilling crews manacled in the cellars until their boats could take them. They just keep the beer down there these days they say. The Town of Ramsgate is a listed building now. It is a narrow old pub with a wooden ceiling and a small deck over the river at the back.There is a sinister black post sticking out of the yellow water. Was this the post on which the pirates died? The Town of Ramsgate isn't saying.

OPEN *11.30-23.00 (Mon-Fri), midday-23.00 (Sat), midday-22.30 (Sun)*
FOOD *midday-15.00 and 18.00-21.00 (Tues-Thurs), midday-21.00 (Fri-Mon)*
CREDIT CARDS *all major cards, not AmEx*
DRAUGHT BEERS *Carling Black Label, Grolsch, Caffrey's, Carling Premier, Cidermaster, Guinness, London Pride, Bass, Worthington*
NEAREST TUBE STATIONS *Wapping, Shadwell*

THE TRAFALGAR

200 King's Road, SW3; 0171 352 1076

This is a pub for teenagers of all ages. Big-screen TV, smaller TVs
everywhere, darts, arcade games, beefburgers, potato skins, steakwiches,
chips (and extra chips) with everything. The Mancunian manager Tony
McDonnell has been making great efforts to clean the place up following
some stormy years. He seems to be succeeding. They now provide table
service for drinks and food, but as it still gets packed in the evenings, this
is sometimes a little unworkable. There's a disco on Friday nights and
bouncers on the door at weekends.

OPEN *11.00-23.00 (Mon-Sat), 12.00-22.30 (Sun)*

FOOD *11.00-20.00 (Mon-Sun)*

CREDIT CARDS *all major cards, not AmEx*

DRAUGHT BEERS *Bass, Caffrey's, Worthington, Carling Black Label, Carling
Premier, Grolsch, Guinness, Dry Blackthorn*

Wheelchair access to venue

NEAREST TUBE STATION *Sloane Square*

THE TRAFALGAR TAVERN

Park Row, SE10; 0181 858 2437

'Pub' is hardly the word for The Trafalgar Tavern, and neither is 'tavern'.
Seat, perhaps, or Hall would be better, so large is it and imposing with its
parade of noble bars and its great ballroom on the floor above. They call
this the Nelson Room, and it is a vast room of quite astonishing splendour
with its classical mouldings, elegant windows and curved wrought iron
balconies overlooking the river. It has elaborate swagged curtains and
no fewer than eight chandeliers. It is currently painted rose. The Trafalgar
was built in 1837 in this dashing Regency style to attract free-spending
grandees from London which indeed it did. It was one of a number of
what were called 'whitebait taverns', noted for their whitebait dinners,
hugely popular and very expensive. No one did them better or charged
so much for them as The Trafalgar Tavern. The gallants and the bloods
careered down to Greenwich in their four-in-hands, the great and the good
came more sedately. Thackeray, Wilkie Collins, Macaulay and Dickens
were all regulars and Ministerial Whitebait Dinners became part of
political life, guests, including the Prime Minister of the day, arriving by
Ordnance Barge. The whitebait taverns had a good run but with the turn
of the century they went out of business one by one.

   The Trafalgar lasted longer than most but in the end it succumbed too
and for the next 50 years it was used as a home for old seamen and
as a working men's club. Then in 1965 it was restored, relicensed and
reopened and there it is, full of swank and swagger again. Even the
whitebait dinners are back. The Saints and Sinners Club gives one in the
Nelson Room every October – 250 members and guests, the whitebait
served with a flourish as the second of five courses and some of the most
amusing after dinner speakers in England doing their stuff. The Nelson
Room is in much demand for wedding receptions but most of the action is
in the lofty main bars downstairs.

OPEN *11.30-23.00 (Mon-Sat), midday-22.30 (Sun)*

FOOD *bar midday-15.00 (Mon-Sun), 17.00-21.00 (Tues-Sat); restaurant
midday-15.00 (Mon-Sun), 17.00-21.00 (Tues-Sat)*

CREDIT CARDS *all major cards, not AmEx or Diners*

DRAUGHT BEERS *Courage Best, Courage Directors, John Smith's Extra
Smooth, Old Speckled Hen, Beck's, Foster's, Kronenbourg, Guinness,
Scrumpy Jack, one guest ale*

Wheelchair access to venue

NEAREST RAILWAY STATIONS *Greenwich, Maze Hill*

TUFNELL PARK TAVERN

162 Tufnell Park Road, N7; 0171 272 2078

This long, low, stylish pub was built in the 30s with room for half of Tufnell Park. If you are seriously into jazz this is your place. There is live music every weekend, Fridays and Saturdays in the big Jazz Bar and it's good stuff too. Most of the jazzmen are professionals. It's a good setting. Moody black and white photographs of jazz greats cover the walls and posters promise evenings of modern jazz, trad jazz, ethnic jazz, boogie blues, jazz funk, rhythm and blues and other treats. The beer garden at the back is big too with picnic tables under struggling sycamore trees, there's a late-night disco upstairs every Friday and the Bound and Gagged Comedy Club upstairs every Saturday. This sort of thing gives you an appetite. They serve breakfast at the Tufnell Park Tavern all day.

OPEN *11.00-23.00 (Mon-Fri), 11.00-24.00 (Sat), midday-22.30 (Sun)*

FOOD *all day*

CREDIT CARDS *all major cards*

DRAUGHT BEERS *Directors, Kronenbourg, Fosters, John Smith's Extra Smooth, Beck's, Guinness, Strongbow*

Wheelchair access to venue and loos. Private room seats 100

NEAREST TUBE STATION *Tufnell Park*

THE TURKS HEAD

10 Motcomb Street, SW1; 0171 245 0131

There is a boring explanation for The Turks Head: a seaman's knot. People seem to prefer the gruesome explanation: the severed head of a Turk said to have once been displayed on a shelf behind the bar counter. Two Turkish tourists looked in recently and asked the inevitable question. A seaman's knot? Well, well! This smart little pub in glossy Motcomb Street has the good fortune to be ringed by five of London's grandest hotels and gets a lot of their staff and some of their guests, also local businessmen and occasional Turks. It has only one bar so it is often packed. It is, remarkably, still lit by gas which makes it cosy on dark nights. Steve Middel, the landlord, does the cooking and sings traditional Scots and Irish songs to his guitar on Saturday nights while his wife runs the bar and a black-bearded man in a golden turban stares fiercely down the streets from either side of the inn-sign. He looks wary and I'm not surprised.

OPEN *11.00-23.00 (Mon-Fri), 12.00-23.00 (Sat), 12.00-22.30 (Sun)*

FOOD *12.00-15.00 (Mon-Sat)*

CREDIT CARDS *all major cards, not AmEx*

DRAUGHT BEERS *London Pride, Bass, Carling, Grolsch, Staropramen, Worthington, Guinness, Strongbow*

Wheelchair access to venue

NEAREST TUBE STATIONS *Knightsbridge, Hyde Park*

THE TWO CHAIRMEN

1 Warwick House Street, SW1; 0171 930 1166

It's difficult to find this pub, which is almost in Trafalgar Square. You can see the entire length of Nelson's column from one end of the little street, but the only people likely to stumble over it are those who pop into the National Lottery office to claim their millions. The Two Chairmen has been there since 1684 and is by far the oldest building in the street, but it looks very well, a narrow four-storeyed house with a cosy, panelled bar on the ground floor and an inn sign showing two sleek fellows carrying a sedan chair. Mrs Rhona Barnett, a life-long publican, signed a 20-year lease on the pub when she was 75, and there she is, at 81, with every intention of signing a new lease in 2011. She pays so much rent – £50,000 a year – and the pub is so small that it is hard to make a profit, but she says it is a pleasure to be there. Indeed it is!

OPEN *11.00-23.00 (Mon-Sat), 12.00-15.00 (Sun)*

FOOD *12.00-15.00 (Mon-Sat)*
CREDIT CARDS *none taken*
DRAUGHT BEERS *Courage Best, Courage Directors, John Smith's Extra Smooth, Marston's Pedigree, Foster's, Kronenbourg, Millers, Guinness*
Wheelchair access to venue
NEAREST TUBE STATION *Charing Cross*

TWO FLOORS

3 Kingly Street, W1; 0171 439 1007

Give this place a chance. It takes a few minutes to get used to the feeling that you're in a bar rather than an empty shop. There is no sign outside and the spartan room – lime-green decorated walls, scruffy seats and slashed bar stool covers – can be off-putting. That isn't the point, however. This bar on two floors is for the young and alternatively trendy with a certain amount of street cred – quite good-lookers too! There are no draught beers but it stocks a decent range of bottles. Don't ask for a glass; you suck your beer from the bottle, that's the cool thing. Spirits are excellent; free-poured doubles (and they are large doubles) are served in large glasses, nicely presented with lots of ice, and decent quality mixers are included in the £3.50 asking price (£4 for premium brands). The downstairs bar is decorated in stripes of orange, brown and cream and has very large cushions where you can sit cross-legged, lie on your belly, or recline in the lap of another. Very laid back.

OPEN *11.00-23.00 (Mon-Sat)*
FOOD *12.00-16.00 (Mon-Sat),*
CREDIT CARDS *all major cards, not AmEx*
Private room: 90 standing
NEAREST TUBE STATION *Oxford Circus*

THE VIADUCT TAVERN

126 Newgate Street, EC1; 0171 606 8476

On your way to the City or possibly to the Old Bailey, you will find this most interesting pub, a small gin palace built in 1869, the year Queen Victoria opened Holborn Viaduct. It was the height of fashion, decorated mirrors, neo-classical paintings, a beaten copper ceiling, an ornate manager's stall behind the bar. The landlord's wife would sit enthroned in it, issuing tokens for drinks. The staff was not trusted with money. Wan soulful ladies gaze down from the wall representing banking, agriculture and the arts. The arts has been holed. A drunken soldier from the London Regiment did it in the First World War. Some say he shot it, others say he charged it with a bayonet. I should warn you that there's something very nasty in the cellars, to whit the debtors' cells. They were once part of Newgate Prison but they are part of The Viaduct Tavern now. The cells are tiny and they used to cram 16 people into each of them. Ventilation holes in the ceilings opened on to the pavement in Newgate Street and prisoners would push their hands through, clutching at passers by. Two of them seem to have been left behind.

Ian Clarke, the landlord, who has introduced all sorts of merchandise – baseball caps, T shirts and so on – takes groups down there from time to time. It is interesting but grisly. You may need a drink afterwards.

OPEN *11.00-23.00 (Mon-Fri), midday-23.00 (Sat), midday-22.30 (Sun)*
FOOD *12.00-15.00 (Mon-Sun)*
CREDIT CARDS *all major cards*
DRAUGHT BEERS *Tetley's, Pedigree, Adnams, Castlemaine XXXX, Carling, Stella, Dry Blackthorn, two guest ales*
Wheelchair access to venue
NEAREST TUBE STATION *St. Paul's*

VIC NAYLOR

38-40 St John Street, EC1; 0171 608 2181

Still tremendously popular. No draught beer but the legal eagles who drink here don't seem to mind. I spotted a dog. In my book all drinking establishments should allow dogs. I'm referring to the Canidae family of course.

OPEN *12.00-midnight (Mon-Fri)*
FOOD *12.00-23.00 (Mon-Fri)*
CREDIT CARDS *all major cards, not Diners*
NEAREST TUBE STATIONS *Farringdon, Barbican*

VICTORIA

68 Pages Walk, SE1; 0171 237 3248

In 1972 a couple of likely lads from Bermondsey were watching the extraordinary scenes going on at this rather splendid pub. The event was the presentation of the *Evening Standard* Pub of the Year award. Brothers Pat and Mike McKenna grew up to own the lease on the Victoria, which is still proving to be a very popular venue. It has a 66-foot horseshoe-shaped bar offering a decent range of traditional ales, but what they're really famous for are the pan-fried steaks, cooked by the McKennas' aunt, available all day during the week. The Victoria normally has quiet background music, but things liven up a little at weekends, when a disco takes over until 1am. You won't have a problem getting there in a black cab – the Victoria is a point on the Knowledge.

OPEN *11.00-midnight (Mon-Thurs), 11.00-01.00 (Fri), 20.00-01.00 (Sat), 12.00-15.00 and 19.30-22.30 (Sun)*
FOOD *12.00-15.00 (Mon-Fri)*
Evening disco's 20.00-01.00 (Fri-Sat), 20.00-22.30 (Sun)
CREDIT CARDS *none taken*
DRAUGHT BEERS *Fuller's, Ruddles County, Webster's, Carlsberg, Foster's, Holsten Pils, Guinness, Strongbow*
NEAREST TUBE STATION *Elephant & Castle, Borough, London Bridge*

WALKABOUT

11 Henrietta Street, WC2; 0171 379 5555

This is possibly the most Australian of all the Australian pubs in London. It was well known as The Outback until recently when it had to change its name, as another company had legally registered it. So the Walkabout it is now. It has plain wooden floors, stout wooden tables, squat wooden stools, and a bar counter that looks as if it was knocked together last night. There's a drinking bit, an eating bit and a huge games bar in the basement. Videos of all major sporting events back home are flown over straight after the match, and enthralled crowds watch them on big screens upstairs and down. There is live music five nights a week and cold lager all day and every day. You don't have to be an Aussie or indeed a Kiwi to drink in the Walkabout, but it helps.

OPEN *12.00-23.00 (Mon-Sat), 12.00-22.30 (Sun)*
FOOD *12.00-20.00 (Mon-Sun)*
CREDIT CARDS *all major cards*
DRAUGHT BEERS *Caffrey's, John Smith's Extra Smooth, Foster's, Stella Artois, Guinness, Dry Blackthorn*
Wheelchair access to venue. Private room: 100 standing
NEAREST TUBE STATIONS *Covent Garden, Charing Cross*

WALKABOUT

58 Shepherd's Bush Green, W12; 0181 740 4339

A colossal music venue on an Australasian theme has recently opened up in Shepherd's Bush, with a 20,000-watt sound system, a 32-track mixing desk and a 200-CD computerised interchange system which could easily shatter the rafters of the bar and its close neighbours at the Shepherd's Bush Empire. If this wasn't enough, there is a 15 x 20-foot large-screen monitor (one of the biggest in the country inside a bar) showing tapes of Australasian sports flown in on an almost daily basis. Should you not be able to see the screen, which is unlikely, there are a further 24 TV monitors throughout the bar.

The food is substantial enough to soak up any amount of beers. The breakfast of steak, bacon, sausage, eggs, chips, baked beans, mushrooms, tomatoes and toast (phew!) is £5.50, crocodile steak with salad and fries is £6.20 and kangaroo kebabs with salad and a fruit relish £5.75. They have a range of bottled beers, including Stein lager, Victoria bitter, Crown lager and Lion Red, which will appeal to any homesick Aussie or Kiwi. Occasionally – at weekends after 9pm and when there's a big sporting event – they levy a small cover charge of £2-£3. They tell me the sound system can be isolated in three different zones within the bar, offering a choice of music along with the DJs and live bands that play there six nights a week – I'll believe that when I hear it.

OPEN *11.00-midnight (Mon-Sat), 12.00-22.30 (Sun)*
FOOD *11.00-20.30 (Mon-Sat), 12.00-20.00 (Sun)*
CREDIT CARDS *all major cards*
DRAUGHT BEERS *Caffrey's, John Smith's Extra Smooth, Foster's, Stella Artois, Guinness, Dry Blackthorn*
Wheelchair access to venue and loos
NEAREST TUBE STATION *Shepherd's Bush*

WALMER CASTLE
58 Ledbury Road, W11; 0171 229 4620
This high-Victorian, distinctly impressive three-storey building about halfway down Ledbury Road is where the good-looking people of Notting Hill chill out. It has a bright, clean and impressive main bar, a smaller, charming little lounge at the back, and a Thai restaurant upstairs, owned and operated by the Pelican Group. You can get some of the menu downstairs: spicy chicken wings (£5.95), dim sum (£7.95) and vegetarian Thai dishes (£5.50). They have an English menu in the bar, which offers a brie and avocado baguette (£3.50) before listing more traditional English fare such as Cumberland sausage, mash and beans (£5.95), and ham, egg and chips (£4.50). The Walmer Castle is not far off being a traditional English pub but with a more modern feel to it. It buzzes at weekends.

OPEN *12.00-23.00 (Mon-Sat), 12.00-22.30 (Sun)*
FOOD *bar 12.00-18.00 (Mon-Sun); restaurant 12.00-14.30 and 18.00-22.30 (Sun-Thurs), 18.00-23.30 (Fri-Sat)*
CREDIT CARDS *all major cards*
DRAUGHT BEERS *Abbot Ale, Boddingtons, Tetley's, Heineken, Heineken Export, Stella Artois, Guinness, Boston Beer, Dry Blackthorn*
Wheelchair access to venue
NEAREST TUBE STATIONS *Notting Hill Gate, Westbourne Park*

THE WARRINGTON
93 Warrington Crescent, W9; 0171 286 2929
The Church of England is down to just a handful of pubs now, a shame really. It used to have so many. Still, it could be a troublesome portfolio as The Warrington in Maida Vale showed. How was the Church to know that all those lively young ladies were not, well, ladies? The Warrington had long since put its past behind it by the time the Church sold it to David and Charles Williams in 1983 and it has become a tremendous star turn, regularly appearing in movies and television ads. It plays what you might call walking-in parts. Cameras love the photogenic entrance with its faience pillars and art nouveau tiling, its mosaic steps flanked by huge wrought iron standard lamps made by Biggs and Co. of Southwark. As for the

saloon bar, it is a sight to behold, the great high room with its cherubs and marble pillars, the marble-topped counter with its ornate canopy, the frieze, the art nouveau glass, the handsome fireplace, lofty ceiling, sweeping mahogany staircase. I like the tap room myself but you would not have found Marie Lloyd in there. The main salon was made for great music hall stars and on a shelf over the fireplace you will see an empty champagne bottle, the last she consumed there. She was in her element in The Warrington. Upstairs, what was the naughtiest bit in the old days, is now in the hands of Mr Songklod Boonyachalayont, known as Ben, whose large smiling staff provides delicious Thai food from 7pm onwards. It is very popular. You have to book.

OPEN *11.00-23.00 (Mon-Sat), midday-22.30 (Sun)*
FOOD *11.00-14.30 then 18.00-22.30 (Mon-Sat)*
CREDIT CARDS *none taken*
DRAUGHT BEERS *Grolsch, Stella, Foster's, John Smith's Extra Smooth, Caffrey's, Guinness, Tennent's Extra, Strongbow, London Pride, Brakspear, Young's Special*
Wheelchair access to venue
NEAREST TUBE STATION *Meadowvale*

THE WATER RAT

1 Milmans Street, SW10; 0171 351 4732
This pub has a beautiful exterior. The white stucco, three-storey building is covered with such masses of flowers spilling from window boxes, baskets and tubs that the Royal Borough of Kensington and Chelsea gives it prizes. Inside there is a big bar, taped music and Sky TV for major sports events. It is a free house, so real ales rule. Absolut Vodkas are big there, too, with home-made variations – Absolut Hot Chilli Pepper, Absolut Raspberry and Absolut Mars Bar, £1.30 a slam on Friday and Saturday nights. They certainly get things going. People from the nearby estates seem to love The Water Rat.

OPEN *11.00-23.00 (Mon-Sat), 12.00-22.30 (Sun)*
FOOD *12.00-15.00 and 18.00-21.00 (Mon-Fri), 12.00-15.00 (Sun lunch)*
CREDIT CARDS *none taken*
DRAUGHT BEERS *John Smith's Extra Smooth, Foster's, Beck's, Kronenbourg, Guinness, Strongbow, three guest ales*
NEAREST TUBE STATION *Sloane Square*

THE WATER RATS

328 Grays Inn Road, WC1; 0171 837 7269
Regard the two faces of The Water Rats. By day it is a conventional Kings Cross local, used by unsuspecting office workers. At the stroke of eight it becomes one of the most influential venues in the music business. With heroic disregard for their hearing, music journalists nightly seek out the next big thing on our behalf here. In 1985 The Pindar of Wakefield was taken over by the Grand Order of Water Rats. The pub was duly renamed and for the next six years it played host to a live version of The Good Old Days. It was not the hottest ticket in town and the management switched from music hall to indie and alternative music. King Rats withdrew to their HQ upstairs leaving the stage to a younger generation and the influential venue, now known as the Splash Club, was born. The vaudeville drapes still hang above the stage and the chandeliers remain, giving the music room a unique appeal to platinum-selling bands like Bush, which came here fresh from 4,000-seater stadiums in the US, and young indie bands fighting their way up the music food chain can be seen here seven nights a week. On a good night, when the hum of excitement buzzing round the front bar is picked up by a band enjoying itself in the music room at the back, there is nowhere better in London for live music.

OPEN *11.00-midnight (Mon-Fri), 20.00-midnight (Sat)*

CREDIT CARDS *none taken*
DRAUGHT BEERS *John Smith's Extra Smooth, Foster's, Kronenbourg, Guinness, Scrumpy Jack*
NEAREST TUBE STATION *King's Cross*

THE WATERSIDE
82 York Way, N1; 0171 837 7118
A railway needs warehouses and there are some new ones behind King's Cross, a group of modern red brick buildings of a strictly necessary kind with high railings to keep you out. The end one is rather different. It has a large board inviting you in. 'The Waterside' it says. A pub-sign yet. So go in. This is not what you have been led to expect. There is a large 19th century Hereford barn inside that red brick shell, oak frame, roof beams, timber and brick walls, an old black plank floor. Left-over timber has been made into plain tables and benches and through the big doors at the end is a wonderful sight. You find that The Waterside is indeed on the waterside. Beyond the deep brick terrace covered in picnic tables is a wide spread of glossy water. This is Battlebridge Basin, a working siding for canal boats. The terrace narrows and follows the basin to its junction with the Grand Union Canal. There is a place behind the railings here where men and boys sit fishing. The Waterside has a Berni Inns food servery in the bar and a barbecue on the terrace on sunny Sundays. It is an unexpected pub which greatly cheers a glum bit of London.
OPEN *11.00-23.00 (Mon-Sat), midday-22.30 (Sun)*
FOOD *midday-14.30 and 18.00-21.00 (Mon-Fri), midday-14.30 (Sat), midday-17.00 (Sun)*
CREDIT CARDS *Mastercard, Switch, Visa and Solo*
DRAUGHT BEERS *Boddingtons, Hoegaarden, Wadworth 6X, Old Speckled Hen, Heineken, Heineken Export, Stella Artois, Murphy's, Guinness, Strongbow, three real ales changed regularly*
Wheelchair access to venue. Semi-private room: 22 seated, 30-40 standing
NEAREST TUBE STATION *King's Cross*

WAXY O'CONNOR'S
14-16 Rupert Street, W1; 0171 287 0255
The interior of this cavernous pub is an Irish Gothic fantasy – 9,000 square feet of bars, galleries, saloons and snugs, each built round the interiors of goodness knows how many Irish churches. There are carved screens, arches, finials, friezes, panels, choir stalls and pulpits. One anteroom has a confessional and a pavement of tombstones. Every space is at a different level. In one the ceiling is so low you have to duck; in another the ceiling is two storeys high. The bleached remains of an ancient Irish beech tree soar skyward. Waxy O'Connor's was an instant success when it opened, and continues to be so. It is quieter in the afternoons, but the design is such that it never feels empty. In the evenings you often have to queue to get in. Irish music is piped through the pub all day, and Irish musicians play five nights a week. The food is Irish, the whiskey is Irish, the poteen is so Irish it is banned in Ireland. It's the most spectacular of all the Irish theme bars, and the service is unpretentious yet efficient.
OPEN *12.00-23.00 (Mon-Fri), 11.00-23.00 (Sat), 12.00-22.30 (Sun)*
FOOD *bar 12.00-18.00 (Mon-Sun); restaurant 18.00-23.00 (Mon-Sun)*
CREDIT CARDS *all major cards*
DRAUGHT BEERS *Caffrey's, Kilkenny, Carling Premier, Carlsberg Export, Foster's, Guinness, Murphy's, Dry Blackthorn, Beamish*
Private room seats 50
NEAREST TUBE STATIONS *Leicester Square, Piccadilly Circus*

THE WELLINGTON

351 The Strand, WC2; 0171 836 0513

The good news about the Lyceum Theatre is good news for London and good news for The Wellington. The famous old theatre is being restored on a grand scale, and it won't be long now before London theatregoers will again be filling the little pub next door as they did in Sir Henry Irving's golden days. It is a small pub but it has an excellent position at the end of the Strand and, like the Iron Duke, has a strong character of its own. Its public and saloon bars each have their own street entrance and there is no mistaking which is which. The public bar has the wooden floor and the saloon bar has the carpet, and hot meals are served in the bar upstairs, a pleasant room with a front window that looks directly across Waterloo Bridge. Anita Smith is manager now. Her husband, Frank, was manager before but he has taken over Drummonds opposite St Pancras Station. Bass is relaunching it this year, another Irish theme pub begorrah.

OPEN *11.00-23.00 (Mon-Sat), 12.00-22.30 (Sun)*

FOOD *12.00-22.30 (Mon-Sun)*

CREDIT CARDS *all major cards*

DRAUGHT BEERS *Bass, London Pride*

Wheelchair access to outside seating only

NEAREST TUBE STATIONS *Embankment, Covent Garden*

THE WELLINGTON

81-83 Waterloo Road, SE1; 0171 928 6083

Grandeur was what one looked for in a railway hotel. The Midland Grand had a 270 foot-high clock tower, an imperial staircase and 250 bedrooms. The Great Eastern had a ballroom. You would have searched in vain for one of them in the South Eastern Railway's hotel at Waterloo. It was, to speak frankly, a modest affair. The Wellington, for so it was called, had two floors of bedrooms and some handsome public rooms but the force was not with it. Almost at once they started rebuilding Waterloo Station. The job took 22 years. There was a war, then a depression, then another war at the end of which it is probably true to say that the bloom was off the Wellington Hotel. By the time Regent Inns bought it in 1994 it had become a large and rather rough pub. Furthermore you could hardly fail to notice that two railway bridges came massively across the road and disappeared into the upper floors. Did trains thunder through the bedrooms?

Regent Inns set about a major refurbishing. Architects, designers, builders and decorators descended and in eight weeks it was transformed: linenfold panelling, sophisticated lighting, new everything – carpets, sofas, armchairs, plants. A glass dome was uncovered in what had been the hotel dining room and they found that the original lobby had had a fine curved ceiling. A mural was commissioned from John Waldon: the Battle of Waterloo, Wellington on his horse, Blucher with the West Prussians, Napoleon surrounded by his Imperial Guards. It is a jolly good ceiling. The new licensee, Jill Keen, presides over this leap up market. There are eight cask beers on the handpumps, including Keen's bitter. There is a cheering sizzle from the grill and there are still 12 letting rooms upstairs, single rooms £28, double rooms £46, get your own breakfast. What about the railway bridges? Don't mind them. This is, after all, Waterloo.

OPEN *11.00-23.00 (Mon-Sat), midday-22.30 (Sun)*

FOOD *Midday-21.00 (Mon-Sat), midday-19.00 (Sun)*

CREDIT CARDS *Mastercard and Visa*

DRAUGHT BEERS *Dry Blackthorn, Stella, Kronenbourg, Foster's, Carling Premier, Carling Black Label, Guinness, Murphy's, Caffrey's*

Wheelchair access to venue, not to loos

NEAREST TUBE STATION *Waterloo*

THE WESTBOURNE

101 Westbourne Park Villas, W2; 0171 221 1332

This big, good-looking pub in deepest Notting Hill is far enough away from the trend-setters to be stylish in its own right. There isn't a quiet spot in the house, so people stand, sit, eat and drink where they can, many flowing over into the delightful forecourt on a sunny day. This is one of the new generation of bistro pubs. It was created by Oliver Daniaud and Sebastian Boyle from a run-down pub located in a run-down part of town, and it opened to astonishing success in 1985, just a few weeks after its near-neighbour The Cow (qv). It has lifted the area and put it on the map as a destination rather than a place to be avoided. It's worth any number of detours to go there now.

OPEN *17.00-23.00 (Mon), 12.00-23.00 (Tues-Fri), 11.00-23.00 (Sat), 12.00-22.30 (Sun)*

FOOD *13.00-15.00 (Tues-Fri), 12.30-16.00 (Sat-Sun), 19.00-22.00 (Mon-Sun)*

CREDIT CARDS *all major cards, not AmEx*

DRAUGHT BEERS *Boddingtons, Kilkenny, Dortmunder Union, Heineken, Kronenbourg, Leffe Blonde, Stella Artois, Guinness, one guest bitter*
Wheelchair access to venue, not to loos

NEAREST TUBE STATIONS *Notting Hill Gate, Westbourne Park*

THE WESTMINSTER ARMS

9 Storey's Gate, SW1; 0171 222 8520

There are nine bars in the House of Commons, one for every 72.2 MPs and they have to share eight of them with visitors and the like. So it's rather a squash. Luckily there are quite a few pubs a short walk away. This is one of them. Until the new Queen Elizabeth Conference Centre was built The Westminster Arms had a clear view of Big Ben and of Westminster Abbey. Now what it sees is the side of the conference centre, not a good swap. On the other hand it gets wave after wave of custom from the new building; in fact it is extraordinarily busy most of the time and MPs can find safety in numbers and reassurance from the division bell in the bar. The bar, crowded most of the day, looks much as it did when the pub was rebuilt in 1913 but as the cellar bar was thoroughly done over in the modern manner recently it looks a great deal older. It is now back in the 1850s with a flagstone floor, drinking booths round the walls, old panelling, benches and wooden tables. There is a pleasant restaurant upstairs, a wine bar downstairs and tables and chairs on the pavement outside. On sunny days they do a brisk trade in ice cream. It is a free house and has seven real ales on the hand pumps.

OPEN *11.00-23.00 (Mon-Sat), midday-18.00 (Sun)*

FOOD *Bar: midday-21.30 (Mon-Fri), 11.00-17.00 (Sat), midday-17.00 (Sun); Restaurant: midday-14.30 (Mon-Fri)*

CREDIT CARDS *AmEx, Mastercard, Visa*

DRAUGHT BEERS *Abbot Ale, Bass, Brakspear PA, Brakspear Special, Caffrey's, Theakston XB, Westminster Bitter, Young's, Carling Premier, Foster's, Stella Artois, Tennent's Pilsner, Guinness, Dry Blackthorn*
Wheelchair access to venue. Private room seats 40

NEAREST TUBE STATION *Westminster, St James's Park*

J. D. WETHERSPOON

New Zealander Tim Martin was so disillusioned with London's pubs that he opened his own in Muswell Hill. That was in 1979 and such was its success that he is now a multi-millionaire and head of one of the fastest growing pub chains around. They are rarely pub conversions; you are more likely to find that in a previous existence the place was a car showroom, a bank, a cinema or even a supermarket. He borrowed the name Wetherspoon from his former, slightly nutty schoolteacher; the J. D.

was added for a certain amount of kudos. Moons appear in many of the names – The Moon under Water (qv), JJ Moons and the Moon and Sixpence. The first of these comes from a short story by George Orwell, who described his perfect pub as a place where he could have a quiet pint with good conversation. Orwell named this fictitious pub The Moon under Water. The other names tend to recognise local history or the previous use of the building, so Bankers Drafts were formerly banks, The Gatehouse is in Highgate, and 179 Upper Street is, well, at 179 Upper Street, of course. There is a strict rule throughout Wetherspoon's pubs: no music of any kind. Even the sound of the gaming machines is muted, and there are no darts, pool or pinball. Each pub stocks several real ales, including Fuller's London Pride – clearly a selling point. Wetherspoon's are also air conditioned, with big no-smoking areas and cut-price beer. Food is served all day and, although hardly Marco Pierre-White, the menu includes substantial dishes at extraordinarily reasonable prices: oven-baked potatoes with a variety of fillings, hot or cold baguettes, burgers and chips, and a Sunday roast.

Branches at:

ACTON RED LION AND PINEAPPLE 281 High Street, W3; 0181 896 2248
   NEAREST TUBE STATION *Acton Town*

ANERLEY MOON AND STARS 164-166 High Street, SE20;
   0181 776 5680
   NEAREST RAILWAY STATION *Penge East*

BALHAM THE MOON UNDER WATER 194 Balham High Street, SW12;
   0181 673 0535
   NEAREST TUBE STATION *Balham*

BARKING BARKING DOG 61 Station Parade, IG11; 0181 507 9109
   NEAREST TUBE STATION *Barking*

BARKINGSIDE NEW FAIRLOP OAK Fencepiece Road, IG11;
   0181 500 2217
   NEAREST RAILWAY STATION *Fairlop*

BARNET THE MOON UNDER WATER 148 High Street, EN5;
   0181 441 9476
   NEAREST TUBE STATION *High Barnet*

BETHNAL GREEN CAMDEN'S HEAD 456 Bethnal Green Road, E2;
   0171 613 4263
   NEAREST TUBE STATION *Bethnal Green*

BEXLEY HEATH WRONG 'UN 234-236 The Broadway, DA6;
   0181 298 0439
   NEAREST RAILWAY STATION *Bexley Heath*

BOREHAMWOOD HART AND SPOOL 148 Shenley Road, WD6;
   0181 953 1883
   NEAREST RAILWAY STATIONS *Elstree, Borehamwood*

BRIXTON CROWN AND SCEPTRE 2a Streatham Hill, SW2; 0181 671 0843
   NEAREST TUBE STATION *Brixton*

CAMBERWELL FOX ON THE HILL 149 Denmark Hill, SE5; 0171 738 4756
   NEAREST RAILWAY STATION *Denmark Hill*

CAMDEN MAN IN THE MOON 40-42 Chalk Farm Road, NW1;
   0171 482 2054
   NEAREST TUBE STATION *Chalk Farm*

CATFORD TIGER'S HEAD 350 Bromley Road, SE6; 0181 698 8645
   NEAREST RAILWAY STATION *Catford*

CHINGFORD KING'S FORD 250-252 Chingford Mount Road, E4;
   0181 523 9365
   NEAREST RAILWAY STATION *Chingford*

CHISWICK JJ MOON'S 80-82 Chiswick High Road, W4; 0181 742 7263
   NEAREST TUBE STATION *Stamford Brook*

CITY HAMILTON HALL Liverpool Street Station, EC2; 0171 247 3579
   NEAREST TUBE STATION *Liverpool Street*

CITY MASQUE HAUNT 168-172 Old Street, EC2; 0171 251 4195
  NEAREST TUBE STATION *Old Street*
CITY SIR JOHN OLDCASTLE 29-35 Farringdon Road, EC1; 0171 242 1013
  NEAREST TUBE STATION *Farringdon*
CRICKLEWOOD BEATEN DOCKET 50-56 Cricklewood Broadway, NW2;
  0181 450 2972
  NEAREST TUBE STATION *Kilburn*
CROYDON GEORGE 17-21 George Street, CR0; 0181 649 9077
  NEAREST RAILWAY STATION *East Croydon*
CRYSTAL PALACE POSTAL ORDER 33 Westow Street, SW19; 0181 771 3003
  NEAREST RAILWAY STATION *Crystal Palace*
DAGENHAM LORD DENMAN 270-272 Heathway, RM10; 0181 984 8590
  NEAREST TUBE STATION *Dagenham Heathway*
EAST HAM MILLERS WELL 419-421 Barking Road, E6; 0181 471 8404
  NEAREST TUBE STATION *East Ham*
EDGWARE BLACKING BOTTLE 122-126 High Street, HA8; 0181 381 1485
  NEAREST TUBE STATION *Edgware*
EDMONTON LAMB 52-54 Church Street, N9; 0181 887 0128
  NEAREST RAILWAY STATION *Edmonton Green*
ELTHAM BANKERS DRAFT 80 High Street, SE9; 0181 294 2578
  NEAREST RAILWAY STATION *Eltham*
ENFIELD THE MOON UNDER WATER 116-117 Chaseside, EN2;
  0181 366 9855
  NEAREST RAILWAY STATION *Enfield Chase*
FELTHAM MOON ON THE SQUARE Unit 30 The Centre, Wilton Road, TW13;
  0181 893 1293
  NEAREST RAILWAY STATION *Feltham*
FINCHLEY TALLY HO 749 High Road, N12; 0181 445 4390
  NEAREST TUBE STATION *Finchley Central*
FINSBURY PARK OLD SUFFOLK PUNCH 10-12 Grand Parade, N4;
  0181 800 5912
  NEAREST TUBE STATION *Manor House*
FINSBURY PARK WHITE LION OF MORTIMER 125-127 Stroud Green Road, N4;
  0171 281 4773
  NEAREST TUBE STATION *Finsbury Park*
FOREST HILL BIRD IN HAND 35 Dartmouth Road, SE23; 0181 699 7417
  NEAREST RAILWAY STATION *Forest Hill*
HAMPSTEAD THREE HORSESHOES 28 Heath Street, NW3; 0171 431 7206
  NEAREST TUBE STATION *Hampstead*
HARROW JJ MOON'S 20 The Broadwalk, Pinner Road, HA2;
  0181 424 9686
  NEAREST TUBE STATION *North Harrow*
HARROW JJ MOON'S 3 Shaftesbury Parade, Shaftesbury Circle, HA2;
  0181 423 5056
  NEAREST TUBE STATION *South Harrow*
HARROW MOON ON THE HILL 373-375 Station Road, HA1;
  0181 863 3670
  NEAREST TUBE STATION *Harrow-on-the-Hill*
 HARROW NEW MOON 25-26 Kenton Park Parade, Kenton Road, HA3;
  0181 909 1109
  NEAREST TUBE STATION *Harrow-on-the-Hill*
HAYES THE MOON UNDER WATER 10-11 Broadwater Parade,
  Coldharbour Lane, UB3; 0181 813 6774
  NEAREST RAILWAY STATION *Hayes & Harlington*
HAYES END MOON AND SIXPENCE 1250-1256 Uxbridge Road, UB8;
  0181 561 3541
  NEAREST RAILWAY STATION *Hayes & Harlington*
HEATHROW AIRPORT JJ MOON'S Terminal 4 Airside, Heathrow Airport, TW6;
  0181 759 0355

NEAREST TUBE STATION *Heathrow (Terminal 4)*

HEATHROW AIRPORT WETHERSPOON'S Terminal 4 Landside, Heathrow Airport, TW6; 0181 759 2906

NEAREST TUBE STATION *Heathrow (Terminal 4)*

HIGHGATE GATEHOUSE 1 North Hill, N6; 0181 340 8054

NEAREST TUBE STATION *Highgate*

HOLLOWAY CORONET 338-346 Holloway Road, N7; 0171 609 5014

NEAREST TUBE STATION *Holloway Road*

HORNSEY ELBOW ROOM 22 Topsfield Parade, N8; 0181 340 3677

NEAREST TUBE STATION *Turnpike Lane*

HORNSEY TOLLGATE 26-30 Turnpike Lane, N8; 0181 889 9085

NEAREST TUBE STATION *Turnpike Lane*

HOUNSLOW THE MOON UNDER WATER 84-86 Staines Road, TW3; 0181 572 7506

NEAREST TUBE STATION *Hounslow Central*

ILFORD GREAT SPOON OF ILFORD 114-116 Cranbrook Road, IG1; 0181 518 0535

NEAREST RAILWAY STATION *Ilford*

ISLINGTON 79 Upper Street, N1; 0171 226 6276

NEAREST TUBE STATION *Highbury & Islington*

KINGSBURY JJ MOON'S 53 Kingsbury Road, NW9; 0181 204 9675

NEAREST TUBE STATION *Kingsbury*

KINGSBURY THE MOON UNDER WATER 10 Varley Parade, NW9; 0181 200 7611

NEAREST TUBE STATION *Colindale*

LEYTON DRUM 557-559 Lea Bridge Road, E10; 0181 539 6577

NEAREST TUBE STATION *Leyton*

LOUGHTON LAST POST 227 High Street, IG10; 0181 532 0751

NEAREST TUBE STATION *Loughton*

MITCHAM WHITE LION OF MORTIMER 223 London Road, CR4; 0181 646 7332

NEAREST RAILWAY STATION *Tooting Junction*

MORDEN WETHERSPOON'S 3 Aberconway Road, SM4; 0181 540 2818

NEAREST TUBE STATION *Morden*

NEW BARNET RAILWAY BELL 13 East Barnet Road, EN4; 0181 449 1369

NEAREST RAILWAY STATION *New Barnet*

NORTH CHEAM WETHERSPOON'S 552-556 London Road, SM3; 0181 644 1808

NEAREST RAILWAY STATION *Cheam Village*

PALMERS GREEN WHOLE HOG 430-434 Green Lanes, N13; 0181 882 3597

NEAREST RAILWAY STATION *Palmers Green*

PINNER MOON AND SIXPENCE 250 Uxbridge Road, HA5; 0181 420 1074

NEAREST RAILWAY STATION *Hatch End*

PINNER VILLAGE INN 402-408 Rayners Lane, HA5; 0181 868 8551

NEAREST RAILWAY STATION *Rayners Lane*

PURLEY FOXLEY HATCH 8-9 Russell Hill Road, CR8; 0181 763 9307

NEAREST RAILWAY STATION *Purley*

PUTNEY RAILWAY 202 Upper Richmond Road, SW15; 0181 788 8190

NEAREST RAILWAY STATION *Putney*

SHEPHERD'S BUSH MOON ON THE GREEN 172-174 Uxbridge Road, W12; 0181 749 5709

NEAREST TUBE STATION *Shepherd's Bush*

SOHO MOON AND SIXPENCE 183 Wardour Street, W1; 0171 734 0037

NEAREST TUBE STATION *Tottenham Court Road*

SOUTHFIELDS GRID INN 22 Replingham Road, SW18; 0181 874 8460

NEAREST TUBE STATION *Southfields*

SOUTHGATE BANKERS DRAFT 36-38 Friern Barnet Road, N11; 0181 361 7115

NEAREST TUBE STATION *Arnos Grove*

SOUTHGATE NEW CROWN 80-84 Chase Side, N14; 0181 882 8758
    NEAREST TUBE STATION *Southgate*
STANMORE MAN IN THE MOON 1 Buckingham Parade, HA7;
0181 954 6119
    NEAREST TUBE STATION *Stanmore*
STOCKWELL BEEHIVE 407-409 Brixton Road, SW9; 0171 738 3643
    NEAREST TUBE STATION *Brixton*
STOKE NEWINGTON ROCHESTER CASTLE 145 High Street, N16;
0171 249 6016
    NEAREST RAILWAY STATION *Stoke Newington*
STRATFORD GOLDEN GROVE 146-148 The Grove, E15; 0181 519 0750
    NEAREST TUBE STATION *Stratford*
STREATHAM THE MOON UNDER WATER 1327 London Road, SW16;
0181 765 1235
    NEAREST RAILWAY STATION *Norbury*
SUTTON MOON ON THE HILL 5-9 Hill Road, SM1; 0181 643 1202
    NEAREST RAILWAY STATION *Sutton*
TOOTING JJ MOON'S 56a High Street, SW17; 0181 672 4726
    NEAREST TUBE STATION *Tooting Broadway*
TOTTENHAM ELBOW ROOM 503-505 High Road, N17; 0181 801 8769
    NEAREST RAILWAY STATION *Tottenham Hill*
TOTTENHAM NEW MOON 413 Lordship Lane, N17; 0181 801 3496
    NEAREST RAILWAY STATION *Wood Green*
TWICKENHAM THE MOON UNDER WATERA 53-57 London Road, TW1;
0181 744 0080
    NEAREST RAILWAY STATION *Twickenham*
UPPER HOLLOWAY DOG 17-19 Archway Road, N19; 0171 263 0429
    NEAREST TUBE STATION *Archway*
VICTORIA WETHERSPOON'S Victoria Station, SW1; 0171 931 0445
    NEAREST TUBE STATION *Victoria*
WALLINGTON WHISPERING MOON 25 Ross Parade, Woodcote Road, SM6;
0181 647 7020
    NEAREST RAILWAY STATION *Wallington*
WANDSWORTH SPOTTED DOG 72 Garratt Lane, SW18; 0181 875 9531
    NEAREST RAILWAY STATION *Wandsworth Town*
WANSTEAD GEORGE High Street, E11; 0181 989 2921
    NEAREST TUBE STATION *Wanstead*
WEALDSTONE SARSEN STONE 32 High Street, HA3; 0181 863 8533
    NEAREST TUBE STATION *Harrow and Wealdstone*
WEMBLEY JJ MOON'S 397 High Road, HA9; 0181 903 4923
    NEAREST TUBE STATION *Wembley Central*
WEST END THE MOON UNDER WATER 105-107 Charing Cross Road, WC1
0171 287 6039
    NEAREST TUBE STATION *Leicester Square*
WEST END THE MOON UNDER WATER 28 Leicester Square, WC2;
0171 839 2837
    NEAREST TUBE STATION *Leicester Square*
WEST HENDON WHITE LION OF MORTIMER 3 York Parade, NW9;
0181 202 8887
    NEAREST RAILWAY STATION *Hendon*
WHITEHALL LORD MOON OF THE MALL 16-18 Whitehall, SW1;
0171 839 7701
    NEAREST TUBE STATION *Charing Cross*
WILLESDEN COLISEUM Manor Park Road, NW10; 0181 961 6570
    NEAREST TUBE STATION *Willesden Junction*
WILLESDEN OUTSIDE INN 312-314 Neasden Lane, NW10; 0181 452 3140
    NEAREST TUBE STATION *Neasden*
WIMBLEDON WIBBAS DOWN INN 6-12 Gladstone Road, SW19;
0181 540 6788

NEAREST TUBE STATION *South Wimbledon*
WINCHMORE HILL HALF MOON 749 Green Lanes, N21; 0181 360 5410
NEAREST RAILWAY STATION *Winchmore Hill*

THE WHITE CROSS

Water Lane, Richmond, TW9; 0181 940 6844
They don't call it Water Lane for nothing. The Thames regularly creeps up
to the doorway of this riverside pub in Richmond, flooding the lane outside.
The floodgates on the cellar flaps and the tidal valves in the drains prevent
the pub's cellar from flooding, so long as the staff remember to activate
them. The pub itself is up a flight of stairs so it always remains dry, and it
has stayed virtually unchanged since it was built in 1835. The saloon bar
has a fireplace under the window, which makes everyone wonder where
the chimney is. Upstairs is a particularly splendid bar with the tiniest of
balconies commanding a spectacular view of the garden and the river.
OPEN *11.00-23.00 (Mon-Sat) 12.00- 22.30 (Sun)*
FOOD *12.00-15.00 (Mon-Sun); snacks available till 19.00*
DRAUGHT BEERS *Young's Bitter, Young's Special, Young's Wheatbeer,
Young's Pilsner, Young's Export, Castlemaine XXXX, Stella Artois, Guinness,
Dry Blackthorn, one guest beer changed regularly*
CREDIT CARDS *Mastercard, Visa, Switch*
NEAREST TUBE STATION *Richmond*

WHITE HART

563 Fulham Road, SW6; 0171 385 1696
The first stop opposite the Tube station is a relatively recent refurbishment
of a traditional pub. I couldn't resist the pint of Adnams offered which I
bought and wished I hadn't. As you might expect from me, I complained,
but it wasn't until I had the full support of other dissatisfied drinkers that
they agreed to replace it. It's an agreeable pub renovation in the modern
bleached-wood genre, and the Thai food appears to be very popular. Not
sure I'll go back, but this is practically the only real ale I found on The
Broadway. To enjoy the late drinking you need to be in before 11pm.
OPEN *11.00-midnight (Mon-Sat), midday-22.30 (Sun)*
FOOD *midday-14.30 (all week)*
CREDIT CARDS *none taken*
DRAUGHT BEERS *Bodington, Strongbow, Carling Black Label and Premier,
Guinness, Bass, Adnams, Tenant's Pils and Extra, Grolsch, Stella Artois,
Caffrey's*
Wheelchair access to venue, not to loos
NEAREST TUBE STATION *Fulham Broadway*

YE WHITE HART

The Terrace, Riverside, Barnes, SW13; 0181 876 5177
A Sunday lunch. A lazy afternoon. A sultry summer's evening. A fine
Victorian pub on the riverside with a beautiful sun terrace, a patio garden
with gazebo, and a generous supply of picnic tables on the riverside
walkway. Where else would you want to be? We manage to secure the
gazebo. I pull on my pint of Young's Special, my companion sips on her
rather good Sancerre. A pleasure cruiser parties by. An eight-blade
training crew powers along, cutting a seamless route through the waters,
creating just the mildest of wakes from which the tiny ripples lap gently
around the reeds of the embankment. A canoeist strokes by and, making
use of a nearby landing, comes into the pub for a pint before gliding
away again. A family of wild geese floats over to investigate us as they
swim home for the evening. A bee bravely bumbles above the nose of a
chocolate-brown Labrador. He doesn't mind. He lies panting next to his
bowl of water, sheltered from the heat under the table of his owners. A red
cardinal butterfly flutters down to say hello, the birds in the trees twitter

their last notes of the day, and the flowers in the garden tubs and hanging baskets close their eyes after a long day's bathing. As the sun finally slips down over the distant horizon, its golden afterglow melts through the lush green trees on the embankment opposite and is reflected in buttery hue on the water's surface. This is a perfect pub, providing the perfect end to a perfect day.

OPEN *11.00-15.00 then 17.30-23.00 (Mon-Thurs), 11.00-23.00 (Fri-Sat), 11.00-22.30 (Sun)*
FOOD *midday-14.30 every day*
CREDIT CARDS *all major cards, not AmEx and Diners*
DRAUGHT BEERS *Castlemaine XXXX, Guinness, Stella, Blackthorn Dry, Young's: Pils, Export, Ramrod Smooth, Special and Bitter*
Private room seats 80, 120 standing
NEAREST TUBE STATION *Hammersmith*

THE WHITE HORSE

1 Parson's Green, SW6; 0171 736 2115

The White Horse should get a mention in any book, article or conversation relating to pubs. It is an extrovert, cheerful place with a distinctly Sloaney clientele. It is known locally as the Sloaney Pony. It has a big, comfortable, U-shaped bar, leather sofas, eating booths, a patio at the front overlooking Parson's Green, and a very efficient troupe of bar staff.

The White Horse is expertly run by Rupert Reeves and Mark Dorber, the latter still leading his double life, by day successful City analyst, by night White Horse cellarman. The food is to be taken seriously – it gets better all the time and is now among the best in London's pubs and bars. A lot goes on at The White Horse. Big beer festivals have spread its reputation far beyond London, and its cellars are remarkable. It claims to be the only place in the world to offer all 15 Trappist brewed beers, houses many European lagers and has up to 100 wines on its wine list. It should almost go without saying that it is an *Evening Standard* Pub of the Year.

OPEN *11.00-23.00 (Mon-Sat), 11.00-22.30 (Sun)*
FOOD *12.00-15.00 and 17.30-22.15 (Mon-Fri), 11.00-22.15 (Sat-Sun)*
CREDIT CARDS *all major cards, not Diners*
DRAUGHT BEERS *Adnams Extra, Bass, Harvey's Sussex, Highgate Mild, Carling Black Label, Grolsch, Staropramen, Guinness, Strongbow*
Wheelchair access to venue. Private room: 60 seated, 120 standing
NEAREST TUBE STATION *Parson's Green*

THE WHITE SWAN

Old Palace Lane, Richmond, TW9; 0181 940 0959

A country lane leads gently down to the river with cottages, perhaps 400 years old, all painted white, little front gardens overflowing with flowers. You see the river ahead, usually flowing by but sometimes coming up the lane to meet you. Large notices warn of flooding. The White Swan, painted white like the cottages, is half-way along and it draws you inside on a cold day with its fires, dark panelling, low ceilings and old settles. It could hardly be more picturesque. It started life as an ale house and until quite recently it could only sell beer. You can get a Scotch there now though and there have been other changes; a small conservatory has been added and there is a flagged garden with picnic tables. It is peaceful there on a summer afternoon and quite a surprise when planes roar overhead and trains thunder past apparently in the bushes. Its original customers were the below-stairs staff of the royal palace that gave the lane its name. It stretched along the river bank and the new little ale house faced its garden wall. Many monarchs lived in the old palace, three died there – Edward III, Henry VII and Elizabeth I who went there on the advice of her astrologer and died of a distemper.

OPEN *11.00-15.00 and 17.30-23.00 (Mon-Thurs), 11.00-23.00 (Fri-Sat), midday-22.30 (Sun)*
FOOD *midday-14.30 (Mon), midday-14.30 and 18.00-22.00 (Tues-Sun)*
CREDIT CARDS *none taken*
DRAUGHT BEERS *Courage Best, Courage Directors, John Smith's Extra Smooth, Wadworth 6X, Foster's, Kronenbourg, Guinness, Dry Blackthorn, one guest ale Wheelchair access to venue. Private room: 35 seated, 50 standing*
NEAREST TUBE STATION *Richmond*

THE WHITE SWAN

The Riverside, Twickenham, TW1; 0181 892 2166
After the match, the discerning rugby supporter takes a walk. He makes his way through the Georgian streets of Old Twickenham, past the church with its medieval stone tower, along the brick-walled sunken lane that winds through the gardens of Yorke House and down to the river. There on the left is The White Swan. This is the old pub he has been making for. The White Swan has been there since 1690. Outside there are terraces and balconies, crooked windows, hanging baskets and troughs of flowers; inside it is old wood and real ale. Bizarre collections cover the walls but the star exhibits are in the rugby room at the back – pictures of scrums and great tries, shirts of the great and ties of the famous, autographed oval balls and Paul Ackford's shorts. These in themselves make this a shrine for toilers in the engine room.

Rugger men are trenchermen and food is important at The White Swan. At lunch times a buffet is laid out on a huge table with a great ham cooked on the premises. On summer evenings and Sunday lunchtimes, landlord Steve Roy mans the barbecue and in the winter he cooks a corking Sunday lunch. The best table is the triclinium. A triclinium, explains Roy, is a room with three walls, the fourth being open, or a table with seats on three sides. The one in the main bar of The White Swan with its view of the river and the terraces is an excellent example of both. After brave resistance TV has now been allowed into the bar of The White Swan. For the rugby of course. For other kinds of football the sound doesn't seem to work.

OPEN *11.00-23.00 (Mon-Sat), midday-22.30 (Sun)*
FOOD *midday-15.00 and 19.00-21.00 (Mon-Fri), midday and 15.00 (Sat-Sun)*
CREDIT CARDS *Mastercard, Visa*
DRAUGHT BEERS *Courage Best, Marston's Pedigree, Webster's Yorkshire Bitter, Old Speckled Hen, Budweiser, Carlsberg, Foster's, Holsten, Guinness, Scrumpy Jack, Strongbow, one guest ale Private room available for evening functions*
NEAREST RAILWAY STATION *Twickenham*

THE WHITE SWAN

214 Vauxhall Bridge Road, SW1; 0171 821 8568
The White Swan is the big Victorian pub you pass as you drive in heavy traffic towards Vauxhall Bridge. The temptation to stop is sometimes great. Drastic things have been happening there. It is now one huge bar in the currently modish style known as Old English Ale House – massive weather-worn timbers, bare floorboards, bare brick walls, chopping board tables, pine benches, ceilings lowered a good yard with introduced bare rafters. The original Victorian ceiling can be glimpsed high above. Real ales, robust traditional food and lots of room make for busy lunchtimes, the latest gaming machines, a juke box and television get a lively young crowd in the evenings and a large white swan in a glass case keeps a beady eye on all around it. There's a beer festival twice a year.

OPEN *11.00-23.00 (Mon-Sat), noon-22.30 (Sun)*
FOOD *during opening hours*
CREDIT CARDS *all major cards, no Diners*

DRAUGHT BEERS *Theakston Best, Courage Best, Theakston XB, Directors, Old Speckled Hen, Old Peculier, Foster's, Beck's, Kronenbourg*
Wheelchair access to venue, not to loos. Private room seats 50
NEAREST TUBE STATION *Pimlico*

WILLIAM IV

786 Harrow Road, NW10; 0181 969 5944
I get the heebie-jeebies whenever I go to NW10. A hundred years ago, when I was a lad, I lived in this much-maligned part of town and found that the safest form of supping was to barricade myself in and consume several pints of wine from a stolen Ind Coope pint glass. Things have changed since my formative years and, happily, there is now a reason for going to this part of town. The William IV calls itself a bar and restaurant, but this is something of a misnomer as it's really one of the better examples you will find in London of that watering-hole genre, the gastro-pub. The bar areas are particularly welcoming and the two eating rooms combine simplicity in design with informality in atmosphere. I had a sirloin steak with what was described as 'big chips' but were really potato wedges (£12.50), and my mate had a less-daunting pan-fried sole with a herb and lemon salad (£8). We wolfed this down with several pints of excellent Wadworth 6X (£2) and then demolished the remains of the barrel of Fuller's London Pride. This is a classic example of what can be done to inject a new lease of life into a London pub. Long may it reign.
OPEN *midday-23.00 (Sun-Thurs), midday-midnight (Fri-Sat)*
FOOD *Restaurant open midday-15.00 then 18.00-22.30 (Mon-Sat), midday-16.00 then 19.00-22.30 (Sun)*
CREDIT CARDS *all major cards, not Diners*
DRAUGHT BEERS *London Pride, Wadworth 6X, IPA, Strongbow, Stella Artois, Heineken, Boston, Guinness, Boddingtons Manchester Gold, guest ales in winter*
Wheelchair access to venue and loos. 2 private rooms, one seats up to 25, the other accomodates 120 standing
NEAREST TUBE STATION *Kensal Rise*

WILLIAMSON'S TAVERN

1 Groveland Court, EC4 (off Bow Lane); 0171 248 6280
You can lose yourself and never be seen again searching for Williamson's Tavern so let me tell you precisely where it is. It is the exact centre of City of London's square mile. A stone in what was the parlour marks the spot. Its history is remarkable. It started off as a grand private house, so grand that it was the official residence of successive Lord Mayors. One of them entertained the King and Queen there, William and Mary, who presented him with a truly royal knick-knack, the wrought iron gates still in daily use. Robert Williamson converted it into an hotel in 1739 and it seems to have been successful. Successive owners worried about fire and one banned matches, which seems to have done the trick, and in the 1930s a new owner made it a pub. It is a distinctly superior pub with a library, two fine panelled bars and the general air of a gentleman's club. It is very popular with City gents who know exactly how to get there also with City women who like its unpubby atmosphere. Between them they fill all three big bars at lunchtime. There is a charcoal grill in one of them and some say its steak sandwiches are the best in London. It is very peaceful in Williamson's in the afternoon with everyone back at work. Then it wakes up again as people look in for a snifter on their way home. Like most City pubs it stays closed at weekends. The City of London is no place for ravers.
OPEN *11.00-23.00 (Mon-Fri)*
FOOD *11.30-21.00 (Mon-Fri)*
CREDIT CARDS *all major cards*

DRAUGHT BEERS *Adnams, Brakspear, Marston's Pedigree, Tetley's, Greene King IPA, Stella Artois, Carlsberg, Guinness, two guest bitters*
Two private rooms: 80-200 standing
NEAREST TUBE STATION *Mansion House*

THE WILTON ARMS

71 Kinnerton Street, SW1; 0171 235 4854
Wilton Crescent, Wilton Place, Wilton Row — as good addresses go, these are hard to beat and The Wilton Arms, named like the rest after the first Earl of Wilton, stands, most respectfully, in the mews. I see it as the comptroller of the household, grand in its own right but knowing its place.

The mews is Kinnerton Street, rough and malodorous in its early days with an open sewer and more horses than people. The Wilton Arms hardly knew where to look. Those days are long gone and for many years The Wilton Arms has had most distinguished neighbours. It has always been a superior public house. It got further improvements in the Whitbread manner a few years ago, and high settles and bookcases now give the big bar a number of pleasantly separate drinking areas. There are some jolly good books in the bookcases. New Zealand Statutes. Public Acts of Tasmania. A conservatory covers the garden now and the flowers have moved into new hanging baskets and exuberant window boxes. There is a kitchen with a presiding chef on the first floor and hot food is served all day.
OPEN *11.00-23.00 (Mon-Sat), midday-22.30 (Sun)*
FOOD *all day Mon-Fri, midday-15.00 (Sat)*
CREDIT CARDS *all major cards*
DRAUGHT BEERS *Heineken, Stella, Boddingtons, Flower's IPA, Abbot Ale, Guinness, Murphy's, Boddingtons Gold, Strongbow*
Wheelchair access to venue. Private room seats 40, standing 200
NEAREST TUBE STATIONS *Knightsbridge, Hyde Park Corner*

THE WINDMILL ON THE COMMON

Clapham Common Southside, SW4; 0181 673 4578
The Windmill is in terrific form. It has a big, wandering bar with tropical fish in tanks, a spacious conservatory for non-smokers, an excellent restaurant and an adjoining hotel that gets three stars and a rosette from the AA and a 'highly commended' from the English Tourist Board. Things are always going on at The Windmill – live music, fiesta nights, opera in the conservatory. In the summer, drinkers spill out on to the Common, and in the winter there's an open fire in the bar. There are cask ales, draught lagers and a plentiful wine list – six reds, eight whites, two rosés and three champagnes. The head chef of the attached restaurant does the bar food. The Windmill gets packed in the evenings and at weekends, and no wonder.
OPEN *11.00-23.00 (Mon-Sat), 12.00-22.30 (Sun)*
FOOD *12.00-14.30 and 19.00-22.00 (Mon-Fri), 12.00-21.00 (Sat-Sun)*
CREDIT CARDS *all major cards*
DRAUGHT BEERS *Young's Bitter, Young's Special, Young's seasonal ale, Young's Pilsner, Young's Export, Stella Artois, Carling Black Label, Guinness, Scrumpy Jack*
Wheelchair access to venue and loos. Two private rooms: 28-45 seated, 35-60 standing
NEAREST TUBE STATION *Clapham Common, Clapham South*

WINDOWS BAR

London Hilton, 22 Park Lane, W1; 0171 493 8000
Despite the distinct severity of the London Hilton lobby, we are all free to take the lift to the 28th floor and imbibe our favourite tipple while surveying what has to be one of the best views in London. Included in the view is the back garden of Buckingham Palace and, apparently, Her Majesty The Queen was so furious about this when the hotel was built in 1963 that she

vowed never to set foot inside. True to her word, she has never done so. But I think this piano bar would make a very decent local for her. I might even do the neighbourly thing and invite her around for drinks one night. The cocktails are quite expensive (from £8.95) but they're well mixed and presented and the smartly attired staff seem to know their armagnacs from their cognacs. Bottled beers start at £3.50 and a premium G&T will set you back £8.25. It may have one of the best (if not longest) wine lists in London with bottles starting at £16.50 and rising as high as you like. The novelty value of this bar dies hard and it always surprises me to find it so under-used. It's a great place to impress a date but, if the evening doesn't turn out as planned, just look over their shoulder at the fantastic view. It will bring a childish thrill to even the most hardened cynic.

OPEN *12.00-15.00 (Sun-Fri), 17.30-02.00 (Mon-Sat)*
FOOD *as opening hours*
CREDIT CARDS *all major cards*
NEAREST TUBE STATION *Hyde Park Corner*

THE WINDSOR CASTLE
114 Campden Hill Road, W8; 0171 727 8491
The Windsor Castle is part of the Eton drinking round, one of a handful of London pubs where Old Etonians meet, and is one of the most up-market pubs in London. It gets extraordinarily busy. The garden is open all year long, and in the summer the numbers treble. The Windsor Castle's kitchen has a high reputation. There is a roster of cooks producing pesto salad, vegetable couscous and such, and from Monday to Saturday there's food all day. On Sundays you can have a traditional roast lunch or just snack on the sausages and mustard, and there is a no-smoking section in the Campden bar at lunchtimes.

A remarkable story is told about The Windsor Castle. When Tom Paine, author of *The Rights of Man*, died in America in 1809, the journalist and social reformer William Cobbett had his bones shipped back to England. Cobbett himself died before he could put up his planned memorial to Paine, and left the bones to his son who, years later, traded them to the landlord of The Windsor Castle to settle a beer debt. They were then lodged in one of the cellars, which was subsequently filled in.

OPEN *12.00-20.30 (Mon-Sat), 12.00-22.30 (Sun)*
FOOD *12.00-22.45 (Mon-Sat), 12.00-22.15 (Sun)*
CREDIT CARDS *all major cards*
DRAUGHT BEERS *Bass, Caffrey's, London Pride, Carling Black Label, Staropramen, Guinness, Red Rock, one guest ale*
Wheelchair access to venue
NEAREST TUBE STATION *Notting Hill Gate*

THE WOODMAN
60 Battersea High Street, SW11; 0171 229 2968
There is, in Battersea High Street, a little country pub called The Woodman. It is at No. 60. A few doors along, at No. 44, is another little country pub. It is called the Original Woodman. Hello, hello? What's this then? Well the ins and outs of this ancient quarrel are long forgotten and the two old pubs get on with their lives as neighbours must. They are, indeed, very different pubs. The Woodman is the pretty one, with cottage frontage, hanging baskets, and it is much the bigger. First comes a little public bar with a sawdust floor, full of real ale and character. Behind it is a saloon bar with a carpet and traditional games – bar billiards, table football, shove-ha'penny. Then comes a much newer bit with a modern food counter and beyond that is a pleasant paved garden with a large pull-out awning. So let it rain. It is an interesting, lively pub. Its regulars send it postcards when they go on hols, there is a pub football team, recently beaten 14-0, empty champagne bottles commemorate marriages and births, and local

horses go for carrots and Guinness every Christmas morning. On Saturdays and Sundays the Woodman opens at 9.30am breakfast, served with the daily papers. The Original Woodman along the road does not go in for this sort of thing. It is very much the local boozer, one small bar and no frills. Some like it better.

OPEN *11.00-23.00 (Mon-Sat), midday-22.30 (Sun)*
FOOD *midday-22.00 (Mon-Sat), midday-21.30 (Sun)*
CREDIT CARDS *Mastercard, Switch, Visa*
DRAUGHT BEERS *Badger Best, Black Adder, Dempsey's, Dorset IPA, Gribble Best, Reggie's Tipple, Tanglefoot, Hofbräu Export, Hofbräu Pils, Hofbräu Premium, Guinness, Taunton Somerset*
NEAREST RAILWAY STATION *Clapham Junction*

WORLD'S END
174 Camden High Street, NW1; 0171 482 1932

World's End in Camden Town has a bold claim to fame. It sells more than a million pints of beer a year. No other pub in the country, it says, sells more. Most of this is lager. The lively and thirsty young customers of World's End are prodigious drinkers of lager, particularly bottled lager, drunk straight from the bottle. They will knock back the draught lager too on occasion, though even a pint glass threatens their street cred. It is a huge Victorian pub, big when it was built, more than twice the size now since the huge atrium was tagged on at the back in the 1960s, with flagged floor, glass roof high above, a big mezzanine gallery with a red spiral staircase, a busy bar counter in the middle. There's hardly any furniture. Furniture takes up valuable standing around and milling about space. Down below there's The Underworld (famous and usually packed) and live bands, some of them very big. Then five nights a week five different clubs take over at 11pm, each with its own style and audience. The Underworld is now considered one of London's top ten venues. The World's End is under siege as the weekend approaches with doormen highly visible at all three doors. There aren't many rules at World's End but three are displayed outside: 'NO DOGS, NUCLEAR WEAPONS OR UNUSUAL PETS', it declares.

OPEN *pub 11.00-23.00 (Mon-Sat), midday-22.30 (Sun); club 19.30-22.30 and 23.00-03.00 (Mon and Thurs-Sat)*
FOOD *midday-15.00 (Mon-Fri), midday-18.00 (Sat-Sun)*
CREDIT CARDS *none taken*
DRAUGHT BEERS *Bass, Caffrey's, Courage Best, Courage Directors, John Smith's Extra Smooth, Kilkenny, Tetley's, Webster's, Carlsberg Pilsner, Carling Black Label, Carlsberg Export, Foster's, Löwenbräu, Guinness, Dry Blackthorn*
NEAREST TUBE STATION *Camden Town*

THE WORLD'S END
459 King's Road, SW10; 0171 376 8946

The World's End is a bus terminus, a garden centre, a council estate, a district and, of course, the pub that gave them all its name. When The World's End was built in 1890 it was called the World's End Distillery, a name which still appears on the oldest of the surviving windows, suggesting the downward path to Gin Lane. It has had many ups and downs since then, and many owners too, some of whom soon decided that this was indeed the world's end. A couple of years ago it became a Harvey Floorbanger's but it was soon taken on by Badger Inns and got its historic name back. For many years now it has had one big bar with an island counter, leaving lots of room for the pinball machine, the table football and the gaming machines. Fresh sawdust is strewn across the floor every day, just as it's always been. Youngsters on their way to clubs in Chelsea and Fulham meet here for a drink, and the music is pumped up late in the evening to get them in the mood. You can get burgers and chips all day.

OPEN *11.00-23.00 (Mon-Sat), 12.00-22.30 (Sun)*
FOOD *12.00-19.00 (Mon-Sun)*
CREDIT CARDS *AmEx, Mastercard, Visa*
DRAUGHT BEERS *Badger, Dempsey's, Tanglefoot, Stella Artois, Guinness, Dry Blackthorn, three Hofbräu lagers*
Wheelchair access to venue. Private room seats 30, 50 standing
NEAREST TUBE STATIONS *Sloane Square, Earls Court*

THE YARD

57 Rupert Street, W1; 0171 437 2652

A doorway in Rupert Street leads into a courtyard fronting this two-storey gay bar. The downstairs bar has a café feel to it – doors opening out on to the courtyard, a scattering of tables and chairs, and people hanging around reading newspapers. Go through the courtyard, up a staircase, and you find a platform where you can lean and keep your eye on who you want to keep your eye on down below. The bar upstairs is more relaxed, with comfortable chairs and armchairs and even more hanging-around space. Unlike some gay venues, The Yard doesn't have a 'heavy' atmosphere, which is probably down to the clientele, who seem to be mainly suits after work. Stick to beers, the wine is unmentionable.

OPEN *12.00-23.00 (Mon-Sat)*
FOOD *12.00-17.00 (Mon-Sat)*
CREDIT CARDS *all major cards (over £10 only)*
Wheelchair access to venue. Private room: 100-150 standing
NEAREST TUBE STATION *Piccadilly Circus*

YATES'S WINE LODGE

Mattock Lane, Ealing Green, W5; 0181 840 0988

Yates's have come a long way since opening their first branch in Oldham in 1884. Gone are the old spit-and-sawdust rough boozers often found near railway stations. In has come a new style of venue. Unfortunately, its progress seems to have got stuck somewhere in the 70s. The Ealing Yates's has a rather pleasant courtyard outside, filled with tables and parasols, which on a summer's day looks very inviting. Inside, the two-level bar is a riot of contrasting colours and designs. The cluttered bar back is so busy with signs, promotions, drinks and gimmicks that it's difficult to know what you're looking at. I suspect the designers were given the brief of transforming the place beyond recognition, and have gone crazy, filling every available space with jokey notices and *objet* crap. The last notice you see as you leave reads 'Mind how you go'. If I were the signwriter, it'd say, 'Mind you don't come back'.

OPEN *11.00-23.00 (Mon-Sat), 12.00-22.30 (Sun)*
FOOD *12.00-18.00 (Sun-Thurs), 12.00-17.00 (Fri-Sat)*
CREDIT CARDS *all major cards*
DRAUGHT BEERS *John Smith's Extra Smooth, Budweiser, Carling Black Label, Carling Premier, Foster's, Kronenbourg, Murphy's, Caffrey's, Carling Premier, Dry Blackthorn, Woodpecker*
Wheelchair access to venue and loos
NEAREST TUBE STATION *Ealing Broadway*

Branches at:
CROYDON 3-11 High Street, CR0; 0181 681 8219
    NEAREST RAILWAY STATIONS *East Croydon and West Croydon*
HARROW 269-271 Station Road, HA1; 0181 863 9470
    NEAREST TUBE STATION *Harrow-on-the-Hill*
HOUNSLOW 1-3 Bath Road, TW3; 0181 570 0091
    NEAREST TUBE STATION *Hounslow Central*
LEWISHAM 67-71 High Street, SE13; 0181 318 6192
    NEAREST RAILWAY STATION *Lewisham*

ZD

289 Kilburn High Road, NW6; 0171 372 2544

The designer frontage of plate glass, wood pillars and copper-clad entrance entices you into this air-conditioned, night-time dance venue. It's part of the Mean Fiddler organisation so you can be sure there's always something going on. Magic Monday is indie, pop, dance and trance. Tuesday's Heatwave is soul, funk and hip-hop. Wednesday and Thursday's Hot Tub is for DJ promo, soul and big house anthems. Friday goes Supersonic, with DJs Danny and Jon playing an eclectic mix of Brit-pop, funk and a 'Pop 'n' Punk' fusion. Saturday sees Climax with DJ L-Tel, featuring vocal and underground garage. On Sunday, All Things End With A Zed, and there's soul, R & B, funk and acid jazz. With cheap drinks, free admission and an impressive light and sound system, this has to be a great deal for the youth of NW6.

OPEN *17.00-01.00 (Mon-Thurs), 17.00-02.00 (Sat), 17.00-22.30 (Sun)*
FOOD *17.00-01.00 (Mon-Thurs), 17.00-22.00 (Fri-Sun)*
CREDIT CARDS *none taken*
DRAUGHT BEERS *Kilkenny, Carlsberg, Carlsberg Export, Löwenbräu, Guinness, Blackthorn*
Wheelchair access to venue and loos
NEAREST TUBE STATION *Kilburn*

ZILLI BAR

40 Dean Street, W1; 0171 734 1853

If you own a bar and your ego's big enough, you make sure that your name is plastered all over it. Aldo Zilli is the man who owns this place. His world-famous restaurant has been feeding visitors to Soho for the past 12 years or so; he acquired the next-door unit about three years ago and opened this bar. I called in when it first opened and didn't go back again for a long time. A mistake. I had been missing out! This is rather a fine bar, attracting a loyal following of Soho media moguls and once-upon-a-time television stars, who help to create a party atmosphere in the evenings. When Italy are playing football, it's almost a carnival. Drinks are ever so slightly on the expensive side, but those who stay until 1am don't mind too much.

OPEN *12.00-01.00 (Mon-Sat)*
CREDIT CARDS *all major cards*
NEAREST TUBE STATION *Piccadilly Circus*

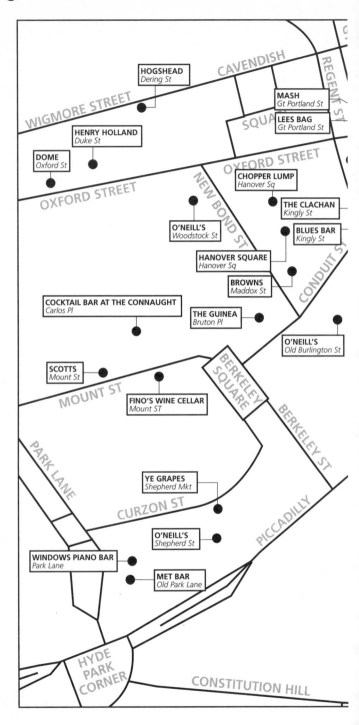

HOGSHEAD
Dering St

CAVENDISH

MASH
Gt Portland St

LEES BAG
Gt Portland St

SQUARE

REGENT ST

WIGMORE STREET

HENRY HOLLAND
Duke St

DOME
Oxford St

OXFORD STREET

OXFORD STREET

NEW BOND ST

CHOPPER LUMP
Hanover Sq

THE CLACHAN
Kingly St

O'NEILL'S
Woodstock St

BLUES BAR
Kingly St

HANOVER SQUARE
Hanover Sq

BROWNS
Maddox St

CONDUIT ST

COCKTAIL BAR AT THE CONNAUGHT
Carlos Pl

THE GUINEA
Bruton Pl

O'NEILL'S
Old Burlington St

SCOTTS
Mount St

BERKELEY
SQUARE

BERKELEY ST

MOUNT ST

FINO'S WINE CELLAR
Mount ST

PARK LANE

YE GRAPES
Shepherd Mkt

CURZON ST

PICCADILLY

O'NEILL'S
Shepherd St

WINDOWS PIANO BAR
Park Lane

MET BAR
Old Park Lane

HYDE
PARK
CORNER

CONSTITUTION HILL

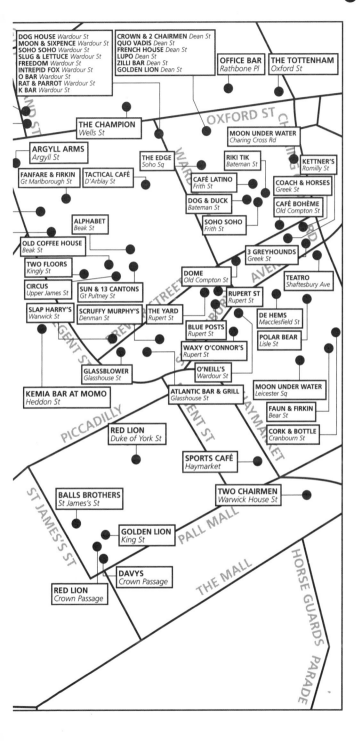

DOG HOUSE *Wardour St*
MOON & SIXPENCE *Wardour St*
SOHO SOHO *Wardour St*
SLUG & LETTUCE *Wardour St*
FREEDOM *Wardour St*
INTREPID FOX *Wardour St*
O BAR *Wardour St*
RAT & PARROT *Wardour St*
K BAR *Wardour St*

CROWN & 2 CHAIRMEN *Dean St*
QUO VADIS *Dean St*
FRENCH HOUSE *Dean St*
LUPO *Dean St*
ZILLI BAR *Dean St*
GOLDEN LION *Dean St*

OFFICE BAR *Rathbone Pl*

THE TOTTENHAM *Oxford St*

OXFORD ST

THE CHAMPION *Wells St*

MOON UNDER WATER *Charing Cross Rd*

ARGYLL ARMS *Argyll St*

THE EDGE *Soho Sq*

RIKI TIK *Bateman St*

KETTNER'S *Romilly St*

FANFARE & FIRKIN *Gt Marlborough St*

TACTICAL CAFÉ *D'Arblay St*

CAFÉ LATINO *Frith St*

COACH & HORSES *Greek St*

DOG & DUCK *Bateman St*

CAFÉ BOHÈME *Old Compton St*

SOHO SOHO *Frith St*

ALPHABET *Beak St*

OLD COFFEE HOUSE *Beak St*

3 GREYHOUNDS *Greek St*

TWO FLOORS *Kingly St*

TEATRO *Shaftesbury Ave*

CIRCUS *Upper James St*

DOME *Old Compton St*

SUN & 13 CANTONS *Gt Pultney St*

RUPERT ST *Rupert St*

SLAP HARRY'S *Warwick St*

SCRUFFY MURPHY'S *Denman St*

THE YARD *Rupert St*

DE HEMS *Macclesfield St*

BLUE POSTS *Rupert St*

POLAR BEAR *Lisle St*

WAXY O'CONNOR'S *Rupert St*

GLASSBLOWER *Glasshouse St*

O'NEILL'S *Wardour St*

MOON UNDER WATER *Leicester Sq*

KEMIA BAR AT MOMO *Heddon St*

ATLANTIC BAR & GRILL *Glasshouse St*

FAUN & FIRKIN *Bear St*

PICCADILLY

CORK & BOTTLE *Cranbourn St*

RED LION *Duke of York St*

SPORTS CAFÉ *Haymarket*

BALLS BROTHERS *St James's St*

TWO CHAIRMEN *Warwick House St*

ST JAMES'S ST

PALL MALL

GOLDEN LION *King St*

DAVYS *Crown Passage*

RED LION *Crown Passage*

THE MALL

HORSE GUARDS PARADE

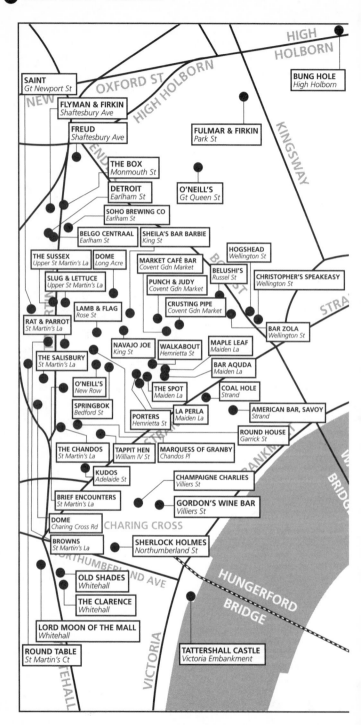

SAINT
Gt Newport St

BUNG HOLE
High Holborn

FLYMAN & FIRKIN
Shaftesbury Ave

FREUD
Shaftesbury Ave

FULMAR & FIRKIN
Park St

THE BOX
Monmouth St

DETROIT
Earlham St

O'NEILL'S
Gt Queen St

SOHO BREWING CO
Earlham St

BELGO CENTRAAL
Earlham St

SHEILA'S BAR BARBIE
King St

HOGSHEAD
Wellington St

THE SUSSEX
Upper St Martin's La

DOME
Long Acre

MARKET CAFÉ BAR
Covent Gdn Market

BELUSHI'S
Russel St

CHRISTOPHER'S SPEAKEASY
Wellington St

SLUG & LETTUCE
Upper St Martin's La

PUNCH & JUDY
Covent Gdn Market

LAMB & FLAG
Rose St

CRUSTING PIPE
Covent Gdn Market

RAT & PARROT
St Martin's La

BAR ZOLA
Wellington St

NAVAJO JOE
King St

WALKABOUT
Hemrietta St

MAPLE LEAF
Maiden La

THE SALISBURY
St Martin's La

BAR AQUDA
Maiden La

O'NEILL'S
New Row

THE SPOT
Maiden La

COAL HOLE
Strand

SPRINGBOK
Bedford St

PORTERS
Hemrietta St

LA PERLA
Maiden La

AMERICAN BAR, SAVOY
Strand

ROUND HOUSE
Garrick St

THE CHANDOS
St Martin's La

TAPPIT HEN
William IV St

MARQUESS OF GRANBY
Chandos Pl

KUDOS
Adelaide St

CHAMPAIGNE CHARLIES
Villiers St

BRIEF ENCOUNTERS
St Martin's La

GORDON'S WINE BAR
Villiers St

DOME
Charing Cross Rd

CHARING CROSS

BROWNS
St Martin's La

SHERLOCK HOLMES
Northumberland St

OLD SHADES
Whitehall

THE CLARENCE
Whitehall

LORD MOON OF THE MALL
Whitehall

ROUND TABLE
St Martin's Ct

TATTERSHALL CASTLE
Victoria Embankment

HUNGERFORD BRIDGE

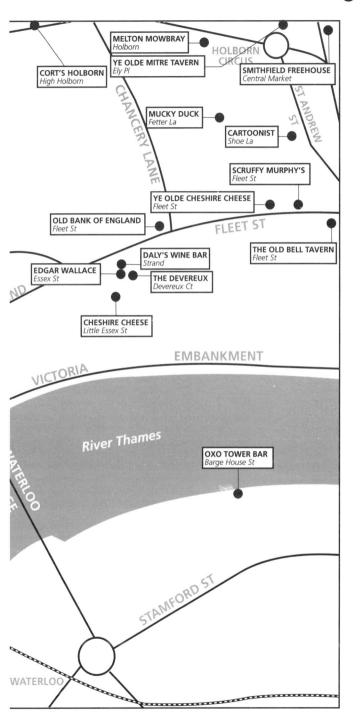

MELTON MOWBRAY
Holborn

YE OLDE MITRE TAVERN
Ely Pl

HOLBORN
CIRCUS

CORT'S HOLBORN
High Holborn

SMITHFIELD FREEHOUSE
Central Market

CHANCERY LANE

ST ANDREW

MUCKY DUCK
Fetter La

CARTOONIST
Shoe La

SCRUFFY MURPHY'S
Fleet St

YE OLDE CHESHIRE CHEESE
Fleet St

OLD BANK OF ENGLAND
Fleet St

FLEET ST

THE OLD BELL TAVERN
Fleet St

DALY'S WINE BAR
Strand

EDGAR WALLACE
Essex St

THE DEVEREUX
Devereux Ct

CHESHIRE CHEESE
Little Essex St

EMBANKMENT

VICTORIA

River Thames

WATERLOO

OXO TOWER BAR
Barge House St

STAMFORD ST

WATERLOO

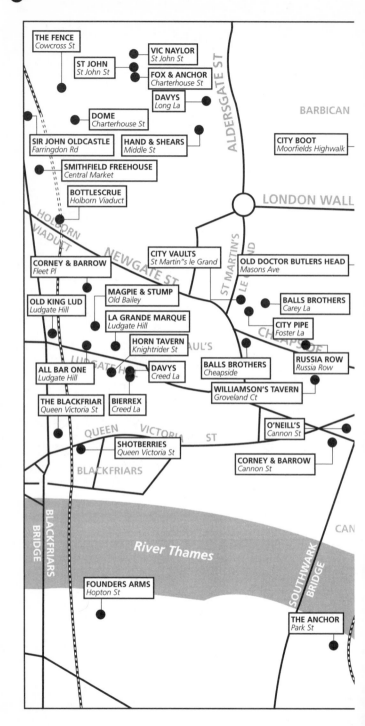

THE FENCE
Cowcross St

VIC NAYLOR
St John St

ST JOHN
St John St

FOX & ANCHOR
Charterhouse St

DAVYS
Long La

DOME
Charterhouse St

BARBICAN

SIR JOHN OLDCASTLE
Farringdon Rd

HAND & SHEARS
Middle St

CITY BOOT
Moorfields Highwalk

SMITHFIELD FREEHOUSE
Central Market

BOTTLESCRUE
Holborn Viaduct

ALDERSGATE ST

LONDON WALL

HOLBORN VIADUCT

NEWGATE ST

CITY VAULTS
St Martin"s le Grand

OLD DOCTOR BUTLERS HEAD
Masons Ave

ST MARTIN'S LE GRAND

CORNEY & BARROW
Fleet Pl

MAGPIE & STUMP
Old Bailey

BALLS BROTHERS
Carey La

OLD KING LUD
Ludgate Hill

CITY PIPE
Foster La

LA GRANDE MARQUE
Ludgate Hill

CHEAPSIDE

HORN TAVERN
Knightrider St

PAUL'S

RUSSIA ROW
Russia Row

ALL BAR ONE
Ludgate Hill

LUDGATE HILL

DAVYS
Creed La

BALLS BROTHERS
Cheapside

THE BLACKFRIAR
Queen Victoria St

BIERREX
Creed La

WILLIAMSON'S TAVERN
Groveland Ct

O'NEILL'S
Cannon St

QUEEN VICTORIA ST

SHOTBERRIES
Queen Victoria St

CORNEY & BARROW
Cannon St

BLACKFRIARS

BLACKFRIARS BRIDGE

River Thames

CAN

FOUNDERS ARMS
Hopton St

SOUTHWARK BRIDGE

THE ANCHOR
Park St

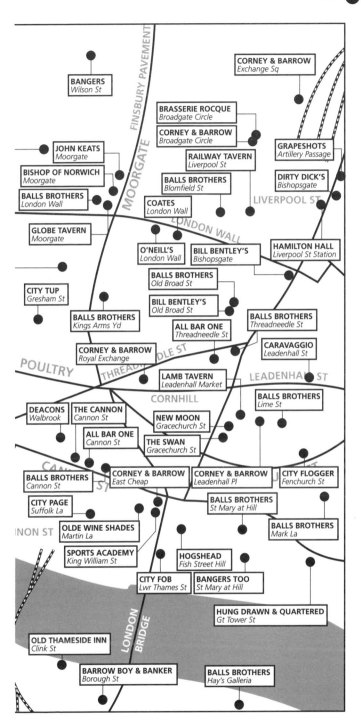

BANGERS
Wilson St

CORNEY & BARROW
Exchange Sq

BRASSERIE ROCQUE
Broadgate Circle

CORNEY & BARROW
Broadgate Circle

JOHN KEATS
Moorgate

GRAPESHOTS
Artillery Passage

RAILWAY TAVERN
Liverpool St

BISHOP OF NORWICH
Moorgate

DIRTY DICK'S
Bishopsgate

BALLS BROTHERS
Blomfield St

BALLS BROTHERS
London Wall

COATES
London Wall

LIVERPOOL ST

GLOBE TAVERN
Moorgate

LONDON WALL

O'NEILL'S
London Wall

BILL BENTLEY'S
Bishopsgate

HAMILTON HALL
Liverpool St Station

CITY TUP
Gresham St

BALLS BROTHERS
Old Broad St

BILL BENTLEY'S
Old Broad St

BALLS BROTHERS
Threadneedle St

BALLS BROTHERS
Kings Arms Yd

ALL BAR ONE
Threadneedle St

CARAVAGGIO
Leadenhall St

CORNEY & BARROW
Royal Exchange

POULTRY

THREADNEEDLE ST

LEADENHALL ST

LAMB TAVERN
Leadenhall Market

CORNHILL

BALLS BROTHERS
Lime St

DEACONS
Walbrook

THE CANNON
Cannon St

NEW MOON
Gracechurch St

ALL BAR ONE
Cannon St

THE SWAN
Gracechurch St

CANNON ST

BALLS BROTHERS
Cannon St

CORNEY & BARROW
East Cheap

CORNEY & BARROW
Leadenhall Pl

CITY FLOGGER
Fenchurch St

CITY PAGE
Suffolk La

BALLS BROTHERS
St Mary at Hill

OLDE WINE SHADES
Martin La

BALLS BROTHERS
Mark La

NON ST

SPORTS ACADEMY
King William St

HOGSHEAD
Fish Street Hill

CITY FOB
Lwr Thames St

BANGERS TOO
St Mary at Hill

HUNG DRAWN & QUARTERED
Gt Tower St

OLD THAMESIDE INN
Clink St

LONDON BRIDGE

BARROW BOY & BANKER
Borough St

BALLS BROTHERS
Hay's Galleria

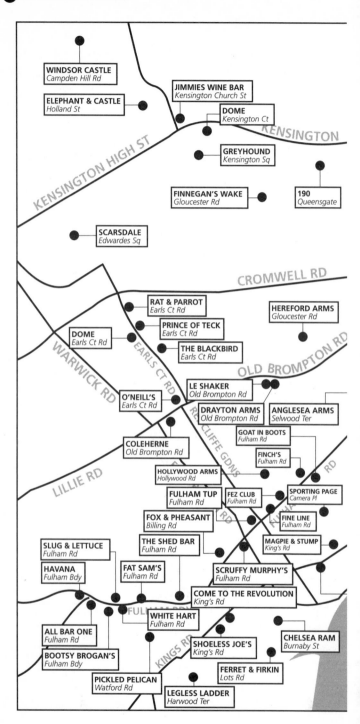

WINDSOR CASTLE
Campden Hill Rd

JIMMIES WINE BAR
Kensington Church St

ELEPHANT & CASTLE
Holland St

DOME
Kensington Ct

KENSINGTON

GREYHOUND
Kensington Sq

FINNEGAN'S WAKE
Gloucester Rd

190
Queensgate

SCARSDALE
Edwardes Sq

KENSINGTON HIGH ST

CROMWELL RD

RAT & PARROT
Earls Ct Rd

HEREFORD ARMS
Gloucester Rd

PRINCE OF TECK
Earls Ct Rd

DOME
Earls Ct Rd

THE BLACKBIRD
Earls Ct Rd

EARLS CT RD

OLD BROMPTON RD

WARWICK RD

LE SHAKER
Old Brompton Rd

O'NEILL'S
Earls Ct Rd

DRAYTON ARMS
Old Brompton Rd

ANGLESEA ARMS
Selwood Ter

REDCLIFFE GDNS

GOAT IN BOOTS
Fulham Rd

COLEHERNE
Old Brompton Rd

FINCH'S
Fulham Rd

LILLIE RD

HOLLYWOOD ARMS
Hollywood Rd

FULHAM TUP
Fulham Rd

FEZ CLUB
Fulham Rd

SPORTING PAGE
Camera Pl

FOX & PHEASANT
Billing Rd

FINE LINE
Fulham Rd

SLUG & LETTUCE
Fulham Rd

THE SHED BAR
Fulham Rd

MAGPIE & STUMP
King's Rd

HAVANA
Fulham Bdy

FAT SAM'S
Fulham Rd

SCRUFFY MURPHY'S
Fulham Rd

FULHAM

COME TO THE REVOLUTION
King's Rd

ALL BAR ONE
Fulham Rd

WHITE HART
Fulham Rd

KINGS RD

CHELSEA RAM
Burnaby St

BOOTSY BROGAN'S
Fulham Bdy

SHOELESS JOE'S
King's Rd

FERRET & FIRKIN
Lots Rd

PICKLED PELICAN
Watford Rd

LEGLESS LADDER
Harwood Ter

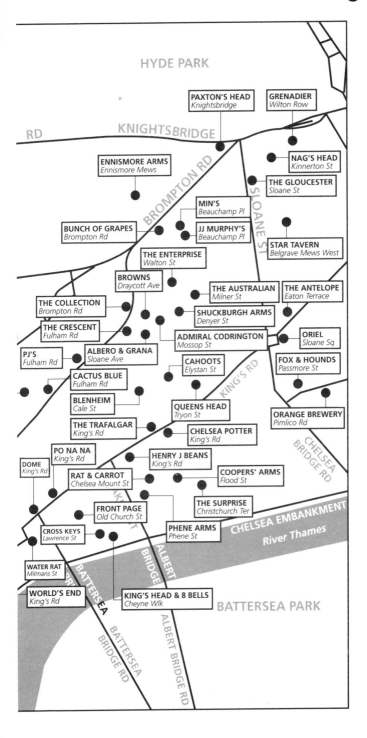

HYDE PARK

RD KNIGHTSBRIDGE

PAXTON'S HEAD
Knightsbridge

GRENADIER
Wilton Row

NAG'S HEAD
Kinnerton St

ENNISMORE ARMS
Ennismore Mews

BROMPTON RD

SLOANE ST

THE GLOUCESTER
Sloane St

MIN'S
Beauchamp Pl

BUNCH OF GRAPES
Brompton Rd

JJ MURPHY'S
Beauchamp Pl

STAR TAVERN
Belgrave Mews West

THE ENTERPRISE
Walton St

BROWNS
Draycott Ave

THE AUSTRALIAN
Milner St

THE ANTELOPE
Eaton Terrace

THE COLLECTION
Brompton Rd

SHUCKBURGH ARMS
Denyer St

THE CRESCENT
Fulham Rd

ADMIRAL CODRINGTON
Mossop St

ORIEL
Sloane Sq

PJ'S
Fulham Rd

ALBERO & GRANA
Sloane Ave

CAHOOTS
Elystan St

FOX & HOUNDS
Passmore St

CACTUS BLUE
Fulham Rd

KING'S RD

BLENHEIM
Cale St

QUEENS HEAD
Tryon St

ORANGE BREWERY
Pimlico Rd

THE TRAFALGAR
King's Rd

CHELSEA POTTER
King's Rd

CHELSEA BRIDGE RD

PO NA NA
King's Rd

HENRY J BEANS
King's Rd

DOME
King's Rd

RAT & CARROT
Chelsea Mount St

COOPERS' ARMS
Flood St

THE SURPRISE
Christchurch Ter

FRONT PAGE
Old Church St

PHENE ARMS
Phene St

CHELSEA EMBANKMENT

CROSS KEYS
Lawrence St

River Thames

BRIDGE

ALBERT

WATER RAT
Milmans St

BATTERSEA

WORLD'S END
King's Rd

KING'S HEAD & 8 BELLS
Cheyne Wlk

BATTERSEA PARK

BATTERSEA BRIDGE RD

ALBERT BRIDGE RD

FRINGE & FIRKIN
Goldhawk Rd

MOON ON THE GREEN
Uxbridge Rd

EDWARD'S
Uxbridge Rd

STONEMASON
Cambridge Gr

HOGSHEAD
High Rd

SECRETS
Glenthorne Rd

JJ MOON'S
High Rd

BLACK LION
South Black Lion La

RAT & PARROT
High Rd

CHISWICK

GEORGE IV
High Rd

THE DOVE
Upper Mall

BELL & CROWN
Strand on the Green

ALL BAR ONE
Chiswick High Rd

OLD SHIP
Upper Mall

HOP POLES
King St

CITY BARGE
Strand on the Green

BLUE ANCHOR
Lower Mall

FINNEGAN'S WAKE
Fulham Palace Rd

BULL'S HEAD
Strand on the Green

YE WHITE HART
The Terrace

KING'S HEAD
Fulham High St

FLOWER & FIRKIN
Kew Gdns Station

SUN INN
Church Rd

SLUG & LETTUCE
Putney High St

THE SHIP
Thames Bank

WHITE SWAN
Old Palace La

ORANGE TREE
Kew Rd

BEIRREX
Putney High St

LWR RICHMOND RD

HALF MOON
Lwr Richmond Rd

O'NEILL'S
The Quadrant

UPPER   RICHMO

BAR M/STAR & GARTER
Lwr Richmond Rd

RACING PAGE
Duke St

HARE & HOUNDS
Upr Richmond Rd West

RAILWAY
Upper Richmond Rd

NEY

MARLBOROUGH
Friar Stile Rd

GREEN MAN
Putney Heath

DOME
Hill Street

CRICKETERS
The Green

HMOND

RAT & PARROT
Putney High St

WHITE HORSE
Water La

ROSE OF YORK
Petersham Rd

RICHMOND RD

DOME
High St

ROBIN HOOD WAY

FOX & GRAPES
Camp Rd

KINGSTON

HAND IN HAND
Crooked Billet

PUZZLE
St James's Rd

SLUG & LETTUCE
Thameside

STON HILL

COOMB

BEVERLE

CROOKED BILLET
Crooked Billet

DRUIDS HEAD
Kingston Market

ROSE & CROWN
High St

NORBITON

COOMB RD

O'NEILL'S
Eden St

ALEXANDRA
Wimbledon Hill Rd

FINANCIER & FIRKIN
Market Pl

GAZEBO
Kings Passage

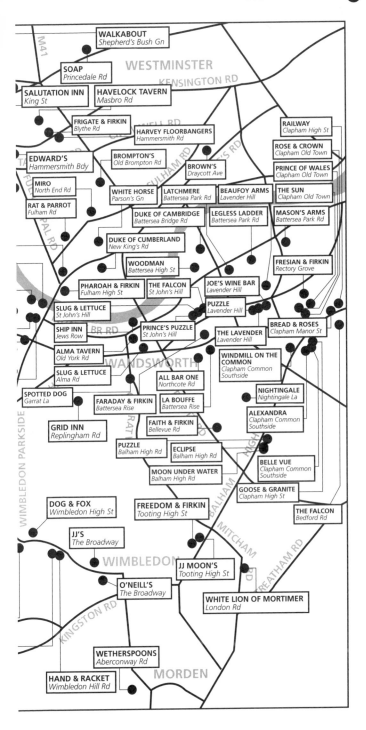

WALKABOUT
Shepherd's Bush Gn

SOAP
Princedale Rd

WESTMINSTER
KENSINGTON RD

SALUTATION INN
King St

HAVELOCK TAVERN
Masbro Rd

FRIGATE & FIRKIN
Blythe Rd

HARVEY FLOORBANGERS
Hammersmith Rd

RAILWAY
Clapham High St

EDWARD'S
Hammersmith Bdy

BROMPTON'S
Old Brompton Rd

BROWN'S
Draycott Ave

ROSE & CROWN
Clapham Old Town

PRINCE OF WALES
Clapham Old Town

MIRO
North End Rd

WHITE HORSE
Parson's Gn

LATCHMERE
Battersea Park Rd

BEAUFOY ARMS
Lavender Hill

THE SUN
Clapham Old Town

RAT & PARROT
Fulham Rd

DUKE OF CAMBRIDGE
Battersea Bridge Rd

LEGLESS LADDER
Battersea Park Rd

MASON'S ARMS
Battersea Park Rd

DUKE OF CUMBERLAND
New King's Rd

WOODMAN
Battersea High St

FRESIAN & FIRKIN
Rectory Grove

PHAROAH & FIRKIN
Fulham High St

THE FALCON
St John's Hill

JOE'S WINE BAR
Lavender Hill

SLUG & LETTUCE
St John's Hill

PUZZLE
Lavender Hill

SHIP INN
Jews Row

PRINCE'S PUZZLE
St John's Hill

THE LAVENDER
Lavender Hill

BREAD & ROSES
Clapham Manor St

ALMA TAVERN
Old York Rd

WANDSWORTH

SLUG & LETTUCE
Alma Rd

ALL BAR ONE
Northcote Rd

**WINDMILL ON THE
COMMON**
Clapham Common
Southside

SPOTTED DOG
Garrat La

FARADAY & FIRKIN
Battersea Rise

LA BOUFFE
Battersea Rise

NIGHTINGALE
Nightingale La

GRID INN
Replingham Rd

FAITH & FIRKIN
Bellevue Rd

ALEXANDRA
Clapham Common
Southside

PUZZLE
Balham High Rd

ECLIPSE
Balham High Rd

BELLE VUE
Clapham Common
Southside

MOON UNDER WATER
Balham High Rd

GOOSE & GRANITE
Clapham High St

DOG & FOX
Wimbledon High St

FREEDOM & FIRKIN
Tooting High St

THE FALCON
Bedford Rd

WIMBLEDON PARKSIDE

JJ'S
The Broadway

WIMBLEDON

JJ MOON'S
Tooting High St

O'NEILL'S
The Broadway

WHITE LION OF MORTIMER
London Rd

KINGSTON RD

WETHERSPOONS
Aberconway Rd

MORDEN

HAND & RACKET
Wimbledon Hill Rd

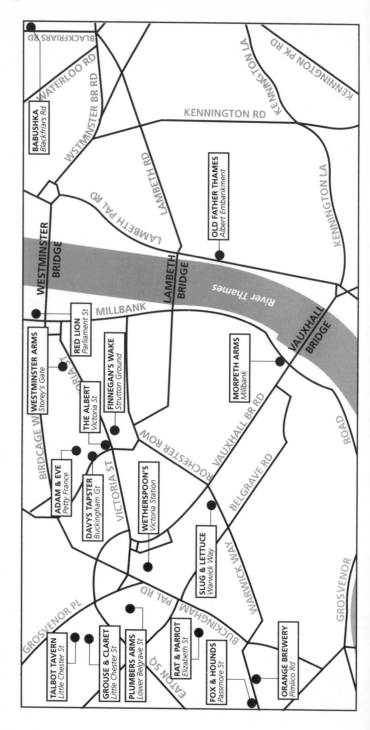

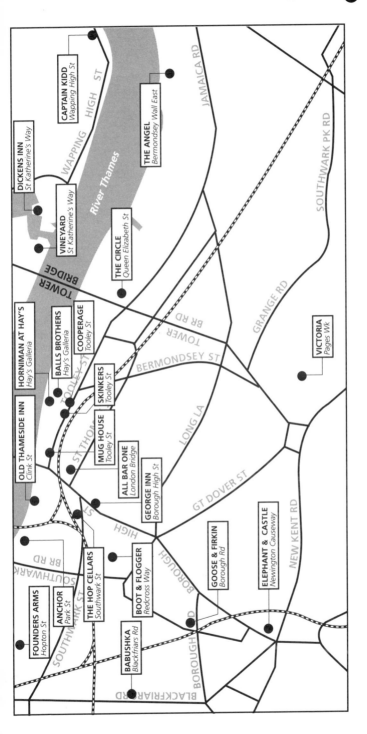

CAPTAIN KIDD
Wapping High St

THE ANGEL
Bermondsey Wall East

DICKENS INN
St Katherine's Way

VINEYARD
St Katherine's Way

THE CIRCLE
Queen Elizabeth St

VICTORIA
Pages Wk

HORNIMAN AT HAY'S
Hay's Galleria

BALLS BROTHERS
Hay's Galleria

COOPERAGE
Tooley St

SKINKERS
Tooley St

OLD THAMESIDE INN
Clink St

MUG HOUSE
Tooley St

ALL BAR ONE
London Bridge

GEORGE INN
Borough High St

GOOSE & FIRKIN
Borough Rd

ELEPHANT & CASTLE
Newington Causeway

THE HOP CELLARS
Southwark St

BOOT & FLOGGER
Redcross Way

FOUNDERS ARMS
Hopton St

ANCHOR
Park St

BABUSHKA
Blackfriars Rd

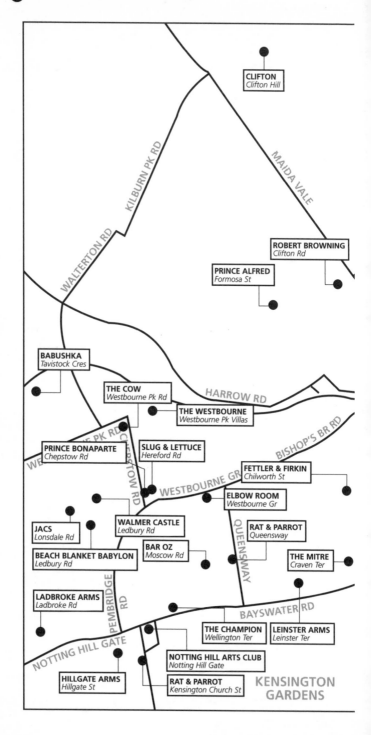

CLIFTON
Clifton Hill

MAIDA VALE

KILBURN PK RD

WALTERTON RD

ROBERT BROWNING
Clifton Rd

PRINCE ALFRED
Formosa St

BABUSHKA
Tavistock Cres

HARROW RD

THE COW
Westbourne Pk Rd

THE WESTBOURNE
Westbourne Pk Villas

BISHOP'S BR RD

PRINCE BONAPARTE
Chepstow Rd

SLUG & LETTUCE
Hereford Rd

WESTBOURNE PK RD

CHEPSTOW RD

FETTLER & FIRKIN
Chilworth St

WESTBOURNE GR

ELBOW ROOM
Westbourne Gr

JACS
Lonsdale Rd

WALMER CASTLE
Ledbury Rd

RAT & PARROT
Queensway

QUEENSWAY

BEACH BLANKET BABYLON
Ledbury Rd

BAR OZ
Moscow Rd

THE MITRE
Craven Ter

LADBROKE ARMS
Ladbroke Rd

PEMBRIDGE RD

BAYSWATER RD

THE CHAMPION
Wellington Ter

LEINSTER ARMS
Leinster Ter

NOTTING HILL GATE

NOTTING HILL ARTS CLUB
Notting Hill Gate

HILLGATE ARMS
Hillgate St

RAT & PARROT
Kensington Church St

KENSINGTON
GARDENS

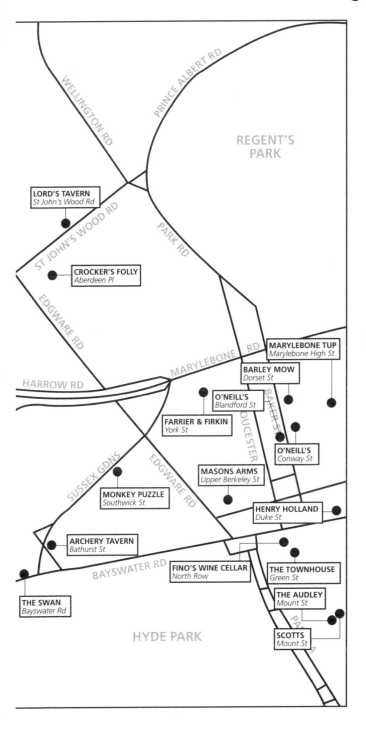

REGENT'S PARK

WELLINGTON RD

PRINCE ALBERT RD

ST JOHN'S WOOD RD

PARK RD

LORD'S TAVERN
St John's Wood Rd

CROCKER'S FOLLY
Aberdeen Pl

EDGWARE RD

MARYLEBONE RD

HARROW RD

MARYLEBONE TUP
Marylebone High St

BARLEY MOW
Dorset St

BAKER ST

O'NEILL'S
Blandford St

FARRIER & FIRKIN
York St

GLOUCESTER

O'NEILL'S
Conway St

MASONS ARMS
Upper Berkeley St

SUSSEX GDNS

EDGWARE RD

MONKEY PUZZLE
Southwick St

HENRY HOLLAND
Duke St

ARCHERY TAVERN
Bathurst St

BAYSWATER RD

FINO'S WINE CELLAR
North Row

THE TOWNHOUSE
Green St

THE SWAN
Bayswater Rd

THE AUDLEY
Mount St

PARK LA

HYDE PARK

SCOTTS
Mount St

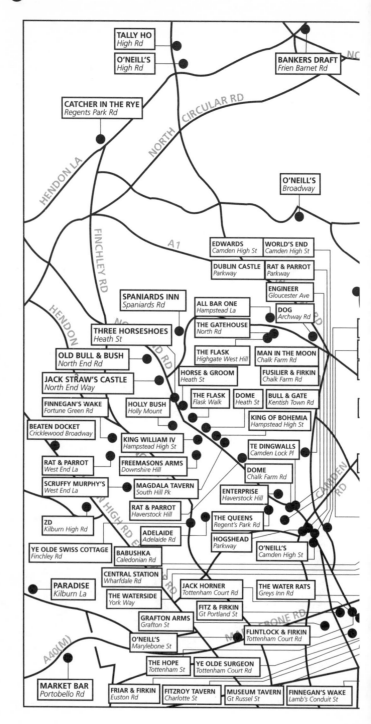

NEW MOON
Lordship La

TOLLGATE
Turnpike La

ELBOW ROOM
High Rd

ELBOW ROOM
Topsfield Parade

HALF MOON
Green Lanes

WHOLE HOG
Green Lanes

OLD SUFFOLK PUNCH
Grand Parade

HOGSHEAD
Crouch End Hill

WHITE LION OF MORTIMER
Stroud Green Rd

FALCON
Royal College St

THE BACKPACKER
York Way

FLOUNDER & FIRKIN
Holloway Rd

ROCHESTER CASTLE
High St

NARROW BOAT
St Peter St

O'NEILL'S
Holloway Rd

COMPTON ARMS
Compton Ave

THE ALBION
Thornhill Rd

FINNEGAN'S WAKE
Essex St

PO NA NA
Upper St

DOME
Upper St

MARQUESS TAVERN
Canonbury St

PUZZLE
New North Rd

THE CORONET
Holloway Rd

HOPE & ANCHOR
Upper St

SLUG & LETTUCE
Islington Green

ISLAND QUEEN
Noel Rd

KING'S HEAD
Upper St

THE CROWN
Cloudesley Rd

FILTHY McNASTY
Amwell St

FINNOCK & FIRKIN
Upper St

HOGSHEAD
Upper St

EAGLE TAVERN
Shepherdess Wk

MATCH
Clerkenwell Rd

EAST ONE
St John St

FALCON & FIRKIN
Victoria Park Rd

BURGUNDY BEN'S
Clerkenwell Rd

CICADA
St John St

COLONEL JASPERS
City Rd

DUST
Clerkenwell Rd

PHEASANT & FIRKIN
Goswell Rd

CAMDEN HEAD
Camden Walk

SEKFORDE ARMS
Sekforde St

BROWNS
Hackney Rd

BLIND BEGGAR
Whitechapel Rd

CANTALOUPE
Charlotte Rd

THE LAMB
Lambs Conduit St

MASQUE HAUNT
Old St

THE GATE
St John St

CAMDEN'S HEAD
Bethnal Gn Rd

ABBAYE
Charterhouse

CROWN & SHUTTLE
Shoreditch High St

O'NEILL'S
Houndsditch

PULPIT
Worship St

TRUCKLES
Bury Pl

O'HANLON'S
Tysoe St

HOOP & GRAPES
Aldgate High St

OLD RED LION
High Holborn

CITTIE OF YORKE
High Holborn

THE EAGLE
Farringdon Rd

HABIT
Crutched Friars

CRUTCHED FRIAR
Crutched Friars

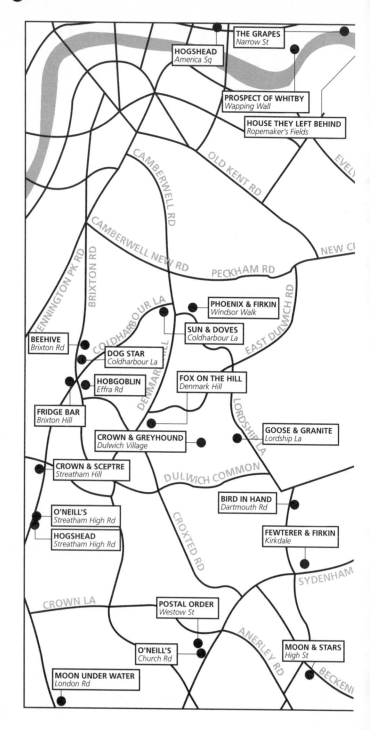

THE GRAPES
Narrow St

HOGSHEAD
America Sq

PROSPECT OF WHITBY
Wapping Wall

HOUSE THEY LEFT BEHIND
Ropemaker's Fields

CAMBERWELL RD

OLD KENT RD

EVELY

CAMBERWELL NEW RD

PECKHAM RD

NEW CR

KENNINGTON PK RD

BRIXTON RD

COLDHARBOUR LA

EAST DULWICH RD

PHOENIX & FIRKIN
Windsor Walk

SUN & DOVES
Coldharbour La

BEEHIVE
Brixton Rd

DOG STAR
Coldharbour La

HOBGOBLIN
Effra Rd

FOX ON THE HILL
Denmark Hill

DENMARK HILL

LORDSHIP LA

FRIDGE BAR
Brixton Hill

CROWN & GREYHOUND
Dulwich Village

GOOSE & GRANITE
Lordship La

CROWN & SCEPTRE
Streatham Hill

DULWICH COMMON

BIRD IN HAND
Dartmouth Rd

CROXTED RD

O'NEILL'S
Streatham High Rd

HOGSHEAD
Streatham High Rd

FEWTERER & FIRKIN
Kirkdale

SYDENHAM

CROWN LA

POSTAL ORDER
Westow St

ANERLEY RD

O'NEILL'S
Church Rd

MOON & STARS
High St

BECKENI

MOON UNDER WATER
London Rd

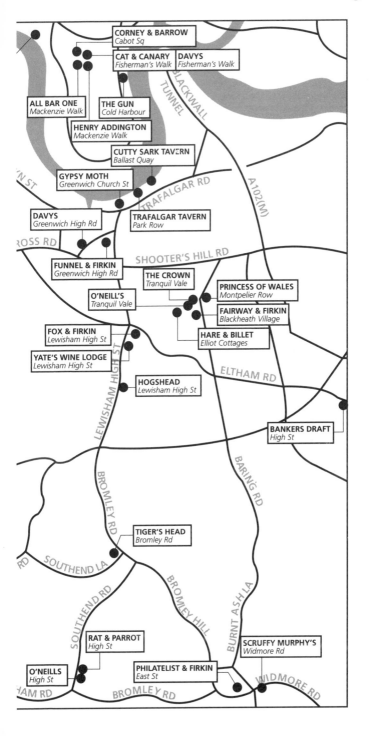

CORNEY & BARROW
Cabot Sq

CAT & CANARY
Fisherman's Walk

DAVYS
Fisherman's Walk

ALL BAR ONE
Mackenzie Walk

THE GUN
Cold Harbour

HENRY ADDINGTON
Mackenzie Walk

CUTTY SARK TAVERN
Ballast Quay

GYPSY MOTH
Greenwich Church St

DAVYS
Greenwich High Rd

TRAFALGAR TAVERN
Park Row

FUNNEL & FIRKIN
Greenwich High Rd

THE CROWN
Tranquil Vale

PRINCESS OF WALES
Montpelier Row

O'NEILL'S
Tranquil Vale

FAIRWAY & FIRKIN
Blackheath Village

FOX & FIRKIN
Lewisham High St

HARE & BILLET
Elliot Cottages

YATE'S WINE LODGE
Lewisham High St

HOGSHEAD
Lewisham High St

BANKERS DRAFT
High St

TIGER'S HEAD
Bromley Rd

RAT & PARROT
High St

SCRUFFY MURPHY'S
Widmore Rd

O'NEILLS
High St

PHILATELIST & FIRKIN
East St

LATE OPENERS

Babushka, N1
Babushka, SE1
Backpacker, N1
Belgo Centraal, WC2
Belgo Noord, NW1
Belushi's, WC2
Black Cap, NW1
Blues Bar, W1
Brendan O'Grady's, SE1
Brompton's and The Warwick Bar, SW5
Browns, E2
Browns, SW3
Browns, W1
Browns, WC2
Cactus Blue, SW3
Café Bohème, W1
Café Latino, W1
Cantaloupe Bar and Grill, EC2
Central Station, E17
Central Station, N1
Circus, W1
Cork and Bottle, WC2
De Hems, W1
Detroit, WC2
Dublin Castle, NW1
Freedom, W1
Friar & Firkin, NW1
Fridge Bar, SW2
Havana, SW6
Kemia Bar at Momo, W1
Kettner's Champagne Bar, W1
King's Head, N1
Kudos, WC2
La Perla, WC2
Lupo, W1
Market Bar, W11
Market Cafe Bar, WC2
Mash, W1
Match, EC1
MetBar, W1
Notting Hill Arts Club, W11
O Bar, W1
Office Bar, W1
Po Na Na, Croydon
Po Na Na, N1
Po Na Na, SW3
Po Na Na Fez Club, SW10
Riki Tik, W1
Saint, WC2
Shoeless Joe's, SW6
Soho Spice, W1
Sports Café, SW1
Spot, WC2
The Beaufoy Arms, SW11
The Crescent, SW3
The Dog Star, SW9
The Edge, W1

The Hobgoblin, SW2
The Polar Bear, WC2
Vic Naylor, EC1

OUTSIDE SPACE

Albion, N1
Alexandra, SW19
Anchor, Bankside, SE1
Angel, SE16
Anglesea Arms, SW7
Audley, W1
Australian, SW3
Babushka, N1
Babushka, SE1
Belushi's, WC2
BierRex, EC4
BierRex, SW15
Bill Bentley, EC2
Black Cap, NW1
Black Lion, W6
Blenheim, SW3
Blind Beggar, E1
Blue Anchor, W6
Bouffe, La, SW11
Box, WC2
Brasserie Rocque, EC2
Bread and Roses, SW4
Brendan O'Grady's, SE1
Brief Encounter, WC2
Bull and Gate, NW5
Bulls' Head, W6
Cafe Boheme, W1V
Camden Head, N1
Captain Kidd, E1
Cat and the Canary, E14
Catcher in the Rye, N3
Central Station, N1
Champion , W2
Champion, The, W1
Chelsea Potter, SW3
Chelsea Ram, SW10
Compton Arms, N1
Corney and Barrow, E14
Corney and Barrow, EC2
Corney and Barrow, EC4
Cow, W2
Cricketers
Crooked Billet, SW19
Crown and Greyhound,SE21
Crown and Two Chairmen, W1
Crown, N1
Crown, SE3
Crutched Friar, EC3
Cutty Sark Tavern, SE10
De Hems, W1
Dickens Inn, E1
Dog and Fox, SW19
Dog Star, SE5
Dove, W6

Ship Inn, SW18
Ship, SW14
Shuckburgh Arms, SW3
Slap Harry's, W1
Slug and Lettuce, SW15
Smithfield Free House, EC1
Spaniard's Inn, NW3
Sporting Page, SW10
Ye White Hart, SW13

GAY BARS

Black Cap, NW1
Box, WC2
Brief Encounter, WC2
Brompton's and the Warwick Bar, SW5
Central Station, N1
Central Station, E17
Champion, W2
Coleherne, SW5
Freedom, W1
Jacomos, EC1
Kudos, W1
Queens Head, SW3
Rupert Street, W1
The Edge, W1
White Swan, E14

DARTS

Australian, SW3
Bulls' Head, W6
Cardinal, SW1
Cat and the Canary, E14
Champion, W1
Chandos, WC2
Cheshire Cheese, WC2
Clachan, W1
Duke of Devonshire, SW12
Duke of Edinburgh, E13
Flask, NW3
George Inn, SE1
George IV, W4
Green Man, SW15
Gun, E14
Hand in Hand, SW19
Hare and Hounds, SW14
Lamb Tavern, EC3
Leinster Arms, W2
London Apprentice, Isleworth
Outpost, NW1
Paxton's Head, SW1
Pharaoh and Firkin, SW6
Plumbers Arms, SW1
Rose of York, Richmond
Ship Inn, SW18
Surprise, SW3
Ye Olde Swiss Cottage, NW3

POOL TABLES

Bar Oz, W2
Beaufoy Arms, SW11
Browns, E2
Bull and Gate, NW5
Bunch of Grapes, SW3
Cardinal, SW1
Cheshire Cheese, WC2
Crown and Shuttle, E1
Deacons, EC4
Duke of Edinburgh, E13
Elbow Room, W2
Elephant and Castle, SE1
Falcon, SW4
Hare and Hounds, SW14
Hope and Anchor, N1
Island Queen, N1
Jolly Farmers, Purley
King's Head, SW6
Magpie & Stump, SW10
Magpie and Stump, EC4
Man in the Moon, SW3
Museum Tavern, WC1
Old Red Lion, WC1
Outpost, NW1
Prince Alfred, W9
Rat and Carrot, SW3
Smithfield Free House, EC1
Sports Academy, EC4
Springbok, WC2
Trafalgar, SW3
Ye Olde Swiss Cottage, NW3

BAR BILLIARDS

Cat and the Canary, E14
Eagle Tavern. N1
Fox & Hounds, Sutton
George Inn, SE1
London Apprentice, Isleworth
Narrow Boat, N1
Nightingale, SW12
Rose of York, Richmond
Woodman, SW11

STRIPPERS

Backpacker, N1
Beaufoy Arms, SW11
Browns, E2
Central Station, N1
Crown & Shuttle, E1
Secrets, W6

WATERSIDE VENUES

Anchor, Bankside, SE1
Angel, SE16
Babushka, N1
Bar M, SW15
Barley Mow, E14
Bell and Crown, W4
Black Lion, W6
Blue Anchor, W6
Bulls' Head, W6
Cat and the Canary, E14
City Barge, W4
Cutty Sark Tavern, SE10
Daly's Wine Bar, WC2
Dickens Inn, E1
Dove, W6
Founders Arms, SE1
Grapes, E14
Gun, E14
Horniman at Hay's, SE1
Old Ship, W6
Old Thameside Inn, SE1
Oxo Tower Bar, SE1
Pitcher & Piano, Richmond
Prospect of Whitby, E1
River Rat, SW11
Ship, SW14
Slug and Lettuce, Richmond
Tattershall Castle, SW1
Trafalgar Tavern, SE10
TS Queen Mary, WC2
Waterside, N1
White Cross, Richmond
Ye White Hart, SW13

10 THEME BARS TO EMBRACE

All Bar One
Balls Brothers
Corney & Barrow
Davy's
Tup Pubs
Hogsheads
O' Neill's
Pitcher & Piano
Slug & Lettuce
Weatherspoon's Pubs

10 THEME BARS TO AVOID

Conran bars
Domes
Edward's
Finnegan's Wakes
Goose & Granites
Puzzle Pubs
Rat & Parrotts
Scruffy Murphy's
Walkabouts
Yates' Wine Lodges

10 GREAT COCKTAILS

Albero & Grana, SW3
Alphabet, W1
American Bar, Savoy Hotel, WC2
Cocktail Bar at Connaught, W1
Collection, SW3
Detroit, WC2
Kemia Bar, W1
Le Shaker, SW10
Match, EC1
Windows, W1

10 OTHER GREATS

Babushka, W11
   (for vodka)
Bread & Roses, SW4
   (for socialist principles)
Christopher's Speakeasy, WC2
   (for quiet times)
Crescent, SW3
   (for wine lovers)
Elbow Room, W2
   (for American pool)
Hogsheads, various locations
   (for real ales)
O'Hanlon's, EC1
   (for Irish atmosphere and beers)
Soho Spice, W1
   (for late opening)
Sporting Page, SW10
   (for Bollinger champagne)
Windows on the World, W1
   (for views)

10 EASY PLACES TO PULL

Goat in Boots, SW10
Fifth Floor at Harvey Nicholls, SW1
Brief Encounter, WC2
Bar Zola's, WC2
K Bar, W1
Waxy O'Connor's, W1
Po Na Na, SW3
Deacon's, EC4
Havana, SW6
190, SW7

10 BEST FOOD VENUES

Al's Cafe Bar, EC1
Churchill, W8
Duke of Cambridge, SW11
Eagle, EC1
Fox & Anchor, EC1
Guinea, W1
Havelock Tavern, W14
La Perla, WC2
Westbourne, W2
Windsor Castle, W8

10 PLACES TO BE SEEN
Alphabet, W1
Collection, SW3
Kemia Bar, W1
Kudos, WC2
Le Shaker, SW1
Lupo, W1
Oxo Tower Bar, SE1
Po Na Na, SW3
Saint, WC2
Soho House, W1

10 PLACES NOT TO BE SEEN
Bar Oz, W2
Coates, EC1
Finnegan's Wakes
K Bar, W1
Met Bar, W1
Rat & Parrots
Sak, W1
Sheila'a Bar Barbie, WC2
Strippers' bars
Teatro, W1

The Guinea
Cutty Sark tai
Trafalgar tai

Admiral Codrington

Ye Olde Cheshire Cheese
Rinos Wine Bar
Fulham Thi
Gordons Wine Bar
Prospect of Whitby